DECONSTRUCTING
GURDJIEFF

OTHER BOOKS BY TOBIAS CHURTON

Occult Paris: The Lost Magic of the Belle Époque (2016)

Gnostic Mysteries of Sex:
Sophia the Wild One and Erotic Christianity (2015)

Jerusalem!: The Real Life of William Blake (2015)

Aleister Crowley: The Beast in Berlin (2014)

The Babylon Gene (novel; 2013)

The Mysteries of John the Baptist:
His Legacy in Gnosticism, Paganism, and Freemasonry (2012)

Aleister Crowley: The Biography (2011)

The Missing Family of Jesus: An Inconvenient Truth—How the Church
Erased Jesus's Brothers and Sisters from History (2010)

The Invisible History of the Rosicrucians:
The World's Most Mysterious Secret Society (2009)

Kiss of Death: The True History of the Gospel of Judas (2008)

Freemasonry: The Reality (2007)

The Magus of Freemasonry: The Mysterious Life of Elias Ashmole—
Scientist, Alchemist, and Founder of the Royal Society (2006)

Gnostic Philosophy: From Ancient Persia to Modern Times (2005)

Golden Builders:
Alchemists, Rosicrucians, and the First Freemasons (2004)

The Fear of Vision (poetry; 1996)

Miraval—A Quest (novel; 1989)

The Gnostics (1987)

DECONSTRUCTING
GURDJIEFF

Biography
of a Spiritual
Magician

Tobias Churton

Inner Traditions
Rochester, Vermont • Toronto, Canada

Inner Traditions
One Park Street
Rochester, Vermont 05767
www.InnerTraditions.com

Text stock is SFI certified

Library of Congress Cataloging-in-Publication Data

Names: Churton, Tobias, 1960- author.
Title: Deconstructing Gurdjieff : biography of a spiritual magician /
    Tobias Churton.
Description: Rochester, Vermont : Inner Traditions, 2017. | Includes
    bibliographical references and index.
Identifiers: LCCN 2016048932 (print) | LCCN 2017012550 (e-book) |
    ISBN 9781620556382 (hardcover) | ISBN 9781620556399 (e-book)
Subjects: LCSH: Gurdjieff, Georges Ivanovitch, 1872-1949.
Classification: LCC BP605.G94 G8728 2017 (print) | LCC BP605.G94 (e-book) |
    DDC 197—dc23
LC record available at https://lccn.loc.gov/2016048932

Printed and bound in the United States by Lake Book Manufacturing, Inc.
The text stock is SFI certified. The Sustainable Forestry Initiative® program
promotes sustainable forest management.

10 9 8 7 6 5 4 3 2 1

Text design and layout by Debbie Glogover
This book was typeset in Garamond Premier Pro with Cooper Hewitt and Gill
Sans MT Pro for display fonts

To send correspondence to the author of this book, mail a first-class letter to the
author c/o Inner Traditions • Bear & Company, One Park Street, Rochester, VT
05767, and we will forward the communication, or contact the author directly at
tobiaschurton.com.

Contents

Acknowledgments

My first thanks are due to Michael Mann, editor at Watkins Publishing, who first put to me the idea that it was time for a new biography of Gurdjieff. Michael had commissioned the previous standard biography, James Moore's *Gurdjieff: The Anatomy of a Myth,* and it was Michael Mann who first generously commissioned me to write what has become this book. It was Michael's desire to see the world truly "wake up" from its current suicidal follies that motivated the commission. I have done all I can with that desire, which ought to be universal but is not. Gurdjieff can help us to understand why that is the case and what we might do about it.

I must express profound gratitude to Jon Graham, acquisitions editor at Inner Traditions International, whose faith in the enterprise and its author has brought this book to final fruition. Jon's friendly and perceptive encouragement has been an invaluable source of inspiration for many years now, and this project owes much to his farsighted consideration and understanding.

Gurdjieff readers familiar with Paul Beekman Taylor's *G.I. Gurdjieff: A New Life*—a work that has successfully corrected many previous errors as to matters of fact made by Gurdjieff's previous biographers—will note at the head of Paul Beekman Taylor's acknowledgments his expression of "an incalculable debt" owed to Michael Benham of Melbourne, Australia, along with Gert-Jan Blom of Amsterdam, the

Netherlands. I have been fortunate to enjoy not only the benefit of what Michael Benham passed on to Paul Beekman Taylor and others from Michael's encyclopedic store of detailed knowledge and very extensive research into Gurdjieff's life and ideas, but also Michael Benham's personal interest and factual contribution to my own biography.

Not only has Michael Benham visted places central to Gurdjieff's early life, such as Kars, Ani, Alexandropol (Gyumri), Tblisi, and Yerevan, but he has also kept in touch with the very latest researches undertaken in Russia and elsewhere. In the process he has assisted Paul Beekman Taylor, James Moore, Dushka Howarth, and J. Walter Driscoll in their accounts of Gurdjieff. As well as having proofread several notable Gurdjieff books, Michael Benham was for ten years entrusted by Dushka Howarth with her drafts for *It's Up to Ourselves: A Mother, a Daughter, and Gurdjieff—a Shared Memoir and Family Photo Album* (by Jessmin and Dushka Howarth), Michael being one of the few who encouraged Dushka Howarth to persist despite opposition and criticism.

Hearing that I was adding what my father would call my "two penn'orth" to the Gurdjieff biographical canon, Michael Benham very kindly undertook to contact me and express his willingness to proofread my biography and check its factual basis. This was an extraordinarily generous and welcome gesture, and the book has truly benefited from Michael's elucidations and comments on a good number of points. Though, thankfully, I had the opportunity to correct a few minor errors, I was relieved to find that in his estimation I had made no substantial "bloomers," save one whereby Michael was able to put right inaccurate information he had previously passed on to another biographer in innocence but which was subsequently found, after fresh research undertaken elsewhere, to be incorrect. This material (concerning Gurdjieff's alleged Masonic Lodge established in Russia in 1909) was a boon, and its inclusion brings this biography well up to "state-of-the-art" in terms of a biography of Gurdjieff intended mostly for the general reader who has heard something about Gurdjieff but would like to explore his life and work more deeply and gain real understanding thereby.

All biographers and writers about Gurdjieff, now and to come, are indebted to the work of the Gurdjieff family, sometime represented by Valentin Anastasieff, and to Jeanne de Salzmann for performing Gurdjieff's will that "everything he had learned about the inner world of man" be shared with "creatures similar to himself."* We have all to thank Gurdjieff's closest friends, disciples, and colleagues, for having translated and disseminated for the world's enlightenment and awakening Gurdjieff's works *Meetings with Remarkable Men; Beelzebub's Tales to His Grandson;* and *Life Is Real Only Then, When "I Am."* If these works do not always provide certain information as to Gurdjieff's life, they certainly provide more than adequate testimony to the nature of the life of Gurdjieff's mind.

---

*Valentin Anastasieff writing "on behalf of the family" in the prefatory note to the 2011 edition of *Life Is Real Only Then, When "I Am."* Jeanne de Salzmann contributed the foreword to that edition, indicating clearly Gurdjieff's wishes for publication of the three books.

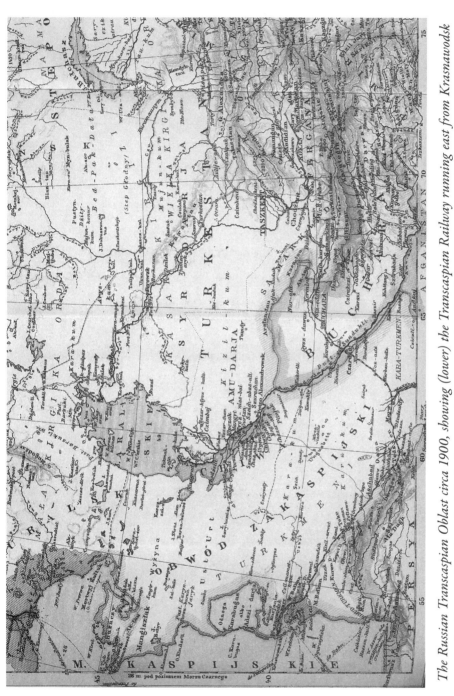

The Russian Transcaspian Oblast circa 1900, showing (lower) the Transcaspian Railway running east from Krasnawodsk on the Caspian Sea through Aschabad, Merw (Merv), Czardzu (on the Amu-Darja River), Buchara, Samarkand, Czernjajewo, and on to Margelan: all places critical to Gurdjieff's accounts in Meetings with Remarkable Men.

PREFACE

*Caveat Lector**

Biographers of Gurdjieff are faced with a serious problem: the extreme scarcity of authentic independent documentation concerning Gurdjieff's life both up to his appearance in Moscow in 1912–13 and, to a slightly lesser extent, between that time and the Russian Revolution in 1917. Gurdjieff was at least forty years old in 1917, his mind, self-appointed destiny, and fundamental attitudes already fully shaped by previous experience. As regards factual support for that experience, Gurdjieff's name finds its way into barely a handful of official documents, themselves not wholly reliable. Seismic tumults from the collapse of the old Russian Empire, aggravated by the twentieth century's immense conflicts and totalitarian vandalism, have sundered and fragmented the historic continuity that might otherwise have yielded collaborative resources from the Caucasus and Transcaucasia regions in which Gurdjieff grew up. Gurdjieff destroyed his own papers during a protracted personal crisis in 1930. We have no volume of Gurdjieff's letters or diaries, however slim, to consult. Personal reminiscences of followers, often highly subjective, are frequently at variance with one another and with verifiable facts.

---

*"Reader Beware"

Self-perceived as a man apart, a kind of spy on a confused, damned world, Gurdjieff persistently objectified the human beings around him; if his relations with people appeared to be natural we have no way of knowing when that was, or was not, a manipulative pretense on his part. Alfred Richard Orage, Gurdjieff's first representative in New York, maintained his master's conduct could not be judged like that of other men; followers tolerated diktats and verbal abuse, or quit. The first thing Gurdjieff's most influential follower P. D. (Pyotr Demianovich) Ouspensky noticed about his teacher in Moscow in 1915 was that Gurdjieff was always acting; Gurdjieff was many men, appeared in many disguises. Was he hiding something, or was he hiding *from* something?

With the fall of the Soviet Union a quarter century ago, Gurdjieff biographer Paul Beekman Taylor has been able to acquaint followers not only with corrections to many misapprehensions and long-standing errors of fact and detail adhering to Gurdjieff, but also with a small number of brief ecclesiastical and provincial administrative entries from Georgia (Caucasus) and Russian Armenia (Transcaucasus), former provinces of the Russian Empire, now constituted as independent outward-looking countries with new borders. Records offer conflicting references to Gurdjieff's immediate and extended family. They can be, and have been, used as support for Gurdjieff's own accounts of his background and adventures, especially that in his peculiar book *Meetings with Remarkable Men,* written after 1924 and published after his death. On the other hand, official records also highlight problems in relating those accounts to historic facts. Here lieth the problem and the caveat.

If independent sources are used to support Gurdjieff's own testimony, it means that we are trusting that testimony and employing documentary sources to prove its veracity. However, both the peculiar manner in which Gurdjieff chose to relate events of his life, and the purposes he intended, apparently, to fulfill by doing so, simply do not allow us to make any such automatic connection with the confidence biographers and historians customarily expect. In simple, legalistic terms we are forced to ask, *is Gurdjieff a reliable witness to his own life?*

One would like to give a straight answer to the question, but we are straightaway faced with a conundrum of the magician's own making.

In the Introduction to *Meetings with Remarkable Men,*[1] Gurdjieff explains that part of his purpose in writing the book is to save himself future trouble in having to answer questions from interlocutors concerning his life and, especially, beliefs. He complains that such questions have been vexatious to concentration on other more pressing matters and regards these questions merely as ones put by "idle curiosity." Those interested in his personal life are described as "shameless idlers." To satisfy their curiosity he has nonetheless, "in revising the material destined for this series [he means this book]" decided to present it "in the form of separate independent tales, and to insert in them various ideas which can serve as answers to all the questions often put to me." The questions put to him are, he says, to do with the "remarkable men" he has encountered; "marvels" seen in the East; questions of the immortality of the soul; whether or not man has free will; the cause of suffering; the credibility of "occult and spiritualistic sciences"; the nature of hypnotism, magnetism, and telepathy; how he first became concerned with such questions; and what then led him to the system practiced in the institute bearing his name.

Gurdjieff had another intention in putting together what at first sight appears to be an autobiography with its curious title.

Meetings with Remarkable Men is in no wise an autobiography. It is interesting that director Peter Brook has turned its tales into a feature film (1979) because, in a sense, Gurdjieff's book could represent the result of a Hollywood treatment of a genuine (though unwritten) Gurdjieffian autobiography: "never let the facts get in the way of a good story"—except that whereas Hollywood would manipulate and invent material for entertainment and profit, Gurdjieff, conscious of writing a "new kind" of book, deliberately shaped and reshaped elements of his life and imagination as *illustrations or parables of his system.* He dramatized *ideas.* Characters may represent those ideas or embody psychic functions (such as instinctive action); they play parts. The ideas might be real but individual characters may not be, though their behavior may be truthful regarding human nature or Gurdjieff's ideas of ideal or misguided action, observed from experience.

The cooked-up book is what the dramatist Bertolt Brecht (1898–1956) would call a *Lehrstück,* a "learning-play" or experimental teaching piece wherein actors adopt roles, postures, and attitudes that exceed conventional distinctions between stage and audience, between idea, image, event, and reality, fact and fiction. Brecht famously declared, "Realism does not consist in reproducing reality, but in showing how things really are." The same remark may be used to describe the parables of Jesus. The story of the Good Samaritan tells us a great deal more about reality and ideal conduct than would a journalistic account of a mugging on the Jericho road.

In the case of Gurdjieff's book, Gurdjieff is principal actor as well as narrator, and elements of his experiences, fantasies, prior reading, and thoughts—and what he considers the fantasies and expectations of his readers—play the parts; Gurdjieff "sings their tune." As we shall discover, such a method was consistent with his upbringing. Gurdjieff's father entertained folk across Transcaucasia as an *ashokh* or traditional bard, a singer-storyteller; enactor of an audio theater of ancient legend, folk history, and accumulated insight, bound by rhythm and melody. Ivan Ivanovich (as his father seems to have been called) could always, like his now-famous son, gather an audience; he could *captivate.* The aim, and means, was enchantment: the reaching into the soul of the auditor, whose own imagination, individual and collective, formerly dormant, provided set and setting for the bardic word from an archetypal store of millennia of human experiences. We can see why Gurdjieff has most appealed to actors, dancers, musicians, painters, impresarios, and storytellers, those especially conscious of the role of symbol and its encoding in artificial forms of address. Artists get or "cotton on" to congenial aspects of Gurdjieff, whereas more prosaic, sometimes troubled minds—perhaps his principal following—struggle with it all, often for years, perennially taking the "black devil" too literally, perhaps too respectfully.

Gurdjieff's idea of science was that of the ancient Magi, not the modern classroom. He barely ever disguised his loathing for what today is called, without irony, higher education. I personally suspect he had a chip on his shoulder about never having graduated from university, so vehement were his repeated digs at "wiseacreing," an ungainly word (in translation) that occurs with tiresome, arguably obsessive repetitiveness throughout all his writings and talks; followers have picked the word up and scatter it like buckshot from self-elevated heights at critics. By *wiseacreing* Gurdjieff means "clever-clever" smart-alecs who can talk the hind legs off a donkey but remain devoid both of common sense and practical know-how, who employ sophistical verbal displays to impress the impressionable or acquire spurious authority, while obscuring lack of deeper acquaintance with truths underlying mere data. In short, such persons are alien to spiritual perception, like those who adhere to a form of religion while denying the substance thereof (cf. II Timothy 3:5–7). Many a barroom philosopher is more palatable than the smart-ass, media-tuned "professional" whose unoriginal thoughts are up for sale and meat for broadcast. Gurdjieff was a "university of life" type of graduate, cynical about cynics. Perhaps to lend authority to conviction, he even invented from the store of reality and myth the archetypal sacred university of wisdom—the Sarmoung Brotherhood—a body of such exalted spiritual purity and genuine universality of insight that its denizens would never soil their elegant hands with the muck of modern education reliant on paper qualifications and bookish memory learning.

Unlike the professional talkers and establishment-acceptable pundits, the self-taught, apparently polymathic, autodidact Gurdjieff could turn his hand to anything and persuade people to do things they never dreamed of doing. He was the man you'd think you'd want in a real crisis. He talked the talk because, as far as he was concerned, he had walked the walk. Unfortunately for historians and biographers he mostly fictionalized the walk. He didn't want people to follow *his* footsteps but to find their own. Inevitably, Gurdjieff's followers may be found in any year hunting about places mentioned in *Meetings with*

Remarkable Men, without encountering the remarkable men Gurdjieff allegedly met, or perhaps meeting such and never realizing it. Mind you, nobody traipsing around Central Asia today is going to have anything less than an interesting time! His book could do wonders for Central Asian tourism; someone somewhere is probably on the case right now. Turkey would doubtless have gone for it had Gurdjieff been a Turkish Muslim rather than an unorthodox Christian. Armenia is a sure candidate for a Gurdjieff Trail vacation; it's a matter of time.

Conversely, Gurdjieff's "Men" are remarkable insofar as they have recognized that the true value of life comes only when that life consciously acquires mythic dimensions, when one, with feet on ground, has yet traversed the stars and touched the beyond. Remarkable men have seen something unremarkable men have not. Such men should engage our attention. Was Gurdjieff himself one of them?

Gurdjieff's *Meetings* (and as such *Meetings with Remarkable Men* will be abbreviated throughout this book) is, he plainly tells us, a series of independent tales for us shameless idlers who want answers. Gurdjieff's idea of an answer is as much a tale as the Good Samaritan is the answer to the question put to Jesus: "Who is my neighbor?" It is well to know that *Meetings* followed on directly from what Gurdjieff called his first series (or book), *Beelzebub's Tales to His Grandson.* In this even more peculiar, often perhaps intentionally ludicrous and unnecessarily elongated work, Gurdjieff adopted the role of Beelzebub, a voyager through time and space who has crossed "the final frontier" as *Star Trek* fans know it. Beelzebub tells his tales; sometimes, it would appear, adopting the role of Gurdjieff! Role-playing and storytelling—such constitute Gurdjieff's "answers" to the questions of the world.

Unfortunately, biographers have with greater or lesser frequency all too easily slipped into the evident trap of confusing fact with Gurdjieff's idea of reality, something that is simply inevitable when in the territory of magic. Authentic magic is concerned with the transformative power of the imagination and Gurdjieff, we might say, was not a self-confessed hypnotist for nothing. Sometimes, Gurdjieff finds that the best way to show how things really are is simply by reproducing reality: telling the factual story "straight," as he remembers it. You can, with intuition, experience, and common sense, often discern when the author is giving us a more or less accurate, though selective, presentation of facts, and discriminate such narrative elements from where Gurdjieff feels instinctively or otherwise that his abstract teaching priorities and story-telling structures, or whims of the moment, require ascending degrees of invention. We can never be absolutely sure, however; one man's tale is another man's lie. A born performer, Gurdjieff knew a trick or two. If Gurdjieff felt his conscience was untroubled by something he did, that was for him sufficient warrant for acting regardless of others' expectations or feelings. Like Saint Paul's idea of the Christian, Gurdjieff was a law unto himself, guided by "love." Arguably a born archimandrite manqué, Gurdjieff identified conscience with faith.

He regarded the details of his life as personal matters and was only inclined to disburse details when conscious of an impersonal need-to-know; that is, as a service to humanity whose earthy representatives he knew from experience were largely unready for unadorned "truth." Other, less obviously noble motives might also entwine themselves. Gurdjieff's revelations of his protracted life of hustling for a buck as a self-made man heading for a self-earned fortune in what he called "The Material Question" later appended to *Meetings* were made in order to persuade potential American donors to the cause that he had always self-funded his operations by sheer hard work and intended to repay any gifts with like energies.

Curiously, and most tellingly, Gurdjieff is almost certainly most reliable as a historian of his own life when dealing with the powerful emotions relating to his childhood: childhood is, after all, already a magical and even sacrosanct world. Arguably, our childhood constitutes the greatest tale of our lives. Even so, there is an underlying message in Gurdjieff's reminiscences of childhood. It can be expressed in the simple commandment given to and by Moses: "Honor thy father and thy mother." Parents are the gods of childhood. Gurdjieff's paternal god died from a Turkish army bullet in 1918.

As stated above, and as reiterated by their most assiduous critic, Paul Beekman Taylor, past biographers have tended to try to meld Gurdjieff's curious accounts in *Meetings* and elsewhere to some known history to produce results that look like conventional biography of an unconventional man. Taylor's *G. I. Gurdjieff: A New Life* has painstakingly debated the veracity of individual details of the received narratives. I do not believe the sources furnish us with material for a conventional modern biography *at all,* and even less for a hagiography. Until the end of the First World War, we only have fragments of material fit for an *investigation* of the man Gurdjieff. However, even where Gurdjieff's narrative of his perennial search for perennial truth is told independently of historical actuality, we may still learn about the man, his ideas, and his motives. Sometimes, we can do better than that.

Perhaps the most annoying factor for the would-be biographer is that it is precisely Gurdjieff's life up to the establishment of his Institute for the Harmonious Development of Man that is, surely to most observers, by far the most stimulating, significant, and attractive part of his life as a whole—if indeed that part of his life is based on fact, a supposition whose factual basis remains unknown. So while there is a wealth of material available for the last thirty years or so of his life, Gurdjieff's activities in Paris and the United States after 1922 utterly lack the color, adventure, freewheeling character, variety, revelation, and audacious magic Gurdjieff attributes to his life up to forty, even if we feel disposed to dispense most of his narrative as didactic fiction. The man his institute's students wanted to meet was the imagined man who had made archetypal journeys in search of absolute truth in mythical lands among truly remarkable beings. They projected this ideal expectation onto the man they met and interpreted all that was strange about him or his demands as the result of this prior, and apparently completed, quest.

What he might have learned of absolute reality remained and remains a personal holy grail to followers.

What is to be believed? What we can believe is that Gurdjieff was a man who told his story in a particular way for particular reasons. Through understanding his way of telling that story, it is possible that we may arrive at an even better picture, a truer understanding of the man than a narrative of events alone might provide. Furthermore, on close examination of Gurdjieff's often confusing accounts apparently based on his life, we find ourselves rather in the position of an interpreter of Christian gospels. We know that the gospels contain history, but they are not primarily historical or biographical documents. They have a more exalted purpose than that. They were composed to demonstrate their authors' conviction that Jesus was the Son of God, savior: truth evident to the composers as being of far greater import than mere "facts" of history, which without inside understanding are deemed devoid of meaning, though for the gospel composers the essential "truth" had undoubtedly *happened,* witnessed by men, women, and children on Earth, "the Word was made flesh." Mere factual journalism perhaps would have left factual narrative with Jesus hanging on the cross, typecast: a failure and testimony to the fate of all who oppose authority too well.

That is to say, there *is* history behind Gurdjieff's narrative and sometimes, in brief, at the forefront of the narrative as well. Gurdjieff's tales of his adventures are rather like palimpsests, with another story vaguely visible behind the dominant ink of the imposed narrative. In searching for the underlying history, we will not so much "prove as true" elements of Gurdjieff's narratives but will gain vital understanding into some of the historic forces and events that shaped his thinking, feelings, and actions, and which, on close inspection, reveal something of his true character, complexities, and intentions, and account for the man's persistent fascination. We shall not have a complete picture, but we shall I think have a more realistic picture than has been attained hitherto.

While a biography of factual certainties concerning Gurdjieff's life prior to his meeting P. D. Ouspensky in Moscow in 1915 is currently impossible, a sound investigation, a search into the mystery of Gurdjieff may, however, be justly attempted, with the caveat that many parts or even the whole may be regarded as propaganda by those who interpret the currently available evidence differently.

For this biographer, or, better, investigator of the evidence, the task is hardly an altogether comfortable one; far from it, but many an uncomfortable journey takes one to places less intrepid adventurers will never see. This traveler is not free simply to enjoy telling a story but must decompose the inherited narrative and interpret it as part of the means of discovering something like a real man. If we understand the man better after the journey, then the effort in making it requires no further caveat.

ONE

The Enigma Arrives

Pier 88, Manhattan, had seen many thousands of refugees, but few had sailed up the Hudson River first class. Not that George Ivanovich Gurdjieff was in any ordinary sense a refugee. He had certainly lost his familial home and was always seeking refuge, but Gurdjieff had come not as an exile, but to invest his spiritual stock in the land of enterprise.

Before passengers from SS *Paris* could descend from the French Line's most celebrated liner into freedom's icy embrace—or as New Yorkers call the area around 12th Avenue and West 54th Street, Hell's Kitchen— U.S. Immigration officers inspected ship's records. Anyone diseased, criminal, or with less than fifty dollars could expect to be ferried across New York Bay with third-class immigrants for processing and possible rejection and heartbreak on Ellis Island. Fashioned in red brick in grand Muscovite style and opened in 1900, the Federal Immigration Inspection Station's four towering cupolas stood sentry opposite that great Tantalus named *Liberty* across the bay. *Liberty*'s famous statue—France's gift to America—still dominates Liberty Island with her fist clenched tight about freedom's torch and her back to the American continent.

As the sun's harsh red orb glared off chilled ranks of the mighty Woolworth Building's skyscraping windows, early morning mission bells echoed across Manhattan's naked skyline, stirring iced souls

1

from Harlem to Greenwich Village, announcing the day as Sunday, January 13, 1924. For Greek Orthodox–raised George Gurdjieff, it was New Year's Eve.

A Department of Labor official scurried through the liner's luxurious Art Nouveau and Art Deco interiors in search of the "Aliens" manifest. Receiving it from a ship's officer, the official scrutinized the typed contents, observing that the *Compagnie Générale Transatlantique's* three-funneled, steam-powered ship had departed Le Havre on January 5, 1924, for an eight-day winter's crossing. So far, so good: all present; but was all *correct?*

The passenger list revealed forty-seven-year-old George Gurdjieff, a married man and self-declared professor, resided at 9 Rue du Commandant Marchand, Paris. Mr. Gurdjieff could write. He could read Russian, English, and Greek. While his race was stated as Greek, the birthplace entry, Alexandrople, indicated Russian nationality. As far as Immigration was concerned, Gurdjieff was a citizen of that distant country whose leader, Vladimir Lenin, had but a week to live and much to answer for.

Who paid Gurdjieff's passage? He had paid it himself. *Did he have at least fifty dollars?* Yes. *Was he an anarchist?* No. *Polygamist?* No. *Health and physical condition?* Good. *Appearance?* Five feet, five inches tall, fair complexion, hair—what was visible of it—black; eyes blue.[1] *Where was he staying?* c/o Mr. Léon Schoumatoff, Napanoch, Ulster County, New York.

Léon Schoumatoff's house in Napanoch was not in fact Gurdjieff's destination, but he had to put something down. Labor Department officials expected travelers not to burden the public purse; a resident family member or friend was the preferred guarantor of an alien's welcome. Top-flight mechanical engineer Schoumatoff was Olga de Hartmann's brother. Twenty-eight-year-old opera singer, composer's wife, and "sacred dancer" Olga de Hartmann was a dominant member of the twenty-three-strong troupe from the Institute for the Harmonious Development of Man whose athletic, shaven-headed, heavily moustachioed "professor" of sacred dances was standing on deck, wrapped in a heavy overcoat, his big luminous eyes scouring the freezing New York pier below for signs of welcome.

Immigration records may not be welcoming, but they can be illuminating.* Since there currently exists a more than ten-year spectrum for Gurdjieff's birth date—from 1866 to 1877—we may note that records subsequent to this, Gurdjieff's first visit to the United States, differed in only minor respects. His French residence address changed, not unexpectedly, as did his stated destination in the United States, but Gurdjieff's given age was consistent with the passing years: fifty-two in 1929; fifty-three in 1930; sixty-two in 1939. Curiously, his height was given as five feet, eight inches in 1929—apparently gaining three inches!—while in 1930 his birthplace moved strangely from Alexandrople (Alexandropol, now Gyumri) in Russian-controlled Armenia, to Essentonki—a scribal error for Essentuki, a spa town in Russia's North Caucasus Krai (the *krai* or district was established in 1924).²

Doubt nonetheless persists over his birth date, as it does over other issues of Gurdjieff's true identity. A *Fremdenpass* issued by New York's German Consulate at Gurdjieff's request in the mid-1930s, for example, indicates a birth date of 1877. Then again, while persistently giving officialdom his date of birth as December 28, Gurdjieff *celebrated* his birthday either on the Old Orthodox Julian calendar date of January 1 or according to the Gregorian calendar date for New Year of January 13 (up to 1899; January 14 after 1900), which, if immigration records are followed, means Gurdjieff could have been born in either 1876 or 1877. While the bulk of extant records weigh heavily toward 1877, Gurdjieff himself, in sundry reported conversations with students, added a further eleven years to his "official" age. Was he trying to preserve pride in the face of time's ravages? At the time of his death in 1949, he appeared

---

*Chapter 1, note 2 in the Notes section (page 316) provides details on Gurdjieff's immigration records.

to at least one familiar interlocutor, nineteen-year-old Paul Beekman Taylor, like a man in his eighties, not his seventies,* as later birth dates would otherwise suggest.[3†]

We do not know why Gurdjieff offered one time-set to officialdom and another to some students in old age; speculation seems vain, though we cannot avoid the fact that Gurdjieff mythologized, manipulated, and fictionalized many aspects of his life story, ever determined to be thoroughly different. For him, as for Martinists, "truth" transcends fact; that which governs the ordinary world imposes fact but is blind to truth. So long as Gurdjieff could move when he wished, he was indifferent to the record. He wrote his life as he lived it—that is to say, as he willed. We shall find further clues to what remains a vexed question as we delve deeper into the mystery of Gurdjieff's life.

So without having taken a single step from his aliens' vessel into his first attempt at challenging the mind—or mindlessness, as he saw it—of the new Western world, we already have a question mark over this Greek's—*or was it Russian's?*—identity.

Who really *was* George Gurdjieff?

---

*Taylor gives a detailed account of extant evidence for Gurdjieff's birth date. While every official record gives a date 1876–1880, Taylor still seems to prefer an 1866 date based on Gurdjieff's oral testimony and how old he looked to him and Gurdjieff's doctor in his final years.

†Michael Benham contributed further information regarding Gurdjieff's birth date in an e-mail to the author (October 4, 2016). Having undertaken extensive research, subsequently supplying Paul Beekman Taylor with some of the Georgian and Armenian records, the only thing Benham would assert with any certainty was that Gurdjieff was not born in 1866. Benham referred to a whole range of documents recording Gurdjieff's birthplace as Alexandropol, and his birth year as 1877. Several give his birth date as 28 Dec 1877. Gurdjieff's German Fremdenpass has the birth date 28 Dec 1877. His Armenian passport, issued 29 Jun 1920, gives his age as 43. His 1936 French driver's license has the birth date 28 Dec 1877. Benham cites an original Russian document, dated 20 May 1918: N° 2274, from the National Soviet of the Transcaucasie of Tiflis, which identifies the person showing it as G.I.GURDJIEFF, a refugee of Alexandropol, 40 years old, who travels in different countries of Russia with two men. According to Benham, these documents are in the possession of Serge Troude. (For more details on Gurdjieff's birth date see chapter 1, note 3, page 316.)

Gurdjieff's New York–based follower, English theosophist Alfred Richard Orage (1873–1934) was in little doubt as to who Gurdjieff was and what he represented. Boarding the ship to assist the troupe through customs, social activist and former magazine editor Orage believed Gurdjieff was the teacher the Western world needed. On January 9, while Gurdjieff's party was suffering a rough crossing with many seasick, Orage had arranged a public talk at the Sunwise Turn Bookshop, situated at the Yale Club Building on 44th Street and Vanderbilt Avenue, across from Grand Central Station. Warm and urbane, Orage inspired eager listeners with the idea of Gurdjieff as a practical mystic who could turn an automatic, inauthentic, and insincere life upside down and inside out. To follow Gurdjieff's teaching involved a new life where one would be tuned in to reality, where nothing could hinder the enlightened will.

Gurdjieff posed a singular question:

How many of you are really alive?

Gurdjieff worked to awaken people from the sleep of the automaton. The automaton was an identity *through which* the will of others, not of the real "I Am," the authentic being, was expressed. Human beings were unconscious of their unconsciousness. They did not know. The cure:

Wake up!

When remembrance of self had been achieved, one's experiences would chime with reality, for one had encountered essence over illusion, wakefulness over sleep, self-awareness over mechanical imitation and conformity. One would walk with the hidden powers of the universe. All one had to do was to *work,* work willingly, and to work on oneself, step by painful step. It all looked like science; that is, an emerging psychological science, not superstitious magic or religion. But Orage's presentation nevertheless rang the right mystical bells mothballed in the wardrobe of the American mind. Gurdjieff, the man coming to New York, whom listeners could soon meet in the flesh, was a revealer of obscured truth: a master who had intimate knowledge of the lore of obscure, romantic lands. The bait was the "True I," the elusive Self, for which some were, and are, ready to pay.

Besotted with Gurdjieff's Asiatic promise, Orage gave several more talks before the master's arrival, telling as many culturally influential New Yorkers as possible about the transformative potential of this spiritual revolutionary from far away. Gurdjieff's ideas about not being properly alive—merely the unconscious agent of external forces—about observing oneself, self-remembering, and coming into the here and now fully conscious suggested listeners could actually stimulate a real change in themselves: nothing need appear the same again. What a relief this might appear to those adjusting uncomfortably to the new physical and temporal regimes of industrial, commercial, urban, and office-constrained conformity, encroaching on the Western soul with another kind of new life in their unnatural wake.

Orage's exposition of Gurdjieff resonated to some extent with the long-standing New Thought movement established as a component of America's extravagant religious potpourri during the previous century. New Thought involved self-help, positive thinking, and oceanic "God within and everywhere" realizations that can soon descend into banalities of speech devoid of substance. The Gurdjieffian twist, however, appeared to carry very little of the religious superstructure of New Thought. It seemed to speak to a more sceptical, postwar, science- and cosmos-aware generation: people who wanted the mechanics-of-being explained to them in a manner that could be applied not just in pious thoughts but in practice, operative in the new, real worlds of ambition, art, education, psychological therapy, and commerce.

A study-vacation in exotic Paris, where Gurdjieff's institute was based, might be convenient—preferable anyway to an ashram, or begging at a dusty roadside in Benares. With Gurdjieff's ancient-new program you could combine the effective virtues of the fakir, the yogi, and the monk (body, mind, and devoted heart) while sporting a clean white shirt and Oxford bags with spats, or twinset and pearls. Orage had the knack of making his obscure master seem modern, even futuristic.

New York was used to gurus, theosophical yogis, and assorted saviors, but here was a guru with a difference: this mystic's territory combined psychology, science, and sci-fi speculation with the hint of primordial Eastern promise. Readers will note that all of this, on analysis, is very general and undoubtedly vague. Did follower Orage, respected editor of the *New Age,* a London journal friendly to socialism and theosophy, *really* know who Gurdjieff was? Perhaps not, but they got on remarkably well, and genial, articulate Orage, restless, sometimes patient, well-intentioned, and ever-willing, could make Gurdjieff, or his ideas, as interesting to others as he was himself devoted to the master.

Orage's welcoming committee of colleagues and well-wishers guided Mr. Gurdjieff due east from Hell's Kitchen through midtown Manhattan's bitterly cold streets to Broadway, which begins its north-westerly arc at Central Park's southwest corner. There was a sense of occasion, a hermetic joy known to a few, but the street atmosphere would scarcely have reflected this.

The United States had submitted to a period of enforced national righteousness. Only a month before Gurdjieff's arrival, Andrew Volstead, framer of U.S. prohibition legislation that from January 1920 forbade the production, sale, and transport of alcoholic liquors, told a Minnesota law-and-order conference that Americans were adjusting comfortably to prohibition. With opposition in decline, Volstead's Act need suffer neither amendment nor repeal: surely music to the big ears of twenty-four-year-old boxing promoter Al Capone, currently serving as right-hand man to bootlegger's enforcer Johnny Torrio in Chicago. Prohibition made criminals, and criminals who survived bitter gangland competition grew very rich from much of the adult nation's desire for a drink with a kick.

At his first State of the Union address to Congress on December 6, 1923, President Calvin Coolidge announced he would beef up the United States Coast Guard to frustrate prohibition-induced crime but was otherwise confident America's problems were chiefly domestic. Its robust economy would reduce the economic impact of crises that beset the outside world. Coolidge insisted every American regard the country's condition "with encouragement and satisfaction." There would be growth in the spring. The Twenties, after all, were "roaring," weren't they? Such confidence was undoubtedly melodious to Mr. Gurdjieff's ears, come to "shear the sheep" of the "dollar-fat" American rich, for their own good and his. Nevertheless, he was annoyed at getting so few dollars for his French francs. Still, the exchange rate would work wonders on the return.

Music was scarce the day Gurdjieff hit Broadway. Sundays were *dark,* as theatricals understood the term, as well as dry; it was said that "satire died in New York on Saturday nights" when the theaters closed. Gurdjieff could only gaze from outside at the latest hit shows, shows such as Florenz Ziegfeld's musical *Kid Boots* with Eddie Cantor and Mary Eaton at Broadway's Earl Carroll Theatre, or *Mary Jane McKane,* the new Oscar Hammerstein–Vincent Youmans musical comedy at Broadway's recently opened Imperial Theatre, while intellectual satisfaction could be found, at least starting Monday, at George Bernard Shaw's *Saint Joan,* produced at Manhattan's Garrick Theatre. That undoubtedly appealed to Orage, a great admirer of Shaw's idea of socialism, and one who had enjoyed Shaw's financial beneficence when Orage established his journal, *The New Age,* in 1907. By 1924 Orage had, out of dedication to Gurdjieff and in accordance with the master's will, sold the journal for £100. It is odd to think of a time when the expression *New Age* betokened middle-class socialism with a dash of the "Jesus was a communist, *really*" brand of theosophy, and stranger is it still to observe that Orage believed it was Gurdjieff who had trumped all that.

MEETING THE PRESS

Orage ushered the Gurdjieff party into the grandeur of the massive Ansonia Hotel at 2109 Broadway, the city's first hotel to boast air conditioning, though it made scant difference in January; there was plenty of "air conditioning" outside. A residential hotel, the Ansonia provided luxury accommodation for New York's movers and shakers. Thanks to Orage's personal connections, Gurdjieff arrived at the top, excited to crown Orage's evangelism with the verbal establishment of New York's own Institute for the Harmonious Development of Man: a bridgehead, he hoped, into the powerhouse of the Western psyche—a rich well for pumping cash back to the country that had given New York her *Liberty*.

New York can be generous to newcomers. Two days later, twenty-six-year-old journalist Nunnally Johnson entered Gurdjieff's suite at the Ansonia to interview the curious arrival from Paris. Frustrated with the trade, Johnson would quit journalism permanently in 1932 for Hollywood, where he produced and wrote John Ford's classic *The Grapes of Wrath* (Oscar winner for 1940's best screenplay) and a career's worth of fine adaptations, such as *The Keys of the Kingdom* starring Gregory Peck (1944), in a career extending into the 1960s with his powerful screenplay for Robert Aldrich's 1967 hit, *The Dirty Dozen*.

Witty, informed, and literate, Johnson's skillful handle on social satire could easily have rebuked the vulnerable mystic Gurdjieff. He didn't. Exhibited in the well-read pages of the *Brooklyn Eagle,* Johnson's article was good-humored, his stance respectful; he merely opined that the no less humorous "Greek" desired to put man in tune with his nature. Well, who didn't? Such ambition had always dominated Greek philosophical discourse; any educated American could click with that. If only, that is, we could establish what Man's nature *actually was.* Our current nostrum is that "it's all in the genes." Quite. *What is?* Johnson's article's tacit conclusion was that America could afford to indulge the amusing Greek with his unthreatening, and possibly intriguing, notions.

While Gurdjieff plus troupe launched themselves, quite literally, into a series of sometimes startling demonstrations to paying audiences of sacred dances at the Neighborhood Playhouse and Carnegie Hall, accompanied by a five-piece micro-orchestra, organized by Olga's husband, Thomas de Hartmann, Orage worked hard to bring Gurdjieff to public attention. Gurdjieff persistently galvanized his closest associates into shearing the sheep of their money, for the cause of the survival of the institute he had formed and of which he described himself, without burden of academic honors, professor.

New Yorkers' perception of Gurdjieff was further enlarged on February 10. An article appeared on page 12 of the *New York Times* Arts section under the headline, "Taking the Life Cure in Gurdjieff's School." The account offered an "Intimate Description of the Russian's Institute in France, Whose Aim is the All-Round, Harmonious Development of Man." That the article's author did not follow Nunnally Johnson's assessment of Gurdjieff as a Greek is not surprising, for the piece came from the pen of Maud Hoffman, well-informed American Shakespearean actress, theosophist, and owner of the famous Mahatma Letters, by inheritance from A. P. (Alfred Percy) Sinnett. These forgeries—consisting of alleged communications from Himalayan Masters, or spirit-beings, Koot Hoomi and Morya, supposedly liberated from all earthly bonds save the desire for human enlightenment—were addressed with Theosophical Society founder Madame Blavatsky's blessing to followers Sinnett and Hume. Maud Hoffman had also coauthored with theosophist and bisexual novelist Mabel Collins *Sensa: A Mystery Play,* a "tragedy of the Soul." Mabel Collins's novel *The Blossom and the Fruit* was recommended reading for Aleister Crowley's Magical Order, the A∴A∴. Maud Collins's belief in what the *Sensa*'s introduction calls "the redeeming Spirit within," which "in the final sacrifice achieves apotheosis and sheds a blessing on mankind," made her highly inclined to sympathy with the ideals that attracted people to Gurdjieff's struggling institute in Fontainebleau, despite the fact that Gurdjieff would himself come to express hostility to theosophy and modern occultism. Nevertheless, without the Theosophical Society's near fifty-year career, it is unlikely Gurdjieff would ever have enjoyed an audience able or willing to grasp the first elements of what he was promoting, as it is equally true that a younger Gurdjieff had himself come under the spell of theosophical concepts, though in his late work *The Herald of*

Coming Good (1932), he implies his interest was essentially subversive. According to Paul Beekman Taylor, Gurdjieff told Orage in 1923 that he spent nine years following in Madame Blavatsky's alleged footsteps, finally arriving in India, where Blavatsky placed the ideological centrum of her movement, and Gurdjieff realized the fruitlessness of his efforts; Blavatsky's theosophy did not have the answers he sought and her accounts, he maintained, were untrustworthy.[4]

What light did Maud Hoffman's article shed on the "Russian" Gurdjieff?

As usual in treatments of Gurdjieff, the man is primarily addressed through his recommendations to students; when he appears in the picture, it is as the sedentary and usually benign conductor of ceremonies, spotlit by adoration. The "light" is not intelligible and revelatory but celestial and reverential.

Gurdjieff challenged minds, but we are still in the dark about him.

Maud Hoffman related how summer 1923 had seen residents of Avon and Fontainebleau join hotel visitors to witness Saturday evening demonstrations at the old Prieuré des Basses Loges. Saturday night was Open Night at the Institute, and in a converted aircraft hangar big enough to accommodate more than sixty pupils and several hundred observers, gymnastic and sacred dance exercises, sometimes referred to as *movements,* were performed by troupes of forty students on a stage surrounded by oriental carpets on floor and walls, interspersed with members' warmly colored paintings and stencils. Below the gaily painted canvas ceiling, goatskins were provided for reclining in Asiatic fashion.

The movements composed a synthesis of esoteric gestures, believed to encode ancient ideas that related the soul to the musical harmony of the cosmos, religious ceremonial movements, Asian folk dances, and ritual dances of Christian contemplatives and Sufi dervishes. Arresting and hypnotic, the effect could be geometrically mechanical yet aesthetically poetic by virtue of disciplined efforts to respect cosmic movement, striving for a totality of motors serving a single dynamic will, while all parts worked as an organic clockwork, endowed with specific purpose related to the whole: microcosms in macrocosm. Collision too could have its purpose, if only to demonstrate the destructiveness of the rogue, ungoverned will. The pinions of global harmony came not from the lateral world, but from above: *as above, so below,* goes the ancient Hermetic principle, or in the Christian paraphrase, "Thy will be done on Earth as it is in heaven."

As a kind of representative or agent of that will, stood the man himself at the side of the stage, or wherever else the deus ex machina wished to be. Visitors to the New York demonstrations were particularly stunned by two tricks Gurdjieff designed to stagger audiences. The first was the stop command when Gurdjieff would make a simple gesture at a moment of choice whereupon the entire troupe would stop stock-still in perfect unison, whatever they were doing, regardless of pain of posture. The complementary trick occurred when the troupe would gather at the rear of the stage, then rush forward toward the stage's edge. The audience would naturally expect an impressive stop signal just in time, but on occasion, showman Gurdjieff would turn away, casually lighting a cigarette while the troupe, defying time and space, leapt unrestrained into the abyss before them, being deposited pell-mell yet frozen into the precise positions in which they fell about one another in the seeming chaos of descent. No injuries were reported.

All this rhythmic magic was accompanied by "mystical and inspiring music": the work of Gurdjieff's devoted Russian composer and cocomposer, Thomas de Hartmann. Much of the music bore a flavor distinctly reminiscent of Erik Satie's *Gnossiennes,* with oriental scales, pronounced incantatory tones, and stately rhythms of self-conscious, mystico-mathematical construction. This was symbolic music, and its natural homeland was the heyday of symbolist art that began to flourish in France in the 1880s and whose blooming in Russia in the early twentieth century would be asphyxiated as the Bolshevik Revolution's concrete social realism banished the ambiguities of genius.

During her stay at Fontainebleau, Maud Hoffman was surprised to find *philosophical* exposition of Gurdjieff's "ideas" in short supply; there were apparently no lectures or classes of philosophical instruction.* Everything proceeded on an individual learning-by-doing basis, designed to break accustomed patterns of behavior and familiar comforts. Nevertheless, American papers referred to the Fontainebleau community as the "Forest philosophers," which had a nice, homely ring about it, redolent of fashionable campfire uniformed movements and the widespread youth subculture of dressing up and living, but not being persecuted, as "red Indians"—a spot of collective savagery to alleviate, or nudge, the uptightness of the bourgeois; hippies in their turn would also don Geronimo bandanas in the 1960s. Gurdjieff's dancers wore loose unisex clothing of the Bohemian Cossack type: workers indeed, but a very different conception of the worker to the allegedly victorious proletariat of the Bolshevik state.

Hoffman found that practically everyone at the institute was English or American. The remnant of Russian followers whom Gurdjieff had led from Moscow to Georgia in 1917, thence like the children of Israel fleeing the Bolshevik pharaoh, through the Caucasus to Turkey and eventually to Germany and France, had their own dining room on the other side of the kitchen, past the dairy. Hoffman failed to notice the absence of French students; the French, whose mystical genii had pioneered the occult revival and the Symbolist movement, had their own gnostic scene seasoned with Gallic unconcern for foreign novelties. Besides, popular French interest in occultism and neo-gnostic spirituality had declined steeply since the late 1890s; the war had practically finished the movement off, its leading lights deceased before the armistice. In a sense, Gurdjieff was bringing coals to Newcastle, after the industry had all but shut down. The latest artistic movements in Paris were Dada and surrealism in abstraction-fueled jazz settings with Lenin a hero; Gurdjieff had no

---

*See chapter 1, note 5 for details.[5]

time for any of them. He hated the foxtrot, preferring to summon the West's chaotic civilization to the timeless steppes of Central Asia.

Maud Hoffman divined the institute's kinship to the outer court of an ancient mystery school, lacking only the sign of Delphi above its gates: *Gnōthi seauton* (Know thyself). There was plenty of work, but the Work's purpose was essentially for what difference the protracted and often painful effort "worked" inside the being of the worker. Self-observation was very important. Breaking bounds of accustomed behavior or self-perception was crucial to the Work: in a sense to open up to unknown potential through wearing out the familiar self and shape of being. Someone might be asked to dig a ditch for new pipes, only to be instructed by Gurdjieff to fill it up again. The "new pipes" he had in mind perhaps were conduits of the psyche. Surprise and shock were administered for therapeutic value. We are now used to the Gurdjieffian concept of "no pain, no gain."

Hoffman understood Gurdjieff's basic challenge to be his assertion that modern man languished in disharmonious unconsciousness—the individual a puppet whose vaunted freedom was illusory. There could be no true refuge in extreme individualism or in collectivism, for the collective was governed by the ignorant pumping dreams into the masses and calling them real.

Speaking from the point of view of the middle and upper classes, Hoffman maintained that "most of the energy in modern life flows into mental activity," so to compensate, there was a need for physical activity. Everyone should be a worker and Gurdjieff spoke of the Work, doubtless purloining and transmuting the traditional activity of the alchemist: the Great Work of psychic and substantial transformation of low into exalted golden or spiritual states. Gurdjieff gave the Work a modernist twist in line with mystiques of fashionable socialism.

The physical labor ran alongside an idea that everyone had emotions and thoughts to express in art; every person was some kind of artist; everyone could participate in a dance, with a bit of training, and the dance would free the body as an expressive, artistic tool. The material employed by the harmoniously developing artist was the combination of one's own mental, emotional, and instinctive energies.

Here is the familiar tripartite Gurdjieffian wisdom—fallen man is three, with three brains: feelings, mentation or ways of thinking, and instinctive physical life. To get all this energy to flow equally into the proper channels, internal conflicts had to be overcome. The self must challenge the self: *Where are you; who are you, and why? Why am I here? Who am I? What am I really doing? What do I know? Do I understand this, or am I swayed by feeling? Have I thought too much and felt too little? Have I felt another's needs while thinking about my own? Am I physically cowardly? Am I a being capable of love? Am I afraid to assert my body? Am I lazy in body, while busy in mind? While running around being busy, do I ever stop to think? Do I respond to instinct? Am I incapable of common sense? Is my life real? Am I really free? Am I a real "I"?* And so on. Gurdjieff wanted his students to learn how to *flow* with the genius and will of unconscious movement, of which the "movements" were symbols. The movements were just as significant when performed alone for purposes of self-remembering, as when danced with and before others.

Gurdjieff was here not completely out of kilter with other kinds of movements in postwar European philosophy. Nietzsche, inspired by Eduard von Hartmann's *Philosophy of the Unconscious* (1869) had prepared some minds for the philosophical value of the unconscious being that could emerge as "superman" from civilization's Götterdämmerung. Nietzsche believed the solar Apollo of Western rationalism had stifled the instinctive, wild, irrational Dionysus of the chthonic id. The concrete formulae of logical prose had choked the air pipe of poetry, wherein lay prophetic truth, not fact. What passed for "intelligence" disparaged inspiration; mere cleverness suppressed genius: the *daimon* who came from the other side of time. There was among some thinkers a suspicion that the Western world had been "thought to death," that it made more useful sense to fly an airplane or climb a mountain than read another book—the future was for *movement*. Into this vortex, bright young things could throw themselves. Along with the "more life at all costs" tendency existed a corresponding thrust toward mechanical movement, being part of something bigger, imitation of fashion, skating on ice for thrills, superficiality of feeling: lack of depth, meaning, understanding, sympathy.

Gurdjieff's institute impressed on Hoffman its claim that harmonious movements could establish a reactionary effect to mechanical civilization's unnatural cramping of humanity's latent style. *Work was good.* There was to this dictum, however, a most vital caveat that fascists and communists utterly missed: *the work must be voluntary and intentional.* It was primarily for the individual's welfare, and only for other individuals as a parergon or side effect. The individual's essential will ought to be revealed and enacted, not suppressed, kept on the right, harmonious track by openness to religious feeling and the life of conscience.

The Work called for mental sweating too. Gurdjieff filled the vacant hours with learning languages or physical and mental tricks: codes that could be incorporated into performances, with numbers representing words and parts of words, or notes for the piano, or movements. Mental agility of yogilike dexterity was cultivated and prized. This work was tough, painful, and only rewarding in the end, when movements could be performed with an immediacy combining instinct, thought, and feeling, almost unconsciously.

Gurdjieff had grasped that a complex philosophy could be transformed into thoughtful actions, just as the Christian saint could express the entirety of God's mystery in acts of selfless love, senseless to the rationalist.

After giving a fairly bucolic description of the French château—formerly a priory for Carmelite monks as well as a property of the famous Dreyfus family—its Empire rooms, its tasteful grounds where the piano was played for the dancing outside amid sun's glare and dappled shades, the basic food, self-help, and communal kitchen routines, Maud Hoffman finally arrived at the man behind it all. Welcoming new students, in hat and overcoat despite the heat, Gurdjieff greets them in the kitchen "with a smile that has both sweetness and spirit-quality." The first impression was a nature "of great kindness and sensitiveness," impressions augmented later on by the sense of "combined strength and delicacy, simplicity and subtlety." According to Hoffman, "he is more awake than any one you have ever known." By *awake* I presume Hoffman meant a combination of spiritual awareness and vivid, hyperalert presence of being.

The article concludes with a blunt statement that perfect being cannot be experienced by intellect alone, or by devotional feelings alone, or by physical strength alone. Basically, you needed Gurdjieff's institute "to fill in deficiencies, correct heredity and habit, and to balance knowledge and being." All this effort brings the by-product of renewal of energies and youth and the making of oneself to be "more efficient for life."

Sold!

Gymnastics and worship of youthfulness were popular pastimes in the 1920s and 30s. "Keep young and beautiful" went Dubin and Warren's hit song—a favorite of Churchill's, incidentally. This was clever marketing. That last line about efficiency was quite pointed for a modern American audience. According to the dicta of capitalist "philosophy," efficiency pursued scientifically was the path to economy and profit. In terms of salesmanship, Maud Hoffman delivered the goods. And it was clear what interested parties could do. They could, if fortunate enough to be admitted at the irregularly attended Prieuré gate, enter a new world in fashionable France, just an ocean liner's voyage away.

And what do we learn from Hoffman about the real George Gurdjieff? Bar trying to please and delight paying guests on arrival with a little tenderness, very little. He remains enigmatic, a source of fascination.

Whichever date he was born, Maud Hoffman and the American public were encountering Gurdjieff in middle age. What kind of life had already shaped the professor of sacred dancing? What lay behind the tender smile of welcome?

Who really *was* George Gurdjieff?

TWO

Reviewing
the Situation

A Birth

It is not surprising that questions persist regarding Gurdjieff's background and identity. Many of Gurdjieff's early problems stem from the fact that his father, Ivan Ivanovich, was Greek. He was Greek, but he was born in Turkey, whose capital Constantinople languished astride the Bosphorus as hub of the great, but long-declining and endemically vicious Ottoman Empire. As Christians in Turkey, Greeks suffered persecution despite, or perhaps because of, the fact that Asia Minor (afterward *Turkey*) had been Greek speaking and anciently Christian until the Seljuq Turk invasion in the eleventh century. Conditions worsened for Greeks with every attempt of the Ottoman Empire's subject peoples, including Greeks, Cretans, Armenians, Bosnians, Albanians, Macedonians, Bulgarians, Romanians, and Montenegrins, to throw off or alleviate the Ottoman yoke. Under Turkish rule, conquered Greeks were subjected to "dhimmi" status, tolerated to live by and large, but not to be treated as equal under Islamic law. Since Christian testimony could not gainsay Muslim testimony in a Turkish court, theft, perjury, fraud, and murder of Greeks could and did pass unheeded as crimes. Persecution had the support of Islamic religious justice.

ARCHIVAL RECORDS

Hearst columnist and old friend of Aleister Crowley William Seabrook, in reporting Gurdjieff's arrival in New York in 1924, gave the family name as Georgiades, a familiar name to Greek immigrants in the United States. Whence Seabrook got what he took to be the original Greek form of the Anglicized Russian Gurdjieff is unknown. *Georgos* means "farmer" in Greek and is the origin of Gurdjieff's Christian name, Georgii. *Georgeades* means "son of George" but as far as we know, Gurdjieff's father's name was Ivan Ivanovich (or son of Ivan). Ivanovich was a common surname in Macedonia and in Montenegro. Nevertheless, the name Ivan Ivanovich Gurdjiff does appear in Alexandropol, Russian Armenia, close to the Turkish border in 1907. A gazette of local families lists this person as married to Eva with two sons: Georgii born in 1880, and Dmitri born in 1883, and a daughter, Sophia.[1] Even though Gurdjieff's mother's name was the Greek Evdokia—meaning "good thought"—which should not strictly be shortened to Eva (Eve), it is probably Gurdjieff's family that is being referred to, despite the doubtful birth dates; Gurdjieff did indeed have a brother Dmitri and sister Sophia, born in 1895 or 1896.

Earlier records complicate the issue of Gurdjieff's father's name still further. While Alexandropol sources from 1883–1918 spell the name in Russian Cyrillic as *Giordzhev* and *Gyrdzhev*,[2] Georgian records, according to Paul Beekman Taylor, state that it was as Vasilii *Kurdjogli* that Ivan's brother Vasilii married Politima Oprikov in September 1867; Vasilii was Gurdjieff's uncle. This apparently Turkish or possibly Georgian form of the surname is also to be found, with a slight variant, in Armenia's Central Archives.[3] There, we find Ivan Ivanovich *Kurchogli,* husband of Evdokia Elephtherovna (born 1852; Russian form of "daughter of Elephther"), whom Ivan is recorded as having married in 1871, aged twenty-three. In Turkish, *oglu* is the common suffix meaning "son of" and *ogli* could be a transliteration of it.

Given the quantity of variants, we cannot be certain what Gurdjieff's name derives from or when it was adopted as a family name. Gurdjieff himself offers no assistance in the matter, but he always pronounced his surname "Gyor-jeff" in the Russian mode. There was, however, a village called Gurdji, part of Armutlu on the Turkish Armutlu peninsula by the Sea of Marmara just south of Constantinople (Istanbul), no longer listed, the scene of Greek army atrocities against Turks during the 1920–1921 Greco-Turkish war waged in western Turkey.[4] Gurdjieff maintained in *Meetings* his family had been Byzantines before the Turks conquered Constantinople (capital of the Byzantine Empire) in 1453, migrating to central Anatolia due to Turkish persecution around Constantinople. The Marmara peninsula had certainly been part of what was left of Byzantium before the capital's overthrow in 1453. To add to the mystery, *Gurji* is also both an Arabic and a Persian word for "Georgian," though if that were the name's origin one might not expect Georgian records to express it as "Kurdjogli" since in Georgia *Gurji* was a familiar patriotic nickname for a Georgian.

Incidentally, toward the end of his chapter on his father in *Meetings,* Gurdjieff states that the last time he saw his father was in 1916, when his father was eighty-two. This date conflicts with the Armenian archive entry above, where, if twenty-three in 1871, Ivan Ivanovich was born in 1847 or 1848; whereas if Gurdjieff was accurate, his father was born in 1833 or 1834. Whom can we believe?

One thing we can be reasonably certain of is that both Gurdjieff's parents were Greek. His mother's maiden name comes from the Greek *Elephtheros,* referring perhaps to the Greek Orthodox saint and martyr of this name as well as the ancient Greek word for freedom: a dangerous surname to have in Turkey in the wake of the bloody 1866–69 Cretan revolt against Turkish rule. Gurdjieff's mother's father Elepheriadis (Greek again) was married to Sophia, whose name was obviously Greek but who was nicknamed in her capacity as midwife *padji,* Turkish for "sister," a clue as to her birthplace. It is worth noting that the Greek *eleutheria* (freedom) is linked to the Greek goddess of childbirth, Eileithyia, helper of women and patron of pregnant women. In some

Greek myths, this daughter of Zeus and Hera was herself born out of wedlock. It is possible that Evdokia's mother Sophia (Wisdom) was a very understanding "sister," even to her own daughter. Eileithya was the mother of Eros, after all. There is a cave of the goddess at Koprana, 9 kilometers from Herakleion in Crete.

Georgia's Central State Historical Archives reveal that Gurdjieff's uncle Vasilii lived in Ekepad, one of a number of Georgian villages settled by Greek-speaking Greeks from Turkey.[5] Ekepad's records were included in those of an adjacent village now called Velispiri near the Pshani River, a fairly dreary flat landscape between Tbilisi and Lake Paravani to the southwest. It is also from Georgian records that we learn that Vasilii married Politima Oprikov in November 1867. The date is interesting for several reasons. First, Gurdjieff states in *Meetings* that his father and his brothers (we only know the name of one of them),[6] while hailing from Gumush Khanei—now Gümüshane—60 kilometers south of Trebizond on the Black Sea coast in northeast Turkey, had escaped Turkish persecution by heading east across the border into Georgia. Gurdjieff states this was "not long before the last big Russo-Turkish war." The war referred to can only be the Russian-Turkish war of 1877–78, a gargantuan armed conflict by any measure. If Vasilii was in Georgia by 1867 when he married, that is really quite a long time before the cataclysmic war of 1877–78, but such levity of Gurdjieff regarding dates seems to be on a par with his statement in the same chapter of *Meetings* that when his father parted from his brothers in Georgia to journey some 100 kilometers south to Alexandropol in Russian Armenia, Alexandropol's name had "just changed" from the "Turkish name of Gumri." In fact, Tsar Nicholas I had renamed this extremely ancient city after his wife Alexandra Fyodorovna as long ago as 1837—and *Gumri* was not Turkish. Restored today to Gyumri in an independent Armenia, after a Soviet-era name change to honor Lenin, its nineteenth-century christening to Alexandropol was a settled matter by the time Gurdjieff's father entered this fascinating city of churches and bells.

Given the dates, it is likely that Ivan and Vasilii's departure from

Turkey to join their ethnic countrymen in Georgia was occasioned by the 1866–69 Cretan Revolt when Greeks in Turkey, especially the Pontus Greeks from the Vilayet of Trebizond where Gurdjieff's father was probably raised, suffered at the hands of angry Turks, conscious that Greeks had come from outside Crete to help their brethren fight Turkish oppression, after the Turks had failed to deliver on legally binding promises of fair treatment for Greeks. The Cretan revolt shocked Europe, a shock compounded after the "Holocaust of Arkadi" when the majority of the 259 Greek defenders along with some 700 women and children taking refuge in the Arkadi monastery died in a deadly conflagration when Ottoman troops stormed the monastery and the abbot ignited gunpowder in the makeshift magazine in a desperate effort to forestall Turkish slaughter.

Pontus Greeks had inhabited the Trebizond region since Homer's day. Their continued presence irritated Turkish nationalists. It has been said that one always hates what one has wronged. Gurdjieff's ancestors may not themselves originally have been ethnic Pontus Greeks with their characteristically antique form of Greek, for he says in *Meetings* that after leaving Byzantium, his forebears had moved to central Turkey, where their substantial cattle herds and flocks of sheep prospered until changed conditions forced them to move northward to the Pontus, where they found long-settled people of their own race and traditions.[7] Gurdjieff's account of his father's eventual, and perhaps traumatic, move from Gumush Khanei to Georgia chimes in perfectly with events of the period.

In the early 1870s, members of Xenophon, a Greek association founded in Trebizond in 1872, were alarmed at the numbers of Pontus Greeks migrating from around a hundred Hellenic settlements in the Pontus to Russian territory or to Greece. Census returns indicate numbers of Greek settlers in Georgia rose from approximately 12,000 in 1865 to nearly 29,000 in 1886. Gumush Khanei was a well-known Turkish source of Greek settlers in Georgia. While migration fever had ebbed somewhat after a high following the Crimean War in the late 1850s, the Cretan conflict provided a fresh, bayonet-sharp stimulus to get away from Turkish harassment and countless unpunished crimes committed against Greeks and Armenians. When Gurdjieff's father left Georgia for Armenia he would have found fellow feeling there with Armenians, as well as Greeks, who also fled persecution in Turkey, though this was still some four decades and more before Turkish military persecution of Armenians and Greeks reached genocidal proportions in the second and third decades of the twentieth century at the time Gurdjieff quit Constantinople, like his ancestors, and tried to reestablish himself in western Europe.

Vasilii's marriage of 1867 to a woman with a Russian surname would fit well with an exit from Turkey sometime around the inception of the Cretan revolt. Can the same be said of Ivan? It is possible, but according to Gurdjieff's account, his father Ivan inherited wealth, by the standards of the region, founded on cattle and sheep, and we do not know what part his brother or brothers played in Ivan's business. It might be that Vasilii went to Georgia to help arrange pasturage for what was, to say the least, a major and conceivably perilous move. We do not know. Nor do we know whether Ivan met his wife Evdokia in the Pontus in Turkey, or later in Georgia, or later again in Alexandropol, for Gurdjieff tells us, as do Alexandropol records, that his father parted from his brothers in Georgia for Alexandropol, without telling us whether Ivan was alone or not, or whether he brought his wealth with him. As for Ivan's marriage, Michael Benham has passed on evidence from Georgian scholar Manana Khomeriki's research indicating Ivan and Evdokia married at Alexandropol in 1871, the information coming from the metric (family) book of the church in Alexandropol held in Armenia's Central Archives, which book also refers to the birth of Vasilii's son. Vasilii's marriage appears in Georgian records in the metric book for the village of Keivan-Bulgason. It is quite possible that Ivan met the Greek Evdokia in Alexandropol's substantial Greek quarter, known as Urmonts, which is recorded as having 363 households during the period when Gurdjieff's cousin, the sculptor Sergei Merkurov's grandfather built a house in Alexandropol (sometime between 1858 and 1869; accounts differ). Merkurov's family was among a hundred other Greek families who migrated from western Armenia (far-east Turkey), specifically the Vilayet of Trebizond in the period before the Russo-Turkish war of 1877–78. Grandfather Merkurov, an architect, would build Alexandropol's Greek Orthodox church, dedicated to Saint George (destroyed by earthquake in 1926). The metric book of the Church of Alexandropol also records the birth of a son Kiriakoz to Vasilii and Politima after the couple, presumably, followed Ivan to Russian Armenia some time after their marriage in November 1867.

If Gurdjieff was born to Ivan and Evdokia in 1877, as many official records maintain, then he was almost certainly a Greek native of Alexandropol, Russian Armenia. There is the possibility that it was the onset of hostilities between Turkey and Russia in 1877, coupled with Gurdjieff's imminent birth or immediate infancy that occasioned a final departure from Turkey to safety with the new baby. In which case, it is possible that Gurdjieff was in fact born in Turkey and that was something he either did not know or did not wish anyone else to know. And if Gurdjieff was telling the truth about his age in his last years, and his parents were not married until 1871 as one record attests, then it would mean that he was born *out of wedlock,* something he may not have known, or something he did not want others to know. Besides, if the received birth date for his mother is accurate (1852), she would only have been thirteen or fourteen if, against the bulk of evidence, Gurdjieff was born illegitimately in or around 1866. Of course, had Evdokia indeed become a mother at that tender age, it would account for the later marriage when eighteen, and the confusion over birth dates. Could there have been a cloud over Gurdjieff's birth? Benham considers this speculation highly unlikely, not only because a birth date of 1866 goes against the majority of documentary evidence, but because Evdokia had already lost two children before Georgii came along.

While it might be convenient or even sensational to solve the mystery of Gurdjieff's birth date thus, there is a significant story that the time-defying Gurdjieff himself tells, and though we might now feel accustomed to treat his testimony with some scepticism, it does enable us to get a more reasonable fix on just when little Georgii entered the world.

CATTLE PLAGUE

In *Meetings,* Gurdjieff describes the greatest disaster that ever befell his father,[8] whom he does not name, such being his awestruck respect for the man. Having successfully settled his family—father, mother, grandmother, younger brother, sister, and himself—in Armenia, much of whose cattle-friendly land is over 3,300 feet, Ivan augmented his mighty stock with several thousand more cattle belonging to local peasants. Repaying them in butter and cheese, Ivan effectively insured their cattle, even against predations by wolves. But catastrophe struck. Within months, Ivan went from a pampered life as the district's biggest cattle owner to penury when a fatal cattle plague (rinderpest*) reached Armenia from Asia. Since Ivan had to repay the peasants for their losses from his personal funds, he was reduced to opening a lumberyard and carpenter's shop with members of his former household; it was a massive comedown and profoundly affected the family and its self-image.

Gurdjieff says he was about seven at the time of the calamity and could still recall the family's shepherds. He recalled also how the lumberyard period lasted for four years, during which time the Russians steadily rebuilt the city of Kars and established the Kars Oblast (region), a strategically significant fist of territory punching right into imperial Ottoman homeland.

Kars was an ancient, formerly Armenian fortress city about 70 kilometers west of Alexandropol across what had been and is now again the Turkish border. While the bulk of casualties endured by protagonists of the 1877–78 Russo-Turkish war had been in Turkey's northwest, the Russians

---

*Rinderpest is a centuries-old infectious disease that killed cloven-hoofed animals. It was finally eradicated; the last known case was reported in 2001.

having invaded through a Bulgaria that had risen furiously against Turkish cruelties, a major wing of the campaign was fought from Georgia in the east. The Russian army was 50,000 strong with 202 guns against a Turkish strength of 100,000. Kars was besieged by the Russians in May 1877, finally falling to the victorious Russian general Ivan Lazarev on November 18 of that year, whereafter five formerly Turkish regions were joined to the Kars Oblast. Russia intended the territory's annexation and with the war's conclusion in 1878 began rebuilding Kars as the Christian city it had been centuries before. It was now joined to the Russian Empire with its environs, including the northerly province of Batumi near the Georgian border on the Black Sea's east coast. By 1881, eleven thousand Muslims had left the Kars region, and economic migrants from Armenia and Georgia, as well as Pontus Greeks from Turkey, were encouraged to settle in their place under Russian military protection. One of these migrants was Gurdjieff's Uncle Vasilii, later followed, alone initially, by Vasilii's brother Ivan, who established his workshop there, leaving his family temporarily in Alexandropol until, presumably, conditions and facilities made moving to Kars sensible.

James Moore's biography of Gurdjieff (*Gurdjieff: The Anatomy of a Myth*, 1991) saw Gurdjieff's account of Asian cattle plague as giving considerable, even decisive, support to the idea that Gurdjieff was born around the year 1866. Moore was aware of an Asian cattle plague striking Armenia in 1873. Rinderpest erupted in the wake of the Russo-Khivan War of that year, fought against the Turkmen's stiff resistance in the Transcaspian Khiva Khanate, just south of the Amu-darya River, now on independent Uzbekistan's southern border with Turkmenistan. Turkmenbashi's seizure in 1869 gave the Russians critical port facilities on Turkmenistan's western coast on the Caspian Sea. Simple arithmetic subtracts Gurdjieff's age of seven from 1873 and produces a birth date of 1866.

There are problems here, especially if one lends credence to Gurdjieff's statement that during the four years *after* the cattle plague, the Russians were rebuilding Kars. Four years after the tail end of 1873, the Russians had only just taken Kars after a violent seven-month siege. Well, if you're desperate you can pick or choose which bits of Gurdjieff's memory you trust, and give or take a year or two or more. In this case, you don't have to.

Intermittent crises of rinderpest constituted a long-standing European and British agricultural headache. Cattle plague had spread in 1865 from the environs of Bucharest in southern Romania to northwest Turkey, its advance believed a result of the Russian army's dependence on infected oxen from the steppes to haul wagonloads of material in their military campaign against the Ottoman Empire in the Balkans. In 1866 rinderpest became a permanent blight on New Russia; that is, Ukraine, Crimea, and the Black Sea coast. Its threat may even have influenced Ivan to lead his herds into Georgia, away from the southern Black Sea coast around Trebizond. Gurdjieff, however, is quite specific that the plague that overturned his family's fortunes came from Asia, the east, as did the plague of 1873. According to Clive A. Spinage's authoritative study *Cattle Plague*,[9] vigorous attempts in western Europe since that time to combat the ruinous disease had pushed its contagion to Russia, where a million cases erupted in 1884, and to the Caspian and Transcaspian regions as a result of poorly policed cattle trading. By 1886 however, Russian authority, recognizing the depth of the crisis, had established two serum centers for areas neighboring on China, Mongolia, and Transcaucasia, including Armenia. This would match an Asian plague carried into Armenia to hit Ivan Ivanovich's fortunes around 1883 and 1884. If Gurdjieff was "about seven years old" in 1884, that would give us a birth date of about 1877, consistent with official records. Such a date would also allow for a proper period for the reconstruction and "Russianization" of the Kars Oblast that started after the conclusion of the Congress of Berlin on July 13, 1878, and would continue as imperial military and economic policy through the 1890s.

Gurdjieff's future destiny hung on a new life at Kars—imperial policy in Transcaucasia and Central Asia provided set and setting. Russian imperial policy conditioned the first forty years of Gurdjieff's life, and removed from the Russian imperial context, Gurdjieff was a fish out of water, forever making baleful judgments on his non-Asiatic hosts.

THREE

War Baby

An Education in Kars

Nothing exerts a stronger psychic effect upon the human environment, and especially upon children, than the life which the parents have not lived. . . . All the father's resignation will turn into consuming ambition in the son. The father's resentment and inevitable feelings of inferiority will make the son an avenger of his father's wrongs. He will wield his sword against all authority, and will do battle with everything that lays claim to the *potestas patris,* as if it were his own father's adversary. What the father lost or had to relinquish—success, fame, a free-roving life in the great world—he will have to win back again. And, following a tragic law, he must fall out with his friends, as the predestined consequence of the fateful bond with his only friend—for psychic endogamy is attended by heavy punishments.

CARL JUNG, *THE SPIRIT IN ART, MAN, AND LITERATURE*[1]

So wrote the great Swiss psychologist Carl Jung of the physician, healer, alchemist, and spiritual teacher, Paracelsus (1493–1541). He might have felt its appropriateness, at least in part, to the case of Gurdjieff, but it would be most unwise to try to explain Gurdjieff with a slick slice of psychological sleight of hand. Nevertheless, there can be little doubt that there is nothing fortuitous in Gurdjieff's having made his father the first of the remarkable men to be met with in his *Meetings*. And we can only guess at the inner, private turmoil undergone by the mostly quiet, steady, wise Ivan in the face of what he had led his family into—a life of perpetual struggle in a violent and unforgiving world. One can perhaps imagine a brief respite of relief when, some time after the failure of his lumber business, and his laboring as a carpenter-handyman, Ivan Ivanovich decided to go west, alone to the frontier fortress town of Kars to make yet another life, better perhaps for his family in the long run: a new start.

What effect all this had on young, proud Georgii we may surmise by the extreme adoration his adult self offers at the shrine of his father's memory, for his father was a man who could do no wrong, whose word was law, whose wisdom sacrosanct, whose integrity matchless, whose example shone, and whose love for the past and its wisdom took Gurdjieff right back through the vicissitudes of time to the ancient Hephaestean workshop of the mind of man. Gurdjieff saw his father as one with his roots at the beginning of man's ascent, having fallen from the stars and beyond. Furthermore, Ivan was a man who knew what work was, who taught his son what work was; Gurdjieff would make his followers work, and it is no accident that what some of them have favored with the term *the Fourth Way* Gurdjieff himself most closely understood as the Work. What was good for his father, and then for him, was good for all. He would set his followers to work; work off the old self, work off the pain, work it all off. Work! It has been said that one can lose oneself in work; one can find oneself in it also, so long, his father taught him, as one does not get too attached to one particular skill. One must keep expanding one's repertoire; one must fight the tendency to sleep; one must enlarge one's consciousness, for the inner life is infinite and only fear sets the bounds.

Gurdjieff's father, if we are to credit the son's testimony, gradually unhooked the boy from dependence on the opinions of others, stressing the importance of individual, hands-on learning through doing. Most notably his father taught him never to trust the word of a man in priest's garb. His father made Gurdjieff question where authority lay.

This stubborn streak in the face of a world that always seems to talk down so that its denizens stop speaking up must have run in the family. One of the first reminiscences from childhood to grace Gurdjieff's first attempt at writing a book concerns sterling advice offered by his father's mother, then over a hundred years old, from her deathbed. Gurdjieff was but a "chubby mite" he says, when his grandmother placed her dying left hand on his head as he kissed her right hand at the bedside and whispered distinctly, "Eldest of my grandsons! Listen and always remember my strict injunction to you: in life never do as others do."[2] When the mite didn't seem to quite grasp the message, she added, a trifle angrily, "Either do nothing—just go to school—or do something nobody else does." At which moment, with commendable restraint, timing, and dignity, she gave up her soul, as Gurdjieff puts it, directly into the hands of "His Truthfulness, the Archangel Gabriel." The reference to Gabriel in this role is worth a moment's digression, since while Jewish and Islamic lore permits Gabriel's role as an Angel of Death who separates soul from body (the Archangel Azrael predominates the role in Islamic traditions), prominence given to Gabriel in this respect is a strong feature of Yezidi faith, where Gabriel is imagined with a knife, ready to sever the soul from the body. Gurdjieff, as we shall see, enjoyed a largely unspoken relationship with Yezidi oral traditions.

Gurdjieff related in *Beelzebub's Tales to His Grandson* (hereafter referred to as *Tales*) how his grandmother's advice had an immediate effect. He said the sacred scene of her death, in a room of great significance to him all his life, filled with the popular incense of "Old Athos"—the Greek Orthodox mountain monastery—drove him to dive into a bin filled with peelings intended for the pigs during Lent and to keep his own counsel despite everyone else's going to the cemetery. On his mother's return she cried over his disappearance, and touched to the heart, Gurdjieff emerged from the bin, rushed to her skirts and began involuntarily stamping his feet and braying like a donkey. When it came to his grandmother's solemn requiem forty days later, whereas everyone else adopted the required stony faces of mourning, he broke from the group and began skipping round the grave singing, "Let her with the saints repose, Now that she's turned up her toes, Oi! Oi! Oi!" From that time on, he would contrive to do as much as he could with the external inventiveness of the literalist, so long as he did it unlike anyone else. If his siblings, for example, caught a ball with the right hand, he would do a somersault, bounce the ball, and when it came to catch it, would use the thumb and forefinger of his left hand. This self-conscious thrust at the genius of originality was probably not quite what his grandmother was getting at, but as Blake reminds us, "If a fool would persist in his folly he would become wise." Gurdjieff cultivated energetic inventiveness as the principal mode of being. Be an individual at all costs.

There is something deeply touching about reading Gurdjieff's determination to paint his cosmos in his own colors as he grew from being a "chubby mite" into what he called a "young rascal," for there is a pulsation that runs right through the almost interminable tales of Beelzebub to this devil's remarkably patient grandson. That pulse is the regular gong of a terrible reminder of the nature of human beings, or as Beelzebub/Gurdjieff is wont to describe the alien species of earthlings, "the three-brained bipeds," who, the grandson is frequently reminded, "would suddenly, without rhyme or reason, begin destroying one another's existence."[3]

Whether one wants to believe Gurdjieff was born in 1866, when that particular Cretan Revolt erupted, or in 1877, when many tens of thousands of Russians and Turks tried to slaughter one another into submission, the historical facts speak volumes. Gurdjieff was growing up in a world of immense insecurity, persistent violence, summary justice, and constant threat of death from many sources. Turkish authorities used Kurds and Circassians to kill and harass Armenians; Greeks were bullied and murdered in the Pontus; Yezidis were slaughtered with impunity in the Ottoman Empire, while in the Kars Oblast Turks were undesirable. The Russian Empire was forever bubbling at its edges, all the way east to the Chinese border, ready to boil over when opportunity arose. The East was as wild as Tombstone, Arizona—wilder, in fact, and he who would walk in the steppes of Central Asia might soon find his feet in Boot Hill. Gabriel had his work cut out for him in Transcaucasia.

While Beelzebub offers explanations to answer the incredulous *Why?* that must emerge in man's conscience in the face of pitiless, self-righteous war, Gurdjieff presents us with a picture of a childhood full of fun and bizarreries, wrapped in love and warmth and mischief. If, as a boy, he stopped to think about what was going on about him in the big picture, he does not let on. It is said that a child accepts the reality in which he or she is raised, but there must be limits to this sort of thing. Children know fear for what it is; they sense when things are wrong. Adult explanations can run out eventually. In most of us, this starts to happen around the time we are expected to "take responsibility" for our actions!

Gurdjieff was a naughty boy, something of a scamp, by his own admission. It is to be suspected his parents gave him all they could in the way of encouragement, doubtless trying to make up in security of love what they could no longer offer in rubles. Gurdjieff's father gave the inestimable gift of himself, teaching his son how to do things and clearly opening up a two-way channel of free communication that was honest, searching, and direct. Gurdjieff maintains his father was always gentle and caring toward him, indulgent of eccentricity and naughtiness, except that is, when it came to basic disciplines. The one bridle Gurdjieff remembered that at the time he obviously chafed under was his father's insistence that the blissful time in the morning when young people feel most cozy in bed, before having to get up, was the time to jump. His father forcefully insisted young Georgii get out of bed and wash in the cold fountain outside, whatever the weather. In his maturity, Gurdjieff thanked his father from the bottom of his heart for this painful discipline, adamant he could never have lived the life he did—indeed, could never have *survived*—had it not been for his father's lesson in foregoing personal comfort for the law of survival and hard self-control, while embracing direct contact with the elements.

One thing Gurdjieff's father perhaps never felt he had to worry about was fear that his eldest son would follow some pied piper into ignominious, ignoble conduct, that he might "go the way of all flesh" and join the gang instead of leading it. Gurdjieff was a fighter, but he definitely had different ideas about conduct and personal pride to those of his father, or rather in addition to those of his father, who, though skeptical regarding much of his religion, adhered to a commercially self-defeating, exemplary standard of personal ethics and fairness in business. Gurdjieff would learn hard lessons from his father's decency and take back from the world what the world had taken from him.

In *Tales* Gurdjieff relates how he and fellow rascals were laying pigeon traps one bright day on a neighbor's roof when a chum offered advice from his zoology teacher as to improving the trap with respect to the pigeon's particularly agile big toe, whereupon another boy, saliva spraying over young Georgii, proceeded with ludicrously pseudo-intellectual long-windedness (wiseacreing) to splutter to the trap technician he was "a hopeless mongrel offshoot of the Hottentots," an "abortion" just like his teacher! Incensed by the know-all cynic, Gurdjieff went for him, charging at the spit-spraying critic and plunging his head bull-like into the shocked lad's solar plexus. Laid out, the boy was unconscious. With just as much rascally casualness in his middle age, Gurdjieff, who may have made the story up completely, of course, asks readers to wonder about what kind of coincidence might have accounted for this sudden ability to fell an opponent. Why, he says, only a few days before, providence had provided him with the appearance at his family's household of a Greek priest fleeing Turkish persecution for his political ideas and convictions. Despite Ivan's suspicion of priests regarding philosophy of life, he nonetheless engaged the priest to teach modern Greek to his eldest son. This too is interesting, since Pontus Greeks were famous for their residual archaic, classical-period Greek, and Ivan obviously wanted his son to be familiar with the lingua franca of universal Greek culture, perhaps envisioning for him a life at a Greek-speaking university or seminary. Gurdjieff says he was marked out for a career as either a priest or a doctor, or both (rather like Paracelsus), so he clearly made an impression as a *mind,* for whose promise his poor father was willing to part with hard-earned coin, or perhaps the priest was allowed to stay for free board and lodging so long as he instructed the hope of the family.

Recalling their conversations and the priest's efforts at getting Gurdjieff to distinguish between different exclamations in ancient and modern Greek, Gurdjieff recollected many years later that while he could not relate what "data" the priest's many convictions and political ideas were based on (typically "Gurdjieffian"; that is, objectively ironic and remote from the rational follies of humans), he was certainly aware this priest dreamed earnestly and vividly of getting to Crete, where he could manifest himself "as befits a true patriot." The priest wanted to knock the Turks "for six," as we might say. And this was Gurdjieff's quite idiosyncratic, roundabout way of saying that it was this bellicose patriotic let's-get-at-'em, pro-Cretan Orthodox Christian avenger of the cruel Turk that taught young Gurdjieff the head tactic, redolent of a Cretan bull on an ancient pot, that reduced his voluble boy-opponent to a static, horizontal silence.

And just in case you think this was the end of the matter and young rascal Gurdjieff had gotten away with it, the story has a dénouement. Fearing his pal dead as a result of Georgii's tactics, one of the frightened lads gave Gurdjieff's face full benefit of wrath with the globe of his fist. Gurdjieff had the privilege of seeing stars in the daytime while his mouth offered up a sacrificial relic. Feeling inside his blood-filled orifice, Gurdjieff extracted a large tooth. Awestruck, the boys examined it against the sunlight. It had seven roots, from each of which was suspended a drop of blood. Each globule manifested what Gurdjieff cunningly calls "one of the seven aspects of the manifestation of the white ray." He means of course—tongue in bloody socket—the colors of the rainbow. This manifestation of light and blood was intriguing to the boys; they delivered the relic to a dentist, who informed them that this was unlike the teeth they were familiar with losing overnight because this was a wisdom tooth (which teaches the archetypal virtue of the number seven). For Gurdjieff, of course, the story is another parable of his path to greater enlightenment, another wake-up call.

In this case, he tells us, with thoughts recollected in relative tranquility after 1924, the ensuing hole in his mouth produced a residue, the origin of which became symbolic along with the tooth of wisdom bathed in rainbow light, a burning sign to him that he must know the truth of the origin of things. He acquired a burning consciousness to know the origin of what people call "actual facts." In pursuit of this aim, nourished by what he calls "a real inextinguishable hearth,"[4] he adopted as his principle the characteristically flippant guideline, "if you go on a spree, then go the whole hog, including the postage." In other words, he found what English visionary William Blake had found a century or so before him—the unstoppable power of spiritual desire; you never know what is enough until you've had too much. You must exceed if you wish to enter Wisdom's palace. Go all the way, all the way from the seven colors of manifestation to the pure white radiance behind them.

As a religious student he was going to be quite a handful, for he was destined to create his own catechism and insist the Lord sign it.

On April 8, 1924, Gurdjieff inaugurated the New York branch of the Institute for the Harmonious Development of Man. This was the occasion that drew from him what was finally published as "The Material Question." Driven to consider his financial education, he thought first of what his father had taught him: "The strongest intentional influence exerted upon me was that of my father, who understood education quite in his own way."[5] Gurdjieff's early experiences had given him "the irresistible urge always to make something new." He was encouraged to do things in quite a special way. Whenever he had familiarized himself with one craft, his father insisted he give it up and try another. This way he got used, he said, to a state of readiness to surmount new difficulties, while overcoming weakness and ignorance. This training undoubtedly affected his own recommendations to those he worked with or taught. His longtime composer associate, Thomas de Hartmann, despite his hard-earned expertise in the field of music, received regular injunctions from the mature Gurdjieff to pack music up and do something else. Imagine telling that to Pierre Boulez, Simon Rattle, or the late Leonard Bernstein! For Gurdjieff, what was done was a means to an end, the way of winning greater vistas of consciousness. One can do far more than one knows. Apart from obvious necessities, work was justified by its contribution or fruitfulness in generating state of mind. Apart from the drug angle, Gurdjieff was pretty much what, as I call them, psychedelions of the '60s and '70s would have called a "head." He was into the perception of things—well in; the best times were to be had gazing at infinity from the standpoint of eternity, there at the center of the circle where, as the Rosicrucians put it, all parts of the globe are equidistant from the center. *In the presence:* presence of God in the mind and the mind in God. In the present. Aware. Now. Truly alive. *I am.*

Growing up in a workshop, watching his father patiently working with his holy hands at stubborn wood for very little money, but creating things, mending and shaping them day by day, taking no advantage from others' folly or misfortune, it all had its effect. Was not Jesus the son of a carpenter, a mason, or a technician? It may be that in dealing with de Hartmann's devotion to music, Gurdjieff projected his father's treatment of himself, treating the composer as the son in need of change, or indeed as a substitute for his own personal wishes and desires, for Gurdjieff told his New York listeners in 1924 that he felt "an urge frequently to change my occupation." This was not a message that seemed to get through very strongly to his followers, who doubtless entertained the idea that his institute was the crown and summit of all his work. Did they not realize that for Gurdjieff, on one level, it was just something else to do, and that his students were tools in the workshop? It had not been Gurdjieff's intention to end his life as the professor of an institute, a teacher of dances. There were other dances; he knew that. But he took on the world, and the world is a heavyweight.

Gurdjieff's father had attitude, and for Gurdjieff it was the right attitude. Recalling coming home from Kars Russian municipal school to work in his father's carpentry shop, he observed how his father's approach was "infecting us all with his freedom from care."[6] Ivan had found the meaning of his work and his work had become a means to living a higher life, not just "a living," as we call it, though half dead. Gurdjieff is plainly using his ideal father image here as a parable and paragon for students to observe, but one senses precious memories behind the construction nonetheless. Regardless of circumstances, it was possible to feel one's true freedom. One might be reminded of the remarkable scene in Robert Bolt's script to David Lean's *Doctor Zhivago* when the family is traveling east in a filthy, freezing Soviet train at the start of the Russian Revolution. They encounter a political dissident played by Klaus Kinski, manacled to the will of an ignorant revolutionary soldier. With bright living eyes, the prisoner tells everyone that he is freer than anyone else in the train, for his mind is free and he speaks truth without fear: that is why he is treated like a wild animal, a slave. He is perhaps the first sign of an unmistakable crack in the communist "utopia."

Above all, it was Gurdjieff's father's knowledge of poetry that seeped into young Georgii's psyche and made him see a world beyond the carpentry shop. Ivan was an ashokh, a traditional bard, a singer of epic poetry. He knew great long, many-versed poems that told ancient stories of mankind, tales of heroism and sacrifice and love and war and loss, stories to stir the soul, folk stories to enchant and lift the imagination, to repaint the starkness of the world with life and light, rhythm, music, and haunting memories. Oh, what we have lost with our reliance on recorded, synthetic music! But no, it is still there. You can still see ashokhs today in Kars, at the shadowy end of a dim-lit street in the cold of night. They gather in old cafés with long-necked lutes and moonlike tambours, surrounded by working men under stark striplights, smoking rough cigarettes, breathing in the smoke with the past as the ashokhs enflesh the ancient word of old songs and beat the old trails and bring tears to the eyes of hard skins and hard knocks in hard times. In *Meetings,* Gurdjieff says he was *spiritualized* by his father's stories; he made wax phonograph roll recordings of his father singing hundreds of songs for posterity. And posterity may one day find them, for Gurdjieff had to leave them behind in Moscow at the time of the revolution, when the "new men" spat on the old things, and who knows what became of them?[7]

It was his father who introduced young Gurdjieff to the realities of travel and adventure, for Gurdjieff says his father took him as a child to Persia, Turkey, the wonders of the Caucasus, Georgia's startling spas and waterfalls, ancient ruins, mysterious dolmens, and graceful houses. Ivan could even sing in Turko-Tartar and introduced his son to singers who came from parts of Turkestan. Then there were the singing contests, held in Van to the south in the region of Ararat, where God made the rainbow as a covenant with man, that he remember to love God. Ivan Ivanovich sang amid the moist emerald green hills of Karabakh in eastern Armenia and Azerbaijan and put his talents up against his peers in Subatan in the Kars region. With his father, Gurdjieff could feel the world was his oyster, for his father imparted to him in all he did a practical inner freedom. This was his father's precious gift, not rubles, but life and spirit of life.

Gurdjieff was also disposed to attribute to his father's agency a realization that became a cornerstone of his teaching: an answer to the question, *why is all not lost with the generations' passing?* How may wisdom, essential knowledge, be passed on through time? For young Gurdjieff was fascinated by the question of the beginning of things; how our kind had reached the madness we take for reality, and how we might wake from it and remember, and remember as his father remembered songs his ancestors knew that their ancestors knew, and on, on, all the way back to the source of creation.

Gurdjieff claims in *Meetings* that there was one epic his father sang that struck him deeply. That was the Epic of Gilgamesh. Gilgamesh is now a very well-known and exceedingly ancient story found inscribed in Akkadian cuneiform in a number of Assyrian versions discovered during British excavations in the Mosul region of northern Iraq initiated under the auspices of Austen Henry Layard in the 1850s. While existing tablets of the epic date from the first half of the first millennium BCE, fragments of or relating to the epic have been found that are considerably older. It is widely believed that the original framework, incorporated into the Assyrian epic of the king of Uruk, Gilgamesh; his friend the wild man Enkidu; and their quest for the plant of eternal life, may date from the first civilization of Mesopotamia, the Sumerians. What is particularly intriguing to us and was no less so to Gurdjieff, as he claimed in his tales in *Meetings,* was that the words inscribed thousands of years ago had come to his father direct and unspoiled through the oral tradition of the ashokhs. For him this was a luminous parable of where one might locate primal spiritual truths of human intelligence before human perception was darkened to such a state that today people perennially cannot bear spiritually awakening truth and daily crucify this "lord of glory" with illusions, lies, and self-deceptions that hold man back from living awareness. Symbolic forms of address, or *art*—poetry, movement, and visual symbol—provided the modes of transmission of truth through time, absorbed by analogous archetypes in the unconscious, arousable as memory from that level by repetition or ritual of remembrance. Of course, Gurdjieff did not come to share the formulation of these nascent psychological ideas in his childhood, and that is just one reason his account of his father's knowing the Gilgamesh epic as an independently inherited ashokh staple arouses suspicion.*

While for Gurdjieff the import of his father's knowing the text was its demonstration that the level of mind appealed to by ancient myths was subconscious, or what Jung and others would call a collective unconscious—as if the unconscious was a place—there are problems in Gurdjieff's account. Gurdjieff claims the essential spark of surprise came when he realized that, apart from the epic his father knew, nobody outside ashokh traditional settings had heard of Gilgamesh for thousands of years, until that is, nineteenth- and twentieth-century Western archaeologists discovered practically identical storylines hidden beneath Mesopotamian sands. It is plain Gurdjieff saw a parallel between the "Tradition" secreted beneath the rubble of time in physical form, discovered by archaeological digging, and the "Tradition" found secreted below the egoistic conscious mind, found by psychic exploration, hypnosis, or psychoanalytic digging. Gurdjieff, as we shall see, liked digging both physically and metaphorically, however painful it might be for others. No pain, no gain.

We too must do some digging.

What struck the man who first discovered the story of Gilgamesh in the stockrooms of the British Museum in London was that the Gilgamesh epic contained an account of a punitive flood launched against mankind for upsetting the gods, an account that shared so

---

*Michael Benham (e-mail to author, October 4, 2016): "This is still a hotly debated subject. In 2005 I [Benham] corresponded with Stephanie Dalley, Ph.D., regarding a note at the bottom of page 173 of her book *The Legacy of Mesopotamia* [Oxford University Press, 2006] that claimed Gurdjieff traveled in Mesopotamia between the two world wars with Soviet archaeologists. She and her then elderly research assistant were unable to find her notes on this and all she could offer was that it was in an old book she had read. She said: 'I have a vague recollection that Gurdjieff visited the excavations in the Dial region of Mesopotamia when Thornily Jacobsen and Henri Frankfort were excavating there; but this may not be correct. Certainly it was Jacobsen whose incorrect translation of the epithet of Ea as "lord of the bright eye" was taken up by Gurdjieff in his attribution to his father of a supposedly unbroken tradition of the Gilgamesh epic. It is this mistranslation that shows Gurdjieff's claim was a false one.' Joseph Azize has written on this and attempted to see the original manuscript of *Meetings* but was unable to get permission."

many elements with the biblical account of Noah and the Ark that, if the Gilgamesh story was earlier, then the biblical story must by some means have been derived from it. In fact, this is the debate that forms the setting for the story in *Meetings*.[8] Gurdjieff states that on that occasion he heard the twenty-first song of the epic so many times it was "engraved on my memory for life":

> I will tell thee, Gilgamesh,
> Of a mournful mystery of the Gods:
> How once, having met together,
> They resolved to flood the land of Shuruppak.
> Clear-eyed Ea, saying nothing to his father, Anu,
> Nor to the Lord, the great Enlil,
> Nor to the spreader of happiness, Nemuru,
> Nor even to the underworld prince, Enua,
> Called to him his son Ubara-Tut;
> Said to him: "Build thyself a ship;
> Take with thee thy near ones
> And what birds and beasts thou wilt;
> Irrevocably have the Gods resolved
> To flood the land of Shuruppak."

This seems a remarkable feat of memory, to say the least. Even the spelling of Anglicized Akkadian words appears intact. Something is amiss here, surely, especially when we bear in mind that *Meetings* was translated from Russian into English, and this allegedly remembered verse obviously reads like an English poetic, even literary transcription with its *thy* and *thou wilt* and pleasant English alliteration (mournful mystery). But it is not simply a matter of a suspicious translation and dubiously sophisticated transliteration. Gurdjieff then tells us that the debate he heard in his father's workshop in Kars on the relative claims of Gilgamesh and Genesis to be anterior to one another conducted between his father and clergyman Dean Borshch, whom we shall meet soon, only became a "spiritualizing factor" in the formation of his individuality much later; that is, just before the First World War.

Gurdjieff writes of how one day he read a magazine article about inscriptions believed to be four thousand years old, accompanied by a "deciphered" text, discovered amid the ruins of Babylon. He said the sight of the story generated in him an "inner excitement" as if his future destiny depended on it, for there was *Gilgamesh,* returned from ancient time, exactly as related by his father. For him, it was, he wants us to believe, a case of startling synchronicity, in accord with his theory of truth transmission through oral and symbolic modes outlined in *Beelzebub.*

Unless he fabricated the circumstance, the story Gurdjieff saw reported was most likely the German discovery shortly before July 1914 made at the site of the old Assyrian capital of Ashur (Qal'at Sherqat, *not* Babylon) of a considerable fragment of the Assyrian edition of tablet six of the Gilgamesh epic. This tablet does not deal with the flood story, nor did any of the fragments of the epic that came to light in the first thirty years of the twentieth century contain the section of the epic Gurdjieff repeats in elaborately translated form in *Meetings.*

In fact, the first discovery of the Gilgamesh text had been made at the British Museum in 1872, before Gurdjieff's birth, by brilliant orientalist George Smith. The account of the contents of tablet eleven of the epic shocked and thrilled London when the papers announced the ecstatic discovery like a revelation; the story spread like wildfire. Such had been Smith's surprise when he first translated the ancient text that he ran around involuntarily, unable to contain his astonishment. He published his first translation in 1873. Such significance and great expectation soon accrued to the discovery that Smith received generous financing to oversee three highly trumpeted archaeological digs in northern Iraq to uncover further textual revelations of ancient times. Between 1873 and 1876 Smith undertook a high-pressure program with the Ottoman government's permission and assistance. Gurdjieff's father could easily have read of the discoveries and excavations whether he was living in Turkey, Georgia, or Alexandropol, as the news was sensational for religious and historically minded people everywhere. Besides, it appears from Gurdjieff's telling of the story that Greek Orthodox scholar Dean Borshch of Kars military cathedral *already* knew enough about the Gilgamesh epic and controversy to debate the issue with Gurdjieff's father in young Gurdjieff's hearing! Borshch clearly cannot have become acquainted with the controversy over whether Gilgamesh was or was not the origin of the biblical Noah story simply by hearing a song from Ivan. Furthermore, Gurdjieff reports his father's opinion that the epic's origin was ancient Sumer, not Assyria or Babylon. This was simply not something one would come to think about from an inherited song without prior knowledge of historical context and the meaning of the curious god names and places.

Lines akin to those in the Gilgamesh epic have in fact been discovered in Sumerian texts—though not featuring Gilgamesh himself—from mounds at Nippur, Kish, and Ur, so the possible Sumerian origin of the protostory became a part of the controversy as it developed. To be fair, it might have seemed to an adoring son at the time that his father had the keys to the tradition if he heard him sing a song about it, but the idea of ashokhs bearing the intact song independently for thousands of years appears as far-fetched as it might appear plausible to willing Gurdjieffian initiates, especially when we look at the textual tradition itself.

In fact, in his initial translation, George Smith transliterated the hero's name as *Izdubar,* which was only corrected to the Latin alphabetic transliteration *Gilgamesh* later with more accurate appraisal of the cuneiform. The first literal translation ran as follows (the numbers refer to lines on the tablet):

1. Izdubar after this manner said to Sisit afar off,
2. "Sisit
3. The account do thou tell to me,
4. The account do thou tell to me,
5. to the midst to make war
6. I come up after thee,

7. say how thou hast done it, and in the circle of the gods life thou hast gained."
8. Sisit after this manner said to Izdubar,

[And here Gurdjieff's extract begins:]

9. "I will reveal to thee, Izdubar, the concealed story,
10. and the wisdom of the gods I will relate to thee.
11. The city Sm-ippak the city which thou hast established placed
12. was ancient, and the gods within it
13. dwelt, a tempest their god, the great gods
14. Ann
15. Bel
16. Ninip
17. lord of Hades
18. their will revealed in the midst of
19. hearing and he spoke to me thus
20. Surippakite son of Ubaratutu
21. make a great ship for thee
22. I will destroy the sinners and life[9]

Critically, Gurdjieff does not say what language his father sang the epic in. It is practically impossible that any language understood in Transcaucasia at the time would have contained the scientifically obtained transliterations of ancient cuneiform names had their origins been anything as ancient as the discovered texts. In fact the texts were worked on thoroughly by Western orientalists after Smith's pioneering discovery. Major new translations appeared, undertaken by Paul Haupt (Leipzig, 1884–91), Peter Jensen (Berlin, 1900), Arthur Ungnad and Hugo Gressmann (Göttingen, 1911), Erich Ebeling (Berlin and Leipzig, 1926), with a more or less perfected English translation of the epic coming out as the work of R. Campbell Thompson in London in 1928, in which most of the proper names are identical to those in the quotation of the epic in *Meetings*.[10]

Plainly, no objective commentator can take at face value Gurdjieff's tale as it appears in the published version of *Meetings*. To be generous, Gurdjieff's essential point about modes of transmission of primordial wisdom through oral tradition stands regardless of the superstructure he has elaborated about elements of his story. There is of course no a priori reason Gurdjieff's father could not sing a traditional story featuring heroic characters, and perhaps angry gods, about the, or *a,* flood. The Bible, as the Gilgamesh epic phenomenon demonstrates, is not the only means of access to traditions of the remote past. If one digs, one does indeed find more of the primordial tradition to stimulate the imagination. It is, for example, highly likely Gurdjieff knew something substantial of the oral tradition that gives life to the religion of the Yezidis, whom he encountered in Armenia and particularly around Lake Van, where once throve the ancient kingdom of Urartu (the *real* Ur of the Chaldees), the homeland of Abraham, where Gurdjieff says his father took him as a boy for the singing.

The Yezidi Kurdish people hold in great respect their special class of *qewwals,* or reciters, who play the sacred instruments of *def* (large tambourine) and *shibab* (flute) and preach to the congregation through their songs and music. Austen Henry Layard (1817–1894), who excavated Nineveh and brought back the tablets Smith translated, described the Yezidis and their sufferings under Ottoman persecution. Gentleman Layard treated them with respect, entreating the Ottoman governors to do likewise. Layard too had witnessed the qewwals and was fascinated by their ancient religion that places so much importance on the sacred number seven, as Gurdjieff would. The qewwals sing a hymn in their language of Kurmanji, an ancient hymn. It describes the Yezidis' own tradition of a ship made to survive a flood. It is called the "Hymn of the Creation of the World" and has been translated by Yezidism's foremost scholar today, Philip G. Kreyenbroek. Here is an extract:

> Our God made a ship;
> Men, animals, and all sorts of birds

He gave a place in the ship, two by two.

Our Lord is at the helm of the ship,
The leader who roams in all four directions.
The ship sprang a leak, water came in,
The snake coiled itself over it.[11]

The Yezidis share with very early Christian Syriac and Babylonian Jewish tradition the later Islamic tradition that the ark settled on Mount Judi (not Ararat, which refers to the ancient region of Urartu wherein the Arabic *Al-Judi* stands) in what was the province of Corduene in Greater Armenia, now close to the Syrian-Turkish border. Yezidis tend to think of there being two flood stories, with theirs the original. Interestingly, the Greeks used the word *Gordyae* for the mountains around Judi, believed derived from the Greek name for the people we today call Kurds, with *Judi* a possible corruption of that name. The roots of Yezidism may represent the ancient religion of practically all Kurds before (often forced) conversion of the majority to Islam. There is a very slim possibility that Gurdjieff's surname may just derive from the Greek for Kurd.

While the Yezidis do treasure, in addition to the hymns of the qewwals, two written works, the *Meshef Resh* ("Black Book") and the *Jilwe,* their spiritual life comes to them primarily as oral tradition, from mind to mind by mode of speech and rite, and for this reason the faith has retained considerable spiritual integrity, as there is no argument about authority in texts or interpretation of words. It is a living religion of the spirit with no orthodox interpretation, embodying from generation to generation the living essence of a spiritual revelation and a complete way of life. In fact, this distinction Gurdjieff would dignify properly with the real meaning of the word *education.* The essential teaching must, in his understanding, be drawn from within, and it is the capacity of oral tradition to maintain this integrity that is the essence of his account of his father and the orthodox, if slightly unconventional Dean, debating the provenance of Gilgamesh the ancient king. According to Gurdjieff, his father knew of an ancient civilization of wisdom from which mankind had deviated with a resultant deformation of consciousness. The idea informs his elaborate treatment of the myth of Atlantis in *Beelzebub's Tales to His Grandson*.

What is really most surprising about Gurdjieff's account of the significance of Gilgamesh in his life is that he makes no mention in his written works of the main story of the epic in which the relation of the Flood by Utnapishtim is but an incident. In the epic, Gilgamesh and his wild friend Enkidu travel to the limits of the known world to locate a man believed to have the "plant that gives life." Utnapishtim tells how the plant had survived the flood, and through Utnapishtim, Gilgamesh obtains the plant and takes it away with him, intending it for his people. He knows he must keep his wits about him and never lose sight of the plant. Unfortunately, even though a mighty hero, the all too human Gilgamesh stops to drink at a pool where, exhausted, he nods off. While he sleeps, a snake emerges from the water and takes the plant back with him beneath the pool. While this story might account for the snake's apparent capacity to rejuvenate by shedding of skin, it adds little glory to Gilgamesh's epic adventure, and the hapless king returns a sadder, wiser, more human man. The story's lesson, one would think, would have almost perfectly encapsulated Gurdjieff's essential message and lodged that message's provenance in the first myths of humanity; that is to say, man loses his greatest potential because of his disposition to *sleep*. Had Gilgamesh maintained awareness and used his intelligence more assiduously, he could have lived forever. The secret, so very, very close, was stolen by one wilier than himself! The snake was awake.

Perhaps it was the case that Gurdjieff was satisfied to point people in a direction and leave the walking and the essential engagement with learning experiences to the individual. We have things given to us, as Gilgamesh was given the plant that leads to life, but it is an unfailing principle of wisdom that we must seek, if we would find, and Gurdjieff was never in the habit of holding back the work from those who would know the secret of life. "Search the scriptures for they testify of me."[12]

FOUR

Dean Borshch and Other Enthusiasms

It is time we tried to get a fix on where we are datewise. One helpful tip has come from recent authentication of one of the main characters of *Meetings*. The book's third chapter deals with "My First Tutor," described as Dean Borsh, the most senior religious figure in the Kars region and dean of the military cathedral in the fortress city. Those who have recognized that the chief characters in *Meetings* might well be unreal from the standpoint of history have doubted whether Dean Borsh, who stands in the "proper guide" role in Gurdjieff's personal pantheon, actually existed at all. However, a journey to Kars undertaken by music scholar Johanna Petsche unearthed the identities both of Gurdjieff's military cathedral and its dean, Damian Ambrosievitch Borshch.[1]

Avetik Melik-Sargsyan has consolidated his local researches into Gurdjieff into an informal "Gurdjieff Center" in Gyumri, Armenia, and in addition to locating the remains of the Alexandropol house lived in by Gurdjieff's family in what was the old Greek quarter in that city (later sold by relatives, the Merkurov family), Melik-Sargsyan was also able to point out that James Moore's photograph in his Gurdjieff biography of the Apostles Church in Kars was not, as Moore thought, the military cathedral. In fact, that honor goes to what is now the Fethiye Mosque, converted for Islamic worship in 1985. Comparing that structure today with its appearance when Kars was part of the Russian Empire makes for a sorry sight. Though its main body is substantially the same at the exterior level—a modest rectangular stone structure with small archway entrances at the center of each side—it was once dignified at both ends by two gorgeous Russian onion domes of the bulbous, fairy-tale type, one of which constituted the bell tower described by Gurdjieff in *Meetings*. These distinctly Russian Orthodox Christian monuments to a hopeful period are now demolished, replaced by standardized tubular minarets erected apart from what is now the mosque at either end, completely out of keeping with what remains of the original building.

Gurdjieff was doubtless harnessing real memories of youth when he described the temporary bell housing constructed next to the cathedral while the cupolas' full glory arose as means became available. He would sit with his mates aboveground on its framework rafters, smoking a cigarette, munching snacks, and trading tales while construction adjacent proceeded. He recalled that when the full bell tower was finally ready to receive the gift of bells, the wooden housing passed to a new Greek church that once stood close to the cathedral. That church has vanished.

Gurdjieff tells us he was attending the Kars Russian municipal school when he heard the new cathedral, dedicated to the mighty name of Alexander Nevsky and to the Cossacks who contributed to the Russian victory in Kars of 1877, needed choristers. Answering the summons for a voice to praise the Lord in song, Gurdjieff quickly came to the attention of a tall, thin man who wrote sacred canticles and exercised loving care over those children who came to sing them. Young Georgii impressed Dean Borshch, and the old dean, then seventy years old, according to Gurdjieff, took the poor boy under his wing. Gurdjieff tells us that in his childhood he himself was known as Tatakh and then in early youth as Darky. Whether the Dean ever called the Greek boy by any nickname is unknown, but according to Gurdjieff, Dean Borshch did enjoy the mischievous, challenging aspect of Gurdjieff's character.

Unlike many a teacher, Borshch obviously recognized the genius and willpower at work in the energy of imaginative, incendiary naughtiness.

Borshch's death certificate has recently come to light. From it we learn that the dean's surname was slightly abbreviated by Gurdjieff (from Borshch to Borsh) and that the old man died, aged eighty, of pneumonia in 1899, to be interred in the grounds around the cathedral. No sign of the grave remains. This fact gives us an approximate date of around 1889 for the time when young Gurdjieff and his father conversed with the dean regarding Gurdjieff's education, for according to Gurdjieff, Dean Borshch encouraged Ivan to remove his son from the municipal school and let the dean find him more appropriate tutors who knew their subjects from experience.

How does this fare with other dating reasonably established so far? If Gurdjieff's father's lumber business in Alexandropol failed four years after the rinderpest outbreak of circa 1883–1884, when Gurdjieff was about seven years old, that would give us a date of around 1887–1888 for the beginning of Ivan's life as a carpenter. On this reckoning Gurdjieff would have been about ten or eleven at that time. Gurdjieff tells us that his father went to Kars and established a workshop there, later being joined by the family. If the family joined the father the following year, say in 1888–1889; where would that leave us? Well, it leaves us smack on the approximate date for when the dean of the unfinished cathedral began discussing young Georgii's future in Kars—given the dean was about seventy in 1889—with the boy's age being about twelve, or coming up to twelve if he was born in December 1877, or coming up to thirteen if he was born in that year's New Year. Now, this detail makes Moore's speculative birth of 1866 thoroughly unlikely; indeed, that particular stool has now lost so many legs, it ain't no stool no more and no use for milking. There is no way that Gurdjieff could have been in his *twenties* when his father and the seventy-year-old dean discussed taking him away from school!

As we shall see, my dating, while approximate given the evidence, makes much sense of what can be gathered about some of Gurdjieff's activities during the 1890s. For example, Gurdjieff regarded 1892 as a critical year in his development, when he decided to go his own way in the matter of study. The decision allegedly took place at the time of acquiring responsibility. In Russia, the age of criminal responsibility was fourteen, the age when most young people who had had the opportunity to go to municipal school, if there was one, left school to enter the world of work, unless destined for higher education, religious seminaries, or military or naval cadet school. In Gurdjieff's account in *Meetings,* the debate of the dean and his father over whether he should stay at municipal school implies strongly that the last years spent at the school would be better spent, for a precocious talent like Gurdjieff's, with tutors rather than in a temptation-filled classroom with less gifted children and less experienced teachers. He could always take any required pass exams at any school at the end of the tutoring period. Dean Borshch obviously knew what he was talking about, and Gurdjieff's father was not the kind of man to look an intelligent gift horse in the mouth. The dean and Gurdjieff's father had ambitions for the lad, who was, after all, the eldest of a once great family. Only the son could restore the fortunes fate had taken away.

Dean Borshch also got on very well, by Gurdjieff's account, with his father. They would discuss religion and history, and while Ivan was speculative, skeptical, and challenging, as well as curious, as he taught his son to be, and Dean Borshch was necessarily more conservative—he disagreed that the Genesis account of Noah was based on the Gilgamesh epic, for example—the latter man doubtless enjoyed meeting a genuine soul who took spiritual matters seriously, and who was also well mannered and intelligent. They also shared a common bond in music and respect for tradition, enjoying a real spiritual intimacy and sense of humor. The father's respect for the dean came from a man who habitually instructed his son that all he need do to lose his faith was to "make friends with a priest." The dean was obviously a chip off another block.

As part of a regular verbal game Gurdjieff calls *kastousilia* the dean would ask Ivan Ivanovich, "Where is God just now?" and Ivan Ivanovich would answer on the lines of, "He is at Sari Kamish" (an area between Russia and Turkey notable for tall pine trees). When asked what God was doing in Sari Kamish, Gurdjieff's father would inform the dean that God was making ladders to assist those desirous of rising to heaven. These curious, elusive conversations always passed in quiet, thoughtful tones, and Gurdjieff loved to listen, nestled in the warmth of wood shavings, bathing his mind in the warmth of the soul bond that enlightened the workshop.

Interestingly, Assyria was another subject the dean much enjoyed discussing. Ancient Assyria also exercised Gurdjieff's father's imagination, Assyria being where the Gilgamesh epic was discovered in the library of eighth-century BCE Assyrian kings of Nineveh. It should also be recognized that Assyria was a major interest and cause of excitement and fascination of cultivated Europeans at the time. Archaeology brought to the public massive sculptures, friezes, and writings of startling novelty and great artistic skill that testified to this once world power, with major implications for understanding the history of religion and the universality of ancient mythologies, as well as the polity, might, and character of the ancient world. Her images were bold, defined, and inwardly arresting. There was a relentless quality about the Assyrian Empire that, according to the Bible record, rendered them fit instruments of God's will in the judgment of Israel. Assyria was forever *on the move.*

During the 1880s, when these discussions took place, similar discussions were held in more superficially refined cafés, salons, and studios among Parisian enthusiasts of what has been called the French Occult Revival (see my *Occult Paris*), where artistic impresario and practical mage Joséphin Péladan called himself Sâr Mérodack after the Assyrian king-god and encouraged Assyrian artistic themes among his artistic friends in the Symbolist movement, as well as in his own series of novels gathered under the umbrella title of *La Décadence Latine* with its damned Babylonian settings and ancient magic of will and love. As we shall see, the intellectual development of Gurdjieff cannot be separated from parallel contemporary developments in the field of esoteric thinking and sciences being assiduously pursued to high levels of sophistication in Paris during the late 1880s and 1890s. Paris's intellectual and artistic influence extended far and rapidly through the French and Russian empires, with groups for independent research into esoteric study and occult phenomena established in Odessa and Cairo linked directly to Paris by 1889.

Gurdjieff makes a point of saying the dean's visits to the Greek quarter, to the poor man's workshop, were undertaken almost surreptitiously because it contravened the city's social system that a dignitary of Borshch's standing should grace a poor Greek with his presence, and willingly too. It is the kind of thing that would make a sensitive and intelligent boy feel he had joined a world apart. Indeed, this sense of being set apart would have been increased by the fact that after lessons with the dean in his austere chamber—principally mathematics among other subjects—Gurdjieff would stay behind, not only to try out new music parts for the dean's canticles, but for deep conversations, conversations that in time led to the dean treating Gurdjieff as an intellectual equal. One thing Gurdjieff emphasizes about Dean Borshch was not only that people thought him peculiar because he had independent thinking on most subjects and looked for the divine aspect of truth, but that he also had decided ideas about how to grow up in the practical sense. Borshch was not afraid to broach the subject of sex directly. He apparently taught Gurdjieff that boys should abstain from sexual intercourse until they had reached full maturity; that is, around their mid-twenties. He was quite adamant that if a boy got physically involved before what was the proper time for his mental development, he could thwart his development and ruin his whole life. The greatest challenge for the mature man was to find the precise complementary character in a woman. Everything depended on this, unless the man chose to "love his own individuality" and stay unmarried. The basis for marriage was the completion of the soul, not mere physical attraction. The bond that upheld marriage was essentially spiritual if the marriage was not to ruin the development of the parties involved. For this reason, the collected wisdom of time had established in civilized cultures elaborate social structures for making sure betrothed couples were truly suited for one another. Girls, the dean recognized, developed mentally earlier than boys: between fifteen and nineteen years. This fact was a problem for precocious boys particularly, and the dean didn't want what he recognized as a real spiritual vocation being spoiled in Georgii. And on this subject, the dean had other independent ideas too.

Like the Florentine Renaissance sage and doctor Marsiglio Ficino, and Paracelsus too, who followed him, Dean Borshch was convinced that a priest could not be a true healer of the soul unless he was a physician of the body as well. The body participated, or could participate, in the *Harmonia Mundi,* a harmony of the world and of Man, related to worlds beyond the visible spectrum. The cosmos was a *sign* of deeper relationships. The body and the soul were intertwined, and it was not always apparent whether the cause of a disease lay in the soul or in the body alone. Both dimensions of the person needed to be attended to and learned from. While we currently in the West have developed a tentative idea of this conception in the well-known idea of psychosomatic diseases, Western medicine has still not fully taken on board a realization as obvious to Dean Borshch as it was to some of the greatest Renaissance minds. Gurdjieff certainly took the idea on board without any great difficulty, though when his father and his ecclesiastical friend, if not brother, the dean pressed him toward a theological and medical mold, his willfulness railed, and he asserted that it was the technical sphere to which he felt the greatest attraction.

It is just possible that this tendency for a technical destiny was at least in part bound up with what we might well perceive as a chip on Gurdjieff's shoulder about his status in the cities of Kars and Alexandropol. When commenting on the remarkable decision of the dean to visit the workshop, Gurdjieff emphasizes the social disparity between the dean and his family with the words, "whereas my father was only a simple carpenter."[2] When he grew from youth to early manhood, Gurdjieff's nickname changed from Darky to the Black Greek. As we shall see, once, in a Transcaspian town far from home, a policeman who knew him simply addressed him as "Black Devil!"—not the last time he would be taken for one of Satan's servants. In later life he was rather amused to be called respectfully, "Mr. Gurdjieff." Gurdjieff was always in a minority.

Through Borshch, young Gurdjieff's horizons undoubtedly widened. He began to encounter educated Russians at close range. In *Meetings,* Gurdjieff states that a Theological Seminary graduate who served as a deacon at the cathedral while waiting for an army chaplain's post, one Krestovsky (meaning "of the Cross," and the name of an island in St. Petersburg), taught him Russian as well as scripture.[3] Russian would have been taught as *the* language by which a young man could wind, or oil, his way up the Russian hierarchy by being plucked from ethnic frontier obscurity into the empire's professional classes via a university in Mother Russia; this was the way to bind the empire and keep it Russian. This would have been something of an uncomfortable challenge to one who in later life admitted that in early youth, while much taken up with philological questions, he preferred Armenian to all other languages, even to his first tongue, which was Greek. He liked Armenian, he said, because it was original, with nothing in common with neighboring languages. Armenian was a road to another place, another identity, as we shall see. When he came to write his first book, *Beelzebub's Tales to His Grandson,* he claimed in the introduction that he would rather have written it in his first language, Greek, but none in his entourage in Paris or Fontainebleau understood it.[4] Besides, he added, tellingly, his native Greek, like the Armenian language, had now been corrupted by those aping the *Russian intelligentsia.*

Gurdjieff had ambivalent attitudes toward the Russian intelligentsia, and the roots of that attitude must have been sown when he came to see in the very bosom of the home of his boyhood that, frankly, his father was looked down upon. It is likely then that a commitment to the technical side of life, though something he could do more than cope with and certainly enjoy, was very much a response to what his father had taught him, and a response to his deep love for his father and his spiritual values. It was also a quick road to ready cash. To take a medical or theological career would inevitably have meant "joining the Russians." Besides we can sense already that Gurdjieff fancied himself top dog and could feel that machines were the gods of the new age. Rinderpest could not touch a machine. There was something as relentless and ambivalent about machines as there was about the Assyrians. The days of cattle herding and sheep grazing were over.

For his eldest son's own good, as he had to see it, Gurdjieff's father encouraged the dean to take on his son and introduce him to alien avenues of intellectual and social advancement. Out of love for father and tutor, young Gurdjieff played the game as best he could. He says he went to ordination candidate Ponomarenko (Russian for "son of a sexton") for geography and history lessons and to Sokolov (meaning "of a hawk, or falcon") for lessons in physiology and anatomy.[5] Lessons with Sokolov took him right out of his comfort zone, to the military hospital at Fort Chakmak, a good three or four miles outside of Kars, and a place where he would encounter an intensification of Russian attitudes and culture, as well as a well-stocked hospital library, which he would scour for books to explain the workings of the mind.

Attending hard to his studies, Gurdjieff had to make his way into different districts to locate the tutors the dean had picked for him. In particular, he had to make his way to the finer houses of Russians and those connected directly to the Russian governing class, who from 1878 had made Kars their home and who intended to make Kars a jewel in the imperial crown. These visits to educated Russians were fraught with interior difficulties for Gurdjieff, which he refers to painfully in *Meetings*. He quite clearly states that he did not want learned people to know that his father was a humble artisan. He was personally embarrassed at his family poverty: "At that time all this deeply wounded my self love."[6] He had a hunger to learn, but it was a painful road, and it took him away from home with mixed feelings of pride, guilt, and shame.

THE CIRCLE OF THE YEZIDI

In *Meetings,* Gurdjieff tells us that around the time of his being tutored, he would holiday with his "uncle" who had a house in Alexandropol. Which uncle this was is not clear. It might have been a second house of his father's brother Dmitri, who we think lived in Kars; it may have been another unnamed brother's house, or it may have been the house of his relative, a Merkurov. Anyhow, Gurdjieff recalled a deeply imprinted memory of sitting in a little grove of poplars by some vacant land near his uncle's house, engaged in making a monogram for a neighbor's niece's wedding, featuring the date 1888—consistent again with our dating—when he was struck by a boy's shriek emitted from a group of Armenian, Greek, Kurd, and Tartar children playing in the vacant plot. The boy made terrified movements, struggling vainly with the curious predicament of having had a circle drawn around him in the dirt. Children jeered. Obviously someone knew the trick and everyone thought it a jolly wheeze to see a boy quaking in the presence of an unexplained terror.

Gurdjieff inquired as to what had produced such a reaction from a circle mischievously, though one might have thought, harmlessly drawn. He was told that the boy was a Yezidi, and Yezidi Kurds couldn't escape from a circle if caught in one, until rubbed away: something they were unable to do themselves. It was obvious the lad was desperate to escape from what appeared a purely imaginary enclosure, but will as he might, he could not allow himself to do so, despite his playmates' taunting. Gurdjieff rubbed away the circle, whereupon the boy dashed out and fled the scene distraught.

The phenomenon, claimed Gurdjieff in *Meetings,* had a profound effect on him. At the time he simply stood rooted to the spot, transfixed by what he had witnessed, unable to comprehend it. He says that although he had already "heard something about these Yezidis,"[7] he had never given them any thought. Now he felt compelled "to think seriously about them."[8] In the context of the *purpose* of *Meetings,* he was asking his readers to think seriously about them and what had happened to him.

In the context of the story he is telling, the incident sparks off a series of discussions among his new, older Russian friends about what kind of forces were involved and whether or not the Yezidis were, as widely rumored, devil worshippers. The discussions basically outline a set of stock reactions to strange, paranormal occurrences or incidences of disturbing psychology that suggested that there was more to it than met the eye. In the context of the story, it is perhaps the major determinative incident in a string of experiences that add up to Gurdjieff's personal quest to explain the essence of the mystery of life and mind. The other experiences involve predictions made that came true—a fortune-teller's warning from his aunt that transpired as predicted—and miraculous healings at a distance: phenomena that had no obvious materialistic, scientific explanation. Gurdjieff was interested in a dimension that seemed to be beyond the ordinary boundaries of space: events related rather by time and meaning than obvious cause and effect, involving ideas of hypnosis and other obscure but potent powers of mind. He notes that this interest was in some way connected to grief at the death of a beloved little sister. Alexandropol records of the period mention a daughter of Ivan Ivanovich called Lukeria, a Russian name, though Gurdjieff and his brother Dmitri both mentioned a sister Luberia. Perhaps in memory of the tragic early death, Dmitiri's first daughter was called Luba, after Luberia. According to Beekman Taylor, however, an 1885 Alexandropol entry refers to Ivan's having daughters called Maria and Anna. In 1875, before Gurdjieff's birth, Ivan and Evdokia had another daughter, apparently their firstborn, Melania, who also died in infancy. Such occurrences were bound to make Georgii brood on the mysteries of life and death, the world of the unseen.

Clearly, the Yezidi incident is a startling example of the sheer power of *suggestion,* something Gurdjieff would explore thoroughly. And in all of this interest, he was perfectly in tune with the intellectual and scientific concerns of his time. As his discussions among "the families who were considered socially higher than mine" demonstrate, what was broadly called *occultism* was all the rage, the regular talk and fascination of the town, at least the Russian part of it. He makes the sad admission, "In the Greek part of Alexandropol, where my parents formerly lived, I had no friends at all."

Gurdjieff took his shock, surprise, and desperation to understand the experience of the terrified Yezidi to his new social circle, children of officers, officials, and clergymen, among whom he had begun to tipple a bit.[9] Opinions on the Yezidi matter differed from outright rejection of any interest to the idea that science would soon understand this. Others considered the Yezidis' painful predicament the inevitable product of being the "Devil's own." Hypnosis was discussed, and hypnosis would soon become a major theme of Gurdjieff's future development.

It is difficult to gain from *Meetings* just how much Gurdjieff knew or didn't know about the Yezidis. He tells readers that Yezidis were natives of Transcaucasia, a "sect" (inaccurate since a sect has separated from another body), especially in the region of Ararat (the Turkish *Agri-Dagh*). "They are sometimes called devil worshippers."[10] To say the least, this is a noncommittal statement. Even though Gurdjieff does not flatly deny the accusation, which he should have done if he were being accurate about Yezidi beliefs, it is certainly a step beyond the ignorant view of Madame Blavatsky, founder of the Theosophical Society, whose works in English at the time insisted the Yezidis practiced black magic.

It is interesting that Gurdjieff's treatment of the phenomenon leaves sufficient doors open to make one think he had a very good idea of what was going on, and that the phenomenon was not simply caused as a result of a hypnotic device from which the Yezidi was unable to break free. Gurdjieff gives the Russian army captain of his debate narrative the opportunity to say that while he had himself experienced a case where some soldiers had drawn a circle around a Yezidi and the poor fellow had besought them with tears to erase it, the captain's view was that the Yezidis were known to take some vow never to go out of a closed circle, and never will, not because they *cannot,* but because they cannot bear the consequences of the broken vow.

The captain's enlightened view chimes with that of a *Pir* (Yezidi instructor) of our time. According to Gurdjieff commentator Henry Korman, who interviewed the Pir on the subject, the Yezidi was taught that the circle represented the Yezidis' entire community of faith, which was the seal of identity and trust for the individual. Therefore, if the community needed to know if a fellow was telling the truth, the circle was put round him. He was then "in the dock," under binding oath of belonging to speak the truth. Release from the circle was the inquiring Sheykh or Pir's prerogative. To break the circle was effectively to excommunicate oneself from the spiritual bond, life, and trust of the community. To speak a lie within it and then leave was to leave the community—a quite unbearable thought, for it meant leaving identity behind and entering, without spiritual protection, a world often deadly hostile to Yezidis. Misunderstanding outsiders, Muslims in particular, used their limited knowledge of the compelling symbol to imprison Yezidis. Younger Yezidis or people who did not understand the deeper meaning of the circle would simply feel compelled to honor the practice and the nature of the vow, which had become part of custom and identity. Outsiders, ignorant of the meaning, failed to see that what was at stake for the Yezidi was their life as a Yezidi; that is to say, their very existence—hence the profound fear.[11]

Of course, Gurdjieff would surely have recognized that while any obviously magical explanation was unnecessary, the Yezidi's identity was nonetheless being controlled from outside, and that external authority had nonetheless become internalized and inseparable from the will of the individual. In short, the individual was being controlled, even when there was no authority figure, only a symbol or sign to suggest the control. The implication is of a "Pavlov's dog" syndrome, and it is notable that Gurdjieff calls one of his Russian commentators on the incident

Pavlov. The famous Ivan Pavlov (1849–1936), known for his physiological studies of conditioning, would shortly begin his dog experiments at the Imperial Institute of Experimental Medicine (1891), founded by Russian Prince Alexander of Oldenburg, probably a later patron of Gurdjieff.

It seems clear Gurdjieff in his narrative was projecting back into the memory of the Yezidi incident what he subsequently learned of the physiology of suggestion. No wonder Gurdjieff found the phenomenon so fascinating. It goes right to the heart of what in his maturity he would consider the automatization of the self. It was of course the individual's will not to break the vow, but the power of will was not necessarily authentically his own, but rather the will of the community or spiritual authority in him. Gurdjieff clearly did not like the idea of people being controlled by the community or by priestcraft. But all of that was a long way off. For the time being, Gurdjieff saw the phenomenon as part of a packet of strange realities that he strove to explain and, crucially, kept finding that the authorities he had begun to favor with his indulgence and time could not explain. Being very young, he just might have been teetering on the brink of a personal crisis.

BOGACHEVSKY AND THE FLYING CHAIRS

Gurdjieff places much of this material within a chapter of *Meetings* devoted to the alleged influence on him of one Bogachevsky (*Bog* is Russian for "God"), who represents to some extent the guidance for the student of objective morality as against subjective morality. The latter changes in time as people apply their ideas of good and evil according to fashion or new emphases, but subjective morals lack universality and temporal integrity (political correctness surely falls into this category, being an anxiety of a period and concocted). Objective morality, forged through time and experience, forms an authentic conscience.

Judging from the manner in which the character Bogachevsky is presented, and certain of his affiliations, there is no reason to think he was a real person, though he may have represented a person or been a composite of aspects of people or ideals that impressed Gurdjieff. The first introduction to him should arouse suspicion in any educated person. Gurdjieff says that Bogachevsky is "still alive" as assistant to the abbot of the chief monastery of the Essenes, situated by the shores of the Dead Sea.

No such place existed during the 1880s, though many wished it did. The Jewish sect of Essenes disappeared from history after the Romans' destruction of the Jerusalem Temple in 70 CE. We owe our knowledge of them to first-century writers Josephus, a Jewish historian; Jewish philosopher Philo; Roman historian Pliny the Elder; and, according to some scholars, documents from the so-called Dead Sea Scrolls. There did exist in Gurdjieff's early life much esoteric interest in the Essenes, particularly among people touched by the theosophical wave that began in New York and swept through Europe to India after 1875. The South Australia teacher Edward Planta Nesbit wrote *Jesus the Essene* (1895), while the fine Irish writer George Moore (1852–1933) was not alone in picking up on such ideas when he wrote his novel *The Brook Kerith* (1916) and a play, *The Apostle* (1911), that featured Jesus in the imaginary setting of an Essene monastery, even after crucifixion. As early as 1821, learned German doctor K. C. F. Krause published his speculation that the Freemasons owed their origins to beliefs shared by the Culdees and the Essenes in *The Three Oldest Documents of the Fraternity of the Freemasons*. Certainly, esoteric interest in historical and imaginary Essenes was well established by the time Gurdjieff wrote *Meetings*. For Gurdjieff, perhaps, *Essene* was a euphemism for spiritually minded Freemasons—he never mentions or criticizes Freemasonry, itself remarkable.

Judging from Gurdjieff's studiedly tentative words on the subject he was at least half convinced that Essenes were transmitters of an ancient spiritual tradition that Gurdjieff himself claimed to have absorbed: "This brotherhood was founded, according to certain surmises, twelve hundred years before the Birth of Christ; and it is said that in this brotherhood Jesus Christ received his first initiation."[12] "It is said," so he says. He also says that Bogachevsky was permitted by Dean Borsh to replace Krestovsky as tutor; so Gurdjieff might have wished, for he has already informed us that he loved fairy tales, liked to see life in such terms, and was captivated by the tale his father told him of the lame carpenter Mustapha, who made himself a flying chair! When Gurdjieff wants to advance his lessons, he invents a flying chair; Bogachevsky and the other remarkable men of *Meetings* who follow him provide the flying chairs. These too are Beelzebub's tales, though considerably better told than those in the brontosauric mass of a book attributed to the mature Gurdjieff's genial version of the "lord of the flies."

Young Gurdjieff was clearly on the lookout for drama, magic, the fantastic, and eruptions of supernatural redemption. When he describes the young students who gathered around his Essene-to-be, he says the gatherings served "to kill time in the monotonous life of the remote and very boring town of Kars."[13] Thus speaks the real Gurdjieff! Boredom is perhaps the first condition of creativity, for the devil makes work for idle hands.

He recalls conversations among army personnel (an engineer and pyrotechnically trained artillery officer) and Russian theological seminarians on the subject of spiritualism (spiritism) and table-turning: "at the time," Gurdjieff says quite rightly, "a subject of absorbing interest everywhere."[14] Various explanations are offered by Gurdjieff's acquaintances for phenomena at séances: magnetism, autosuggestion, laws of attraction, and of course spirits. Everyone, he points out, accepted that things did actually happen and needed accounting for. This is a clue to Gurdjieff's later personal discoveries—everyone, that is, or so he implies, but himself, who at the time did not know. It is at this point that he says these subjects, new to him, made a particularly strong impression on account of his favorite sister's recent death. Her untimely death had stirred involuntary thoughts about life beyond the grave. It was, he maintained, as if the discussions he was listening to were occurring as a direct result of his own questions, questions that had arisen "unconsciously." Life events answered, so to speak, the yearnings of his soul.

Gurdjieff recalls an experiment where the informal group of conversational loafers closed the windows and held their hands on the table in a particular way. The table began to move and answered questions about their individual ages by the tapping of one of the table's three legs. Gurdjieff says he felt afterward that "vast unknown fields" had thus opened up before him, but when he asked the dean about them, he was told not to bother his little "garlic head" thinking about them, as they were unnecessary for the living of a "tolerable existence." That last phrase is very telling. Dean Borsh in the narrative advises only so far. He has wisdom to make something tolerable of this life, and this is the wisdom of the man of the world: a kind of resignation. Gurdjieff was not satisfied with it.

Gurdjieff says he put the dean's response partly down to his age; perhaps born when science was not so advanced, Borsh was satisfied with its categorical rationalism. Gurdjieff says Bogachevsky gave him books relating to his inquiries but does not say what they were. Bogachevsky begins to sound somewhat like the freelance teachers who toured the country giving instruction that went beyond orthodox teaching. Often they were Protestants, believing in the "priesthood of all believers." Frontier places on the empire's edge enjoyed considerably better opportunities for learning than was available to peasants in the Russian mainland.

Time passed, and Gurdjieff would go to Alexandropol to make things and to mend them, to earn money for clothes and books and to help his family, who at the time suffered great poverty. He got used to caring for them, as the eldest, as he would try to do for his followers who came with him from Russia to Constantinople at the end of the First World War, and those who came to him in Paris subsequently. He needed family. He could turn his hand to many trades: embroider a cushion, fix a lock, build a stove, mend a watch. He could shape metal, wood, and stone. Recounting his entry onto the world of the street-level entrepreneur to Americans in "The Material Question," he emphasized that coming "from a poor family and not being materially secure," through his energy and dexterity, he became "an expert, cunning old blade."[15] In Alexandropol during holidays he earned a lot of money; he did his money earning in Alexandropol because, he said, he would have been ashamed if his older, educated Russian friends in Kars knew that he was working with his hands to keep his family from the breadline. This double life might have been a projection of his later double life in Paris, where he would run the institute in Avon while maintaining a flat in Paris for his multifarious business activities, about which his students knew next to nothing. On the other hand, it seems more likely that the pattern, a pattern of necessity, was established in early life and became habitual. So long as he could keep the poles apart, the spiritual and the material, he could live reasonably freely. He only had to think of money when he needed it; the rest of the time he could devote to his researches and mystical life. For if there was a "Material Question" that he could address for those potential donors who wanted to know, there was always and always had been, the "Spiritual Question." Perhaps it was tragic that in Paris, after the World War, the two questions got confused, and with that confusion came what this author considers the long disaster of Gurdjieff's already difficult and laborious life.

FIVE

The Spiritual Question

Gurdjieff maintains in *Meetings* that he was first stirred from the cozy rationalism of his formal and informal education when his aunt—possibly the wife of "the esteemed Giorgii Mercurov"[1]—told him in Alexandropol during Easter holidays that before his arrival at their house she had consulted a "half-witted" fortune-teller called Eoung-Ashokh Mardiross, who had made several predictions, some of which had come true and were harmless and two that had yet to come to pass. First, he would have a nasty sore on his right side, and second, more threatening, he was in danger of a serious accident with a firearm. He should be cautious wherever shooting took place.

His aunt's warnings came second to responding to those he considered at the time the "intelligentsia" of Alexandropol's Russian quarter, where he says he found all his friends. Two friends, one the son of a company commander in the Baku Regiment, insisted he join them on a wild duck shoot at the lake below Mount Alagheuz, one of the highest peaks in the Caucasus. Gurdjieff considered such an adventure a pleasant break from absorption in neuropathology. Unfortunately, shooting low for his first duck, the "orderly of commander Gorbakoun" fired a rifle bullet that passed through Gurdjieff's leg, missing the bone but wounding him badly. A further visit from the old, sick fortune-teller yielded more predictions, which, Gurdjieff relates, all came true.[2]

MIRACLES

Through the tutors arranged for him by Dean Borshch, Gurdjieff became familiar with the world of Armenian theological seminaries. His first visit to the still-thriving seminary at Echmiadzin was not, according to his testimony, to put his toe in the water of what being a theological student for the priesthood might entail, as one might expect, but was occasioned, he says in chapter 4 of *Meetings,* by his seeking an answer to the question of supernatural phenomena.

The Gevorgian Seminary is today a distinctive, elegant, classically inspired two-story structure of Roman arched windows, squared buff-colored ashlars, and decorated cornices, dominated by a central tower supported on wide arches surmounted by a monumental copper dome, set amid tranquil hedgerows and trees. It does not look the kind of place where satisfaction on nonorthodox spiritual issues might be obtained, and so it proved. What Gurdjieff did find there, he says, was a companion in his quest called "Mr. X or Captain Pogossian," allegedly an Armenian from Turkey whose family moved to Kars after the Russians took it in 1877. Again, a person of similar background might well have been a friend to Gurdjieff, but Pogossian—who represents the virtue of the active, instinctive, working life—seems a composite or complete invention. Precisely how much of their ensuing adventures were pure fantasies is impossible to tell.

Gurdjieff states in *Meetings* that their encounter followed Pogossian's parents in Kars asking family friend Gurdjieff to deliver their son a gift of linen, since Giorgii was heading for Echmiadzin in search of answers.

Echmiadzin, or Vagarshapat, was a mecca for Armenians. When Gurdjieff first went there he joined a party of pilgrims, keeping his bags in a wagon belonging to the Molokan sect of unorthodox "spiritual Christians" from Alexandropol. Gurdjieff's approach to religion is expressed throughout *Meetings* as strictly ecumenical. He is interested in all faiths and respects the faith that keeps people's faith.

While Pogossian was probably a fictional character or name, it appears Gurdjieff's familiarity with Echmiadzin was genuine. He states he and Pogossian resided there, care of Archimandrite Surenian. Gevork Surenian had been called by Catholicos Gevorg IV, leader of the Armenian Apostolic Church (1866–1884), together with Archimandrites Vahan Bastanian, Vahram Mankuni, and Aristakes Sedrakian, to reestablish a theological school to educate the clergy at the Mother See of Holy Echmiadzin in summer 1872. Despite the seminary's newness, Pogossian was unhappy with what may have been the strictly historical nature of the teaching. It was probably intended as highly conservative, to establish Armenian orthodox tradition for the country's welfare: a valid motive in the mature, but one bound to stymie expectations in frustrated young minds seeking spiritual meaning and national self-assertion in a modern, science-oriented world, especially when many of their relatives were subjected to humiliating Turkish oppression and Russian suspicion. Gurdjieff says that Pogossian found the priests' teaching contrary to his own ideals (Gurdjieff's ideals?), while Gurdjieff states that his three weeks spent under the archimandrite's hospitality left him deeply disillusioned.

From other comments in *Meetings,* set in the political context of the early 1890s, such disillusionment may not only have resulted from inadequate answers to questions about supernatural phenomena. Perhaps the religious establishment at Echmiadzin was considered insufficiently engaged politically in the growing national "awakening" or reawakening of Armenia, as news poured in constantly from Turkey that, as in Crete, official treaty obligations and promises made to the British government at the Treaty of Berlin in 1878 to respect the integrity of Armenians in eastern Turkey, as well as Greeks, were flouted by Turks determined to keep Armenians down as low as possible by whatever means could be arrayed. Of course, any move to Armenian independence would upset the delicate balance of the Armenians' relationship with Russia, which dominated the larger part of what had once been the historic kingdom of Armenia. It is impossible to imagine young Gurdjieff not being moved by the powerful political waves of the times, especially as his own family owed their security to the Russians, who protected them from what Greeks and Armenians both had cause to fear: Turkey.

Gurdjieff's search for an explanation of the supernatural had already, he says, taken him in a religious direction, visiting monasteries and meeting pious men of common knowledge, while seeking nourishment from the scriptures and lives of the saints. He says he served as an acolyte of Father Yevlampios at Sanahin Monastery for three months, as well as undertaking pilgrimages to the holy places of the "many different faiths in Transcaucasia."

Sanahin Monastery is a place that ought to light anybody's inner being. Built in the tenth century on a plateau by a tributary of the Debed River in Armenia's northern Lori province, Sanahin is a collection of stone buildings and ancient gravestones of intense beauty, partly overgrown with ivy and lush bushes, with distinctive, Romanesque-like architecture, low carved arches, and unusual conical tiled roofs, like medieval castles are imagined to have in our dreams. The wonder of the location—think of Wordsworth's "Tintern Abbey"—may have touched Gurdjieff's eager imagination, but the instruction he received apparently did little to slake his thirst for reliable knowledge. However, he will certainly have been assured that miracles do happen, and that they happen in religious contexts. This he was about to experience directly for himself.

Traveling with pilgrims from Alexandropol to Mount Djadjur for a religious festival, he witnessed a paralytic ex-soldier, lame at thirty, borne in a cart by friends and family from his village. On the way, Gurdjieff helped carry the man into the private house of an Armenian, custodian of an icon of the Savior in the village of Diskiant, where the poor fellow desired earnestly to pray. Later the pilgrims arrived at the mountain Djadjur, on whose slopes the distant sight of a little church welcomed them in their various wagons and carts. Leaving their transport, pilgrims ascended the path for a quarter of a mile, some barefoot, others on their knees out of respect for the tomb of the saint they had come to see. The paralytic meanwhile resisted all attempts to carry him, insisting on dragging himself toward the place of miracles. After three hours he embraced the tomb and fell unconscious at the center of the church. Gurdjieff helped the priests to revive him with water. Eventually, the invalid came to. Then, realizing the new feeling in his body, he sprang up and made *dance movements,* before pulling himself together and falling to prayer with a great cry. The priest gathered the throng and held a thanksgiving to the saint.

On another occasion, Gurdjieff recalled a terrible drought that hit Kars and its surroundings, blighting crops with scorching heat and bringing famine's awful prospect to bear on the people. It happened, according to Gurdjieff, that the same summer, an archimandrite from the patriarchate of Antioch (today Antakya in southeast Turkey, while the see itself is based in Damascus) arrived in Russia with a miraculous icon, having an especial interest in those parts of the empire with Greek populations. The visit seems to have been stimulated by the need to provide relief for Greeks suffering the effects of the Cretan War—rebellion against the Turks would erupt again in 1896.

The Russian authorities welcomed the dignitary to Kars with due honors, and all the clergy welcomed the icon as it was carried to bless all the city's churches. It then became known that a service would be held to entreat divine assistance in the matter of drought. Processions gathered with banners and icons to approach the sacred icon that would form the centerpiece or center presence of the celebration and entreaty. Armenian, Greek, and Russian Christians all joined together from their churches and cathedrals to hear the archimandrite lead a solemn service outside of Kars. As the population returned toward the city, the sky suddenly darkened, and before they could shelter themselves, everyone was soaked to the skin with the downpour of life-giving rain. Yes, Gurdjieff says, it could, as a phenomenon, earn that favorite word of "our so-called thinking people" *coincidence,* but who could deny that this coincidence was "almost too remarkable?"[3]

Gurdjieff follows this story with an experience he claims to have had when his family moved out of Kars and back to Alexandropol for a short time, living next door to Gurdjieff's aunt. She had let rooms to a lodger, a Tartar. He worked as a clerk in local government and dwelt there with his old mother and sister, having just married a good-looking Tartar girl from nearby Karadagh. Shortly after the marriage, however, his wife fell very sick, and neither the town doctor nor a former army doctor, despite regular injections, could relieve the poor girl's condition. One day, Gurdjieff's family invited the doctor's assistant to table, whereupon they inquired after their neighbor's health. The doctor's assistant was doubtful the girl would survive; she had tuberculosis.

While those at table absorbed the sad news, the sick girl's mother-in-law arrived in tears. She asked Gurdjieff's mother for rose hips from the garden, telling of how during the night the girl had been visited by Mariam Ana, the Tartars' name for the Virgin, and Mariam Ana, in a dream, had instructed the girl to be fed with rose hips, boiled in milk. The doctor's assistant, Gurdjieff says, could hardly restrain his laughter, but Gurdjieff's mother helped the old woman gather the fruit. Gurdjieff saw the medical opinion out of the house and was duly astonished when, the next day, the sick girl appeared on her feet with her mother-in-law, leaving the Armenian church of Sev-Jiam (*Sev* means "black"), a church housing a miraculous icon of the Virgin. The town doctor said her recovery "was a matter of chance."[4]

Religion provided miracles, but not explanations, it seemed. As we have observed, Gurdjieff recounts how he brought his questions not only to religious authorities but also to the educated Russians of Kars, among whom he names Pavlov, a treasury official; the fortress church deacon Father Maxim; an artillery officer Artemin; a Captain Terentiev; and the teacher Stolmakh; and at one point refers to himself being employed as an interpreter in Armenian when an acquaintance of his uncle's,

Dr. Ivanov, a general and chief physician of the Thirty-Ninth Division, was called to see a poorly Armenian neighbor. Addressing the doctor as "Your Excellency" since he was a general, Gurdjieff asked what *he* thought about the Yezidi and the circle, an inquiry greeted with, "Ah, you mean those devil-worshippers? That is simply hysteria."[5] Gurdjieff says he knew what was meant by *hysteria,* as he had absorbed every single book on neuropathology and psychology available at Kars's military hospital.

That Gurdjieff was either at the time or in later life familiar with at least the rudiments of the latest science from France regarding hypnotic states is revealed in a speech he puts into the mouth of teacher Stolmakh. Stolmakh tells Gurdjieff confidently that what currently was held to be metaphysical in origin would soon be explained by physical causes and that such mysteries were already being brought into scientific paradigms by "those magnetic phenomena which are now being investigated by scientists at Nancy."[6]

Gurdjieff's exchanges precisely mirror the contemporary debate then raging between Hippolyte Bernheim (1840–1919), based at Nancy, and Jean-Martin Charcot of the Salpêtrière Hospital in Paris. Publishing his main findings in 1884,[7] Bernheim believed ordinary people could be manipulated through hypnotic means of suggestion, maintaining this capacity was natural and innate. Charcot, on the other hand, believed the whole phenomenon to be a mental disorder based on abnormal states of hysteria, especially in women (*hysteria* comes from the Greek for "womb"). Charcot conceded to Bernheim in 1891, and the therapeutic value of hypnosis was officially recognized. It is notable that not only Freud studied under Charcot (Freud held dubious ideas about hysteria, which he applied to female patients), but also the dominant protagonist of the French Occult Revival, Dr. Gérard Encausse (1865–1916), known as Papus.

Papus observed hypnotic phenomena at the Salpêtrière Hospital as part of *his* medical training while pursuing satisfaction of an omnivorous appetite for esoteric knowledge no less pressing than that of his younger contemporary Gurdjieff. In Papus's mission statement printed at the beginning of every issue of his monthly magazine *l'Initiation,* founded in 1888, Papus wrote, "experimental science has led the scientists, despite themselves, into the field of purely spiritual forces by hypnotism and distance suggestion." For Papus, as for Gurdjieff, hypnotic phenomena pointed to dimensions that grossly materialistic conceptions of science only touched on but did not explain or encompass. "Materialism," Papus wrote pointedly in his mission statement, "has had its day." The fundamental question involved was, *when is matter not matter?* The flip answer being, when it is *mind.* Gurdjieff would come to claim that by the early 1900s, his extraordinary development of practical knowledge had reached the point where he could, if he willed, kill a yak ten miles distant by mind power. How could anyone have normal relations with Gurdjieff if they knew this and believed it true?

Gurdjieff's debt to the "Nancy School" is revealed in a note in his chapter on his father, when he recalls involving his father in later life in Alexandropol in the hypnotizing of "the half-witted Armenian woman, Sando."[8] Gurdjieff was at the time apparently operating as a freelance "psychic researcher." Unlike members of the contemporary British-based Society for Psychical Research, however, he was not only investigating but actively using mediums for research purposes, bringing people ("guinea pigs") of many different types into various degrees of hypnosis to understand the phenomenon whereby painful sensations could be transferred at a distance, or, as he put it, what "learned hypnotists call the exteriorization of sensitivity." What Gurdjieff claims to have done in his father's presence was to rub parts of the medium's body with a blend of olive and bamboo oil. This oil was then rubbed into a rough wax, clay, and fine shot image of the woman under hypnosis. He and his father then observed that pricks made in the image were registered in the medium, even to the point of spots of blood emerging from the woman's skin. He wouldn't get away with it today.

Gurdjieff states that he brought the woman into the hypnotic state by "a branch of science which has come down to our day from very ancient times" called "loss of initiative." He elsewhere claims he learned this art in a monastic context, as we shall see, and it was called *mekheness.* Anyhow, he ratifies his practice by saying that loss of initiative corresponds to the "contemporary classification of the School of Nancy" known as the "third stage of hypnosis." Gurdjieff wants to assure us that while he is aware of the science on the subject, he is working with an older and deeper understanding whose full ramifications had not been grasped due to a myopia in the makeup of "controlled" minds.

SPIRITUALISM AND HYPNOSIS

It is intriguing and not at all coincidental that Gurdjieff's quest for understanding of supernatural knowledge coincides with a brief period when science and paranormal phenomena enjoyed a mutual, if uneasy, coexistence, even though scientists concerned with the issue still kept their occult sympathies private, if they had them, to be expressed in the fields of esoteric Freemasonry, spiritism, theosophy, and magnetism, which Papus was concerned to unite as a bulwark against the damage inflicted on the European psyche by materialistic rationalism. There were, however, opportunities for legitimate cross-investigation.

In 1888, Prince Alexander Petrovich Oldenburgsky (1844–1932) received imperial approval for his Institute for Experimental Medicine, established with his own money, in Moscow. To its portals came the famous Pavlov, with his interest in the psychology of suggestion and the nascent science of behavior, and if we are to believe strong hints of Gurdjieff in *Beelzebub's Tales to His Grandson,*[9] Oldenburgsky also patronized Gurdjieff himself in some way, as part of the aristocrat's patrician efforts to stem alcoholism in Russia.[10] Gurdjieff would use hypnotism to effect cures for alcoholics. While all that is still ahead of us, it is, nevertheless, important to know of developments parallel to Gurdjieff's youthful obsession with the subject of the invisible world—developments that were shaping the intellectual culture of the time, especially in Russia, where the need for some kind of rapprochement between traditional religious devotion and science and academicism was keenly felt. Occultism could be related to science because it dealt with *forces,* while the nature of those forces touched on religious conceptions of the spirit; so efforts to understand the supernatural could serve as a bridge for troubled minds to cross an unhappy gulf that had opened up in Russian culture. The Orthodox Church, of course, liked neither science nor what Church leaders tended to lump into their idea of a collective pseudoreligion they called Freemasonry, or "Illuminism." What need of all this, they argued, when the Church had nearly 1,900 years of illuminated miracles behind it?

In September 1889, supported by his magazines *l'Initiation* and the *Veil of Isis,* Papus helped to organize the Spiritist & Spiritualist Congress in Paris, to which forty thousand people came to hear delegates divided in basic outlook into two schools: those who believed spirits did the things attributed to them in séances and whose activity proved the soul's immortality; and second, occultists who believed mediums were themselves responsible for the phenomena. Occultists wished to learn ancient skills—like Gurdjieff, who always seemed to write as if he was practically the only person in the world who really cared about mastering these things.

Five hundred delegates from seventeen countries belonging to thirty-four different groups attended the extraordinary Paris Congress: theosophists, kabbalists, Swedenborgians, magnetizers, theophilanthropists. While occultists parted with spiritists, both adopted a ternary constitution of man—as would Gurdjieff. For spiritists, man was material, spirit, and "perispirit," a fluidic link they believed provided a new body to the spirit in the afterlife.

Perispirit was a term of Allan Kardec's, first used as item 6 of his introduction to *The Spirits' Book:* "The link, or perispirit, which unites the body and the spirit, is a sort of semi-material envelope. Death is the destruction of the grossest wrap. The Spirit retains the second, which is for it an ethereal body, invisible to us in the normal state, but which may accidently become visible and even tangible, as do the appearances."

Occultists of the time believed man to be composed of a material body of the soul, a spiritual mind believed to be of divine essence, and the astral body, which, unlike perispirit, dissolved completely after death. In the irenic spirit natural to Papus and necessary for a combined front against encroaching nihilism, Papus believed all differences could coexist and mutually enlighten one another under the umbrella of his Independent Group for Esoteric Research, which established branches throughout the world, and quickly too, and which included correspondents in Odessa and Cairo.

Just how specific the issues of Papus's Congress were to Gurdjieff's development is apparent from the section of *Meetings* dealing with Gurdjieff and his father's hypnotic causing-pain-at-a-distance experiment on Sando, the Armenian woman. Gurdjieff describes going back to see his father some years after that experiment and asking his father straight whether he believed in life after death. His father's answer shows an obvious awareness of the issues between Kardec and the occultists gathered in Paris in 1889. According to Gurdjieff's account, Ivan replied to his son's question by saying he believed in a soul, which is to say that "in the course of a man's life 'something' does form itself in him: this is for me beyond all doubt." This *something* had a life "almost independent of the physical body" but was of "much finer materiality." "The sensitivity of its perception is in my opinion such as you remember when you [Gurdjieff] made that experiment with the half-witted Armenian woman, Sando."

Gurdjieff's father believed that the *something* outlived the body for a time but then ended its existence. This position is basically a halfway house between Kardec and the occultists and allowed for, and explained, folk beliefs in Kars of a dead person's spirit being hijacked after death by a *gornakh,* an evil spirit made visible by impersonating the dead. Particularly susceptible, Gurdjieff tell us, were Tartars, who were customarily buried close to the earth's surface. Gurdjieff described this strange phenomenon in *Meetings:* something for which he sought an explanation vainly from Church authorities and rationalist intelligentsia.

To illustrate independently of Gurdjieff how keenly these issues were felt outside of Paris at the time, we need only consult a contemporary periodical entitled, *Light: A Journal of Psychical, Occult, and Mystical Research,* published from 2 Duke Street, Adelphi, London WC. In its issue for Saturday, September 7, 1889, its editor, who called himself "M.A. [Master of Arts] Oxon. [Oxford; that is, he had an Oxford Master's Degree]," contributed "Spirit Teachings No. XLIX," wherein he wrote, "For you the Supreme exists in His works, for you spirit is only objectively manifest by its operations. Not by ascetic life, but by active discharge of duty; not by perpetual meditation, but by energetic work; not by aimless aspirations, but by zealous activity does the incarnated spirit gain progressive knowledge. . . . We do not lay exclusive stress, but we insist, in your present phase of being, on the religion of the body and of daily life." Remarkably prescient of Gurdjieff's later, developed attitude, this was from page 1 of *Light* under the title, "Harmony of Religions: Ancient Religions of India."

M.A. (Oxon.) also gave a preliminary account of the Paris Congress in *Light* in the Saturday, September 28, 1889, issue, page 463: "It is a truism which states: 'Facts are only of use so long as they act as bases from which truths are deduced.'" This principle is certainly applied by Gurdjieff himself in dealing with the facts of history and his own life. Of "The Paris Congress" (page 467) the editor of *Light* refers to the *Moniteur Spirite et Magnetique* (a French specialist periodical of September 15) that informed him the Congress opened on Monday "under the most happy auspices." Papus was secretary; the president was Papus's colleague Jules Lermina; and thirty-five members of the committee were chosen from international delegates made up of Russians, Spaniards, Belgians, and Italians ("most numerous").

As we have seen, one of the principal accounts of spiritist phenomena to be discussed in Paris was attributed to French theorist Allan Kardec. Kardec is referred to *directly* by Gurdjieff in the introduction to *Beelzebub's Tales to His Grandson* with a jocular and cynical reference to a revelation from Allan Kardec's "Life-principle" in an "absolutely secret spiritualistic séance."[11] The principle enjoined, which Gurdjieff liked often to repeat, was, "If you go on a spree, go the whole hog including the postage."

Allan Kardec's real name was Hyppolyte Léon Denizard Rivail, and his *The Spirits' Book* of 1856 provided the basic text for understanding the spiritist phenomenon. Gurdjieff continued his allusion to Kardec in a joke he began to tell in *Tales* about his coming to Russia and what he endured there. Of that time, he wrote, "As for me, unfortunately doomed, while still living, to experience the delights of 'Hell,' as soon as I had cognized all this . . ."[12] The allusion is to Kardec's *Heaven and Hell* (1865) subtitled "Divine Justice according to Spiritism." Hell as a punishment in the afterlife was, Kardec held, a misconception; the state of spirits in the afterlife was not definitive, but there was always hope. Kardec explained in detail why "good people are doomed to suffer." Clearly, Gurdjieff regarded his life in Russia in this light: an ambivalent hell reserved for the well intentioned—Gurdjieff claimed he swore in 1911 to use his powers only for the good.

It is also worth noting that Gurdjieff's dislike for theosophy, and almost personal disappointment with Madame Blavatsky, evident in his works, was somewhat mirrored by Papus, who also would go to the "hell" of Russia on a mission in the early twentieth century and who, in 1890, had quit his theosophical lodge in Paris, while maintaining links with theosophical friends.

It is abundantly clear that the basis and much of the substance of Gurdjieff's developed world of related ideas comes from his early, teenage fascination with hypnosis, pursued during a historical period of intense interest in spiritualism, and that he associated the compulsion to understand its phenomena with his desire to account for what ordinary people regarded as religious miracles—miracles that he himself observed occurring, and explanations for which offered by either ecclesiastical or scientific authorities appeared impotent to satisfy what he called the "worm of curiosity"[13] that gnawed constantly at him and drove him into stranger and stranger lands.

SIX

Mad about the Girl

Or How to Get to Tiflis in a Hurry

Since the middle-aged Gurdjieff was known to have intimate relations with a number of his female pupils, and children by several of them, it might come as a surprise that sex is not a subject often raised in his writings other than in the context of pleas for straight teaching on the subject, highlighting the dangers of prudery, or to show the moral decline of individuals who succumb to protracted vice. He does offer us one glimpse of his adolescent romantic nature, though, in chapter 9 of *Meetings,* though typically the tale is embedded in a setting concerning inner development and the importance of spirit.

The story begins with him still singing in the choir at the Kars fortress cathedral. The time must be circa 1890–92. He is bored with Kars; his parents have discussed moving back to Alexandropol, and the idea has its attractions, especially as Dean Borshch has taken leave of absence due to illness while favorite tutor Bogachevsky has left to pursue a spiritual career, culminating in his becoming abbot of an "Essene" community and an ideal Christian. Georgii dreams of going to Tiflis (Tbilisi) in Georgia, where, in his youthful "self-love" and undeveloped thinking capacity, he hankers to join Tiflis's Archdeacon's Choir. Furthermore, he says that things he had done at the Kars artillery range, on the city's mountain rim, troubled his conscience.

He was friendly with a boy his own age whose name, he says, was Riaouzov or Riaïzov, whose father distilled vodka, and whose sister, aged twelve or thirteen, attracted Georgii greatly. This chapter of *Meetings* is devoted to Piotr Karpenko (from the Russian for "fruit" or "profit"), alleged son of an artillery officer, and Karpenko is introduced as another young friend equally enamored of the same girl, who is not named, perhaps to protect the innocent. Georgii impresses the girl with his guitar playing, but Karpenko's family is better off. Coming out of choir early to escort the girl home, he finds Karpenko has had the same idea, and Gurdjieff boils with jealousy. Like two romantic knights, Gurdjieff says, they both take her to her home, where they part from the beloved. Georgii precipitates a fight, and Karpenko comes off worst. Strong, Gurdjieff was always up for a fight if necessary. Gurdjieff went off for his "club"; that is, his mates, gathered on the beams of the temporary bell housing by the military cathedral. One of the lads, he says, was named Korkhanidi, from the Greek quarter of Kars.[1] Gurdjieff says this boy grew up to be an author, which is probably true. P. Korkhanidi's educational *Zhivoe slovo: pervaia kniga dlia chteniia v shkolie i sem'ie*, that is, "The Living Word," was published in Tiflis in 1912. Korkhanidi's aunt, we are told, provided the schoolboys with *halva,** but pleasure in the aunt's gift was rudely interrupted by the arrival of a bandaged Karpenko with two Russian pals. After Karpenko made a pretentious speech, Georgii told him what he could do, whereupon another boy reminded the rivals that fisticuffs was fit only for Kurds; proper people reasoned their way out of disputes or had a duel.

Karpenko said the world was not big enough for them both, so a duel it must be. It was then suggested that God could decide the matter of which of them had a right to a place in the world, so it was suggested

---

*Halva is a favorite candy dessert of the Middle East made with honey and sesame seeds.

they both go to the artillery firing range, secrete themselves behind the targets, and endure the judgment of destiny.

The artillery range in the mountains about Kars was familiar to the boys because they were in the habit of going there secretly at night to gather copper from spent shells and scattered pieces of lead to hand over to two older Russian boys who acted as a fence, selling the metals for good money. This was highly dangerous activity, but being youths who hardly knew what was what in the world they dreamed in, they did it nonetheless. Similar lack of reality informed the appalling decision to conduct a duel with the unwilling assistance of Russian artillery.

The boys duly crawled onto the range and found shell holes about 100 yards from the targets. Their accomplices waited by the banks of the river Kars Chai. When day broke and the firing began, Gurdjieff experienced fear such as he had never known in his life. He felt "fated to die." As the terrific storm of shells rained down close to him, his being was transmuted into pure terror, in which he "thought and experienced more than during an entire twelvemonth." [2]

This experience is intended to convey to the reader an essential fact of Gurdjieff's teaching, that the true experience of the self is not the normal experience of the self, and it might take a shock or series of shocks to shake one into awareness, or remembrance of who one is really. Sure enough, while Georgii quivered tight in his shell hole, "Simultaneously, there arose in me for the first time the 'whole sensation of myself.'"[3] He knew himself and valued his existence facing death's imminence. He became aware of the existential facts: what he called in *Tales* "The Terror of the Situation," "an unconquerable living terror."[4] From this moment, in retrospect, Gurdjieff traced his fearlessness in thought, as well as his sympathy and understanding of others' fear: important lessons he immediately applies to his getting up after the deluge to find rival Karpenko unconscious in a shell hole, wounded by shrapnel. Though Karpenko's wounds transpired to be slight, Gurdjieff was nonetheless seized by remorse and pity. From that moment he feels Karpenko is his brother; the girl suddenly of no consequence. What he had considered undying love evaporated. The deeper, more real fraternity comes from understanding in a shared ordeal.

He says Karpenko was soon taken to Russia for several years of education but nevertheless developed enthusiasm for their common ideas seven years after the duel, when he would participate in some of Gurdjieff's adventures in travel and exploration whose tales dominate *Meetings* after the first three chapters. Karpenko's experience proved "fruitful," in tune with his name. Unless the number seven is merely symbolic, Gurdjieff here indicates that "our recently formed group Seekers of Truth"—which seems to be Gurdjieff's ideal Work group—came together circa 1897,[5] but the name has euphemistic qualities and since its membership has proved to be very likely entirely fictional and ideal, we have no compelling reason to cling to the idea of its existence as much more than a useful device for teaching and inspiring. Besides, *Seekers of Truth* is an expression that covers all Gurdjieff's spiritual or quasispiritual activities. However, while he seems to have operated in Central Asia and elsewhere very much as a one-man band, he also liked to have a coterie, gang, or club around him when he was in the mood, and life being what it is, it is unlikely he was able to maintain a continual group, so he may have idealized those times when he had colleagues or friends, for a time. However, it is equally possible that he was bound by secrecy not to reveal his closest connections. One cannot help thinking of him, especially with his conscious ecumenism and devotion to universal truth, as embodying the essence of a sincere Freemason, and one who followed to the letter the rule of never revealing his membership. Many did not, in those days, under any circumstances, since being able to keep a secret was seen as a primary test of character. On the other hand, later attested colleagues never mention Gurdjieff in relation to Freemasonry in Europe or America, but that could be explained by Gurdjieff's multiple lives, if one had to. But one does not have to. Gurdjieff did not concoct his cast of characters so we might believe they were real people, but for what they might tell us about ourselves and the search for truth.

FEDEEV AND BLAVATSKY

There is possibly at least one hidden aspect to the tale Gurdjieff tells in his account of the duel at Kars. He confesses that he was involved not only in theft of military hardware—spent as it was—from the artillery field, but also of cigarettes from his uncle's cigar case. These he would use to keep "in" with an army clerk member of the military cathedral choir. We are told that this fellow gave Georgii advance notice of serious trouble heading his way.[6] The panting clerk blurted out to his young friend that he'd overheard fortress commandant General Fadeef discussing with the chief of mounted police the arrest and cross-examination of persons involved in suspicious activity at the artillery range. Gurdjieff's name was mentioned. While it is likely, from Gurdjieff's accounts, that his name would already have been known to the military community, presumably as a precocious and interesting, even promising chap, and perhaps to the general himself, the name here that may count the most is General Fadeef or, as the surname is also spelled in English, *Fedeev*.

Fedeev was one of the most illustrious names in the Russian army and Russian statecraft, a name famed particularly in connection with Tiflis, the Caucasus, and—note—Kars itself. Bearing in mind the way senior jobs in the Russian army were meted out to favorites of aristocratic members of the state, it seems likely that General Fedeev, commandant of Kars who heard young Gurdjieff's name, was kinsman to General Rostislav Andreevich Fedeev (1824–1883), who had died in Tiflis less than a decade before. Tiflis was central to the military administration of the Kars Oblast. It was General R. A. Fedeev who had defeated the Turkish army when the Russians besieged Kars fortress in 1855 during the Crimean War. Furthermore, as the great Russian diplomat Sergei Witte (1849–1915)—General R. A. Fedeev's nephew—explained in his memoirs concerning his admired and favorite uncle, Fedeev,[7] the general had converted to Christianity the night before the battle at Kars. While the other officers were getting drunk, Fedeev prayed to God to take him into divine care. Surviving the battle, Fedeev became a sincere

Christian—he later refused to lead a military force against Abyssinians because they were Christian—with a strong interest in spiritualism, mysticism, and theosophy.

The most surprising fact about General Fedeev from our point of view, however, is that he was the uncle of Helena Petrovna Blavatsky (1831–1891), cofounder and leading light of the Theosophical Society, which itself grew out of the vogue for spiritist séances joined to her existing enthusiasm for Russian illuminism, gnostic magic, and what we today call comparative religion. Madame had deep connections with the Caucasus; her name, *Blavatsky* came from a brief, ill-sorted marriage to an elderly Armenian diplomat of that name, contracted when she lived with her family in Tiflis, Gurdjieff's next destination.

Gurdjieff would admit to Orage, as we have noted, that he had spent nine years following in Blavatsky's footsteps but in the end rejected her Hindu-Buddhist solutions to life problems, as well as her addiction to séances. I intuit that despite the disparities, there could have been elements of Blavatsky in Gurdjieff's fictional tutor Bogachevsky, who also follows a checkered career before arriving, in his case, at inner peace and harmony, albeit in a fictional setting.

The links between Fedeev, Blavatsky, and Witte are straightforward and intimate. Diplomat Andrey Mikhailovich Fedeev (or Fadeyev) married Princess Helena Pavlovna Dolgorukov in 1813.[8] Of their four children, daughter Elena Gan married Peter von Hahn. Peter and Elena were Helena Petrovna Blavatsky's parents. General Rostislav Andreevich Fedeev was Elena's brother, and thus Madame Blavatsky's uncle. Uncle Rotislav Fedeev served as general at Kars and was the scorched-earth subjugator of jihadism in Chechnya and the Caucasus. Fedeev became Witte's admired outspoken diplomat, spiritual Christian and pan-Slavic imperial ideologue, believing Russia should take Constantinople and rule an empire uniting all Slavs behind a victorious banner of Christian progress.

Elena's sister Ekaterina Andreevna was Sergei Witte's mother. Witte was arguably the most brilliant diplomat in Czar Nicholas II's government. Elena and Ekaterina's younger sister, Nadejda Andreevna, would become active in her niece's Theosophical Society. The Theosophical Society might never have existed had Elena's maternal grandfather, Prince Pavel Dolgorukov (died 1838), not possessed hundreds of books and manuscripts on alchemy, magic, Freemasonry, and Rosicrucianism.

After Elena's death in 1842, Helena Petrovna joined her grandmother's household, gaining unrestricted access to the late prince's library. According to K. Paul Johnson in *The Masters Revealed,* absorption in the library brought Helena to the idea of "Unknown Superiors" familiar to "Strict Observance" Templarist and neo-Rosicrucian Freemasonry. Young Helena's experience directly shaped her perception of "the Masters."[9]

In 1847, sixteen-year-old Helena Petrovna moved with her family to Tiflis when her grandfather, Andrey, became a member of the Council of Secret Governance for the Transcaucasia region. There, Tiflis resident Prince Aleksandr Golitsyn, Freemason, magician, and seer, paid call on Helena's grandparents, greatly impressing young Helena. According to the memoirs of Madame Ermolov, wife of Tiflis's governor, such a passion was ignited through their long conversations that the couple ran away, an adventure that led to Helena's family condoning the hasty marriage of General Fedeev's granddaughter with the considerably older Nikifor Vladimirovich Blavatsky, vice-governor of Erevan, Armenia, on June 7, 1849. Ermolov suggested it was Prince Golitsyn who gave Helena contact details for Coptic magician Paolos Metamon, considered Blavatsky's first "Master" in occultism.[10] At this point, Blavatsky's life becomes something of a pre-echo of the life structure the considerably more humble Gurdjieff gave himself, or himself as "alter-ego," in *Meetings.*

Escaping marriage, Helena went first to her relatives in Tiflis, then to Odessa where she took the English sailboat *Commodore* to Kerch before moving on to Constantinople. In Constantinople she met Russian countess Kiseleva, with whom she traveled to Egypt, Greece, and central Europe. In Cairo in 1851, Blavatsky met American writer, artist,

Freemason, and archaeologist Albert Leighton Rawson (1828-1902). Fascinated by ancient and esoteric religion, Rawson was a member of American fringe Masonic orders (95th degree Rite of Memphis; 32nd degree Scottish Rite; *Societas Rosicruciana Americae,* among other fringe sodalities). In later life Rawson recalled of their encounters—he and Blavatsky were together in Paris and the States in the early 1850s— how she claimed her destiny was to liberate the human mind, a work not hers but of "Him who sent me," a phrase from Saint John's gospel attributed to Jesus.

In 1871 Blavatsky began a spiritualistic, magical society in Cairo to study mental phenomena, inspired by Paolos Metamon, whom Rawson and Blavatsky first met in Cairo in 1851 and whom K. Paul Johnson surmises to be the real identity behind Blavatsky's "Master Serapis."[11]

Readers familiar with *Meetings* will of course note Gurdjieff's heading for Constantinople with Pogossian, after a trip through Armenia and northern Mesopotamia, whereupon they take an English warship (!) to Egypt where Pogossian envisages an English destiny for himself as an engineer and goes his own way, and where, in a separate account, Gurdjieff will encounter a Russian prince and archaeologist while working as a guide in Cairo, trying to understand the Great Sphinx. How much Gurdjieff's following in Blavatsky's footsteps was physical and how much imaginary is impossible to ascertain.

Blavatsky left Cairo in 1872, passing through Palestine, Syria, and Constantinople before settling a while at Odessa, where she opened a shop selling artificial flowers. Readers of *Meetings* will again note Gurdjieff's claim that when running a workshop in Ashkhabad, he specialized in making artificial flowers, among other profitable activities. Blavatsky's cousin Sergei Witte recalled her colossal talent for absorbing anything very quickly and that she had the hugest blue eyes he had ever seen in his life. Both statements could equally be made of Gurdjieff, of course.

According to *Meetings,* on hearing that a General Fedeev of the Kars fortress had heard Gurdjieff's name mentioned in connection with irregularities at the artillery range, Gurdjieff says he resolved to leave Kars the very next day. If he'd had doubts about leaving, surely fate had now played a decisive hand. Get out—or else! His destination, from the logic of previous remarks, was that fateful opportunity enabled him to do what he had dreamed of doing; that is, head for Tiflis. The sole reason he gives for choosing Tiflis is a vain ambition to distinguish himself in the archdeacon's choir there. This seems insufficient as a motive, but disingenuous as it may be, it is the only motive Gurdjieff offers, other than the negative desire to get out of boring Kars, and frustrations due to interruptions in his education occasioned by the absence of sympathetic tutors, Bogachevsky, and Dean Borshch, the latter on account of illness.

There seems to be a tie-in of dates with Gurdjieff's curious account of parts of his life in his short work *The Herald of Coming Good* (1932), a work that Orage, for some reason, advised Gurdjieff to repress, and that in Gurdjieff's similarly curious "third series," posthumously published and titled *Life Is Real Only Then, When "I Am,"* he actively urged potential readers to ignore, perhaps on Orage's advice. We, however, cannot afford to ignore what Gurdjieff chose to communicate in 1932.

The essay opens with the statement that it was now twenty-one years since he began a period in his life that only now, in 1932, was ending. He says he took an oath in 1911 to lead an "artificial life" promoting his ideas and working his powers solely for the liberation of mankind. He says the root of this mania occurred when, on the point of attaining responsible age, an irrepressible urge to understand the significance of life on Earth imposed itself "by the Will of Fate." He then says that in the year 1892 his researches reached a point when his contemporaries could assist him no longer and he would perforce have to go for a period of complete isolation where he could assess what he should pursue in the matter of research. While he then says this self-isolation took place in Central Asia, where a friendly "street barber" got him access to an unnamed Muslim monastery—the proper word for which in Central

Asia is *khanqah,* which Gurdjieff never uses—in which he meditated on his future, the high-sounding language in which he expresses himself seems to add up to the simple fact that Gurdjieff left his tutors in Kars and pursued his own path. He would have been, we may surmise, fourteen or fifteen. He had reached the end of his formal and informal education, and if he had indeed been in as serious a predicament in relation to the law in Kars as suggested earlier, he would not have taken any exams there and was therefore in a fix as to getting a decent job. But then, he has decided to let "Fate" have her way, while presumably seeking not only guidance as to the supernatural, but supernatural guidance as well. He's going to have to live on his wits.

We find very similar language and concerns, less pretentiously expressed, in chapter 6 of *Meetings,* where we are introduced to the "remarkable" person named Abram Yelov, of Tiflis, fortuitously a bibliophile. Gurdjieff meets Yelov, he says, during his "preparatory age"; that is, "a short time after I had lost all hope of discovering from contemporary people anything real concerning those questions in which I was wholly absorbed."[12] *Yel* is Russian for "fir" or "spruce" and symbolizes time and evaluation. There is nothing in this account, or version of things, about Central Asian monasteries. Rather, Gurdjieff says he was *returning* to Tiflis from Echmiadzin, Armenia, where he had stayed at Archimandrite Surenian's home with Pogossian, exploring all the religious sites, an account of which extended visit is related in the previous chapter devoted to Pogossian or Captain X.[13]

Gurdjieff says that on returning to Tiflis—he gives us no information as to what he was living on, or how—he immersed himself in ancient literature. He then says the attraction for returning from Echmiadzin to Tiflis was because the city gave access to any rare book in any language, whether Armenian, Georgian, or Arabic (nothing about wanting to be in the archdeacon's choir!). Just how he might have been able to understand Arabic, or even Georgian, is not revealed, though if he was going to make any kind of life in Tiflis, capital of Georgia, he would have to acquaint himself with a good working knowledge of the tongue.

TIFLIS

In the "Yelov" chapter of *Meetings,* Gurdjieff says his first residence in Tiflis was in the Didoubay district. From there he would travel some distance to the Soldiers' Bazaar, held on a street off the west side of the Alexander Gardens, which still exist, though the narrow streets around have been much cleared. Most of Tiflis's bookstalls were in the Soldiers' Bazaar and have now gone, though there is a flea market down by the river. Gurdjieff records that among the book peddlers and small traders was a young *Aïsor,* or Assyrian, known in youth as Abrashka Yelov: "an artful dodger if ever there was one, but for me an irreplaceable friend."[14]

Yelov plays the part of provisioner of Gurdjieff's reading matter—being a veritable "walking book catalogue." Gurdjieff says he used to accompany this book catalogue in the Alexander Gardens or in the *Moushtaïd,* discussing philosophical themes, the same Moushtaïd where in his chapter on Pogossian, Gurdjieff says he walked with Pogossian talking about whether the latter could find employment at Tiflis railway station, where Gurdjieff presents himself as working.[15]

The nature of the Moushtaïd is also revealed to us in a remarkable travel book, written by Englishman Harry de Windt and published in London in 1891. This makes it practically contemporary with the time Gurdjieff says he was living in Tiflis. Since Gurdjieff gives us practically no description of what Tiflis was like when he was there, Windt's amusing travelogue greatly helps to color in Gurdjieff's sojourn in Tiflis, as seen by one frustrated by Tiflis authorities' delay in granting permission to enter Transcaspia to enable him to continue his "Ride to India across Persia and Baluchistan," the title of his book.

One hears a deal, in Europe, of the beauty of the Circassian and Georgian women. Although I remained in Tiflis over a week, I did not see a single pretty woman among the natives. As in every Russian town, however, the "Moushtaid," or "Bois de Boulogne" of Tiflis, was daily, the theatre nightly, crowded with pretty faces of the dark-eyed, oval-faced Russian type. The new opera-house, a hand-some building near the governor's palace, is not yet completed.[16]

I suspect what de Windt was saying—though we should allow for some journalistic license—was that the Moushtaid was where you went to pick up pretty girls. The Bois de Boulogne, of course, was notorious for prostitutes.*

Tiflis, capital of the Caucasus, is about midway between the Black and Caspian Seas, and lies in a valley between two ranges of low but precipitous hills. The river Kur, a narrow but swift and picturesque stream spanned by three bridges, bisects the city, which is divided in three parts: the Russian town, European colony, and Asiatic quarter. The population of over a hundred thousand is indeed a mixed one. Although Georgians form its bulk, Persia contributes nearly a quarter, the rest being composed of Russians, Germans, French, Armenians, Greeks, Tartars, Circassians, Jews, Turks, and Heaven knows what besides. The name Tiflis is derived from Tbilis Kalaki, or "Hot Town," so called from the hot mineral springs near which it stands.

Tiflis is a city of contrasts. The principal boulevard, with its handsome stone buildings and shops, tramways, gay cafes, and electric light, would compare favourably with the Nevski Prospect in St. Petersburg, or almost any first-class European thoroughfare; yet, almost within a stone's throw, is the Asiatic quarter, where the traveler is apparently as far removed from Western civilization as in the most remote part of Persia or Turkestan. The Armenian and Persian bazaars are perhaps the most interesting, I doubt whether the streets of Yezd or Bokhara present so strange and picturesque a sight, such vivid effects of movement and color. Every race, every nationality, is represented, from the stalwart, ruddy-faced Russian soldier in

---

*Years later, Gurdjieff would return to the lushness of the Moushtaïd Garden when his group gave a final movements demonstration there before Gurdjieff left Georgia forever in 1920 (Michael Benham, e-mail to author, October 5, 2016).

flat white cap and olive-green tunic, to the grave, stately Arab merchant with huge turban and white draperies, fresh from Baghdad
or Bussorah. Georgians and Circassians in scarlet tunics and silver
cartridge-belts, Turks in fez and frock-coat, Greeks and Albanians
in snowy petticoats and black gaiters, Khivans in furs and quaint
conical lamb's-wool hats, Tartars from the steppes, Turkomans from
Merv, Parsees from Bombay, African negroes—all may be seen in
the Tiflis Bazaar during the busy part of the day.

The Hotel de Londres was the favourite rendezvous after the play.
Here till the small hours assembled nightly the élite of European
Tiflis. Russian and Georgian officers in gorgeous uniforms of dark
green, gold lace, and astrachan; French and German merchants with
their wives and daughters; with a sprinkling demi-mondaines from
Odessa or Kharkoff, sipping tea or drinking kummel and "kaketi"
at the little marble tables, and discussing the latest scandals. Kaketi,
a wine not unlike Carlowitz, is grown in considerable quantities in
the Caucasus. There are two kinds, red and white, but the former is
considered the best. Though sound and good, it is cheap enough—
one rouble the quart. Tobacco is also grown in small quantities in
parts of Georgia and made into cigarettes, which are sold in Tiflis
at three kopeks per hundred. But it is poor, rank stuff, and only
smoked by the peasantry and droshki-drivers.[17]

It should be of interest that de Windt refers to Tiflis's map store,
regarding the maps of Central Asia superior to those sold in England.
Gurdjieff had much to say, when he encountered Russian military
mapmakers in Afghanistan of their occasionally loose commitment
to precision. Aleister Crowley made the same observation in his
assessment of military maps of the Karakorams made by English
topographers!

Tiflis has a large and important garrison, but is not fortified. Its
topographical depot is one of the best in Russia, and I managed, not

without some difficulty, to obtain from it maps of Afghanistan and Baluchistan. The latter I subsequently found better and far more accurate than any obtainable in England. The most insignificant hamlets and unimportant camel-tracks and wells were set down with extraordinary precision, especially those in the districts around Kelat.[18]

Gurdjieff might have added in years to come that they might have looked accurate down to the last detail, but that the last detail might have been wrongly sited in the first place!

De Windt's account of waiting on Tiflis station for the steam train to Baku is highly evocative, insofar as Gurdjieff tells us in *Meetings* that he eventually got a job there as a stoker. This task in a railway context would normally suggest what in England is more familiarly known as a "fireman," who shovels coal into the boiler next to the locomotive driver. However, in terms of railway hierarchy, if the Tiflis to Baku railway was anything like British or French

Тифлисъ. Станція 3 Ж. Л. - Tiflis. Station de chemin de fer

Contemporary postcard of the Tiflis Railroad Station

railways, the position of fireman was something that had to be worked for quite some years after entering service as an apprentice "cleaner," the job of fireman being only one down from the coveted position of engine driver. Since Gurdjieff does not mention journeys undertaken on the footplate of an engine, only as a passenger, the likelihood was either he stoked the furnace used for heating the station itself, or that he sometimes worked stoking "shunters," or locomotives used in the goods yard for switching, though this latter possibility too is unlikely. The station furnace seems his most likely place of work, though with his technical bent, one can well imagine him eyeing the engine driver's job with envy. In those days, to a young person especially, being an engine driver was like being an astronaut in the 1960s—something to aspire to.

De Windt took the train eastward from Tiflis shortly before the Greek Orthodox New Year, on January 12, his 11 p.m. train having been delayed down the line by a violent storm. It seems he only slightly missed having been warmed on his way by young Georgii Gurdjieff.

> It was again snowing hard, and the east wind cut through my bourka [a long, sleeveless coat made of goatskin] as if it had been a thin linen jacket. Seeking shelter in the crowded, stuffy waiting-room, we solaced ourselves with cigarettes and vodka till past 2 a.m., when the train arrived. Another delay of two hours now occurred, the engine having broken down; but the carriages, like those of most Russian railways, were beautifully warmed, and we slept soundly, undisturbed by the howling of the wind and shouting of railway officials. When I awoke, we were swiftly rattling through the dreary monotonous steppe country that separates Tiflis from the Caspian Sea.
>
> The Russians may, according to English ideas, be uncivilized in many ways, but they are undoubtedly far ahead of other European nations, with the exception perhaps of France, as regards railway travelling. Although the speed is slow, nothing is left undone, on the most isolated lines, to ensure comfort, not to say luxury. Even

in this remote district the refreshment-rooms were far above the average in England. At Akstafa, for instance, a station surrounded by a howling wilderness of steppe and marsh; well-cooked viands, game, pastry, and other delicacies, gladdened the eye, instead of the fly-blown buns and petrified sandwiches only too familiar to the English railway traveller. The best railway buffet I have ever seen is at Tiumen, the terminus of the Oural railway, and actually in Siberia.[19]

The combination of books and railway work, while sounding implausible to some, need not make us doubt such a combination. A fellow writer and retired civil servant I know, back in the sixties, traveled across the United States in the cab of a train whose engineer had a bookcase installed there whose contents he discussed with his young English friend on the very long journey west to an eventual job in the UCLA library! However, precisely what Gurdjieff did, and when, rather depends on whether you are reading the chapter on Pogossian—where Gurdjieff tells his railway stories—or Yelov, where we are treated to Gurdjieff's successful attempts to wheedle the secret formula out of a local Greek street trader for making plaster of Paris busts for decorating local houses. In this matter, as in so many of his necessary trading activities, Gurdjieff showed himself not to be a mimic of his father's "subjective morality" but of the objective need to survive, and made his money with cavalier unscrupulousness. With regard to the Greek who took Gurdjieff on as a helper, Gurdjieff "pretended to be a blockhead," playing on his patriotism by speaking Greek. His role playing as one "so foolish and harmless" prepared him, we might observe, for acting as a way of life.[20]

Before we look more closely at Gurdjieff's important acquisition of connections on Russian railroad projects, we need to address the question of the kinds of books Gurdjieff might have been obtaining from Tiflis booksellers, whether or not one of them acquired the name *Yelov* in order to feature as a "remarkable man" for Gurdjieff to meet in his web of stories.

Now, if we read the biography of any figure with distinction in the life of the mind, we do not have to go very far to discover what particular books and authors most inspired them. Aleister Crowley, for example, was absolutely specific on what he read and what he most appreciated and had been inspired by. He even supplied, for the use of his pupils or other interested persons, a long bibliography of varied books idiosyncratically chosen.

Not once does Gurdjieff let us know what he was reading—the rare mention of Kardec in *Tales* being a kind of slip in this regard. Sometimes, as we shall see, we can make an educated guess. But Gurdjieff gives no credit to any author, living or dead. The suggestion is that he made his system up in the condition of the archetypal but romanticized genius. According to Beekman Taylor, however, when Russian gnostic intellectual Boris Mouravieff (1890–1966) asked Gurdjieff in Paris about Christianity's relation to his system, Gurdjieff replied, "It's the ABC. But they [the church fathers] didn't understand at all." "Is the system yours?" asked Mouravieff. "No . . . ," replied Gurdjieff. "Where did you find it? From where did you take it?" "Perhaps," replied Gurdjieff, "I stole it." Was Gurdjieff intuiting that this was what Mouravieff was actually thinking, and so gave Mouravieff his ironic twist on the skeptic's doubt? Gurdjieff always claimed his insights were of ancient provenance, though not from India!

Indeed, it is not theft to take one's ideas from different sources. If it were so, no student would be safe from copyright lawyers. "There is nothing new under the sun," my father used to repeat, and he was, where essential ideas are concerned, right. We can no more steal ideas than we can steal our mother's milk. We share ideas, and that is the joy of it all.

However, in Gurdjieff's case, there is a little more than irony in his riposte. There lurks a chip on the shoulder and a real fear of, and suppressed anger at being exposed to, analysis and criticism, which, had he waded through the misery and mirth of a university education, he would have been considerably more accustomed to.* Amateur writers become far more nervous when the reader of their work brings out the red pen than the professional, since the professional is used to editorial priorities scrubbing excellent work for any number of reasons. I should go so far as to say the best writing may improve perhaps only from fear conditioning of losing the "good stuff." If you want the good stuff in, it had better be damned good! Never did Gurdjieff recommend as a matter of instructional aid the work of another writer, unless of course that writing was the Bible or other ancient scripture, dignified by that expression that looms behind Gurdjieff's knowledge-theory, or fantasy: *the Tradition.*

---

*Michael Benham would defer from concluding definitively that Gurdjieff never attended a university or studied for a degree, citing first, two newspaper interviews A. R. Orage gave in Boston in February 1924, prior to Gurdjieff's visit. In the first Orage has Gurdjieff attending Athens University, and in the second Gurdjieff is presented as graduating:

> "We aim to bring Eastern psychology to the West, in the Western form," said Mr. A. R. Orage, who was for fifteen years editor of the *New Age* (London), in an interview with a CRIMSON reporter, yesterday afternoon. Mr. Orage has written several volumes on economics, literary criticism, and psychology. He is author of the revolutionary Social Credit Theory. Mr. Orage represents the Gurdjieff Institute, which was founded two years ago at Fontainebleau (near Paris), by the Russian George Ivan Gurdjieff.
>
> "Gurdjieff," said Mr. Orage, "after graduating from the University of Athens, spent thirty years traveling through the East, gathering as much knowledge as possible of Eastern tradition.
>
> "The Gurdjieff Institute," he continued, "conducts along with its other activities, a set of special exercises, which we call 'movement,' but which appear as dances. Mr. Gurdjieff didn't invent the dances, he discovered them. They consist of ancient Greek, Egyptian, and Buddhist and early Christian sacred classics—4000 all told."
>
> The Institute is at present touring the United States, giving demonstrations of these "movements." Mr. Orage is in Boston principally for the purpose of arranging for a demonstration here. March fifth is the probable date. ("Uses Dancing to Convey Eastern Ideas to West A. R. Orage Lauds Russian Institution of Gurdjieff as Affording Perfect Balance of Body and Mind," *Harvard Crimson,* February 27, 1924.)

Benham also cites in support of Gurdjieff's studying for a degree the following extract

Gurdjieff had the pride of the self-taught man, and that pride made the admission of deficiency a habitual irritant. He opens his *Beelzebub's Tales to His Grandson* with an excessively long-winded attack/defense explaining why his book does not read like anyone else's; in particular, why it is not written in *bon ton* manner. Needless to say, conscious of the hurdle he has created, he asserts that if you find problems with his writing, you can always ask for your money back! But don't bother criticizing what you don't understand! He was as he described himself "a cunning blade," a dude, a street dealer relying on sheer presence and a hypnotic face to cast aside a challenge.

We who seek to understand something of this man's life cannot take *No* for an answer. As we have seen, Gurdjieff's interests, regardless of the egoistic manner in which he expresses his commitment to them, followed tracks well worn already in the culture of western and

---

from notes of conversations with Gurdjieff by writer, editor, and sometime secretary of Gurdjieff, Solita Solano (1888–1975), whom Gurdjieff nicknamed Kanari (Canary).

Notes of trip to America, April 1939:
Fifth day. He [Gurdjieff] remarks, "Time slowly pass." I tell him how extraordinary are the three Russian-Greek anatomical books he has lent me for my work at the Hospital St. Louis. "Just from those books," he says, "I studied for my degree. Old German printings are some diagrams, very rare. But of course I found later much better in one Chinese monastery. Such for detail as you could never see even in dream. Only they were hard to learn to read because they not show negative picture, as all other books, but in this case, positive. Must study positive while holding always picture in mind of negative. Not one of your Western scientists can even know there is such a thing. This book also show at same time function. Also this not one of your idiot doctors can understand" (Michael Benham, e-mail to author, October 5, 2016).

The author of this book considers this as evidence only that Gurdjieff claimed to have worked for a degree and rather suspects that for him the "University of Athens" may have meant he considered himself adept at dialectic in the Socratic mode. The word *degree* also has initiatic, esoteric undertones, and may of course refer to Freemasonry rather than formal tertiary education. The Masonic 2nd degree is concerned with the study of the "Seven Liberal Arts," which formed the traditional basis of Western university education. The 2nd degree also encouraged the Mason to study "the hidden mysteries of nature and science." Orage was in no position to assess the historical background of Gurdjieff's early life.

central Europe. Culturally as regards his social, economic, and racial position, there is no doubt that his personal experience was far removed from that of the average Parisian or English or Berlin-based intellectual. Gurdjieff had *street cred:* something we might value highly today, or say we do, but in his time he would be, and we know he was, definitely conscious that he came from the wrong side of the tracks—socially speaking, and as regards academic sophistication at the formal or arguably superficial level. He was right to assert in *Tales* that none of this mattered where *essential truth* was concerned. Plato might have been an academic of sorts, but the prophets were not, and truth required neither tuxedo nor starched shirt and pince-nez for the right to join the party. And aristocratic sages got nowhere at all unless they left their protected environs and got down to the streets and close to nature. The Buddha had to leave Mama with no credit card to lean on. But Gurdjieff was, as he says, an omnivorous reader and would have us believe he had read everything and more that there was to read on what interested him.

What then can we say of his reading matter, since Yelov is not telling us?

SEVEN

Books

Furniture of the Mind

It should not really surprise us that Gurdjieff chose Tiflis as the next step in his self-education adventure. Whereas in old Russia debate still raged over whether imperial policy should advocate two years of basic education for peasant children; in the southern and eastern frontier lands, to which Georgia gravitated, children of settlers had had over a century to enjoy education provision between the preconfirmation ages of seven and fourteen—Gurdjieff was one of them.[1] With relative improvements in education, and distance from the power centers of the Russian Orthodox Church and the court, came other liberties prevalent in the frontier areas of the Russian Empire. Women enjoyed more freedom—as the career of Helena Petrovna (Madame Blavatsky) demonstrates—and there was a more liberal atmosphere and encouragement to progressive thinking. The cultural air, we can say, was fresher. In Georgia the overall atmosphere benefited from healthy spas, mountain breezes, mineral baths, and proximity to the mysteries and varied faiths of Transcaspia.

During the 1890s, the kindly Chamuel (Lucien Chaumel) of Paris, working chiefly for Papus, published a large number of ancient and modern texts on every aspect of esotericism. Combined with profuse, often high-quality articles in *l'Initiation* and the *Veil of Isis,* as well as the host of basic texts of gnostic traditions published and edited by members of the Theosophical Society in Great Britain, it would not take long for an enthusiast with sufficient pocket money and knowledge of French and English to build up a reasonably comprehensive esoteric source base. According to Maria Carlson's *No Religion Higher Than Truth: A History of the Theosophical Movement in Russia 1875–1922,*[2] much of the French material soon found its way to Russia and to Freemasons of various hues everywhere. Translations into Russian of much of the new material, however, were not available straightaway. The works of Papus on Paracelsus, tarot, spiritism, Kabbalah, hypnosis, and magnetic medicine did not acquire Russian editions until after 1905, following Papus's visits to Russia with the miracle worker Monsieur Philippe, which made him deeply valued by the Russian royal family and much spoken of throughout the empire, becoming at last an embarrassment to the French government (see my book *Occult Paris*). The Parisian Hermetic movement, small as it was, was nevertheless written about in articles that appeared in Russian literary journals, and there would be translations by Bal'mont (1867–1942), Briusov (1873–1924), and Russian symbolist writers. The golden age of Russian occultism, or revival of occultism, built up steam throughout the decade following Gurdjieff's arrival in Tiflis and accelerated even faster after censorship was eased by law on October 17, 1905. More than eight hundred occult titles were published in Russia between 1881 and 1918.[3]

Vladimir N. Zapryagaev, an interesting editor of esoteric literature, including works on astrology and the tarot, translated an astrological work by Papus's friend, Henri Selva. A pseudonym of A. Vlès, Henri Selva's main work was the *Traité théorique et pratique d'astrologie généthliaque* (Paris: Chamuel, 1900). Selva's theory that astral influences were caused by the integration of suprasensitive forces by the nervous system, in the form of rhythms indicated by light, would almost certainly have interested Gurdjieff had the book come his way. In 1907

Zapryagaev published the third edition of Papus's colleague Paul Sédir's *Les miroirs magiques* ("Magic Mirrors"), translated as Магические зеркала (*magicheskie zerkala*), published for the first time in Russian in 1894.[4] It is hard to imagine Gurdjieff ignoring such a work had he become acquainted with it. All we can say for certain is that it was available to him.

Since Gurdjieff specifically refers to old and rare books, he may have come across the prolific publications of Moscow Masonic Rosicrucians Nikolai Novikov and Ivan Lopukhin issued through the Moscow University Press and the Moscow Typographical Company during the reign of Catherine the Great until their business was suppressed and Novikov imprisoned by the czarina on the advice of the Russian Orthodox Church leadership and her political advisors. They feared that Freemasonry, coming from Germany, was subversive of nationalist sentiment. Between 1783 and 1785, the Novikov-Lopukhin circle published Russian translations of Paracelsus' *Chymischer Psalter and* Michael Sendivogius' *Novum lumen chymicum,* as well as the German alchemical tales *Chrysomander* and *The Cradle of the Philosophers' Stone* (*Kolybel kamnia mudrykh*), among many other illuminist works.

Among the Masonic holdings of the former Imperial Library in St. Petersburg, indefatigable scholar of Rosicrucianism Carlos Gilly in the early 1990s was shown Russian translations of the *Corpus Hermeticum,* under the title *Poemander,* based on the German translation of 1781, as well as Comenius's *Lux lucens,* in Russian, and much else besides. Moscow's Russian State Library "V. S. Arsenyev collection" holds seventy-four copies of manuscript versions of works by Jacob Böhme, mainly translated by Semen Ivanovich Gamaleia (1743–1822), as well as two complete copies of the *Corpus Hermeticum* translated into German and Russian. Gnostic works by writers influenced by Paracelsus, such as Robert Fludd, abound. In fact, there is hardly a name in Western esoteric tradition, including all of the Neoplatonists, who are not represented in the Russian State Library's collections.

THE TRADITION

Gurdjieff's conception of Tradition is central to the enlightenment he claims to have received through the agencies of a number of monasteries, principally it appears—from the numerous references to dervishes in *Meetings*—of a Sufic or Sufi-influenced character. It is possible that Gurdjieff's conception of a persistent, authentic Tradition may also have been influenced directly or indirectly at some point by the thought of French esotericist Antoine Fabre d'Olivet (1767–1825), whose ideas about the Tradition strongly influenced contemporary occultist Saint-Yves d'Alveydre (1842–1909), the Parisian Martinists led by Papus (Gérard Encausse, 1865–1916), and the author of the highly influential book *The Great Initiates* (1889), Édouard Schuré. While the Yezidis regard themselves as the inheritors and guardians of what they too call the Tradition (*sunna*), it is clear that Gurdjieff's ecumenical, universalist view of a primordial spiritual knowledge that has been passed through all religions in spiritually resonant symbols and moral teachings is consistent with Fabre d'Olivet's influential account of human civilization. Fabre d'Olivet is a key—if physically absent—figure of the French esoteric movement of the 1880s and 1890s. The Russian State Library today only has one Russian translation of a work by Fabre d'Olivet: Фабр д' оливе ("Fabr d'olive"); Космогония Моисея (*Kosmogoniya Moiseya*); пер. В. Н. Запрягаева (per. V. N. Zapryagaeva); Вязьма, типо.-лит. Р. Писаревской 1911 (Vyazma, tipo. lit. R. Pisarevskoy, 1911).[5]

What had Fabre d'Olivet to say of the Tradition?

Between 1800 and 1805, impacted by the ideas of Pythagoras and his followers, Fabre d'Olivet underwent a spiritual crisis. Pythagorean ideas concerning how numbers related to abstract truths about the structure of the world and the nature of the soul in the world burst into Fabre's world view as a profound revelation leading him to embrace the idea of a unity behind all phenomena, a unity that was also the alpha and omega, the origin and purpose of all. D'Olivet emphasized the idea that the life process we live is a working out of reintegrating diversity and duality into unity. Salvation lies in the return to the One. Fabre then introduced an idea that would have a massive impact on Martinism. Martinism had been established in Russia at the time of Novikov and enjoyed a revival exactly contemporary to Gurdjieff's years of searching.

Recognizing that his spiritual experience was not peculiar to himself, and attempting to account for it, d'Olivet posited the existence of what he called the Tradition. For Saint-Yves d'Alveydre the Tradition became a kind of historical force whose social opponent was anarchy, where anarchy was simply understood as *life without the Tradition.* In Gurdjieff's understanding, anarchic disintegration is expressed as *disharmony,* for which his Institute of the Harmonious Development of Man offered the cure.

What did Fabre mean by the Tradition?

The idea is closely linked to the Rosicrucian-Hermetic understanding of the Dignity of Man: the restoration of the primitive; that is, original human understanding. Fabre concluded the Tradition must exist in all people at some level, since he had inherited it as a revelation from within himself to himself. It must have been passed on from long ago, for it is evident in all ancient civilizations. For d'Olivet, this "primitive" world was not one of unevolved ignorance but of paradisal harmony, pure, original, and profoundly simple.

For Fabre the Tradition must predate the earliest civilizations (dated at 4500 BCE), since the civilizations were only possible with its guidance, and where deviation took place, collapse would follow. Applying this theory to the nineteenth century, decay of civilization was the result of loss of contact with the Tradition. The arts must represent the Tradition.

According to Fabre, the identifiable process of transmission of the Tradition was from the Egyptians to Moses and from Pythagoras and Orpheus to Jesus. This idea would be taken up by Schuré as the essential structure for his book *The Great Initiates,* which insightfully saw the French Decadents as the seed ground for renewal of spiritual understanding. Schuré would see it chime in with similar ideas of esoteric transmission promulgated by Madame Blavatsky. According to Fabre d'Olivet, the great initiates named above were divine men in full reception of the Tradition; hence Jesus could say, "Had ye believed Moses ye would have believed me" (John 5:46). Having fully realized the Tradition, these men could work the essential task: to bind Will to Providence. By *providence* is meant God's foreknowledge, the mind that sees before we see, expressing God's will to provide what is necessary for the Good.

D'Olivet had answers for Gurdjieff's questions about miracles. Somewhat anticipating Éliphas Lévi's mid-nineteenth-century idea that miracles had explanations if one knew the magical science required, d'Olivet cured deaf mute Rodolphe Grivel by putting the fifteen-year-old in a "magnetized sleep" (following Mesmer's hypnotic ideas), whereupon he awoke in the mute the volitive faculty, that is, *the will,* by drawing it forth by sympathy transmitted in the "universal vital fluidity" posited by Mesmer. Treated in January 1811, when the cure hit the newspapers, Fabre was forbidden by Napoleon Bonaparte from doing it again, as it contradicted what men of science had made of Mesmer's theories.

Judging from the manner in which Gurdjieff expounded stories from his own life, he seems to have at least shared d'Olivet's view of conventional history as a kind of deaf mute, incapable of yielding intelligible faculties unless it was, as it were, magnetized by sympathetic understanding. D'Olivet claimed that understanding. He applied it to contemporary philosophical problems. Where Immanuel Kant insisted that philosophy was not equipped to assess the truth value of revealed statements, thus erecting a divide between matters of faith and reason, Fabre assessed Kant as one ignorant of the Tradition, by which Man is body, soul, and spirit. Kant, he said, confused rationality with reason. Rationality is of the soul (mere thinking); reason is of the spirit, according to Fabre. Reason for Fabre is better rendered as "intellect informed by spirit" or spiritual intellect, equivalent to the Greek *nous* or higher reason—the King faculty, as Plotinus called it. It draws, according to Fabre, on the spiritual source of the universe's intelligibility. Fabre's Reason is a mirror of heaven, reflecting the divine mind. It is the means by which humankind receives higher knowledge. Rational statements divorced from this faculty lack universality. They may be logical within their own terms but are maimed in application, being dependent on sense experience alone. The soul is understood here as the human passions and feeling; the spirit belongs to the higher unity, surpassing ordinary understanding. Spiritual teaching addresses this faculty. The mind receives, and what the higher mind receives constitutes the Tradition.

Kant, along with a vast quantity of post-Kantian philosophy attempts vainly, according to Fabre, to submit a higher faculty to a lower one. Reasons derived from the soul, unenlightened or illuminated by the spirit are insufficient in essential judgments. Here Fabre was offering to the artists who came after him the essential tools to combat the concretion of scientific rationalism that was producing, and is still producing, sclerosis in the spiritual dimension of the culture. And still the churches condemn or are indifferent to esotericism!

In his book *Cain, the Dramatic Mystery of Lord Byron* (1823) written to rebut Lord Byron's popular play *Cain,* which Fabre believed would promote a loss of faith in England when England's problems necessitated faith, Fabre represented Cain as "Will," Abel as "Providence." The separation of Will and Providence is ruinous for humankind, engendering perpetual cycles of conflict between *hommes volatifs,* who rely on their own will, and *hommes providentiels,* who trust in God's love for humanity. The murder of Abel then is the Luciferian suppression of Providence by Will and is a sign of human history. How history turns out depends on how "Man" responds to Will, Providence, and Destiny. In *Cain,* Adam and Eve respond to Abel's murder by producing new son Seth. He represents Destiny or blind fate, and history then becomes a conflict between sons of Seth, who submit to necessity and work with nature through science, and sons of Cain, who champion anarchic liberty. The conflict is endless, and though humankind cries out for Providence, the "providential men" no longer walk the Earth. All we have is our limited knowledge of a few such beings—men like Moses, Orpheus, Buddha. Providence can only work indirectly, through channeling humanity's willfulness toward an ultimate *apocatastasis:* the reintegration of Adam and establishment of the Ideal. The *potential* is there in the essence of the individual, like the germ of a seed, but its realization requires an active, guided Will.

The theory is easily compatible with an enlightened medicine. The ordinary doctor sees only an incomplete human being (an impression), but the good doctor sees health in the completion of the being's potential: drawing forth the hidden will and "magnetizing" the mute capacities.

One can see straightaway the confluence of these potent ideas with Gurdjieff's interest in awakening the faculties of the unconscious through an application of a tripartite conception of the human being. Emphasis on the threefold aspect of man was traced to its chief exponents by Gnostic Church leader Jules Doinel in the August 1892 issue of *l'Initiation* (page 121), where Doinel writes forcefully of the "Ophite or Naassene Gnosis": "They established as first principle THE IDEAL MAN and the son of this man . . . the mystical Adam . . . generator of the Eons . . . celestial Citizen! Man by essence (Man worthy of the name)!" This idea that man is only *potentially* worthy of his name occurs in Gurdjieff's frequent caustic comments about his fellow "three-brained bipeds" who seem incapable of even approaching the idea due to some primal blockage of perception that has set their faculties at odds.

Doinel's article describes how the "homotype" manifests on Earth as a triple being: "he is intelligible, psychic, terrestrial," or spirit, soul, earth/body. "The commencement of perfection," says Doinel—appointed bishop of Montségur after a séance at the Parisian home of Madame Blavatsky's friend, Lady Caithness—"is to know MAN. To know GOD is the absolute perfection." This wisdom he attributed to the Naassene Gnostics. Based on the triple essence of man, Doinel informs us, the Naassenes were able to classify the three kinds of human being, typified by the aspect of the triple essence that had gained supremacy. Thus, there were three churches: the Elect (pneumatic, or spiritual), the Called (psychic, or soul-conscious), and the Captive (hylic, or material). When Gurdjieff came to reorganize his clubs of students in New York in 1931 he divided the membership into exoteric, mesoteric, and esoteric. The rule of three he habitually employed is familiar to thinking Masons.

The Gnostic conception of body, soul, and spirit, evident in Fabre d'Olivet, becomes for Gurdjieff the basis for therapeutic interest in *reharmonizing* bodily instinct, feelings (soul), and thinking or mentation (mind) to generate awakening from the dream of ordinary, externally directed consciousness, to a higher being or state of being. To quote the Gnostic Jesus, "It is those who are awake I have addressed" (Sophia of Jesus Christ, Nag Hammadi library).

The keynote of Western esotericism is the idea of the fallen faculties, and the *redemption* of esotericism is the *reconstitution,* or raising, of the fallen faculties to their primitive dignity (apocatastasis). Gurdjieff was aware that this tradition could be found in ancient literature and residual custom and folklore, but for some reason he found it impossible to hand any credit to those of his *own* time who worked to the same or analogous ends.

THE BROTHERHOOD OF THE ROSE-CROSS

Scholar of Rosicrucianism Christopher McIntosh has noted on many occasions that there is an obvious resonance between Gurdjieff's elusive Sarmoung Brotherhood, which provides *Meetings* with its most durable thread, and the equally elusive brotherhood of the Rose-Cross, whose existence was announced in Rosicrucianism's foundation document, the *Fama Fraternitatis* (published in 1614 in Kassel). In the *Fama,* the revelation of knowledge stimulated by the unseen fraternity of initiated brothers was so that "Man might recover his true dignity and worth," an accomplishment attributed to Wisdom (*Sophia*) "poured out so richly" on mankind by "the only wise and merciful God." Its signs included the renewal and reducing of "all arts to perfection" and the restoration of the faculties of Man to divine fullness. The Russian Masonic-Rosicrucian Novikov's friend I. P. Turgenev made a notable Russian translation of the *Fama*. At Moscow's Central State Archives of Ancient Acts, Carlos Gilly inspected a manuscript of the *Fama* as well as the classic *Secret Symbols of the Rosicrucians*—both in Russian.[6]

The *Fama* (or Fame of the Fraternity), which first appeared in a German manuscript of 1610, contains the allegorical story of the discovery of the tomb of Christian Rosenkreuz, who, the document stated, having in his youth got bored of Western Christian monastic life—like Gurdjieff and his perhaps imaginary friends Pogossian and Bogachevsky—quit in search of transcendent wisdom. Traveling to Damar in Arabia—misstated as *Damcar* or *Damascus* in different versions—Rosenkreuz encountered pristine wisdom, essential *magia,* protected by Arab sages, both there at Damar and at Fez in Morocco. Ignored by academic savants on returning to Europe, "C. R." founds a fraternity of the Rosy Cross whose brethren meet regularly in an invisible "House of the Holy Spirit," where they work for the healing and enlightenment of mankind, sharing their discoveries, in preparation for the last times, which times will be preceded by a general enlightenment effected by a divinely inspired, total reformation of learning and reorientation of the heart. Is it possible that Gurdjieff somehow absorbed this story into his own version of it when, as we shall see, he would tell how he and his "remarkable" friends came mysteriously upon the monastery of the Sarmoung Brotherhood in *Meetings*?

Even more prescient perhaps of Gurdjieff's own traveler's tales is Thomas Vaughan's preface to the first published English translations of the *Fama* and *Confessio Fraternitatis* (1653), wherein London-based Vaughan is struck by the ability of the Rosicrucians' "Spherical Art" to show an inner conformity that reconciles different schools of ancient

Wisdom. Vaughan compares Philostratus's account of the natural philosophy of magus Apolonius of Tyana with that of the RC Brothers, noting how Apolonius (circa 15–100 CE) describes with respect the "Brachmans" (Brahmins) of the Ganges (India). Vaughan offers a fascinating story about the Brachmans. By the banks of the Ganges, the Brachmans have formed secret fraternities of wisdom. In tune with the exalted thoughts of the Jewish Kabbalah, the Brachmans are privy to what Vaughan calls the "Sphiristical Order," referring to the Spheres or "Sephiroth" of the kabbalistic Tree of Life, while also suggesting the "Spherical Art" known to the RC Brotherhood.

Further, Vaughan says that conqueror Alexander the Great never reached the holiest, most secret places of the Brachmans. Their stronghold stood on a hill between the Ganges and the River Hyphasis (the Beas River, which rises in the Himalayas). Out of respect for their mysteries, Alexander did not seize it, though respect may have been engendered by fear, for Vaughan tells us that the Brachmans had perfected—apparently by alchemy—a security system within their gated refuge, which is to say they could inflict defeat upon enemies without by means of "Thunder and Lightening" [*sic*]. Vaughan is quick to remind his readers that while the experience of gunpowder would have shocked Apolonius, nothing could now be more familiar to his readers—on account of the explosive English Civil Wars—nor indeed, he adds, would such fires and terrors of the sky have surprised thirteenth-century adept Friar Roger Bacon.

Vaughan notes that Roger Bacon, while discoursing on "several wonderful Experiments," confided to readers the existence of "a secret Composition, which being form'd into Pills, or little Balls, and then cast up into the Air, would break out into Thunders and Lightenings, more violent and horrible then those of Nature." Vaughan quotes Bacon to the effect that only a "thumb-measure" of the substance could "cause a horrible report and show a brilliant flash, and this can be done in many ways, by which a city or an army may be destroyed."

The idea of a secret redoubt somewhere in Central Asia holding the most ancient Tradition was a staple of theosophical circles, and it is hard to imagine Gurdjieff being unaware of it. Saint-Yves d'Alveydre took many of Fabre d'Olivet's ideas and passed them off as his own work. However, one idea d'Alveydre did not get from Fabre was the concept of Agarttha, the name coming instead via Saint-Yves's somewhat manipulative Sanskrit language teacher, Hardjji Scharipf. Saint-Yves elaborated on Tibetan Buddhist and Hindu legends of a place, Shambhala, held to be a pure, peaceful land from which the Golden Age would arise, as from a root. Saint-Yves offered his version in a place he called *Agarttha,* of like import, revealed to him as located somewhere underground in the Tibetan Himalayas. In this place, the Tradition of "Ram," supposed patriarch of enlightened religious awareness, held sway through a "king of the world," a conception fundamentally akin to the neo-Rosicrucian idea of the secret direction of the world by Secret Chiefs, and analogous to the Sufic idea of the Axis: the *Qutb* or perfect, universal human being, who leads the saintly hierarchy and brings to each generation the desired knowledge of God. Jimi Hendrix sang a song of how the Axis was "Bold as Love" and knew everything. From Agarttha, an oriental Atlantis—though not damned as in the Greek legend told by Gurdjieff in *Tales*—the modern, anarchic industrialized modern anthill could yet be redeemed should it accept Saint-Yves's "Trinitarian Synarchy" as its means of renewal.

Having found his mission in life, Saint-Yves believed that sense of mission should be shared by professional groups he addressed in a series of influential "Mission" books. In 1882 *The Current Mission of the Sovereigns* was laid out. The workers received their Mission in 1883, the Jews theirs in 1884. The most thorough work on Agarttha did not appear until 1910: *The Mission of India.* The Russian State Library has it in a Russian translation: Сент-Ив д' Альвейдр Миссия Индии ("Missiya Indii"; *Mission de l'Inde*), published in St. Petersburg in 1915. They also have a copy of the Martinist journal, the *Veil of Isis,* apparently in Russian from 1913, catalogued as Изида ("Izida").

Regarding books on spiritualism (spiritism), the spring 1875 issue of Russian periodical *Vestnik Evropy* ("Herald of Europe") published the first declaration by a Russian scholar of belief in mediumism.[7] The writer was Nikolai P. Wagner, professor of zoology at St. Petersburg University. Aleksandr M. Butlerov echoed similar beliefs in *Russkii Vestnik* ("Russian Herald") a few months later. One may wonder whether subconscious memory of such titles might have stimulated Gurdjieff when he entitled his 1932 printed pronouncement, *The Herald of Coming Good.* Following the appearance of Wagner and Butlerov's articles, Dmitri I. Mendeleev and members of St. Petersburg's Physical-Chemical Society formed a "Medium Commission" to investigate spiritist phenomena. After surveying eight séances, the commission concluded that the practice was superstitious. Officially proscribed in Russia, the subject was illegal in published works. Such proscription would have increased the subject's attraction for the fearless young Gurdjieff.

Equally undeterred was Aleksandr Nikolaevich Aksakov, a scholar whose interest in spiritism had been sparked in 1855. Aksakov published his thoughts in the journal *Psychische Studien* in Leipzig, Germany, after 1874. It took four years to produce his hoped-to-be comprehensive study of the subject *Animizm i spiritizm* ("Animism and Spiritualism") in 1893. Telepathy and telekinesis were, he believed, psychic phenomena exteriorized beyond the body: "The soul is not an individual 'I' . . . but an envelope, a fluid, or an astral body of that 'I,'" wrote Aksakov.[8] He believed the cause of the manifestations was not only external to the medium, but "beyond the sphere of our existence."

Aksakov invited and paid for mediums to come to Russia while funding the journal *Rebus,* which began its life in 1881, persecuted by the censor. Though *Rebus's* contents were modest, the censor would not even permit biographies of authors to be printed. Innumerable complications ensued in getting anything published at all. By the mid-1880s, however, *Rebus* was printing articles on Russian folklore, as well as material on séances and information about the spiritualist movement in American and European societies investigating the psyche. *Rebus* featured Baron Karl du Prel's occult series *Filosofia mystiki* ("the philosophy of mysticism"), which appeared separately in 1895.

Rebus first mentioned Blavatsky in the late 1880s. In 1893 well-known writer Vsevolod Solov'ev expressed disillusionment with her in a book that received a fiery response from Blavatsky's sister, Vera P. Zhelikhovskaia, whose title called Blavatsky "a contemporary prophet of truth" (published in St. Petersburg, 1893, by Izdanie A. S. Suvorina). As a result of the debate, Blavatsky attracted even more followers—one was probably Gurdjieff—and her serial *Zagadochnye plemena* ("The Mysterious People") that had graced the journal *Russki Vestnik* in 1883 was published a decade later as a book. These were hot works in the 1890s and may well have contributed to inspiring Gurdjieff to set off east, or south, or both. When more of Blavatsky's books were being prepared for publication after the Theosophical Society was founded in St. Petersburg in 1908, the Soviet government confiscated a Russian translation of *The Secret Doctrine*.

Western occult literature appeared in the 1880s and 1890s, just in time to fill young Gurdjieff's head with strange ideas. It's odd to think of him shoveling wood or coal into a furnace at Tiflis station with his eager mind buzzing with titles such as *Spiritizm v Indii: Fakiry ocharovateli* ("Spiritualism in India: The Fakir-charmers") by Louis Jacolliot, 1883; Charles Richet's *Sonambulizm, demonizm i iady intellekta* ("Somnambulism, Demonism, and the Diseases of the Intellect," 1885); *Statii po mediumizmu* ("Articles on Mediumism") by Butlerov, 1889; Edwin Arnold's *Svet Azii* ("The Light of Asia"), 1893; Helena P. Blavatsky's *Iz peshcher i debrei Indii: Zagadochnye plemena na "Golubykh Gorakh"* ("From the Caves and Jungles of India: The Mysterious People of the 'Blue Mountain'") of 1893—Gurdjieff must have read that!—and Frank Podmore, Edmund Gurney, and Frederic Myers's *Prizhizennye prizraki i drugie telepaticheskie iavleniia*

("Phantasms of the Living and Other Telepathic Phenomena"), also published in 1893.*

One can imagine a highly imaginative and intelligent young man seizing on a conception of the human being that was entirely based on inner potential and the development of the *new body,* rather than social conventions that people accepted because everyone else did. These ideas gave Gurdjieff's feet wings; he must have bubbled at the thought of a different kind of future.[9]

---

*Regarding Gurdjieff and books: Michael Benham (e-mail, October 6, 2016) has drawn my attention to aspects of Gurdjieff's table talk recorded by Solita Solano, in the company of "the Englishman Pindar [Major Frank Pinder 1882–1962], Miss G [Elizabeth Gordon, 1876–1945], Sardine [actress and theatrical manager Louise Davidson], K ["Krokodile" Kathryn Hulme (1900–1981), a member of the 1935–39 "Rope" group of women followers of Gurdjieff]" at a time in Paris when Gurdjieff's brother Dmitri was "very ill." On Friday, 13 April 1937 Gurdjieff announced at table, "I am unique for the number of books I have read in my life from all countries. When could not read a language, I had someone translate. Five or six a day I read, often before sleeping. Now I nothing read." The previous day, he had said to Madame de Salzmann, Miss Gordon, Dmitri's doctor, Sardine, and the American Nick Putnam, "Other people read books, but I verify"—meaning, presumably, that whereas others absorbed or repeated what they read, he would challenge what he read and assess the truth-value of the work. This further implies that Gurdjieff would not quote an author as an authority but would make the read content his own by personal testing: thus he possessed his own conclusions. He was saying that lazy academics and ordinary readers generally parrot what they have read without fully challenging supposed authorities.

EIGHT

In Search
of Brotherhood

While Gurdjieff's young mind was full of Don Quixote–type ambitions, ambitions he claimed to share with his friends, he still had to survive. Trying to sort out his working life from his inner life is a practically impossible task when examining what can be known of Gurdjieff in the 1890s. There are so many loose ends, fragmented stories, bits of fact mingled with fiction, fantasy, and didactic teaching material to contend with. For example, his activities in Tiflis are curiously divided around adventures with what first appear to be interesting friends, Pogossian and Yelov, but by the end of the accounts devoted to these personae, they seem to have morphed into two principles: *spirit* and *work,* with Pogossian always working with a will to be willing, and Yelov probing mysteries. And when the friendly principals discover an intimate fraternity between themselves, one is aware Gurdjieff is trying to make a point that work and spirit, combined as intentional suffering, are like loving brothers and make for spiritual development and a taste of the kingdom of heaven within.

According to *Meetings,* Gurdjieff crafted plaster of paris busts at a workshop in Tiflis before working on the railways. The Yelov chapter does not mention Gurdjieff's job as stoker. He does, however, say that after selling the workshop to two Jews for a good price, he had to vacate his rooms and move to Molokans Street near the elegant white railway station, constructed in 1872.[1]

The Molokan Spiritual Christian pacifist sect had a meeting house on Molokans Street (*Molokonskaia Ulitsa*) on the first floor of a two-story house, and it is to be suspected from what Gurdjieff wrote about leaving his bags in a Molokan wagon during a pilgrimage earlier, that he perhaps had made their acquaintance, as they were an independent spiritual group, and such groups interested him. They had their own graveyard in Tiflis's Akhalia Kukia district. In the 1860s the Molokans set up the market, which was known as the Molokan Bazaar, a popular market persisting until the 1960s. The Molokans traded fish, vegetables, salt, and dairy products. They worked mainly as coachmen and owned the best phaetons in the city. Providing the base of support for the Russian administration in the Kars Oblast, Molokans provided transportation services for the Russian army during the 1877–78 war with Turkey and were employed on the railways. It is possible Gurdjieff got his job as stoker through such a connection.

Gurdjieff says in *Meetings* that he had gotten to know an engineer on the railways called Yaroslev.[2] The word *engineer* here and elsewhere could mean Yaroslev was an engine driver, or a construction engineer engaged on track maintenance and tunnel, cutting and embankment work, probably the latter. The engineer allegedly wrote a letter of introduction to Tiflis's stationmaster to help Pogossian obtain a job as stationmaster's locksmith. We are then offered a more historically reliable tidbit of information that should help us to date the succeeding events quite closely to historical realities.

Gurdjieff says Yaroslev introduced him to another engineer, Vasiliev. Vasiliev had just arrived in the Caucasus to survey a proposed new railway line from Tiflis to Kars. Though Gurdjieff does not tell us this, the railway scheme he refers to was in fact a vital component of Russian imperial policy. It was overseen by the military since it was intended to consolidate the Kars Oblast territories gained in 1878 so that in the event of further conflict with Turkey, troops could speedily reach the

Turkish border. It would also be a major economic benefit to the people of the Kars region and was hoped to encourage Russian migration and settlement, though, as it turned out, most Russian settlers could not stand the climate or rough country. An enlightening study of the building of the railroad has recently been published: *The Construction of the Tiflis-Aleksandropol-Kars Railway (1895–1899)* by Sonya Mirzoyan and Candan Badem.[3] It greatly assists us in getting inside this fascinating, epic slice of history that Gurdjieff himself treats in the most cursory and disinterested manner, as he seems to treat most politically motivated physical endeavors undertaken by mere mortals (unremarkable men). One doubts, however, whether Gurdjieff had attained anything like Beelzebub's preternatural objectivity when he labored at Tiflis station.

After meeting Vasiliev a few times, young Gurdjieff obviously made an impression on the Russian employed to make an engineer's assessment of what was going to be a state railway, meaning, for those in administrative roles, they would be on the state payroll. The Russian engineer apparently proposed employing the young man before him as overseer and interpreter. That seems quite a responsibility for a youth. How old was young Gurdjieff?

On March 11, 1894, a special council chaired by Russia's minister of war came to a decision concerning railways in the Caucasus: "In 1894 [we will] carry out a final survey for the connection of Tiflis to Kars and Erivan and in 1895 we will begin the construction of the aforesaid lines." Emperor Alexander III approved the conclusion.[4]

Preliminary surveys had already been undertaken. On September 19, 1892, the director of the Transcaucasian Railway petitioned the minister of communications to reverse existing policy and to allow foreigners to be hired both as employers and employees. Permission was granted "in view of exceptional conditions." In 1892 and 1893 foreign subjects (Persians, Turks, Italians, and Belgians) could be employed as contractors, subcontractors, artisans, and workers.

Since it is plain that any hiring of Gurdjieff was due to linguistic skills and because his on-the-ground familiarity with the region would have made the Russian new to the territory feel considerably more secure, it would seem his being taken on as interpreter and overseer was with a thought to unfamiliar languages being spoken. An energetic, useful fixer, Gurdjieff had broad tolerance for different cultures—an asset considering Molokans, for example, had settled in villages along the highway from Alexandropol to Kars; they would find work on the railway. Most of the population in the villages spoke Armenian, Gurdjieff's favorite language. In addition to well-paid administrative staff, the construction would exploit, sometimes quite cruelly exploit, the labor of Turks, Armenians, and Kurds from outside the Russian-controlled Oblast, so Gurdjieff's colorful background, as well as his ability to converse intelligently with Russian officials, and his (mostly) good relations with Russian military men, rendered him ideal to have around. Young he might have been, but he was tough, polite when necessary, energetic and streetwise. It would appear then that Gurdjieff was around fifteen or sixteen—seventeen at the outside—when he seized the opportunity to work for the Russian government as a subcontractor. If he was good, and recommended, one doubts if too many searching questions were asked.

Gurdjieff states plainly that the salary was almost four times what he was getting as a stoker; a job he said that was already interfering with his "main work."[5] Besides, how could he resist?—the position allowed him lots of free time. According to Mirzoyan and Badem, salaries on the Aleksandropol–Kars railway ranged from 18 rubles per month to 2,700 rubles per year, with generous bonuses for work well done. A ruble was worth about 77 U.S. cents, when one pound sterling was worth about $4.86.

Gurdjieff says he spent three months traveling with the engineer through the narrow valleys between Tiflis and Karaklis: a credible itinerary, as documents show some seventy-five foreign workers would live in Karaklis once construction got under way. Gurdjieff earned a great deal of money, much of it under the table. He refers to "several unofficial sources of income of a rather questionable character."[6] Since he already knew which villages the railway would pass through, he could "send someone" to the bigwigs of local towns and villages and basically fleece them in exchange for putting their village or town's case for official recognition of a station. Parties involved found it hard to resist the spurious offers, and Gurdjieff's pockets, he says, bulged accordingly. When you play with the world, Gurdjieff believed, you had to know when to play hardball.

In fact, the railway's construction would be riddled with petty corruption, usually to the detriment of workers' safety. The Ottoman Empire's consul in Kars, in his report to the Ottoman Ministry of Foreign Affairs in May 1898, wrote that corrupt Russian officials did not conduct business properly, while greedy contractors used limestone for embankments, which did not last, vanishing after showers. While bitter workers eventually unionized and struck for better conditions, this was still an imperial gravy train if you knew the right man. Gurdjieff could have "done even better," having been on the job from the beginning, but true to character, once he realized he'd amassed sufficient cash to pack up work, he retired from the railway to concentrate on his consuming interest: finding that "certain something" that people had once known but seemed to have been forgotten.[7]

Meanwhile, a joint resolution of the Committee of Ministers and the Economic Department of the State Council received the emperor's approval on May 12, 1895, and construction of the Tiflis–Aleksandropol–Kars railway began in earnest.

THE ARMENIAN QUESTION

It is fairly true to form that when Gurdjieff does mention a book by name, it is almost certainly an invention of his own. In *Meetings* he says that despairing of finding answers in contemporary literature or science, he and Pogossian were driven to seek inspiration solely in ancient literature, since it was now plain to them what they sought had been left behind in the shifting sands of time. They would have to dig.

The book he mentions he calls *Merkhavat,* and judging from what he wrote earlier about Pogossian's focusing exclusively on ancient Armenian literature, we may presume the book to be Armenian too.[8] To students of Hebrew Kabbalah, the title will appear as a variant transliteration of Merkabah or Merkavah: that form of kabbalistic speculation concerned with the throne or chariot of God as revealed in the first chapter of Ezekiel and further elaborated in the thirteenth century *Zohar* and other kabbalistic works. The aim of Merkabah, or throne mysticism, is to ascend and approach the divine being, primarily through the image of God, which appears in the form of a man: the perfect Man. Beyond that image, divinity has no form. By a twist of literary sleight of hand, Gurdjieff establishes an ambiguity about "Merkhavat," for it is immediately conflated with the word *Sarmoung,* which Gurdjieff tells us he found in the book *Merkhavat,* with reference, apparently, to a brotherhood in possession of great knowledge and the key to many mysteries. Without specifying what *this* refers to—either Sarmoung or Merkhavat—Gurdjieff writes, "This word is the name of a famous esoteric school which, according to tradition, was founded in Babylon as far back as 2500 BC, and which was known to have existed somewhere in Mesopotamia up to the sixth or seventh century AD; but about its further existence one could not obtain anywhere the least information."[9] What a magician with words! Well, Merkabah mysticism is rooted in an arguably gnostic vision of what Gnostics later called the *Anthrōpos* experienced "by the rivers of Babylon" in about 500 BCE and that was pursued by mystical Jews in Babylon and elsewhere from at least the first century BCE to the medieval period—and was of interest to authors of some of the Dead Sea Scrolls as well. As for the Sarmoung Brotherhood, it is clearly a catchall for an ideal combination in tune with all surviving elements of the "Tradition."

Pogossian's immersion into Armenian literature is something of a clue to the times we're talking about, especially in view of what will ensue after the next episode in Gurdjieff's search for the great knowledge. It cannot be an accident that Gurdjieff, now he's got the cash, however earned, wants to get away to somewhere peaceful to study, away from Tiflis, to contemplate his search, nor can it be coincidental that the place chosen is Ani.

ANI

Ani, a plateau of extraordinarily abundant and quite hypnotic ruins about 30 miles west of Alexandropol, was once the capital of Armenia, when Armenia was a fabulous kingdom—the first Christian kingdom in the world: a place of exquisite beauties—and what we're really seeing here, reflected behind the main drama Gurdjieff is concocting, is the deep need of Armenians to recover the fullness of their national identity. Gurdjieff of course never says that he himself is interested in recovering national identity, indeed, he seems most intent on *losing* any such thing at the first opportunity, judging by his linguistic claims—eighteen languages at one point!—hobnobbing with Russians, his passion for disguises, his "universal face," and eventual literary transmogrification into an archangel, albeit a suspect one, in *Tales*. No, he projects his own feelings about Armenia—home of his favorite language—on to Pogossian and lets Pogossian bear the burden of the pain of a people. He does not intend to suffer for Armenia. In fact, he seems more like a young man on the run.

We need some hard history, and hard history should come as a shock perhaps for those who have read *Meetings* entirely through and within its own frame of reference. From the history, we can be reasonably confident in deducing that the date in which Gurdjieff's story is set precisely parallels the historical completion of the final survey for the Tiflis–Kars railway. The year is clearly 1894: a particularly hard year in Armenia's tragic history.

The Treaty of Berlin that formally ended the Russo-Turkish war in 1878 internationalized the Armenian question, the essence of which question was that there were Armenians in large numbers on Turkish soil and large numbers of Armenians on Russian soil, but there was no Armenian soil. Armenia as a kingdom had gone, but the Armenians remained and remembered they were Armenians and remembered their country, and they remembered that their once beautiful capital had suffered destruction by Seljuk Turks, Georgians, Mongols, and earthquake. Turkey remembered too, and after World War One, demolished even more of the stately shells and thousand churches, all ruined, of the once astonishingly beautiful capital. Today the truly extraordinary ruddy brown site of Ani, ghostly and silent, like glowing embers of a dream at dawn and sunset, suffers inadequate state protection and is regularly vandalized, while locals run the ticket concession, with graves desecrated by treasure seekers. Many in the Turkish state want to forget, if not obliterate, the country's Christian history, and the historic preservation policy, especially beyond Istanbul, follows suit.

By the terms of the 1878 Treaty of Berlin, Sultan Abdulhamid II promised Great Britain reforms and protection of Armenians from Kurds and Circassians. These promises were not kept, even though Britain had effectively guaranteed them. Patriotic Armenians felt themselves forced into secret groups and political parties. Gurdjieff's take on all this in *Meetings* is remarkably distant. He says "a violent political explosion was taking place, such as recurs from time to time in Armenia, with the usual train of consequences."[10] Perhaps he had some sympathy with the Russian point of view. Ottoman and Russian archives contain many documents about Armenian armed groups illegally crossing the Turkish-Russian border.[11]

From the early 1890s, Armenian revolutionary organizations had begun importing weapons from Russia to Turkey in pursuit of Armenian autonomy. In 1891, deaf to calls for reform, Sultan Abdulhamid assented to the use of irregular Kurdish tribal cavalry. These "Hamidiye" regiments were immune from prosecution. Resisting them was deemed rebellion against state and sultan. Robbing and terrorizing Armenians, Hamidiye troops were granted pastures on the Russian border to establish an Islamic barrier between Russia and the Armenians.

In 1894, the year Gurdjieff apparently got away from Tiflis for a bit of peace and quiet to study and explore Ani, Armenians were massacred in Sasun. More massacres occurred the following year in Trabizond, Erzurum, Marash, Sebastia (Sivas), Van, Bagesh (Bitlis), Harput, Diyarbekir, and elsewhere. The massacres of 1894–1896 led to mass migration of thousands of Armenians to different countries. Transcaucasia was obviously closest. Most of these refugees remained in the Kars Oblast and the "gubernia" of Erivan.

From 1890 to 1896, General Sergei A. Sheremetev served as supreme administrator of the Caucasus. General Prince Gregory S. Golitsyn (1838–1907) succeeded him. Distinctly reactionary, Golitsyn was known for his anti-Armenian policy. His administration wanted to cold-shoulder Armenians fleeing into Russian territory. Intolerant of Armenian patriotic activity within Russian-controlled Transcaucasus, Golitsyn closed some Armenian nongovernmental organizations and censored Armenian periodicals, while persecuting Armenian cultural leaders identified with independence and autonomy. A law was passed to confiscate Armenian Church property while Golitsyn tried to take the title *Catholicos of all Armenians* from the Catholicos of Echmiadzin.

Golitsyn exaggerated dangers posed by Armenian refugees from Turkey to his superiors and even tried to send them back across the border. The fact was that the imperial government did not want to populate the Kars Oblast with Armenians, for whom there was considered to be insufficient land anyway. The policy demanded preference to Russians and Anatolian Greek settlers. One can imagine this must have posed a few questions in young Gurdjieff's mind, if not conscience.

Between 1894 and 1902 Turkish and Russian diplomats argued the toss over Armenian refugees. Sultan Abdulhamid would not accept them back, calling them "troublemakers and rebels." It would be on Russia's conscience if they returned to Turkey and experienced unpleasant consequences. Among his ministers, Sultan Abdulhamid accepted that some of the blame lay with local governors not exercising authority over loose-cannon Kurds, and his administration in Constantinople accepted that indigenous Armenians were mostly peaceful but saw present and future danger with Armenian nationalists coming out of London. However, any broadening of perspective was not something the Sublime Porte would communicate to Russia while any chance remained that Russia would take Armenians out of Turkey permanently. It took until 1900 before the czar finally assented to the admission of Armenian refugees. Golitsyn was recalled to St. Petersburg four years later.

It seems almost churlish, even irrelevant, to cut from the all-too-grisly facts of history to the story Gurdjieff tells of his contemporary activities in the ancient Armenian capital of Ani, a ghost city unlike any other in the world, and just then, there might have been more ghosts than usual. There is no mention in *Meetings* of the gaping, aching political meaning of Ani—what the ruined city of Ani *represented* in the context of the times. What we get instead is a fairly ludicrous story of Gurdjieff and his (imaginary) pal Pogossian reading and studying there in a self-made hut while "for a rest" indulging in a bit of do-it-yourself archaeology. It might be remembered that Gurdjieff was mentally assembling this yarn during the afterglow of the amazing Tutankhamun discoveries of November 1922 that took place just as Gurdjieff and his entourage were settling in to their first winter at the Prieuré des Basses Loges in Avon, France. Everyone was fascinated by what might lurk undiscovered underground.

Curiously, Gurdjieff's own account of the Ani "dig" in the Pogossian chapter does not mention there a completely different account of the Ani excavations inserted into the much later chapter devoted to Piotr Karpenko.[12] Neither Karpenko nor any other members of what he calls in the later chapter "our recently formed group, the Seekers of Truth" who descend on Ani are mentioned in the key, determinative account of Ani that concerns Pogossian. The reason is pretty obvious; when Gurdjieff dreamed up the tale around Ani's hidden secrets he hadn't considered bringing either Karpenko into it or his apparently imaginary Seekers of Truth. That was an afterthought.

The brief Ani account in the Karpenko chapter begins with Karpenko on his way to Kars for his holidays, stopping off in Alexandropol to find Gurdjieff working there "in solitude."[13] Karpenko is shown Gurdjieff's large stable, which he has converted to a kind of laboratory, an "original kind" of course. Karpenko is captivated by Gurdjieff's experiments. These involved subjecting "various types of human beings as well as other forms of life" to the influence of sound vibrations. Somewhat prescient perhaps of Doctor Who and fashionable sonic experiments of the late 1960s (*chez* Pink Floyd, Jimi Hendrix, sometime doyen of Apple Records "Magic Alex," and Warhol associate Chuck Wein's "Rainbow Bridge Vibratory Color-Sound Experiment" in 1969 Maui), Karpenko's interest leads him to contact other members of "our group" and to join "some excavations among the ruins of Ani." We are then told Karpenko left but at the end of three years became a full member of "our original society," after which he participated in several "serious expeditions of ours in Asia and Africa."[14] Perhaps the "hippy trail" really starts here.

While this second account of Ani strikes one as pure fiction, the experimentation on human beings seems part of other activities Gurdjieff repeatedly claimed to have undertaken during the following decade and a half (circa 1895–1911), while the reference to becoming a full member after three years cannot fail to strike one as highly reminiscent of traditional Masonic practice with regard to staggered disposition of the three degrees of initiation. The basis of the Seekers of Truth, even if only imaginative, may be a Masonic Lodge, though probably of an irregular obedience, such as the Ancient & Primitive Rites of Memphis and Misraim, attractive at the time to French, Italian, German, Swiss, and British theosophists and esotericists. *Seekers of Truth* does strike one as a euphemism for Freemasonry whose three principles may be expressed as Brotherhood, Truth, Charity. It may have been in Gurdjieff's mind to find what he considered *the source* of Freemasonry. Such would explain his claims of interest in the mystery of the Sphinx and the dervishes. Bektashi dervishes had long observed similarities between themselves and the first European Freemasons in Constantinople (see my book *Freemasonry: The Reality*). In the late 1860s, British Freemason Charles Warren excavated the Temple Mount in Jerusalem; Masons had a vested interest in the archaeology of ancient civilizations since Masonry and antiquarianism had been closely tied since at least the mid-seventeenth century when "Free-mason" Elias Ashmole (1617–1692) first invented the technique of using pottery for site dating.

It may also be noted that the Masonic "center of the circle" whereat the "Master Mason cannot err" can serve as a symbol of the unconscious, as well as the presence of God.

One might also consider that this precise period in Armenia saw the formation of a number of secret societies, though the part Freemasonry could have played in these has not yet been researched. "Grand Orient" Masonry stemming from France and Italy were the jurisdictions most sympathetic to political liberation through universalist philosophy in the late nineteenth century; both were quietly active in Transcaucasia and Transcaspia. It should be borne in mind that Freemasonry had been banned in Russia in 1822, with a fairly short-lived but significant liberalization of the ban occurring in 1906. Russian subjects seeking initiation had to travel abroad, and membership was kept strictly secret. British, Italian, and French Masonic rites flourished in Egypt during Gurdjieff's lifetime. If Gurdjieff was a Freemason, in his youth or at any other time, it is highly unlikely he would ever have disclosed the fact to non-Masons. That from a strictly Masonic point of view Gurdjieff was a minor in 1894–96 is no objection; lying about his age meant nothing to Gurdjieff, or many other people of the time. You were truly as old as you felt. Initiation was discreetly available in Constantinople and relatively easily accessible in Cairo, both places Gurdjieff claimed to have visited during his youthful adventures. If he had Masonic friends he would hardly have said so in a book like *Meetings*. While it may be deemed unwise to speculate over a relationship between Gurdjieff and continental Masonry, it is one of those speculations whose value lies in its being able to unravel at a stroke, rather than add to, some of the mysteries of Gurdjieff's development.

So we return to the image of Gurdjieff and Pogossian digging, apparently alone, at Ani. He says they were exploring underground passages when they found nothing less than a more or less intact monastic cell filled with broken pots. The underlying myth here—if we may call it such—appears curiously close to Masonic Cryptic Rites where revelatory texts are discovered in crypts. As Gurdjieff tells it, though the furniture in the cell had mostly rotted, parchments remained in a niche. Some turned to dust, others were retrieved to their hut. While at first sight appearing somewhat fantastic, excavations at Ani beginning in 1915 chime in with Gurdjieff's matter-of-fact style account. Gurdjieff could, of course, have drawn on the 1915 and subsequent Italian excavations of underground wonders secreted at Ani for his narrative,* but his story is not without a factual aspect.[15] The parchments were written, Gurdjieff teases us, in a forgotten form of Armenian, but with the advice of surprisingly handy experts in Alexandropol, they found they had stumbled on ancient monastic correspondence. One of the writers was a "father Arem." This sounds like folk etymology of the origin of the name *Armenia,* attributed to a patriarch called Aram, curiously close to d'Alveydre's ancient patriarch, Ram, alleged origin of Rama and Ab-ram (Brahmanic and Hebraic tradition). Anyhow, the letters, now perfectly legible (!) inform us that "Father Telvant" has discovered the truth of the "Sarmoung Brotherhood." How happily we are linked to the very Sarmoung referred to in the alleged Armenian book *Merkhavat,* which of course no one has found since!

From the letter, the two intrepid researchers find that the Brotherhood migrated from Siranoush (Syria?) to the valley of Izrumin, three days from Nivssi (Nineveh?). The pair then learn that Nivssi is now called Mosul. The site of ancient Nineveh is joined to modern Mosul, whose precious antiquities are (as I write) being violently demolished by IS fanatics. The two explorers date the migration to the persecution of Aïsors (Assyrians), driven by Byzantines out of Mesopotamia into Persia in the "sixth or seventh century."[16] Gurdjieff thinks the school must have been an Aïsor school, situated three days from Mosul

*See chapter 8, note 15 for a recent account of Ani's archaeology that uses Gurdjieff's story as a source.

between Urmia (in Persia) and Kurdistan. The Aïsor reference ties Pogossian in with Yelov, who is described as being descended from the ancient kings of the Aïsors through his mother's line.[17] We then learn some facts about "Assyrians" today. The majority, Gurdjieff tells us, are "Nestorian" Christians who don't accept Jesus's divinity, with the minority of them Maronites, Catholics, Gregorians, while some of them "though not great in number" are also "Yezidis, or devil-worshippers."[18] Gurdjieff laments Assyrians having been pawns of British and Russian policies, exposing them to massacres by "the Kurds and the Persians," only to be saved thanks to the U.S. consul.

According to the narrative, their decision to seek the Brotherhood is rudely interrupted by "a great nationalist movement among the Armenians," with everyone talking about freedom-fighting heroes like "young Adronik." Everywhere, Gurdjieff rightly tells us, among Turkish, Persian, and Russian Armenians, parties and committees were formed, with attempts at unity thwarted by "sordid quarrels" between different factions. One wonders how much he knew about such quarrels, and then we get a clue, as Gurdjieff relates a telling coincidence of interests.

He was, he says, on his way to bathe one morning in the river Arpa Chai at Karakuli in Alexandropol when a breathless Pogossian caught up with him to tell how the priest Z had learned "the Armenian Committee"—of which the cleric was presumably a member—planned to choose volunteers from "the party" to dispatch to Moush on a special mission. *Wasn't this a great opportunity to make an expenses-paid trip to find the Brotherhood?* Not being a member of the party, Gurdjieff was unconvinced. Pogossian insisted arrangements could be made with the party if Gurdjieff accepted the plan. Gurdjieff says he wished "at any cost" to get to the valley "once named Izrumin" and didn't care how he got there. He'd travel on the *devil's back* if he had to. This was perhaps a clue, or two.

The historical reality behind this tale is clear. The Armenian Revolutionary Federation (ARF or *Dashnaktsutiun*), founded in Tiflis in 1890, organized the arming of groups to defend Armenians from Ottoman persecution while also attempting to secure long-promised reforms and eventual autonomy. Poster propaganda and scattered acts of minor sabotage—cutting of telegraph lines and damage to government buildings—sparked harsh reaction. In 1892 Andranik Ozanian (1865–1927), referred to above by Gurdjieff as "the young Andronik," joined the ARF and with Aram (*note!*) Manukian and other brave Armenians, led the resistance.

August 1894 saw the fourth Turkish army march on Sasun, attended by massacres at Erzerum, Bitlis, Zeitun, Cilicia . . . and *Mush:* the Holy Apostles monastery site and destination of Pogossian's vaunted secret mission. Kurdish chieftains assisted the Turkish harrying of Armenians, of whom it is estimated between 80,000 and 300,000 had perished by the end of 1896. In 1899 Andranik became head of Armenian forces, commanding some thirty-eight villages in the Sasun-Mush region of western Armenia. Andronik would fight a great battle, widely reported, at the monastery of Mush in November 1901, and it may be memories of this later period also that informed Gurdjieff's story of his alleged secret mission to Mush.

Mush, in western Armenia (Turkey), would take the explorers just under 300 kilometers southwest of Alexandropol to the region just west of Lake Van. But did this journey ever begin? We have no way of knowing whether Gurdjieff himself undertook such a journey, or if he did, when, or for whom he undertook it. Did he participate at some level in covert Armenian resistance? Could he have spied on it, perhaps for the Russians? If he did contribute to Armenian resistance, he does not give himself any credit for it, saying he simply took the Russian, Turkish, and Armenian money, provided by the party for the resistance effort, happy to use it for his own purposes: behavior consistent with his approach to money from adolescence to his life's end. He was quite mercenary in pursuit of his aims. He was emphatic in his maturity, at least, that all persons caught up in "war-fever" on whatever side, were suffering a psychosis, and were consequently

manipulated. Gurdjieff's identity was superficially fluid. He was prepared to ride "on the devil's back." After World War I, Gurdjieff was
effectively a "stateless person."

Gurdjieff says he undertook certain obligations and attempted, as
far as possible, to carry them out. However, he maintains pointedly that
he never "lost sight of our real purpose," whose itinerary did not always
coincide with the places he was expected to visit. However, Gurdjieff
says he had no hesitation in leaving such commitments to others
unfulfilled—omissions that he makes plain did not cause "any great
remorse of conscience."[19]

South of Alexandropol, he crossed, so he says, the Russian-Turkish
border at the River Arax, with the help of Kurds who had been sent to
help them: an odd detail, since Kurds are otherwise presented as enemies of Armenians in this context. Could they have been Yezidi Kurds?
It is pointless to speculate; they may never have existed.

Gurdjieff says he and Pogossian were forced eastward, over to Mount
"Egri Durgh"; that is to say, Mount Ararat, which is 250 kilometers
northeast of Moush, or Mush—quite a detour, and one attributed to
avoiding the peril of encountering Kurdish and Turkish detachments
determined on pursuing Armenians. They then head southwest toward
Van, being almost due north of Mosul in northern Mesopotamia. The
stakes were high. It was rumored that Aïsors had flayed Englishmen alive
for transcribing inscriptions—archaeology had its perils too! Gurdjieff
says he and Pogossian disguised themselves as Caucasian Tartars.

At this point, the account begins to slither into a strange, serpen-
tine movement as both original foci are lost in a sequence of storytelling
meanderings. Not only obligations to Armenian resistance disappear,
but so does the Sarmoung Brotherhood, or hidden school of Aïsors in
a valley. Perhaps the reader's attention is being deliberately mesmerized.
Real sense of time and space evaporates. Gurdjieff says that two months
after having crossed the River Arax, they come to "Z," a certain pass
toward Syria (which is west). In the pass, before the waterfall "K" they

were to turn off toward Kurdistan—on that road they expected to find what they had come to see.

Fate intervenes, somewhat predictably, and they endeavor to deliver a resistance letter to an Armenian priest in the town "N": something they'd hoped to avoid as it was out of the way of their intended destination (work that out!). The sudden use of secretive capitals rather echoes similar usage in the Rosicrucian manifestoes, with the intended sense of mystery. Pogossian suffers a bite from a yellow phalanga, a tarantula-like spider. Such could prove fatal, and getting him to treatment helps to divert all attention away from the point of the journey. They find the priest, who takes his friend in, and with him, the reader, for we really do now find ourselves in a fantasy, as if proximity to the Brotherhood has rendered all historical reality of no account and everything becomes enveloped by a mist emanating from the "school," a kind of spiritual mirage, like tents appearing out of a haze in the barren desert as the story's compass is deranged.

Pogossian's temperature starts to drop "on the third day," a phrase from the Bible that appears many times in Gurdjieff's tales. *On the third day he rose again from the dead.* Like a good Mason, Gurdjieff believes in the rule of three, symbol of construction, ascent, and resolution of opposites.

Living with the priest for a month, Gurdjieff is shown a map left with the priest by a Russian prince who has come to him with the support of a Turkish bey. For some reason the map fulfills "precisely what I had spent long months of sleepless nights thinking about! It was a map of what is called [by whom?] 'pre-sand Egypt.'"[20] This idea of an even more ancient Egypt flourishing in verdant glory before obscurity amid the sands of time is picked up later in *Meetings* and seems to have been an interesting idea that preoccupied Gurdjieff: that beneath the deserts lay evidence of another world, a lost protocivilization, with secreted resources. He somehow heeded the old prophetic call to make a path in the desert where prophets traditionally venture to find God, or be found by God.

Anyhow, Gurdjieff says curiosity got the better of him, and he outraged the laws of hospitality and broke into the priest's family heirloom chest so he could make a copy of the map. He knew the act culpable, but a "man's gotta do." After that, the Sarmoung thread is lost; it takes four months to get to Smyrna—a very long time—but why go west through Turkey to the Aegean anyway? The idea of the map wafts them strangely by British warship to Alexandria after they acquaint themselves with English sailors, and then somehow Pogossian's destiny is fulfilled when he goes to England to study marine engineering (perhaps a secret wish of Gurdjieff?), proving the validity of Pogossian's intentional suffering—that significant Gurdjieffian principle. We are then treated to a small sermon on the virtue of conscious work, with Pogossian as epitome of its virtues and rewards. There is a subtext perhaps that *the Brotherhood is always working,* often through the unexpected twists and turns, and that to *find* the Brotherhood, it only requires one to *seek* it. And that means *work.* Even Pogossian's vacant moments are spent marking time with his feet and making manipulations with his fingers: all suggestive of the famous Gurdjieffian "movements" and performance tricks to come. Pogossian says his love of work is not *in his nature,* but he loves it with his common sense. He then adds more Gurdjieffian emphases. The *I* he is talking about that loves work is not that *I* that is only a part of him (egoistic, partial, superficial, and conscious self). It is not simply a question of heeding reason; no, the *whole of his nature* loves it and is accustomed to it. He is self-harmonized. No conscious work is ever wasted; sooner or later, someone pays for it. *Conscious,* willing work is the thing; a Karabakh ass, after all, works all day and night but derives no essential benefit from the effort.

And what about the Sarmoung school?

Well, had we not been sidestepped by the phalanga spider, we might have realized that the directions originally set out *can* in fact give us a real place, both real and *more than real.* The ancient school in possession of the keys is said to be three days' walk north of Mosul, between Urmia in Persia and Kurdistan.

Some 50 kilometers north-northeast of Mosul is the region known as the Sheykhan, whose most holy place is the valley of Lalish. Lalish is the sacred center of the Yezidis, and the qewwals sing that Lalish is no ordinary place; Lalish came down, whole, from heaven. At its center, close to the tomb of the Sufi master Sheykh 'Adi, is the "market of mystical knowledge."

While subsequent tales in *Meetings* bring us to other holy men and secret monasteries of allegedly profound knowledge, it seems clear to this author that while Gurdjieff was not actually identifying his ideal brotherhood with the Yezidi tradition, he is clearly more than implying that the Yezidis are at the very least a pointer or conduit to the great Tradition that should be sought in the process of reharmonizing the warped human being.

It behooves us then to look at the beliefs of one of the most persecuted peoples, and one of the most inspiring spiritual traditions, on Earth. I do not think we can understand Gurdjieff properly unless we do.

NINE

The Yezidis

Unto the persevering mortals the ever-present
guardian angels are swift to assist.

ZARATHUSHTRA

It is not entirely curious that Gurdjieff relates the Yezidis to the
Assyrians. So it probably appeared to an inquisitive Armenian-speaking
Greek in the 1890s. The Assyrians today are an Aramaic-speaking
people indigenous to northern Iraq. The Kurdish autonomous region
government calls Assyrians "Kurdish Christians"; they are frequently
ill-treated. Many live in close proximity to the Yezidis, who are also
persecuted. The designation *Assyrian* also refers to any member of
the Assyrian Church of the East, the oldest Christian church in
Mesopotamia, founded by Thomas the Apostle; members survive in
present day Persia, and are not to be confused with the Chaldaean—
Roman Catholic–affiliated—Church.

Also mostly Kurds, Yezidis probably have Persian, Assyrian,
Armenian, and Arab forebears as well. At less than a quarter of a million, numbers have declined over a thousand years of persecutions. They
survive in the Sheykhan, north and east of Mosul, in the Jebel Sinjar,
west of Mosul, in southeastern Turkey, and in Georgian Armenia.
Due to perilous conditions in Iraq, Syria, and Turkey—mass murders

and other appalling, genocidal crimes committed in God's name by jihadists—some Yezidis have today sought asylum in Germany and elsewhere.

By the time Gurdjieff came to write *Meetings* in the 1920s, the Yezidis had become a hot subject for students of the East. While Gurdjieff himself simply says, "They are sometimes called devil-worshippers" (*Meetings*, 66), attaching no negative connotations to the phrase himself, nor subscribing to its implication of wickedness, many others have taken the all-too-commonplace assumption of ignorant outsiders to Yezidism at face value and, enflamed by propaganda and atrociously misplaced zeal, have very recently gone to the far extremes of depraved genocidal murder, enslavement, and torture.

Gurdjieff's use of the phrase "devil-worshipper" may derive in part from awareness of graduate Isya Joseph's* 1919 publication *Devil Worship: The Sacred Books and Traditions of the Yezidis*.[1]

Joseph (Isya Muksy Yusef) refuted the speculation that the "sect" of the Yezidis derived from ancient Mesopotamian civilization, something, one suspects strongly, Gurdjieff did himself believe, as he believed the Assyrians were also derived from the first civilization of the East, the Sumerians, ancient authors, he believed, of the Gilgamesh epic. For Protestant Christian Isya Joseph, on the other hand, the Yezidis were predominantly a schismatic Islamic sect whose worshipful angel was a devil. We may suspect Gurdjieff rather regarded Yezidi tradition as one linked to that of the exalted company of the archangels of planetary destiny, a conception that makes perfect sense within the Yezidi angelic system.

---

*Isya Muksy Joseph (Yusef) was born in 1872, in a village 15 miles south of Diyarbakir near the Hakkari Mountains (now southeast Turkey) from a learned family that included several bishops of the Assyrian church. A graduate of a U.S. mission school, he was based in Mosul in 1892, where he witnessed the persecution of Yezidis. The late 1890s saw persecution of Syrian Orthodox Church members (Jacobites) and Protestants. Joseph's father-in-law was killed in the persecutions; Protestants and Jacobites emigrated. Joseph came to New York in August 1898. In 1907 Joseph received his master's degree in philosophy at the Union Theological Seminary, New York.

THE GOD OF THE YEZIDIS

The word generally employed by Yezidis for God is the Kurmanji word *Khudê,* which, according to Ethel Stefana, Lady Drower (1879–1972), was ever on the lips of the pious Yezidi people she encountered in northern Iraq in 1940.[2]

Other words for the divinity are related to the name Yezidi itself, a name that first appears in writing in the eleventh century CE. Theories compete as to its origin. One frequently denied by Yezidis is that the name derived from a peculiar and, for their opponents, disreputable respect for the Umayyad Caliph Yazid ibn Mu'awiya, despised by Shia Muslims for his part in the death of the Prophet's grandson, Hussein.

The word *Yezid* itself goes back further. Some consider it stems from *Ized* (angel, God) or *Yazata* (worthy of worship), words found in the Avesta, the sacred writings of the Zoroastrians. Other words bear similar meaning. Variants of the Persian *Izd,* or *Ized* include *Azidi, Izidi, Izdi,* or *Yazata,* or *Yazd* in Pahlavi, or *Yajata* in Sanskrit. All of these terms generally mean "worthy of worship." The reference is usually to an angel who intercedes between God and man, supervising the affairs of created men, but in practice the reference suggests simply the English word "Godly."

Persian roots may lie behind some Yezidi words for holy beings used to this day. *Yazdan* may be behind the Yezidi *Êzdan,* another term for God.[3] *Sultan Êzî* or *Êzîd* are alternative names for the Yezidi's world governor, Tawûsî Melek (in the Kurmanji or Kurdish language), the archangel of the supreme heptad of seven angels created by God. The former names are also identified with Sheykh 'Adi, the twelfth-century Sufi founder of what would become the vital Yezidi community at Lalish, north of Mosul.

It is a fascinating aspect of Yezidi religion that names and beings are interchangeable in a way that we, with our written traditions, could hardly tolerate. Figures of Yezidi history may also be divine angels— Jesus is regarded as an angel. It is taken that persons distinguished in divine service were not solely the offspring of human agency; Yezidis are joined to the holy beings above and within them—though they may have descendants. This remarkable awareness makes Yezidi spirituality something almost "natural" as opposed to being thought about, or cut to reason's measure.

Names may change, but values remain. God is the ultimate force of nature; his names are, in a sense, the laws of nature. Thus like God, nature's laws are eternal, omnipotent, omnipresent, and so on, their "will" immutable and absolute. To grasp them is wisdom, which comes from God. A Yezidi would have no problem in seeing a Sheykh as manifesting a divine power, once he or she was convinced such power was indeed manifested in that person.

In Yezidi religious discourse, God operates in phases of being perceptible in people and nature, in places and in stories, in everyday life and the life hereafter. These phases are given names but are neither asserted dogmatically nor held as definitive. Oral tradition reigns. Yezidis have been reported possessing a curious acuity of spiritual perception; they may be described as panentheists: God is in all nature, but God is not encompassed by nature.

Lady Drower visited the Yezidis' holiest sites at Lalish in 1940 and wrote movingly of the experience:

> I am glad, too, that I rose early and saw the shrine at its holiest moment of first dawn. For it was then that I became convinced that some Yezidis, inarticulate and vague as they are about their own dogmas and beliefs, possess to a rare degree a faculty as sensitive as the antennae of an insect, which makes them conscious of things outside the material. They have the instinct to be still and worship, which is the very essence of religion. And of all holy places I have ever visited, during 60 years of life in West and East, the valley of Shaikh 'Adi, the Mecca of the most sorely persecuted and misrepresented people in the world, seems to me the loveliest and holiest. Here one may find the spirit of the Holy Grail, or perhaps rather of

the glad piety of the Saint of Assisi. Something lingers here unpolluted, eternal, and beautiful: something as quiet as the soul and as clear eyed as the spirit.[4]

This perceptiveness suggests that in no way does the tradition's fluidity bring confusion; rather, the deliberate keeping of the tradition to a nonwritten form, and learned by mind to mind and heart to heart, is a positive benefit to maintaining the living spirit of the faith.

The implication seems to be that while the laws of the world we know derive from the spiritual world, that world is not subject to them. What *our* world is subject to, according to the Yezidis, is the governance of the archangel known as the Peacock Angel, or Melek (Lord or King) Tawus.

MELEK TAWUS

According to Yezidi tradition, God consigned his creative work to seven angels, the seven created in the "Pearl," God's first creative expression. Their names vary according to the source of information. A version of the *Meshef Resh* ("Black Book") obtained by Carmelite monk Father Anastasius from a Yezidi ("a tall devil with big black eyes and long hair") in May 1904, gives the following names for the angels.[5] It should be noted that most members of the heptad (the Seven) are also considered as manifest in beings with a terrestrial role in Yezidi historical traditions.

> 'Ezra'îl = Melek Tawus (the Peacock Angel)
> Derda'îl = Sheykh Hesen
> Irafîl = Sheykh Shems (the divine power of the sun)
> Mîka'îl = Sheykh Obekr
> Jibra'îl = Sejjad el-Dîn (Sejadîn); *Jibra'îl* is "Gabriel."
> Shemna'îl = Nasir el-Dîn
> Tûra'îl = Fekhr el-Dîn

This list is not consistent in Yezidi traditions but is a fair representation. Note the significance of the number seven. In *Tales* Gurdjieff refers time and again to what he extravagantly calls the "heptaparaparshinokh" or sevenfold creative principle.

The focus of Yezidi identity is their special guardian, Melek Tawus, represented through the form of a peacock. His name is also given as 'Ezazîl where 'Ezra'îl is Secad el-Dîn (the Browne-Guest version).[6]

There may be a link between the Yezidi tradition concerning the angel 'Ezazîl and the angel appearing in late antiquity as Azazel. Azazel is singled out for censure in the famous Book of Enoch (9:6) as one that revealed to men "the eternal secrets which were in heaven which men were striving to learn" and who is condemned for it. In circa 180 CE, Irenaeus ranted against the Gnostic Marcus, magician and follower of "fallen and mighty angel,"[7] Azazel. The Yezidi perspective on the angel 'Ezazîl bears some functional resemblance to the Gnostic being, but comparison should definitely not be pushed, for in this matter, interpretation is all. In the Yezidi tradition, Melek Tawus is the unrepentant, stern benefactor of mankind, set by God to govern the destiny of the human race. He does not delight in evil or attempt to trip up human beings into immoralities.

In the *Meshef Resh,* Gabriel leads Adam into Paradise, where he is told he may eat of all the fruit of paradise but not of wheat. Adam remains in Paradise for one hundred years, whereafter he is visited by Melek Tawus, who asks Adam how he can expect to have progeny if he doesn't eat wheat. Melek Tawus teaches Adam the ways of agriculture.

As written, Adam gets bloated on the grain. Melek Tawus leads him out of Paradise, whereupon he is left to his own devices—and a bloated stomach. God sends a bird that pecks at Adam, creating his anus and simultaneous relief.[8] Man will have to learn by experience. And he must pass wind.

Very Gurdjieffian.

The *Meshef Resh*'s provenance is still unresolved. It is not a dogmatically authoritative source for Yezidi beliefs. Melek Tawus has arguments with the absolute God, but he is not cast out; he is *not* a fallen angel. In fact, God recognizes his exemplary loyalty and lets him manage human affairs. Melek Tawus offers human beings knowledge and freedom. There is even a folk story among Yezidis that the tears of the angel put out the fires of hell, a charming, fascinating myth.

Knowledge and freedom: this is the majestic message of Melek Tawus' self-revelation recorded in the *Jelwe,* the "Divine Revelation" or "Effulgence," attributed to the Tawus-inspired mind of Sheykh 'Adi.

Such a being or conception of a being is not congenial to the monotheisms of orthodox Christianity, Judaism, and Islam. Not content with dubbing the mighty angel Melek Tawus a devil, persons hostile to the Yezidis have regarded him as the, or *a,* "sheitan."* This mistaken conception has been and *is* being used to justify genocide. It is a travesty of the truth. In 1940 a Yezidi qewwal complained to Lady Drower, "They say of us wrongly, that we worship one who is evil." Lady Drower's thoughts on concluding her conversation with the qewwal bear repeating here:

> It seemed probable to me, after this talk, that the Peacock Angel is, in a manner, a symbol of Man himself, a divine principle of light experiencing an avatar of darkness, which is matter and the material world. The evil comes from man himself, or rather from his errors, stumblings, and obstinate turnings down blind alleys upon the steep path of being. In repeated incarnations he sheds his earthliness, his evil, or else, if hopelessly linked with the material, he perishes like the dross and illusion that he is.[9]

Deeply grieved by hideous caricatures of their religion, the Yezidis forbid the saying of the word *sheitan* or even words that sound like it. The Englishman Austen Henry Layard visited the Sheikhan (Yezidi territory in northern Mesopotamia) in the 1840s and left a remarkable

---

*The term *sheitan* (equivalent to Satan) is usually applied in the East to a clever, cunning, or daring fellow.

description of their life, troubles, and beliefs. He described the horror of the Yezidi people when he accidentally emitted the forbidden word.

> One of these urchins . . . had forced himself to the very end of a weak bough, which was immediately above me, and threatened every moment to break under the weight. As I looked up I saw the impending danger, and made an effort, by an appeal to the chief, to avert it. "If that young Sheit—" I exclaimed, about to use an epithet generally given in the East to such adventurous youths:[10] I checked myself immediately; but it was already too late; half the dreaded word had escaped. The effect was instantaneous: a look of horror seized those who were near enough to overhear me; it was quickly communicated to those beyond . . . it was some time ere the group resumed their composure, and indulged in their previous merriment.[11]

What of the Yezidis' own conception of Melek Tawus? We now have examples of the Yezidi *qewwals,* sacred songs translated by the leading scholar of Yezidism, Philip Kreyenbroek. They offer a picture of Melek Tawus as the ancient one, the eternal one. He was not born and does not give birth; he is the king of the world, lord of men and jinns—this is important; he is not a jinn himself. Making Adam eat forbidden food, he helped him to live in the world. He has come to Earth to help the Yezidis. He is Angel of the Throne; Master of firmament, moon, and sun; Judge; remedy; healer; the living one; the glorious one. Here are extracts from the twenty-one-verse "Hymn of Melek Tawus":

> Oh my Lord, by your eminence, by your rank and by
>   your sovereignty,
> Oh my Lord, you are generous, you are merciful,
> Oh my Lord, you are forever God,
> You are forever worthy of praise and homage. (v.1)

Oh my Lord, you are the angel who is king of the
    world,
Oh my Lord, you are the angel who is generous king,
You are the angel of the awesome Throne.
Oh my Lord, from pre-eternity you have always been
    the ancient one (v.2)

You are the eternal one, you dwelt in the source of
    light,
You are the eternal one, you are the living one, the
    glorious.
You are one, praise is due to you. (v.5)

Oh my Lord, you are the judge of the entire world,
Oh my Lord, you imposed repentance on man,
Oh my Lord, you are the judge of intercession. (v.15)

You are wise, we are aliens,
Oh my Lord, you always know where our remedy is,
Oh my Lord you are an intimate friend to strangers.
    (v.18)

Oh my Lord, you are the creator, we are creatures,
You are the desired, we are the desire. (v.21)[12]

As far as we know, Gurdjieff himself never uttered the sacred name
Melek Tawus, though by the mid-1920s—when Gurdjieff was compos-
ing his two main series—he had numerous opportunities to acquaint
himself with the name. At least half a dozen manuscripts of the Yezidi
sacred books were available for study by 1900.[13] Père Anastase made
copies of these works in the Jebel Sinjar in 1904, creating a stir in the
world of oriental scholarship. It was suspected Yezidi beliefs might ante-
date the Mosaic revelation. Gurdjieff may have felt he knew sufficiently

already. Had he sometime in the previous decade visited the Yezidis' most sacred precincts; namely, the shrines of Lalish? He may have seen the famous door from the stone courtyard (called "the market of mystical knowledge") to the Shrine of Sheykh 'Adi. There, carvings depict a comb (to unravel or plat Fate?), the staff of the religious leader, intertwined triangles (the seal of Solomon?), the stars, the sun, and a lion. Most prominent of all is a striking black serpent, the height of a man, renewed in its coloring by a local dye administered by the shrine's guardians.

Perhaps Gurdjieff loved Lalish too much to spoil it with literary attention. For the sensitive, Lalish exhibits that union of matter and spirit that Gurdjieff aimed for. Hear Lady Drower's response to a privileged performance of qewwals, on the third day of the great Spring Festival at Lalish, the sixth day of Nisan (April 19) 1940:

> But what pagan spirit had usurped the shrine of the Saint? The night's vigil with its turbanned worshippers, its chants, and its prayers might indeed have passed as the devotions of a Sufi sect, mystical and eclectic indeed, but still Moslem in outward appearance. Today the mask was away and I seemed to see a laughing face peering from behind it. It was a glad god, an ancient god, a young god, that would dance in before long, naked and unashamed.[14]

YEZIDI BELIEFS

Lady Drower described Yezidi religion as a "mystical pantheism." Yezidis call it "the Tradition." In their own understanding, they are sunnites. The Tradition is vouchsafed by Melek Tawus, who governs the world with the blessing of Khudê, the absolute deity. "His ocean is deep"[15] — such is God's perfection and limitlessness. Yezidis must have great faith to endure so much for God.

Until recently, Yezidis learned their religion exclusively from oral tradition; literacy among the *Mirids* (laity) was frowned upon. That has changed. A number of their religious songs have been published along with the *Jilwe,* a short epiphany of Melek Tawus attributed to Sheykh 'Adi b. Musafir (1073–1161).

A descendent of the Umayyad line, the Sufi Sheykh 'Adi, fellow student with some of the greatest names in Sufism, arrived in the Hakkari Mountains after having left his birthplace in the Bekaa Valley in Syria to study theology in Baghdad. His arrival at Lalish transformed the practice of the religion that existed before his arrival. Sufism changed the older religion, but it is clear the older religion changed the Sufism also.

One is born a Yezidi—as with being born a Jew; religion, racial, and family identity are one. They believe they are in Melek Tawus's special care. The Peacock Angel may communicate his will through the *Kocheks,* traditionally the seers and visionaries of the faith. Above the Kocheks are the Sheykhs, who come from distinct clans. It has been observed that the Sheykhs appear to be physically different from the laity. The *Baba Sheykh* is the ruler of the Kocheks.

Religious guidance is sought from the order of *Feqirs,* the Sheykhs, and the Pirs. Every Yezidi should have a Pir as guide. The head of the Sheykhs is the Baba (Father) Sheykh who is always of the Fekhr el-Dîn branch of the Shemsani Sheykhs.[16]

There are three branches of Sheykhs: the Shemsanis, Qatanis, and the Adanis. The princely house—the Chol family—is thought connected to the Qatani branch of Sheykhs. The *Mir,* currently Tehsin Beg, is the ruling prince of the Yezidis, and the royal residence is traditionally Ba'drê castle in the Sheykhan. The Mir's person is held to be a manifestation of the divine; he is entitled to money and services.

Far from the Sheykhan, the religion came traditionally to Yezidis through the travels of the qewwals. The qewwals embody the mystical essence of the faith in their religious songs and playing of *def* and *shebab* (tambour and flute). They also carry the small number of *senjaqs* to the disparate clans of Yezidi people. According to Philip Kreyenbroek, who visited Lalish in 1992, this system is suffering greatly today.

Senjaqs are bronze images of the Peacock Angel that have survived many attacks on the faith; the qewwals receive money for showing the senjaqs. Money is also paid to the guardians of the many shrines at Lalish. They collect dust from the shrines, roll it up with water from the sacred *Kanîya Sipî* spring at Lalish and give it to the believers as trusted remedies for many ailments. These little balls are called *berat*.

Yezidi religion consists in honoring God, being truthful, being clean, respecting their prince, giving to the poor, and maintaining the Tradition. This includes regular visits to Lalish for festivals. Yezidis follow strict rules of marriage; the Sheykhly branches are endogamous. Many Yezidis experience baptism at special cisterns at Lalish, though this is not vital. They abstain from some foods, such as lettuce. Yezidis are taught to respect the religion of others, while never forsaking their own. Much knowledge and inspiration consists in participating in the qewls.

Yezidis believe in paradise, but not necessarily in hell.* They do not believe in a dualistic conflict between God and a dark power. Evil comes from men's hearts, and men are responsible for what they think and do. A bad life will lead to compensatory reincarnation. A Yezidi was recently asked what he thought would happen to Saddam Hussein. The Yezidi suggested he would return as a donkey; he would have to bear the load of others.[17]

Care for graves and the shrines (*mezar*) is a vital duty. Wednesday is a Yezidi holy day, and the eve before it also.

> Yezidis observe a special respect for the sun as a living symbol of God. A Yezidi is to kiss the ground where the sun first strikes. Prayers may also be said at midday and sunset. A reflection of this duty is perhaps visible in chapter 7 of Beelzebub's Tales to His

---

*Though *hell* may be used as a comparative. For example, when entering the valley of Lalish, the paradise of this "Site of Truth" (as it is called) is contrasted with the hell of the ordinary world outside it. Punishments and consequences occur in the world about us.

Grandson, concerned with essential duties. Beelzebub's grandson is instructed not to forget one thing: Every day, at sunrise, while watching the reflection of its splendor, you bring about a contact between your consciousness and the various unconscious parts of your general presence. Try to make this state last and to convince the unconscious parts—as if they were conscious—that if they hinder your general functioning, they, in the period of your responsible age, not only cannot fulfill the good that befits them, but your general presence of which they are part, will not be able to be a good servant of our COMMON ENDLESS CREATOR and by that will not even be worthy to pay for your arising and existence.[18]

The old life of the Yezidis holds many fascinations for people interested in the Near East's ancient customs. A bull is sacrificed at the Shrine of Sheykh Shems in Lalish. Sheykh Shems is both historical figure and the divinity of the sun. The name *Shems* reminds us of the Mesopotamian god Shamash (the Sun) known throughout the East.

Sufic mysticism or gnosis is important to the Sheykhs, but it has been suffused with a profound vision of the divinity hidden in or expressed by nature. Water is very important; caves and mountains, trees, and valleys have religious significance. Yezidis believe in nature spirits, subject to Melek Tawus; Lalish is the site of Truth that descended from heaven.

God's will is expressed in the creation; to be close to it is to participate in the proper governance of Melek Tawus. All inspiration comes from God. Only God knows everything; his knowledge utterly transcends man's reason. What we know is thanks to him.

Yezidi people are permitted to drink alcohol; this may partly explain why they have a long-standing association with the Caliph Yezîd, criticized in Shia tradition for his tolerance of life's pleasures, as well as his part in the death of Hussein.

Yezidis are taught that Jews, Christians, and Muslims are latecomers to religion. Where their beliefs agree with their own, well and good. Where not, Yezidis must reject contrary beliefs.

They date their origins to Adam, the first man. According to variant texts of *Meshef Resh,* Adam and Eve had an argument about which of them was capable of bringing forth progeny. Each put the product of their fertility in a jar. After a season, Eve's jar was opened, revealing a putrid mass; Adam's jar opened to reveal a boy and a girl. "Now from these two our people, the Yezidis, are descended. . . . After this Adam knew Eve, and she bore two children, male and female; and from these the Jews, the Christians, the Moslems, and other nations and sects are descended. But our first fathers are Seth, Noah, and Enosh, the righteous ones, who were descended from Adam only." [19]

This genealogy is very similar to the "Priestly" genealogy of Seth given in Genesis 5:1–30 as Adam, Seth, Enosh, Kenan, Mahalel, Jared, Enoch, Methuselah, Lamech, Noah. It may be contrasted with the genealogy of Cain given by the "Yahwist" in Genesis 4:17–18 as Adam, Cain, Enoch, Irad, Mehujael, Methushael, Lamech. [20]

The role of Seth in offering a new future to the human race after the denigration of Cain has inspired many myths. Josephus wrote in the first century CE of how Seth was "a virtuous man" who left children of "excellent character" who "were the inventors of that peculiar sort of wisdom concerned with the heavenly bodies, and their order." Interestingly, the invention of astrology has traditionally been seen as the work of the Chaldaeans of Urartu—the land about Ararat in southern Armenia.

ORIGINS

Anthropologist Sami Said Ahmed told an interesting story of how a Yezidi friend gave him two papers on Yezidi beliefs. [21] In them, legendary tales were taken as fact; each paper contradicted the other. Ahmed eventually found the papers contained real facts and genuine articles of Yezidi belief, disguised. When told of this, the Yezidi replied, "The book which I presented to you contains only one (fact) of the thousands (of facts) of Yezidism." The friend declared, "Yezidism is the mother of all Eastern religions."

It is understood that Yezidism in its contemporary form is the product of years of struggle with neighboring faiths, leading to cross-faith but transvalued language use. Jesus, for example, may be regarded as a manifestation of Sheykh Shems. Furthermore, the impact of Sheykh ʿAdi's sojourn in Lalish generated a revolution in the hierarchy of the faith—though it would seem from the evidence that Sheykh ʿAdi and members of his family were themselves immensely affected by what they discovered among the Yezidis. After his death, hostile observers believed Sheykh ʿAdi's disciples had gone much further than Sheykh ʿAdi himself—in particular, indulging in an excessive veneration for the Sheykh.

Sheykh ʿAdi's Sufi *tariqa* (the "path" of the *ʿAdawiyya*) was regarded as Islamic, though suspect by a number of medieval Islamic commentators.[22] It spread to Syria and Egypt.[23] Its Lalish manifestation developed quite differently from elsewhere.

Manuscripts discovered in the Sinjar attributed to Sheykh ʿAdi show their author regarded himself as having achieved in himself divinity: "How dare ye deny me when I am truly your God and I wipe out and I write down [destiny]. . . . How dare you deny me . . . when I, the Ancient of Time, created the world? And ye ask me about my lower abode. I tell you of the dominion which was established on the rock."

Furthermore, "I am a unique Sheykh; and it is I, myself, who created things. It is I who received a book, a book of good tidings. It came from my God piercing the mountains. It is to me that all men come. They come in submission and kiss my feet."[24] Little wonder that Yezidis take the Sheykh as a manifestation of God.

Links between Yezidism and ancient Sumerian religion have not been, and are unlikely to be, established. Those being oral traditions, there is no possibility of proving whether a thing believed three hundred years ago was believed thirteen hundred years ago. Furthermore, it is impossible to place the Yezidi religion with certainty, before it was first referred to in the texts of opponents in the eleventh century.

Kreyenbroek believes we should look to Zoroastrian Iranian traditions as well as thirteenth-century Sufism for features of Yezidi traditions.*

Why did Gurdjieff repeat the phrase "devil-worshippers" regarding Yezidis? Gurdjieff himself gives no obvious guidance on the issue, except that throughout his works he maintained common knowledge is not identical to common sense. One needs a strongly developed sense of irony to understand initiated reference to the "devil." Jesus was accused of getting his power from the devil. There is always something "devilish" about the exercise of any power, for it can be used for good or ill, and what anyone thinks is good or ill may be temporal and subjective— save, as Gurdjieff maintains, an objective morality still stands rooted in faith and conscience, stabilized by time and tradition in such injunctions as: *do unto others as you would have them do unto you,* and *love thy neighbor as thyself.* In general, it might be said that a devil is any god of a person other than that worshipped by oneself. Thus, the more ignorant missionaries in British India identified gods of the Hindu pantheon as devils, insofar as worship of them did not lead acolytes to accept Jesus as unique savior.

It is no accident that in his first series of writings for the use of pupils, Gurdjieff took the role of Beelzebub, a devil, if not *the* devil, presented as a cool, detached archangel with a tail, zooming around the universe in the "Karnak," a spacecraft—which perhaps gives us an idea of how Gurdjieff saw ancient temples function. Beelzebub, like Melek Tawus, has seen humankind from its beginnings and occasionally offered beneficial suggestions to aid humanity's evolution, persistently

---

*Note especially, "All that can be confidently asserted, therefore, is that the religions of the Yezidis and the Yaresan have sprung from intensive contacts between Islam and a cult of Iranian origin which contained both Zoroastrian elements and traits that cannot be traced back to mainstream Zoroastrianism" (61). And "the cultural environment in which these faiths originated appears to have had a genius for adopting alien elements and integrating these into its traditional system. As a result, isolated elements of various origins abound in the Yezidi and Ahl-e Haqq traditions. These are hardly of major significance, however, for understanding the early development of these systems" (61 n. 130).[25]

thwarted by endemic resistance to truth, experience, and good sense. Gurdjieff doesn't mind a bit when a lawyer calls him "Black Devil!" His point seems plain enough. Enlightenment may look satanic to the earthbound. Dense matter of itself cannot comprehend spirit. "Lucifer" brings light from the stars, and using that light to its full advantage requires toughness, ingenuity, determination and hard work, not neurotic oversensitivity and fear of offense. Those who live in darkness fear the light and project onto its manifestation images generated from those fears. Such become self-terrifying, panic reactions. Rejecting knowledge, truth is feared. The unenlightened reject awareness of their true selves, for the unenlightened ego cannot bear exposure to its isolation. It crucifies the light-bringer, ridicules him or her, trying to bring the "devil" down, while destroying himself in the process. Those shouting about "Satan," those who hatefully point the finger are always themselves devilish, cunning, murderous, and cruel in the ordinary destructive sense, insulated in their unconsciousness of their unconsciousness. The one who visits Earth to teach is the "devil," worshipped blindly or hated, or both. The Lucifer of legend is a fallen angel because he came to Earth, a "morning star" or herald of dawn: the light-bringer. The enemies of light try to destroy those touched by the light. "There is light within a man of light, and he lights up the whole world" (Gospel of Thomas, Nag Hammadi library).

Gurdjieff was looking for a way to guarantee that men and women would not fall under the spell of darkness, the hypnotism of the fearful, that they might be able to think truly for themselves and discover and remember the light buried in the ocean of human sleep.

TEN

Do-It-Yourself Gurdjieff and Unaccountable Journeys

I saw plainly that what is most peculiar to them [the Sufis] cannot be learned from books, but can only be reached by immediate ecstasy and inward transformation.

ABU HAMID AL-GHAZALI (1058–1111)[1]

It is impossible to establish anything like the precise truth of Gurdjieff's many and conflicting accounts of journeys outside Russian Armenia, whether to Georgia in the north, Turkey and Constantinople in the west, Egypt to the far south, or to Crete, Palestine, Syria, or Central Asia between the Caspian and the borders of Afghanistan and China. Not only do details, times, places, and names of companions conflict and elide into one another, but actual purposes and activities engaged in also conflict with one another. The three main selective autobiographical accounts left to us, those in *Life Is Real Only Then, When "I Am,"* "The Material Question," and *The Herald of Coming Good,* also conflict and sometimes confusingly overlap with the mixture of fiction, fantasy, and history to be found in *Tales* and *Meetings*. To English ears and eyes particularly, Gurdjieff, always in translation, comes over with the burden of an exasperating mode of self-expression. Outside of *Meetings,* which can mostly be read with degrees of pleasure, Gurdjieff's habitual discourse is filled with pseudo-objectivity, where the plainest statements are dressed in quasi-scientific terms, reaching, in *Tales* particularly, fantastic levels of repetition, invented words, and arch pretentiousness. Simple objects and subjects are very frequently conceptualized, expressed as though addressing an academic pedant from another planet. The idea in part seems to be to alienate habitual conceptions while obviously rendering human beings ridiculous. Observing humans as "guinea-pigs," Gurdjieff intends to show how human behavior appears to a true outsider, which Gurdjieff believes he (or "Beelzebub") is. Humanity is reduced to, and by, science. The sad thing, I suspect, is that Gurdjieff's genuine personal vision was poetic, creative, and imaginative, but he was bent on addressing the Westerner with an inflated, self-consciously acted and ironic, quasi-academic style whereby the innate humor of his point of view is skewed repeatedly into sourness. In combating what he calls "wiseacreing" he often sounds like the most irritating wiseacre of all. This, surely, is the main reason his writings have enjoyed limited currency. Gurdjieff himself, as we have seen, had nothing against annoying people who took an interest in his ideas; as far as he was concerned, overcoming resistance was part of the process of overcoming habitual responses. Nevertheless, his approach may evince a lurking chip on the shoulder syndrome, ameliorated in a private joke (*is not most academic-speak pseudo-objective babble?*): a shame perhaps, because if one applies exemplary patience, the content is often wise, urgent, and insightful.

We shall approach that content in due course. For the time being, the biographer is faced with the question, *how can we describe Gurdjieff's life from the mid-1890s to the first years of the twentieth century?*

In an attempt to encourage "dollar-fat" Americans to shed some of their overload upon his schemes, Gurdjieff presented his travels in

"The Material Question" (April 8, 1924) primarily as the adventures of a hard-grafting entrepreneur. He says he engaged in "the most varied enterprises, sometimes very big ones," such as carrying out private and government contracts relating to supplying and constructing railways. He had some experience here. In blazes of energy, he claimed he established stores, restaurants, and even cinemas, only to be sold upon becoming profitable. He kept to his father's teaching and his grandmother's last words: always try something new, and always be different. He claimed to have led rural enterprises, such as driving cattle into Russia—perhaps his father's experience was of use here—chiefly from Kashgar in far western China. Such prosaic activities do not feature in the account in *Meetings* of his journey to Kashgar. Oil wells, fisheries, and combinations of all these activities pursued simultaneously, and above all, a passion for buying and selling antiques and carpets, he claimed dominated his commercial life until arrival in Moscow, where he put much of his profits into his institute, in many respects more conceptual than real in this period.[2] Such is his apologia as delivered for American capitalist consumption in 1924.

Before these substantial-sounding business ventures, Gurdjieff used his wits to place himself in the repair-of-foreign-goods market—typewriters for the frontier army, for example. One of his most charming statements on his *I'll-do-anything-practical-for-money* period comes when he tells us how he put one over on corset sellers by redesigning existing corsets: "I need only say that I bought up and sold in the towns of Krasnovodsk, Kizil-Arvat, Ashkhabad, Merv, Chardzhou, Bukhara, Samarkand, and Tashkent more than six thousand corsets."[3] Just imagine this number of women holding their own in Central Asia in a "corset by Gurdjieff"! It might seem odd to the romantic imagination that associates most of these Central Asian place names with oriental mystery and mysticism—Merv, for example, once the city of rose gardens and the glorious Persian Empire before Chingiz Khan's barbarism—that they have come to mean for George Gurdjieff sky-high profits from retailored ladies' underwear.

Addressing who knows what audience in his barely coherent 1932 public manifesto and "Supplementary Announcement," *The Herald of Coming Good*—a manifesto Orage urged Gurdjieff to suppress—Gurdjieff presents us with a very different account of his life after abandoning the teachings of his contemporaries in, he says, 1892. In this peculiar account of his development, three pursuits are highlighted. First, monastic discipline; second, hypnotism; third, spiritism or spiritualism. Trade does not come into it. A sympathetic observer might say that what we are dealing with here is simply the Gurdjieffian "double-life." He works at his trades and enterprises in order to fund, more or less simultaneously, his researches into the life of the conscious and unconscious mind. Well, that is not an impossible scenario, but I should have thought it might have proved something of a strain to combine retirement to monastic isolation and ascetic one-pointedness with flogging corsets and repairing typewriters. The alternative possibility is that he operated in alternating periods: a period of work and enterprise ending in selling his former assets, followed by reimmersion into travel for research or meditative purposes. But then, we must contend with other elements that enter the scenario, and which we shall look at in the next chapter: his apparent participation in, or observation of, military conflicts—a kind of addiction to danger, expressed, not altogether convincingly, as research into human behavior.

What follows is his account of a life devoted to experimentation into the psyche in *The Herald of Coming Good*.

Giving up on his contemporaries, Gurdjieff decides on retirement from the "outer world." Thanks to meeting a street barber in Central Asia he is accepted into an Islamic monastery, where he enters a deep spell of private meditation as to where he is and where he is going. Sticking to an idea of conduct emerging from this meditation he resumes his wanderings, still without a definite plan of action: a not untypical state for a young man who has not found his métier.

He "liquidates" his affairs—a favorite expression—and combines his resources into collecting oral tradition and literature "still surviving among Asiatic peoples" with regard to what he calls "Mehkeness," a branch of science highly developed, he says, in ancient times. "Mehkeness," he says, signifies "taking away of responsibility." According to Gurdjieff, modern hypnotism only contains an insignificant portion of an allegedly ancient science for removing conscious inhibition and discernment.

Having assembled all the knowledge he can, he goes to "a certain Dervish monastery." Dervishes are also known as Sufis, of course, and everyone has heard of the whirling dervishes permitted occasionally by the Turkish state to perform mystical dances in Konya and Istanbul today. The proper name for a Sufi monastery in Central Asia and Afghanistan is a *khanqah*. They often house hospices and hospitals for travelers in Persianate societies and welcome non-Muslims. Gurdjieff, however, does not specify where this particular place was situated. He says he had been there before. It might have been near Constantinople, for we have a brief account of a youthful visit to the dervishes of Constantinople in *Meetings*. In the Ottoman Empire and Bosnia, Sufi monasteries went under the name *takije*.

He says he settled in this monastery studying his acquired material on the theoretical side of mehkeness. He says after two years familiarizing himself with theory, he needed *practical* verification as to the mechanics of the "subconscious sphere." He says he got his practical verifications by passing himself off as a healer, a healer of many vices, and gained knowledge from his practice as well as genuinely relieving the afflicted. The vices, from later comments, included drug and alcohol addiction, conditions he addressed by hypnosis.

He then refers to an oath taken with respect to using his knowledge conscientiously to help sufferers; the oath apparently specifying a period of four or five years for the task. We do not know if this was an oath insisted upon by persons who instructed him—there are passages in *Herald* that suggest so—or whether it was self-imposed. It should be noted that he says, during this period of four or five years, his practical

investigations of his powers constituted his "exclusive preoccupation"—
no time then for setting up restaurants or cinemas. By his oath, he was
not to use the knowledge for egotistical, personal ends. To such a degree
did his investigations benefit from practical experience that he claims to
have achieved results without precedence or equal in "our day." Perhaps
the aforementioned return to Kars, where he involved his father in an
experiment with the Armenian woman, Sando, should be included in
this alleged period of exclusively experimental activity. Gurdjieff also
became convinced that observations of man's conscious behavior were
as important as observing man's "unconscious mentation" in solving the
problems of the human psyche. This switch of emphasis seems to signal
a move from hypnosis alone to observing spiritist séances.

He next refers to a two-year period of wanderings on the continents
of Asia, Europe, and Africa. This two-year period may be the same as the
two-year period mentioned earlier when he familiarized himself with the
theory of mehkeness. In that case he repeats himself, and strangely so,
for he states in *Herald* that "reflections," which "recurred periodically"
during the two years' wanderings, led him to employ his exceptional
knowledge of "the so-called 'supernatural sciences'" by entering "these
pseudo-scientific domains" as a "professor-instructor": phrases that he
himself puts in quotation marks, indicating his ironic critique of modern
knowledge and its asserted inferiority to ancient wisdom in these fields.
Either we have here two ways of saying the same thing, that is, he worked
on theory for two years and then became a healer, expressed also as two
years' wanderings culminating in his becoming professor-instructor,
or we have consecutive activities, the first culminating in his practical
research period as a healer, and then subsequently, two years of wanderings culminating in making contact with pseudo-scientific domains. It is
hard to believe that this confusion was not in some degree intentional.
Alternatively, his mind was very confused at the time. Unfortunately,
this kind of dreamlike timekeeping is endemic to Gurdjieff's accounts.
Most people reading Gurdjieff probably just try to trip over the verbal
treacle to arrive at a point, but the point keeps shifting.

So we have a two-year period anyway of wandering across continents, at the end of which he decides he will not only use his knowledge of "so-called 'sciences'" but also reveal his skill in producing different "tricks."

His principal motive for giving himself out as professor-instructor resulted from what he calls "a widely prevalent and specific psychosis." This psychosis was well established, he says. It had led to people surrendering to "woeful" ideas, ideas that are "spheres of quasi-human knowledge," which have been called different things in different epochs. In the current epoch, he says, these psychosis-inducing quasi-sciences go by the names of occultism, theosophism (theosophy), and spiritualism. Later in *Herald* he will throw in Rudolf Steiner's system of "anthroposophy," which was not launched as such until 1912, after Steiner's split with theosophist leader Annie Besant. Gurdjieff's rejection of theosophy as known in the 1890s, and probably the 1930s too, compares interestingly with Aleister Crowley's contemporary critique of what *he* dubbed "toshosophy" and his rejection of spiritism, which Crowley regarded as cruel tricks played on the vulnerable bereaved. It is significant that Gurdjieff does *not* tar Freemasonry, Rosicrucianism, or Martinism with his contemptuous brush.

Having "dissed" so much of the 1890s' reactions against materialism in favor of his own vein of allegedly ancient knowledge, it may seem surprising that Gurdjieff then declares that his next step was to direct all his capacities to coming into contact with members of these "vast organizations": theosophy, occultism, spiritualism.

It is difficult not to see this period of alleged engagement with existing organizations as having taken place principally in Tiflis, Georgia, and the Cossack Caucasus *stanitsa* (village or district) Yessentukskaya, centered on Essentuki (or "Yessentuki"), some 70 kilometers beyond Georgia's northern border, and perhaps other places in old and new Russia, or even Cairo. The period would then probably have to be after censorship reform that followed abortive attempts at socialist and democratic revolt in 1905 in Russia. Theosophists with esoteric interests often called their gatherings "lodges," following the Masonic example.

In *Herald* Gurdjieff says that within six months of having decided to commit to engaging with existing organizations, he succeeded not only in contacting a great number of their members but very quickly was taken by them as an "expert," "well-known," and a trusted guide to evoke "so-called 'phenomena-of-the-beyond.'" He accomplished what are plainly implied to be perceived manifestations of spirits of dead or distant persons, within a "very large 'circle,' as they called it." The word *circle* refers to spiritist gatherings. Theosophists and spiritists frequently interacted, while both designations often applied to the same person.

It is plain then that Gurdjieff had entered on a curious campaign of deception, generating impressive spiritist phenomena, perhaps through trickery and attention-deflecting hypnosis, in order, he says, to study the psyches of those involved. Whether he obtained cash for his alleged exploits is unstated and unknown. He offers a no-punches-pulled collective description for spiritist séances. He calls them "workshops for the perfection of psychopathism." Members and their families hailed him, he claims, as a "maestro" of everything under the banner of "supernatural knowledge." He performed "so-called 'manipulations'" in the realm of the beyond in the presence of many members of the spiritist circle that welcomed him. To Gurdjieff, these dupes were there to be studied and observed: their psychological "waking state" had been provided for him by destiny; they were "trained and freely moving 'Guinea Pigs.'" This kind of activity allegedly persisted for more than three years, and he set up groups of his own, in three cities he says, and at great personal expense, by which he could continue his observations of human conscious behavior. Of course, *any* activity might be justified as providing opportunity for objective observation of human behavior.

The period in question is referred to in *Tales,* where on Beelzebub's sixth descent to Earth, he becomes a "physician-hypnotist" responsible for making "Pythias," "pythonesses," or mediums in order to explore "subconsciousness."[4] In this period took place many scientific investigations of mediums as to their reliability or falseness; it was a hot issue internationally. The British Society for Psychical Research was very active in the field, to whose activity there may be a reference in *Tales* when Beelzebub refers to the investigation of "Makary Kronbernkzion."[5]

When Gurdjieff felt he had the requisite working knowledge of the human conscious and subconscious, he thought he should establish his own institute. This period of deliberation took place between 1911 and 1912. He says in *Herald* that it was difficult to choose the best location, but that in consideration of Russia's condition immediately before World War I—"peaceful, rich, and quiet"—he decided on Russia. Decision made, he immediately began to "liquidate" his affairs (again), dispersed throughout Asia, to collect all his wealth and to move to Moscow "two years before the so-called 'Great-World-War'": itself as clear a demonstration of the disharmonious nature of the human psyche as could be wished for, and a clarion in concrete terms of why Gurdjieff's Institute for the Harmonious Development of Man was, he believed, so urgently necessary.

MISCELLANEOUS ADVENTURES

While it seems likely that Bogachevksy, Gurdjieff's tutor in objective morality, was an imaginary person, certain details related in his regard might give one to wonder if there was not an actual individual who fulfilled the role of a skeptical but ultimately spiritual priest, a man well traveled whom young Gurdjieff would, or indeed did, meet later (himself?).

Gurdjieff says it was soon after Bogachevsky left Kars that he in his turn departed for Tiflis (circa 1892). However, they would, he says, meet again "much later."[6] The place of meeting was the Iver monastery, whose monumental and imposing red, square towers stand so grandly today at Samara, 1,000 miles north of Georgia, by the Volga. Deprived of Christian worship under the Soviet regime, the monastic complex was restored to the Russian Orthodox Church in 1992. It seems unlikely Gurdjieff would have invented the detail of Samara. He added that the priest at first did not recognize the grown-up before him who had "changed a great deal." Gurdjieff says he had caught up again with news of Bogachevsky when he happened to be in Broussa (now Bursa), on the Sea of Marmara, 80 kilometers south of Constantinople, where lived a Turkish dervish friend of Gurdjieff's. In days gone by, Broussa accommodated a flourishing colony of Armenians; it was a center for Armenian commerce and for the Gregorian Church in the Ottoman Empire. It is impossible to say whether it was the dervish friend or the fact that there was a Gregorian theological seminary at nearby Armasha in the vicinity of Ismid (Izmit) that brought Gurdjieff to Broussa. Acquaintance with Broussa, and the dervish, may first have occurred during another youthful trip to Constantinople: a visit Gurdjieff uses as the setting for his meeting "remarkable man" Ekim Bey.

Gurdjieff says he learns from the dervish at Broussa about Bogachevsky's experiences in Palestine. It is just possible that the details concerning the priest's becoming an Essene may have come from experiences in Palestine that occurred after Gurdjieff's claim in *Life Is Real* that Greeks took him to Jerusalem in 1896 after he had been wounded during the Cretan uprising against Turkey. The link with Essenes is highly curious and perhaps came from the following source.

Gurdjieff says he heard from the dervish that Bogachevsky went to Mount Athos but subsequently abandoned the priesthood, whereafter he went to Jerusalem, where "near the Lord's Temple"—which ceased to exist in 70 CE! (the Essenes disappeared from history in the same period)—his friend met a rosary vendor who happened to be an Essene monk, who brought the ex-priest in stages *into the brotherhood,* in which brotherhood Bogachevsky rose to become assistant to the abbot of the chief monastery of the Essenes. While it may be that Gurdjieff's reference to "the Lord's Temple" may just allude to the Dome of the Rock shrine, or the site thereof on Jerusalem's Temple Mount, Bogachevsky has nevertheless jumped in time into Gurdjieff's peculiar conflation of the first-century Essenes and an Orthodox monastery. A clue comes from a letter sent, says Gurdjieff, through his uncle's agency. The letter contained a photo of Gurdjieff's friend dressed as a *Greek monk,* and views of holy places "in the environs of Jerusalem."[7] The Greek monk's costume might be the vital clue here.

Lena Cansdale's *Qumran and the Essenes: A Re-evaluation of the Evidence* cites information from French explorer F. De Saulcy's *Narrative of a Journey Round the Dead Sea and in the Bible Lands,* undertaken in 1850 and 1851, where the explorer De Saulcy describes descending from the truly remarkable ancient Greek Orthodox monastery of Mar Saba. Making his way along the Wadi Kedron, De Saulcy was struck by "walls of natural rocks, perforated with caves, but at present inaccessible. The entrances are barricaded by piles of stones without mortar, which indicated they have formerly been inhabited. By whom? The true solution appears to be that we have before us numerous samples of the retreats inhabited in ancient days by the primitive Essenes."[8]

Between Jerusalem and the Dead Sea, today under the governorship of Bethlehem, Mar Saba is only 10 kilometers from the Dead Sea shore. Cansdale makes the valid point that here is a possible site for an Essene base (other than Qumran) that has not been pursued by contemporary scholars. It just might, however, have been taken seriously by George Gurdjieff!

Gurdjieff seems to have been at pains to make the point that the original Christians were *Essenes,* pointing allegorically thereby to the authentic presence in the past of the "true knowledge." A similar case he also makes in an equally understated and elusive manner to the Yezidis and shows if nothing else that he was not following Blavatsky here at all—a path that led pointlessly, he believed, to India—but his own remarkable intuition. Bogachevsky stands for the man who has found the Way and has been able to live by it (*bogach* means a "rich man" in Russian).

That a youthful Gurdjieff may have visited Constantinople before leaving for Tiflis circa 1892 is indicated in the chapter of *Meetings* dedicated to Ekim Bey.[9] Gurdjieff says he went to the Ottoman Empire's administrative center before he even went to Echmiadzin. He was seeking answers to the questions that ran around his brain. So intense was his questioning that he says "most contemporary people" reckoned his brain was "sick with psychopathy," which is an idea not pursued anywhere else; that is, that people thought Gurdjieff had gone mad in asking himself unanswerable questions. Did he himself wonder also that he might have entered into the realm of the insane? Did he experience schizophrenia? Or was it just excessive introspection?

He says Constantinople drew him on account of marvels said to be accomplished there by dervishes. He says he arranged to stay in the Pera district, and from there made visits to dervish monasteries of the different orders, perhaps the means by which he got to know a Turkish dervish in Broussa. He says he lived in the company of "dervish zealots" thinking about "all kinds of dervish nonsense," that is to say, nothing practical, when suddenly it dawned on him that he was broke. He girded his loins and went swimming for coins dropped by visitors from the steamers by the bridge between Pera and Stamboul by the Galata shore, having seen other boys do the same. Before taking up this laborious means to a meager income he had been on the bridge pondering the "continuous movement" of the whirling dervishes, which superficially appeared to be unconscious or automatic, uninhibited by conscious thought; then the practical need to earn seized him and took his mind off the issue of what made the dervish whirl. When Gurdjieff took Ouspensky to see the whirling dervishes in Constantinople in 1920, he confided to Ouspensky's surprise that they did it by counting; he had every reason to know (ballroom dancers too).

While Gurdjieff goes swimming "to get hold of that contemptible something which for contemporary man is almost the sole stimulus of his life" (cash), we shall take a closer, timely, and timeless look at what makes Sufis tick.

THE SUFIS

The name *Sufi* first appears in the late tenth century in Mesopotamia, apparently derived from the Arabic *tasawwuf*, meaning "to wear wool," pure wool (*suf*): the garment of the ascetic.

A Sufi order or brotherhood is called a *tariqa* ("path"; plural *turuq*). The path is to *haqiqa*, or inward reality. Sufi philosophy stresses the eye of the mind, the noetic faculty, the spirit manifested in the mind as intuition of higher things. One of the earliest of the turuq was founded by Shitab ad-Din as-Suhrawardi (circa 1144–1234). He recognized that the one God of the Islamic revelation could accommodate the more ancient Hermetic monist doctrine, with its universalist, gnostic content. Sufis have been esoteric students of the Qur'an, endeavoring to experience the prophet Muhammad's mystical experience, a process involving *ma'rifa;* that is, gnosis or spiritual knowledge that outshines ignorance.

Sufis aspire to *baqa*—pure "subsistence," beyond all form—preceded by the extinction (*al fana*) of the ego, or common idea of self.

Sufic insight has given us the dramatic picture that the spirit (*ar-Ruh*) and the soul (*an-nafs*) are in conflict for possession of the essential faculty *al-qalb*, the heart: their common "son." Like the demiurgical ego of the cosmoclastic Gnostics, an-nafs, the soul, mistakes herself as an autonomous whole and, in doing so, veils the heart. The soul is the world's accomplice, subject to the world's passions, whereas ar-Ruh is above all that. Sufis hope spirit will be victorious over the soul so that heart may be transformed into spirit while transmuting the soul with spiritual light. Then the heart may be revealed in its true dimension: as a tabernacle (*mishkat*) of the divine mystery (*sirr*) in humans. A gradual awakening needs to be initiated, or begun.

One can already see a kindred dynamic with Gurdjieff's picture of the three fighting brothers: bodily instinct, feeling, and thinking—Gurdjieff's "three brains" working against each other disharmoniously, each overpowering the other. However, Gurdjieff's interest in nascent psychology, suggestion, and hypnosis has psychologized the spiritual dynamics into a behaviorist scenario. Gurdjieffian thought does stress the idea of two selves, the ego as disharmonious identity, and a real "I Am," which is to all intents and purposes, God, or one's inner God, formed or even acquired through a life process. Gurdjieff's idea of "removing the ego" is to subtract consciousness from the mind, leaving what he takes to be authentic subconsciousness. Mehkeness, whatever that may have been to him, taught him to "take away responsibility" in the sense of conscious inhibition. The ego is intentionally isolated and comes under observation as if it were an unruly criminal and certainly an idiot subject to punishment for the sake of psychological salvation (harmony). It may be objected that this is not a spiritual dynamic but a psychological game played within an objective thinking process. Is this not a *psychic,* rather than a pneumatic or spiritual life process? The conception is aggressive, spurred on by shocks in order to highlight personal delinquencies and shove the process on. But Sufism is not psychology. It seems to me that Gurdjieff has either confused the spiritual with the psychic, eliminating the spiritual, or simply regarded the spiritual as a state of special powers attendant on the acquisition of interior psychic and bodily harmony.

Sufism shares with Christianity the path of love (*mahabba*), adding the way of gnosis (ma'rifa). Love was important to Gurdjieff too. He could never let go of his family or the Orthodox virtues of faith, hope, and love; they remained vital to him, reappearing time and time again in *Tales,* as the flower of the active conscience, inspired by what he calls "objective morality" and what the Sufi would accept as *shari'a* (law) or outward conformity.

The essential organ of cognition in Sufism is the heart, not the brain. The heart is a throne for the spirit or mind of God, which transcends mental or rational forms, and which cannot therefore be encompassed by wiseacreing, or indeed any particular human system.

Like Western esotericism in general, Sufism sees humanity's tragedy as a fall of the faculties, a fall of being: the ego, obsessed with the visible, tangible, and apparently objective world deflects the heart from its true center, rooted in the eternal. Thus the consciousness of people in their ordinary state is as if imprisoned in a kind of dream state, an amnesia: forgetfulness (*ghafla*). "Wake up!" is the perennial cry of the gnostic prophet. This doctrine clearly impacted greatly on Gurdjieff, but it was filtered, it appears, through a prior focusing on the hypnotic characteristic of life lived "unconsciously."

The Sufi medicine for the state of worldly sleep is *dhikr*, meaning "recollection" or "mindfulness," as well as "contemplation" or "invocation." *Awareness* might be succinct. Starting from dhikr as a repetition of the name of Allah, Sufis generated a path of purification and illumination, predisposing the soul to attain to gnosis, defined as the knowledge of the attributes of the divine unity, peculiar to the saints, who behold God with their hearts. The whirling of the dervishes in their remarkable dance is an act of dhikr, of remembrance of the raising life of the eternal God. Gurdjieff found the inspiring dance a communication medium of primordial wisdom. Doing things differently, Gurdjieff invented his own, according to what he took to be ancient principles, or principles he took to be of the Tradition.

Obviously, we have in the Sufi dhikr much of the basis for Gurdjieff's emphasis on "self-remembering" and recollection: attempting to isolate ego-consciousness from the "real life" perceptible, according to Gurdjieffian doctrine, only in *the present*, when "I Am."

"I am that I am" is of course the meaning of the divine name revealed to Moses whose Hebrew is transliterated *Jahveh* (or Yahweh), and the Gurdjieffian practice aims at an apotheosis of Being. It should be recognized, though, that using the present tense for the divine name does not indicate an obsession with being alive "in the now," necessitating the avoidance of thinking about past or future; it is simply the grammatical means to say that *God always is*. He is in and beyond our sense of time: no more in the present, and no less, than he is in what we consider past or future. God is eternal, of the *aions*, and time, as Plato reminds us, is "the moving image of eternity." Besides, common sense tells us that the "now" has no specific spacial content, the present is not now—there is no stasis; the now *is* constant change, since from the moment we think of "it," it is of course already past. The now is not the present as you perceive it, but the ever present. The now is always past, present, and future and of the enigma, or if you prefer "illusion," of time. Eternity becomes intelligible only with the dissolving of the sense of time altogether.

There are other problems involved in the transposition of Sufi recollection into Gurdjieffian self-remembering. Due to the psychological character and independence of the Gurdjieffian student in the act of self-remembering, there lies the danger of existentializing the divine. Given the peculiar development of the Western mind (our ego is ourself), the pitfalls can come first as egos blown up to imagined God-size—what psychology calls a psychosis or psychic illness—or second, the loss, or dissipation, of ego with nothing to stand as the identity of the person: extreme nervous breakdown. It really doesn't do anyone any good to go around thinking, "I am bad; I am ego." Just add LSD (for example), or extreme stress, and you have an emptied existence, a Dionysian psychic dismemberment, a defeat of the mind only kept from utter disintegration by prescription drug therapies or the tantalizing memory of a healthy mental state. The verb *to will* requires a first person to activate it.

Sufism is a *spiritual* process. The human being bows gently in relation to higher being, and the heart is maintained. Religion becomes psychology at a terrible price. Beware of behaviorism!

It was the Persian Sufi Abu Yazid of Bistam who developed the doctrine of *fana:* the passing away of the false self (ego), with, *note,* its positive counterpart, *baqa,* the absorption of the heart in its full integrity into the unitive life in God. The "unitive life in God" should not be identified with the "unconsciousness," which is merely a psychological term. Among the sayings attributed to Abu Yazid are, "Creatures are subject to 'states,' but the gnostic has no 'state,' because his vestiges are effaced and his essence is noughted by the essence of Another and his traces are lost in Another's traces"; "I say that I am my own mirror, for 'tis God that speaks with my tongue, and I have vanished."[10] One might then ask, of course, who was the "I" who said he had vanished? Was this a new self or a self-delusion?

The Sufi dhikr among the followers of *Mawlana* ("Lord"— "Mevlana" in Turkey) Jalal-ud-Din Rumi (1207–1273)—whom Gurdjieff never mentions—was aided by the whirling dance of devotion. Rumi's disciples are the *fuqara* (plural of *faqir*, meaning "poor," "poor in spirit"; that is, *dervish* in Persian). They perform the dance to support their dhikr, invocation, or quintessential prayer. This is important. The essence of the "remembering" is not an act of self-analysis, but a self-offering and surrender in prayer. The Work is *God's:* He raises the heart.

There is a common idea of Gurdjieffian teaching that it is a "fourth way," the first three ways being those of the faqir, the yogi, and the monk. This threesome is of course identified with the familiar three brains of Gurdjieffian human caricature: the training of the body (faqir), the thoughts (yogi), and the feelings, or life of devotion (the monk). The fourth way is supposed to combine all three into a harmony able to be practiced outside of any specific sacred setting while pursuing one's ambitions in the world, though with benefits accrued through group work and mutual observation, like Alcoholics Anonymous. Well, the specifying of the monk, faqir, and yogi to separate faculties is essentially artificial, since devotion to God traditionally already calls for the whole person, the entire being: "Thou shalt love the Lord thy God with all thy heart, with all thy soul, with all thy mind, and with all thy strength" (Mark 12:30). There is no fourth way; there is only the way, and Gurdjieff surely knew this, as it is evident throughout *Tales* that he fully accepted the spiritual teaching of Jesus and the revelation of the prophets and was buried according to the rites of the Orthodox Church.

It ought to be stressed here that Gurdjieff did not pour Sufism down his followers' throats. His priorities were clearly influenced by dervish teachings, but it was chiefly his later follower, John Godolphin Bennett (1897–1974) who went out of his way, especially after Gurdjieff's death in 1949, to link Gurdjieffian ideas to the doctrine and practices of Sufis, such that persons with experience of Bennett's communities frequently identify the teachings as a single revelatory stream. Bennett became convinced that a remote and highly refined Sufism was Gurdjieff's "secret" source. Interestingly, Gurdjieff first encountered British intelligence officer Bennett in Constantinople in 1920, during the period Gurdjieff indicated his understanding of the secret of the whirling dervishes to Ouspensky.

A last word from Sufi master Rumi: Rumi recognizes the imprisonment of the soul, and its anguish, as well as any existentialist. But he also knows that the world is a prison in which we find our freedom: "'Tis wonderful that the spirit is in prison, and then, (all the time) the key of the prison is in its hand."[11] Rumi's formula for the person who has found his or her role in life is simple:

> If you are putting trust in God, put trust (in Him) as regards (your) work: sow (the seed), then rely upon the Almighty. . . . He (God) said: "I was a hidden treasure": hearken! Do not let thy (spiritual) substance be lost: become manifest![12]

Thy will be done. The spiritual work is God's; he can reach where we cannot. The Hypnos of *hypnosis* was the Greek god of sleep, and his children were dreams.

BACK TO WORK WITH GURDJIEFF

According to Gurdjieff's account of his relations with Ekim Bey, whom he allegedly met in Constantinople on his first youthful visit when he dived for coins by the Galata shore, he would meet Ekim some "four years later," perhaps around 1895. The location is interesting. Gurdjieff says they climbed the Suram (or Surami) Pass, a little to the north and some 80 kilometers west of Tiflis. This would be no light stroll. The Suram Pass divided the eastern from the western Caucasus in Georgia's Likhi range (altitude 949 meters). The rocks are jagged and the slopes very steep. Given Gurdjieff's claims to have worked on railway contracts and oil wells, and his presence in oil-rich Baku in Azerbaijan on the Caspian, it is possible Gurdjieff was involved in some way with the surveying or contracting for the most profitable railway in Georgia.

In 1883, Alphonse Rothschild of the French branch of the Rothschild Bank arrived in Baku with capital to open up an "Oil Road," or steam railway, from Baku to the Black Sea: a hugely ambitious project, crossing from Baku across the desert, following the valley of the River Kura up to Tiflis, then over the Suram Pass, and down the River Rioni to Batumi. Baku kerosene could now be shipped from the Black Sea coast through the Bosphorus to markets all over the world. The Caucasus became an epic construction zone, with embankments, tunnels, cuttings, and bridges, making the Caucasus the industrial heartland of the Russian Empire. The oil cars were mainly owned by the Nobels and the Rothschilds; the latter invested the equivalent today of 2.2 billion pounds in the Baku oil industry. Improvement in the railway became a necessity. An oil pipeline was built alongside the railway, and a new tunnel (Sruamski Tunnel) was opened at the Suram Pass in 1895 to speed up the passage of the profitable cargo. The opening was celebrated with a popular fair. Could it have been that Gurdjieff's account of Ekim's visit coincided with this popular event, celebrated with tents, sideshows, and bunting?

Gurdjieff says he spent the summer in the area, exploring also the beautiful mountain resort of Borjhomi, where in 1894 Mikhail Romanov had just built a mineral water bottle factory, 100 kilometers west of Tiflis, making the town even better off with new investment for its spa facilities.

Gurdjieff says he and Ekim Bey took pleasure in encountering peoples who had not yet been "exposed to the effects of contemporary civilization." He says they even visited the famous Khevsurs, who "have driven all the learned ethnographers mad."[13] Interestingly, the Khevsurs recur in Gurdjieff's stories (in *Life Is Real*)—this time after his having been shot in the leg, so he claimed, during a revolt in the Caucasus at the end of 1904.

The Khevsurs looked rather like crusaders and dressed in chain mail with crosses adorning their combat clothing. Traditionally, they were linked to lost crusaders and remained fiercely independent mountain warriors. While Christian, they also held secret rites at sacred places in the mountains. In *Life Is Real,* Gurdjieff claimed to have attended a "secret meeting" of his "immortal neighbors."[14]

Gurdjieff's story in *Meetings* has Ekim Bey as excited as Pogossian, Yelov, and Karpenko about their shared "psychopathy" and their "Don Quixotic aspirations." Their romanticism unquenchable, Gurdjieff says he and his "friends" (Don Quixote and Sancho Panza being themselves fictional, with Quixote prone to hallucinations) joined a larger party at Nakhchivan—then part of the Russian Empire, now an autonomous exclave of Azerbaijan—led by one imaginary Prince Yuri Lubovedsky to explore Persia.[15]

ELEVEN

Traveling Tales and Bullets in the Leg

Prince Lubovedsky was fictional; was the expedition? Who can say? No evidence external to the narrative has arisen to support it. Gurdjieff says it was set to begin the following January—if the summer at the Suram Pass was set in 1895, an expedition to Persia could have taken place in 1896.

Gurdjieff's narrative takes us to Tabriz in northwestern Persia to encounter a Persian dervish who contradicts Gurdjieff on what he has learned about hatha yoga and gymnastics (note that these are activities sanctioned by theosophy); this seems to be the point of the narrative. Gurdjieff even claims to know the dialect of Persian that enables him to receive the considerations of the holy man who is said to work miracles. This is Gurdjieff's chance to knock a couple of holes in theosophy and yogic practices, practices that have since caught on around the world: chewing food extremely thoroughly, for example, is dismissed by the holy man as weakening the capacities of the stomach, which needs to get used to strong challenges. *Pranayama,* or breath control, is likewise dismissed as dangerous for lung, heart, and organs, as there is, we are told, a delicate unconscious balance between the organs; how they process what Gurdjieff characteristically calls our "second food" (air) through blood rhythms is crucial to health. One should not interfere with natural rhythms and flow, which should be unconscious, but understand their inner life where possible: trust nature; don't impose on it. All the parts of the body combine to make the "bread of life."

Gurdjieff promises that the astounding information from the dervish about hypnotism and man's physical body will appear in his third series, or book. Such never occurred, leaving one wondering if there really was much more to say. They then head for Baghdad as if it were a quick hike. Baghdad was 550 kilometers away, so the reason given, that his friends were sick, seems barely adequate.

Having dispensed some of his views on hatha yoga and gymnastics, Gurdjieff next treats us to some accounts of hypnotic experiments performed on people who consequently regard him as a "redoubtable magician and wizard."[1] He says some of the people who met him, and others who had only heard of him, began to fear him, while some became exaggeratedly respectful and even "began to lick his boots." This may be a comment on the way people responded to him in Paris as well, or New York; he attributes it in part to the "servility of human nature." As Crowley would put it, "the slaves shall serve" (Liber *AL* vel Legis, 2:58).

Gurdjieff gives away a few tricks. A medium might want to hold a person's hand. Why? Because a movement of the thoughts in a definite direction "is always accompanied by a tension of the muscles in the same direction"—a useful trick indeed for one bent on exposing spiritualistic frauds! The movement is, he says, unavoidable because it is "unconscious" in origin.[2] The body registers thought ahead of vocalization. Muscles reveal intention. This simple guide to the relation between unconscious acts and the nervous system explains certain "miracles." Muscles are "subject more to the subconsciousness than to the consciousness."

Ekim Bey performs experiments to "determine the causes of hypnotic influences." He gives the example of guiding a hand over letters and numbers: common theosophical-spiritualist practice at the time. Ordinary people may ascribe the medium's knowledge to spiritual influences whereas Gurdjieff and his friend share "laughter at the stupidity and naivety of people."[3]

The journey continues, perhaps by Mustapha's flying chair, or perhaps its itinerary has more to do in fact with Gurdjieff's claims that he brought cattle in from China and elsewhere, because before we know where we are, we find ourselves at Yangishar in Kashgar, on the border of Tajikistan and Kyrgyzstan (*Yangishar* is a variant name for the city of Kashgar on the Silk Road). Then—just like that!—we're off to the Hindu Kush![4] He says he passed through Irkeshtam toward Russia. Irkeshtam is a border crossing on the Kyrgyzstan side of the border with Xinjiang province, China.

"After many adventures" and without following the usual roads from Kashgar, all of which led to Osh—the second largest city in Kyrgyzstan, in the Fergana valley—they reached Andijan. Andijan is today in Uzbekistan, 30 kilometers southeast of Osh, on the southeast edge of the Fergana region. In fact, Osh is on a straight line from Kashgar to Andijan, so there seems no point in taking different roads to those going to Osh. Was he trying to avoid something at Osh that he isn't telling us? Or had memory faded?

At Margelan he and his alleged party supposedly bought rail tickets. The railway line only went into service in 1898, so he seems to have jumped in time as well as space. Margelan is west of Osh and southwest of Andijan. It seems to make no practical sense to have gone to Margelan via Andijan and not Osh. The train was supposed to take them to Krasnovodsk (now Turkmenbasy) on the east bank of the Caspian Sea, where a train ferry operated across the Caspian to Baku. On account of having no money for food or clothes, he says, they only went as far as "Chernyaevo" (Czernjajewo) and then took what was in fact, from 1898, the brand-new spur north to Tashkent (now the capital of Uzbekistan) where money was secured by telegraph.

He says he and Ekim Bey put up posters in Old Tashkent with police permission and placed ads in the papers to attract people to see the amazing magic of Ekim Bey as "Ganez" or "Ganzin" and his assistant Salakan (Gurdjieff). They sold their hypnotic skills for money, he says, shamelessly: "We finally brought them into such a state of hypnosis. . . ." They used two unemployed men—so effectively hypnotized that "you could stick pins in them."[5] This may tell us little about what Gurdjieff was actually doing in 1896—or 1898—but it says something about his approach to scientific methodology.

He boasts that he earned much more money than was needed.

He then gives us a stern lecture on how much Europe had to learn from Asia: "for example medicine, astrology, natural science and so on, without any wiseacreing or hypothetical explanations, have long since attained a degree of perfection which European civilization may perhaps reach only after several hundred years."[6]

In *Life Is Real,* Gurdjieff creates an interweaving narrative of three bullets: all of which were strays, all of which hit him in the leg (which leg?), and all of which affected the course of his life. It all seems very far-fetched, for he has forgotten a fourth bullet—the one that passed through his leg when hunting with his Russian friends when living in Kars. That was a rifle bullet and somehow missed his bone: also somewhat incredible, but then, it did fulfill the prediction of a fortune-teller. Still, a rifle bullet that missed the bone, and also vital arteries. . . . Clearly, Gurdjieff believed in providence, and his story of three bullets in his leg also has the feel of providence. Four bullets would have spoiled the symbolism, presumably: the number three being very important to Gurdjieff.

The story of bullet number one is set a year before the Greco-Turkish war on the island of Crete. On February 4, 1897, Greece claimed Crete. The Turks did not take kindly to that. What Gurdjieff might have been doing on Crete the previous year is anybody's guess but his own. The only motive we have is that which he gives us: he had a passion for going to places where the tensions in people's psyches reached extremes. He was, he implies, addicted to danger, or at least his understanding required observing such conditions. He claims no heroic role, possibly because there was none to be claimed, but one cannot be sure; one might say he was mad enough for anything. Many Greeks were swept up in a patriotic rush of passion to support their Cretan brothers against the cruel Turk. He had been prepared, it seems, to throw in half a hand with the Armenian resistance; perhaps he thought he could spare the other half for the Cretans.

Anyhow, Gurdjieff misses the main conflict as the stray bullet renders him unconscious, and in such a state he claims, somewhat improbably, to have been carried by "unknown Greeks" all the way to Jerusalem. Why Jerusalem? Possibly because this was the base of the Greek Orthodox Patriarchate of Jerusalem, which body surely had a role to play in the conflict. Even so . . . Gurdjieff says he was in the company of other "seekers of pearls in manure," which must mean something, perhaps a cynical reaction to war or the world in general. He then says he made his way back to Russia on foot: a remarkable feat—forgive the pun—for one shot in the leg. There is nothing about going to visit his old friend Bogachevsky at the Essene monastery; but then, *Life Is Real* is supposed to be, well, real. He took four months to get home, a journey that, he says, should have shortened his life, but he was gifted. Nevertheless, a list of ailments suffered offers some indication of the physical misery he wants us to believe he endured: "Kurdistan tzinga" (scurvy), Armenian dysentery, and influenza. Did he perhaps call in at Lalish, north of Mosul, which was on his way north?

Following some months at home in Transcaucasia—it must now have been 1897 if there is any fact at all in this story—he undertook various trips through all kinds of "bush and jungle."

In order to get an idea of what this journey entailed, we need only look at what he amusingly calls the local "delicacies"; that is, diseases: Ashkhabadian bedinka, Bokharian malaria, Tibetan dropsy, Beluchistan dysentery, and "many others." So he went, it seems, to Ashkhabad, capital of Turkmenistan in Central Asia—a place to which he would apparently return and profit greatly from—Bukhara (or Bokhara), the ancient, stunningly beautiful city now in Uzbekistan, a place filled with the kinds of bazaars where Gurdjieff could work his trade in carpets, antiques, and anything else that came along that looked profitable; to Tibet (who knows why, or if); and Beluchistan, between Rajasthan, India, and Iran, south of Afghanistan, now a province of Pakistan. The reference to Beluchistan is curious, the date telling.

In July–August 1897 the siege of Malakand brought relief to British forces harried by Pashtun tribesmen in Britain's Northwest Frontier, an occasion that marked Winston Churchill's first taste of combat (and war journalism) as tribal unrest rippled through the borders of British India, closely observed by Russia. In September 1897, the British Sixth Bengal Cavalry marched through the Kohat Pass in Beluchistan to engage with the Orakzais, led by rebel Beluchistan chiefs, one of whom, Hadda Mullah, hoped to attack Dir, as the clans there supported British forces. Northern Beluchistan bordered on the volatile Northwest Frontier. A thrilling scene from the campaign opens Richard Attenborough's movie *Young Winston* (1972).

Scattered references elsewhere to crossing British border posts into India might suggest Gurdjieff's danger addiction took him to Beluchistan for some action. The other possibility is that he took Russian money to engage in spying on British forces. Anyone familiar with the history of the "Great Game" will know that Russians and British intelligence never took their eyes off one another wherever territories of mutual interest adjoined. References to Tibet and Beluchistan in 1897 from a Russian speaker and independent traveler and businessman would have been examined closely by British intelligence. Alas, the name Gurdjieff has not emerged from documents of the period, but then, if he retained his liberty and his secrecy, they would not.

SOLOVIEV AND THE KUSHKA LINE

It seems there was a Russian military angle lurking around the story in *Meetings* Gurdjieff weaves around his acquaintance with a character he calls Soloviev—named perhaps out of respect for the contemporary Russian spiritual philosopher of that name. The historic background appears to be the building of the Kushka Line, a military-inspired railway construction between Merv and the highly sensitive Afghan border that began, under cover of a news blackout about it, in November 1897.

Hypnosis is the basis for Gurdjieff's encounter with the almost certainly fictional Soloviev, destined to die of a camel's bite in the Gobi Desert. Soloviev has taken to drink out of shame. This was a common cause Gurdjieff claimed to have found uniting many alcoholics. Soloviev felt he had failed his father and escaped his responsibilities, but in escaping, wound himself ever deeper into the prison of his vice, or indeed, the vice of his prison. Gurdjieff reminds us, "At that time I already knew a great deal about hypnotism, and, after bringing a man into a certain state, I could influence him by suggestion to forget any undesirable habit."[7]

All interesting, no doubt, but perhaps even more interesting is the story Gurdjieff weaves around Soloviev's decline. The story goes that Soloviev had been attached as a telegraphist to the railway battalion of the Transcaspian Railway, at the time militarized and concerned in 1897–98 with extending a spur from the Central Asiatic Railway station at Merv to the Afghan border.

Of very recent construction, the Transcaspian, or Central Asiatic, Railway ran from Krasnowodsk on the east coast of the Caspian, southeast through Turkmenistan ("Obwod Zakaspijski") to Ashkhabad, thence east to Merv, northeast to Bukhara in the Emirate of Bukhara, then east again to Samarkand in Turkestan—completed in 1888—before heading farther east into Ferghana, until running out of steam at Andijan near Osh, being completed in 1898. It is highly significant then that Gurdjieff's accounts of his wanderings leading up to meeting Soloviev find him exclusively on the main stations of the Transcaspian Railway, which at the time were effectively military bases. He says he goes to Bukhara (where the Emir had his own railway spur from the main station outside the city) to find the essence of Muhammad's religion and "to meet Bukharian dervish acquaintances of various sects," including his "great friend" Bogga Eddin.[8] From New Bukhara Gurdjieff goes to Samarkand, another luminary along the old Silk Road and four stations eastward on the railway. In old Samarkand he says he made fake canaries for cash and did not follow his father as an honest trader who stayed poor. He keeps a dog there, Philos, who has an instinct for love.[9] We then find him back in New Bukhara meeting Bogga Eddin and his dervish friends again while making paper flowers, as Madame Blavatsky used to make in Odessa.[10] It is at Bukhara that Gurdjieff says he encountered Soloviev working on the railway, discharged from the army due to jaundice, engaged in a counterfeit banknote scam with a man from Warsaw who failed to show up.[11]

Gurdjieff appears to have been wandering by train from military base to military base, offering his services wherever possible to the mighty railway construction that edged its way southward and eastward, like extending veins in the flesh of empire, toward the British zone of interest. His previous experience, linguistic skills, fearlessness, and familiarity with Islamic customs must have been assets to receiving occasional employment. One could describe him perhaps as one occasionally "servicing the military" while doing what he could for himself on the side.

The Merv–Kushka railway ran for 293 versts (313 kilometers) along the valleys of the Murghab and Kushk rivers to terminate at the military Kushkinski Post, established in 1890 as the southernmost outpost of the Russian Empire and seed for the town of Kushka (now Sehetabat). Work on the railway began on November 15, 1897; it was opened on December 4, 1898. Had the tracks crossed into Afghanistan, Britain would have regarded the incursion as provocative. As it was, the line was of top-level concern. In 1900 Russia's minister of war organized an experiment, sending troops by rail from Tiflis to Baku, then across the Caspian Sea to Krasnovodsk, and on to Kushka. It proved the Russians could get troops from the Caucasus to the Afghan border in eight days. News of Russia's "secret railroad" 220 miles long and threatening Herat, Afghanistan, was sprung on the British public in spring 1899. An incredulous press demanded to know how, in these days of telegraph and newspapers, news of its construction had remained secret; St. Petersburg had denied its existence. Britain feared the line's extension to Herat, providing support for a Russian army to launch an attack on British India, or simply to tie up British resources, giving Russia political leverage in the West.

In London, Henry Norman, MP, advocated immediate extension of Indian railways into Afghanistan. Railways were of enormous strategic and political significance. Russia had the money and the motive to invest, and Gurdjieff doubtless fancied a share of it. As it turned out, the Afghan government wanted no railways either from Russia or Britain entering its territory. That would not have stopped covert surveys, however, and it did not.

TOWARD THE SARMOUNG MONASTERY

After encountering Soloviev, Gurdjieff's *Meetings* narrative takes us on a 300-kilometer journey southeast of Bukhara toward the great Amu-darya River that made the border of the Russian-controlled Bukhara Emirate and Afghanistan. By Bogga Eddin's agency, Gurdjieff will finally enter the imaginary Sarmoung monastery. Bogga Eddin's name, by the way, may be a play on Sia-*Eddin*, the next but one railway station up east from Bukhara; *Bogga* could be a pun on *Bokhara*, now written as Bukhara. On the other hand, Bogga Eddin may be derived more directly from the fourteenth-century Sufi master Bahauddin Naqshband, nicknamed "The Designer," born near Bukhara and buried there. An aspirated *H* is pronounced *G* in Russian and may tell us that Gurdjieff's Sufi director was named Bahauddin in honor of the Naqshbandi path he adhered to. Masonic scholar Thierry Zarcone has observed that in the Ottoman Empire, Masonic Rite was translated as "Sufi Path" and Bektashi dervishes in Turkey found common symbolism in Western Freemasonry, which they adapted. The word for lodge in Turkey became a *tarikat*—from *tariqa*—while the Ancient & Accepted Rite became the "Ancient & Accepted Sufi Path." Bektashi poet Ahmed Rifki (died 1935), a member of the secret Virtuous Order—*Tarikat-i-Salahiye*—established by Ottoman Masons and Bektashis in the 1890s, perceived the link between Renaissance Hermeticism in Masonry and Islamic Hermeticism in Bektashism, shared by the Melami, Hulufi, and Batini brotherhoods with their esoteric sympathies and bonds of secrecy. In July 1892 Papus's journal *l'Initiation* announced that Constantinople would soon have a representative of Papus's Martinist Order–linked "Independent Group of Esoteric Studies" to encourage esoteric spiritual universalism (see my *Freemasonry: The Reality,* 177–78).

Bogga Eddin introduces Gurdjieff to a member of the Sarmoung Brotherhood "of which the chief monastery is somewhere in the heart of Asia."[12] Note: somewhere in the *heart*—like God; like the heart of Sufi mysticism; like the heart that is first appealed to symbolically at the initiation of Entered Apprentice Freemasons.

Like the fictional wise men of Damcar in the *Fama Fraternitatis* who greet Brother CR as one long expected, the "extraordinary being" from the brotherhood knows all about Gurdjieff. Gurdjieff says Bogga Eddin is staying at Kishlak near New Bukhara. A kishlak is a wintering place for seminomadic people. Gurdjieff then describes a meeting "near Yeni-Hissar" on the banks of the Amu-darya.[13] I cannot locate a "Yeni-Hissar." *Hissar* means a "fortress" and Hissar is the name of a village about 150 kilometers south of Samarkand, 30 kilometers southwest of Dushanbe (today the capital of Tajikistan), on a northern tributary of the Amu-darya—not really the "banks" of the main river.

Only 4 kilometers from Hissar is a place one might think would have interested Gurdjieff. The Hissar historical reserve is today one of Tajikistan's great monuments, consisting of an imposing gray-brown, sixteenth-century fort, two madrassahs, a caravanserai, the grave of Khodja Muhammad, the mausoleum of Mahdumi Abzam (also sixteenth century), and, most interestingly, the Sangin ("stone") mosque.

Within the twelfth-century walls of the domes are features that surely would have captured Gurdjieff's imagination: four resonators made of four bottomless jugs serving as acoustic enhancers, presumably for sermons and prayers—medieval amplifiers, in fact.

Gurdjieff says the party encountered four Kara-Kirghiz to whom they swore oaths to keep secret the monastery they were being taken to—reminiscent perhaps of oaths of secrecy connected with Masonic degrees; note also the "blindfolding" of the hooded aspirants. Gurdjieff says that from "the character of the surroundings," he must have been traveling through the valley of the Pyandzh River (1903 Russian maps have *Pandz*). Today the *Panj* River forms the largest part of the Tajikistan-Afghan border. Just to confuse even more, Gurdjieff also likens the territory to the Zeravshan ("spreader of gold" in Persian). The Zeravshan, however, is some 300 kilometers to the north of the Panj, flowing west through Panjakent toward Samarkand in Uzbekistan.

From this already vague setting, Gurdjieff's terrain becomes so confusing that without resort to the occasional "monument" no traveler could avoid getting lost. Interestingly, perhaps, Masons refer to significant "landmarks" or "cornerstones" of the Craft that maintain the path. It may also be noted that the Wakhan region features peculiar stone cairns at the top of many hills. One suspects this journey is allegorical and the "monuments" are faith, hope, and love—central principles encountered on the Knight-Mason's symbolic journey in the 18th degree of the Ancient & Accepted Rite—together with a Gurdjieffian combination of feeling and instinct. The reference to changing "horses and asses" several times might also be allegorical, for changing "bodies," possibly a refinement of being, the body being the notorious "ass" of the mystic.[14]

Crossing the bridges required great courage and balance. Europeans, he opines, lack "heart" and cannot cross bridges like these. One of the first questions an Entered Apprentice Freemason is asked is, "Do you feel anything?" as a divider is placed on his heart. There were offerings made at the monuments. Generosity is a sign—again a spiritual message is expressed allegorically; Entered Apprentices are asked if they have anything to give.

Directions are deliberately vague, but if they were heading in the general direction in which they appear to have been going—east, of course (whence comes the light of the Mason)—they would be approaching the Pamir Mountains, 300 to 400 kilometers southwest of Osh: "On our right, and in front of us, but a little to the left, we could see snow-capped peaks." He makes out something like a fortress on the banks of the Amu-darya or the Pyandzh. The man at the monastery speaks "Pshenzis." Perhaps the tongue is related to the town of Kalai Pendz on the River Pendz in the Wakhan district of the Pamir in what was southeastern Bukhara province.

To his astonishment, Gurdjieff once more encounters Prince Lubovedsky, who is at the monastery already, congratulating Gurdjieff that "it proves to me that during this time you have not been asleep,"[15] even though blindfolded with a hood on the journey: heavy, and rather obvious symbolism! The Prince then makes a long speech about how his life took him to rock bottom, and how, through an inner battle, he had intimations that he should join the desire of his mind to the desire of his heart; that he should become indifferent to externals; that he should consciously die to the life he had lived up to that time; then a wise man says he should "liquidate" all his affairs.[16] This is something Gurdjieff seems to do regularly in *Meetings,* as in his life, and is the advice he would give plainly to his disciples, such as composer Thomas de Hartmann. Gurdjieff was a perennial liquidator, an alchemist of worldly goods. One thinks of the Gnostic injunction: Become passersby. The prince takes the tip and finds himself among the wise, ready to welcome Gurdjieff and show him the ropes, and how to loosen them. The prince's speech is without doubt redolent of a paraphrase of the symbolism of the Masonic 3rd degree, wherein the aspirant must go to the bottom of the grave and be raised to conquer the King of Terrors (death) that takes all things away before the

Master Mason may advance beyond reason toward the very throne of Almighty God.

In Gurdjieff's Sarmoung narrative, Masonic intimations with Sufist coloring deepen. After "days" spent acclimatizing to the monastery, "one day we were called into the third court."[17] The reference to the third court seems plainly Masonic, for the third part of the Temple is related to the completion of the 3rd degree, the step beyond rational thought toward the throne of God (see I Kings 6:8). Indeed we may see the whole of Gurdjieff's account as an illustration of William Preston's famous definition of Masonry as, "a peculiar system of morality, veiled in allegory and illustrated by symbols." In the center of the third court is a building like a temple. The building of Solomon's Temple is of course a primary symbol of Freemasonry, and we might bear this in mind when we recall Gurdjieff's meeting Bogachevsky at the "Lord's temple" in Jerusalem, when Bogachevsky is an officer in the Essene order (Essenes have been compared many times in their practices to Freemasons, and therefore, not surprisingly, linked as to origin).

Gurdjieff next witnesses young priestesses come to hear the sacred music, to which when matured and perfected in movement, they will dance. As there are priestesses, this is plainly no Sufi or Islamic monastery, nor Orthodox Christian for that matter; it is an ideal, though the priestesses also invoke the symbol of the Graces, as well as the genii of the seven liberal arts (the proper study of the Fellow Craft Mason), and perhaps above all, the Nine Muses, with Terpsichore ("delight in dancing") as goddess of dance and chorus. And Gurdjieff is doubtless preenacting, as it were, his ideal institute. Indeed Gurdjieff notes, "the prince, well knowing my great and absorbing interest in the laws of movement of the human body and psyche"—to readers of *Meetings,* it's the first *we've* heard of it!

We are now introduced to Gurdjieff's fundamental insight concerning sacred dance: dance is a communications medium of profound harmonies and spiritual truths. He illustrates an odd term he invented for *Tales,* relating to sevenfold patterns in creation, the *heptaparaparshinokh.*

There are in the temple constructions for demonstrating "the alphabet of these postures," whose intention is that "the brethren may read in these dances one or another truth which men have placed there thousands of years before." This concept he has called "legominism" in *Tales;* the passage of truth through art and through time, the keys to which are esoteric.

When finally he sees the older priestesses performing the sacred dances with extraordinary precision, he is struck forcibly by their "automatized human manifestation . . . this purity of execution."[18] We might say it is paradoxically robotic, or put another way, like a fine Renaissance astronomical mechanism. Gurdjieff was always fascinated by automatic movement: automata in machines and unconscious movement in people, and he of course is himself the deus ex machina, or spiritual impresario.

Despite a date given to Soloviev's death, 1898—the date of the completion of the Kushka Line—we are soon back in unreality, and Gurdjieff's story of the crossing of the Gobi Desert, which follows the sojourn in the Sarmoung monastery, reads like a Jules Verne story that's drunk too much. We get no concrete details of travel but much allegory. Having worked for the "attainment of his individual perfection" (Knights of the 18th degree of Ancient & Accepted Masonry are "perfected"), Soloviev joins the "Seekers of Truth," which sounds like a cloud of Gnostic saints who have (almost) left this world, or simply a body of enthusiastic Masons embracing their guiding principles of brotherhood, love, and truth.[19]

Soloviev's death is by camel bite in the Gobi, a place where Gurdjieff's theme of pre-sand civilization is implied again, this time with the idea that the party could survive in the desert by living on sea shells, on the basis that what was now desert was once a seabed. The idea is interesting and scientifically valid, but *living on old dry shells*? Seven camels are loaded with the stuff in a story reminiscent of the seven basketsful of food left over from Christ's feeding of the five thousand. I think Gurdjieff is saying there is nourishment on the grand scale under the deserts when we come to grips with ancient conditions on Earth prevailing in prehistory. *This is not a lie,* as professional prospectors will tell you today, if you're lucky enough to meet one.

The daftest idea in this tale, however, is that they could avoid the worst of the sandstorms by making and mounting 60-foot stilts on which they could stride across the desert while winds bite below their knees. One might be forgiven for saying, stick to the dancing, professor!

It is of course unlikely that Gurdjieff would have welcomed this remark. Michael Benham brought to my attention the following exchange, recorded by Solita Solano (whom Gurdjieff nicknamed Kanari, or Canary) from a lunch of July 8, 1937, with Gurdjieff (G) and Elizabeth Gordon (Miss G), which casts some light on what Gurdjieff felt about his desert and stilts story:

G: I know of course a little but I not know canary *behind* like sparrow. Sparrow I know like myself.

Miss G: Yes, you used to paint them to resemble canaries. I always wondered if that was true or a fable like the ladder in the desert. Stilts in sand and ladder.

G: No, those stories true, only ten percent fantasy. That reminds me how I suffer when Soloviev dies. For three months I not myself. Such friend was—more than brother. I love him more than a mistress.

Anyhow, Soloviev is buried in the "heart of the desert" and Gurdjieff can leave the "accursed place"—though not for as long as he might have liked, it transpires.

In his 1924 apologia on institute financing, later titled "The Material Question," Gurdjieff established that he wanted students of his system to believe that there really was a "Community of Truth Seekers" who gathered for expeditions. It was not just a working fiction of *Meetings*; so would he have students, or rather donors, believe. He seemed to evoke a particular memory of members agreeing to assemble at Transcaspian Chardzhou (now Turkmenabat) on January 2, 1900, to sail up the

Amu-darya to the Pamir region and wild parts about India, though the *precise* purpose was not stated. However, before that occasion, presumably during 1899, he says he was alternating between his parents' home back in Alexandropol and Baku (now the capital of Azerbaijan), 200 kilometers southeast of Tiflis on the Caspian's west coast. He does not say he was in Baku for the oil industry, which was massive, but because there was a society there, mainly made up of Persians, who were studying ancient magic, and he had been a member of it for a long time. I should bet this "society for studying ancient magic" was a euphemism of some kind, though it might impress the impressionable as it stands.

It may have been a Masonic Lodge, for regular Freemasonry in Persia still had to wait just a few years before *official* establishment in 1906, affiliated with the French Grand Orient. In Russia, Freemasonry was still officially proscribed, but there was significant Persian interest in Freemasonry nonetheless, on account of diplomatic and mercantile contacts with India, England, France, Russia, and Turkey.

The earliest evidence of Persian contact with Freemasonry is found in the Indian memoirs *Tohfat al-'ālam,* written by merchant Mīr 'Abd-al-Laṭīf Šūštarī (died 1805), where Freemasonry is described as open to non-Europeans, irrespective of religion: "among the Indians and the Persian-speakers of India [it is known] as *farāmūšī* (forgetfulness), which is not inappropriate, given that their automatic answer to any question (concerning Freemasonry) is: 'I cannot remember.'" A Lodge was known in India and Persia as *farāmūš-kāna* (house of forgetfulness), as well as *jadu ghar* (magic house) in India. Enlightened Bukharan statesman, reformer, and writer Ahmad Dāneš (1826–1897), who worked for Bukhara's Amir Abdulahad (who ruled 1885–1910) also used the popular word *farāmūšī* for Freemasonry, and the word *farāmūš-kāna* to designate an initiate as well as a Lodge.[20] Devoted to science, poetry, and his country, Dāneš also ran a literary and musical salon in Bukhara. I can't help suspecting some kind of interior connection between Gurdjieff's mehkeness (or taking-away-of-responsibility) and the somewhat ironic euphemism farāmūšī (or forgetfulness) for Freemasonry.

Gurdjieff told his New York audience in 1924 that he was living in a caravanserai in Baku, short of money, when he spent much of what he had left on an old Edison phonograph, to which he added a few features. "Liquidating his affairs," he took the first boat 200 kilometers across the Caspian, to Krasnovodsk, where he got hold of a local Tekin street musician to record some favorite local songs on phonograph rolls. Guessing that phonograph rolls were fairly rare east of the Caspian, he went to the bazaar with his Edison phonograph and four ear tubes, set up a booth, and charged five kopecs a tube to listen to his traveling "jukebox." This may not have been his first killing with an Edison phonograph. According to *Meetings,* he'd used the contraption on another occasion, to spice up a boot-shining concession in Rome, and with equal profitability. There was never a spare tube, and Gurdjieff brought smiles to many faces, including his own; he'd have done well in the straight music industry, or even movies if he'd gotten in on the ground floor.

From Krasnovodsk, he went six stops, or about 300 kilometers, southeast up the Central Asian railway line to Kizil Arvat (now Serdar). Gurdjieff and his singing box were welcomed into the homes of wealthy Turkomans in nearby villages, where he earned much *tiangi* ("dough") and once even was given two excellent Tekin carpets. Next stop: Ashkhabad, another 300 kilometers up the line. On the train he says he met the fearless Vitvitskaia, who appears as a remarkable female character in *Meetings.* Vitvitskaia always wore men's clothes, but this was never explained—though it can be, easily: when Blavatskaia went to Egypt with Countess Kiselev, the countess asked her pretty companion to dress as a gentleman student. Madame Blavatsky also dressed as a man in India. Draw your own conclusions.

Vitvitskaia had been on expeditions to Asia, Africa, and even Australia and neighboring islands, so we are told. She was apparently part of the new breed of intrepid female explorers, or Gurdjieff's ideal of the type. Having free time, she had decided to go from Warsaw to Andijan to see a sister. Her husband, a representative of the Polish textile firm *Poznansky* (mentioned in *Meetings* as having a presence in Transcaspia, at a port on the river Amu-darya), must have been a man of rare understanding, or indifference. Vitvitskaia intended to rest at Andijan before assembling with the other "Seekers" at Chardzhou. At this point the narrative becomes peculiar. Gurdjieff and Vitvitskaia have a dispute and a wager, and Gurdjieff's original plan to go to Ashkhabad for phonographic profits seems forgotten. Anyhow, instead of going to Andijan, Vitvitskaia joins him at Ashkhabad.

At Ashkhabad, Gurdjieff makes a large advertisement: UNIVERSAL TRAVELING WORKSHOP, offering repairs to every kind of machine.[21] Obtaining permission from the police to distribute the ads, he rents a room at the town center. He might have recalled Craft instruction, perhaps, that "at the center of the circle the Master Mason cannot err" and avoided dividing himself between the two distinct parts of Ashkhabad: the one part Russian, the other Asiatic. He cannot help passing on the news that the "honesty of the local population was as yet unspoiled by contemporary civilization."[22] He lamented how Transcaspian journalism tended to blow up the glories of the West and its machines; everyone wanted to buy a machine from the West, even if they didn't know what it was strictly for, or what to do when it broke down. Like all upstarts, Gurdjieff says, they imitated anything "fashionable." This was all good profit for him, however. The new inventions invariably broke, and soon he was assailed, happily on the one hand, with all the trash of modern mechanized society. In short, "owing to their stupidity" (how unkind!), there were machines every-where![23] While he observed that ignorance and naïveté are open to advantage, he preferred to take advantage of the fool who had done worse to others. He chose to make a personal example of "a rich, fat Armenian." There was nothing wrong with the sewing machine the Armenian put his way for repair; the man just didn't understand how to operate it. Gurdjieff did and told him it might take three days, at the end of which Gurdjieff was twelve rubles and fifty kopecs better off, without having had to lift a finger.[24]

Next to fall under Gurdjieff's judgment were Russian officers: "Russian officers of that period never spoke to anyone except to give orders." One such imperious example of the breed visited him to ask how he fared with typewriters. "Long before this," Gurdjieff confides, "I had already become an old hand in the art of playing a role. So, assuming the expression called by real actors 'respectful timidity and bashful deference,' and employing special and pompous terms borrowed from various Russian technical works," Gurdjieff went to work on the Russian officer. Once he examined the offending new typewriter (just one of many, it turned out, suffering the same technical malady), Gurdjieff quickly assessed it was simply a matter of rewinding a spring attached to the ribbon mechanism. Any fool could do it, so Gurdjieff made any fool the butt of the joke and got one over on the Russian officer class without a prison sentence! Acting as angel of judgment, "beneath an expression of naïve innocence, I knew how to punish such insolent persons very venomously."[25] Eighteen rubles per typewriter! He was on a roll.

This is the point at which Gurdjieff let it become known that he had made a fortune from buying up cheap, from shops with unsellable stock, dozens and dozens of unfashionable corsets, so as to give employment to Vitvitskaia and two Jewish boys who, with minimal adjustment, extracted unwanted whalebone and, with a little deft cutting and sewing, produced a *mignon* corset of the latest Parisian design! Seeing them sold at a handsome profit, shopowners who'd initially unloaded their unwanted corsets on Gurdjieff's representative had to buy back the corsets, not at their sale price of ten or twenty kopecs but at three and a half rubles per corset. From the gusto with which he related his exploit, clearly this was one of the best moments of Gurdjieff's life.

After hitting Krasnovodsk, Kizil-Arvat, Ashkhabad, Merv, Chardzhou, Bukhara, Samarkand, and Tashkent with his corset scheme, he had the Central Asiatic Railway ladies' accoutrement scene sewn up: more than six thousand corsets sold! You could say his future was all in front of them. After only three and a half months of the corsetry workshop—a workshop, mind, that drew on the talents of the daughters of local worthies for experience—the poor boy from Alexandropol had made fifty thousand, yes, fifty thousand rubles, at a time when the average Russian public official with a family took home thirty-three rubles and thirty-three kopecs a month! One suspects that if Vitvitskaia existed, she must have had a great sense of humor, though with her predeliction for men's clothing, she had scant use for the product, though neither did Gurdjieff. The corsets represented something bigger than their contents. The huge profit was, Gurdjieff confessed proudly, "owing to my merciless attitude toward those weaknesses, present in me as in everyone, which through repetition, form in man what is called laziness." Here was a clear example of Jung's dictum that the greatest influence on the man Gurdjieff was *the life the father did not lead* (see page 28). It is odd, from the psychological perspective, that Gurdjieff observed in himself, during this period of manic buying, selling, and sewing, that he had enormous stores of energy and hardly needed any sleep at all. He was pure energy. Perhaps by overcoming the example of his father, he had somehow unblocked a psychic scotoma and liberated himself, receiving a requisite "shot in the arm" rather than his leg. For someone who regarded himself as a great psychologist, it is odd perhaps that Gurdjieff never seems to have made the connection.

He told his New York listeners that some day he intended to write a book about this and similar periods of what he calls the "commercial fiber" of his working life, but he never did. Pity.

Why didn't his followers get it? Gurdjieff was a businessman, a salesman; he had to have something to sell. He knew how to exploit a weakness, and to turn it into a power.

To take Gurdjieff's surviving writings at face value, there might appear to have been three different expeditions related to Chardzhou and the Amu-darya River. "The Material Question" offers the picture of the Community of Truth Seekers gathering at Chardzhou (Turkmenabat) on January 2, 1900, for a trip through the Pamir to India. The chapter of *Meetings* dedicated to Karpenko speaks of "one of these big expeditions, when we [Karpenko and Gurdjieff] were intending to cross the Himalayas from the Pamir region to India." [26] Then, in the chapter devoted to fictional archaeologist Professor Skridlov, we have a colorfully described expedition to the very remote region of Kafiristan (where the main action of Kipling's *The Man Who Would Be King* is set) that begins with Skridlov and Gurdjieff leaving the ruins of old Merv before catching the train to Chardzhou, where they set off up the river Amu-darya that farther east becomes the Pyandzh referred to in the Sarmoung monastery narrative. [27]

It is impossible to sort out elements of fact from weight of fiction in these narratives, except to say that the elements in common suggest there was possibly at least one expedition of some kind that left from Chardzhou for the Pamirs and Hindu Kush, and it may have begun in January 1900.

On the other hand, the entire body of narratives could be composites of other people's experiences, plus an engaging interest in maps. If one wished to go down this route, one might cite the preamble to the Karpenko account, where Gurdjieff makes an informed whine about the practical uselessness of "special military topographic maps of many countries" he has pored over. Due to their fanciful inaccuracies, he says it would be better if maps of uninhabited areas did not exist. While this may be true in certain cases (and Crowley said much the same thing in the same period of maps of the Karakorams in his *Confessions*), it would certainly leave the path open for pure imagination, as well as direct experience! [28] Gurdjieff seems to be saying, "Make your own map!" Of course one could use the quotation to suggest Gurdjieff had access to reserved military maps and was involved in surveying or spying for the army.

Indeed, at one point in the Karpenko tale, Gurdjieff describes map production undertaken by the Turkestan Military Topographic Department in a valley near the peak of a Turkmenistan mountain dedicated to Alexander III (Russia having seized Merv in 1884, the tsar promoted consolidation of the region until his death in 1894): "The chief surveyor was a certain colonel, a good friend of one of our traveling companions, and because of this we made a special visit to their camp." The staff officers "welcomed us with great joy."

Gurdjieff comes upon a military mission with a young officer and two soldiers involved in surveying. The officer interviews an old Kara-Kirghiz who provides information. Gurdjieff calls the officer a "rather good artist." Despite the artistry, he had nonetheless confused the local's words for *in front* with *behind* and had put the details given him in the wrong place! When the error was brought to the tired officer's attention, he cursed, "Oh, well, devil take it!" and slammed his sketchbook shut. [29] This does sound like an imaginative picture dreamed up to explain errors, but it might have happened.

Another possibility to explain aspects of Gurdjieff's narrative might have been to "trump the ace" of Helena and Nicholas Roerich's U.S.-funded and Soviet-backed expedition to Central Asia, which began in 1924, the year Gurdjieff was launched in New York by Orage. Mad keen theosophists, the Roerichs went in search of Shambhala and anything else they could gather of ancient spiritual civilization in the Himalayas. Gurdjieff may arguably have been at pains to show that he'd gotten there first. This might explain the rather sarcastic comment in *Meetings* where Gurdjieff cheekily seems to contrast his self-funded, modest but successful expedition in the company of Karpenko, with the grandiose, press-trumpeted, almost official progress embarked upon by the Roeriches: "Of course, for journeys undertaken on behalf of some government or other for a certain political aim, or on a journey for which large sums are disbursed by a banker's widow, an ardent Theosophist, one might hire as many porters as one wishes to pack and unpack everything." [30] The Roeriches' tortuous expedition, halted in its tracks, turned out to be little short of a disaster. The Roerichs never found Shambhala, but they did find how obstructive Chinese officialdom could be. We already know Gurdjieff's view of theosophy, and he probably knew of the Soviet secret service agenda involved in the Roeriches' expedition. Aleister Crowley also commented on the expedition in a satirical painting, *Four Red Monks Carrying a Black Goat across the Snow to Nowhere* (see my *Aleister Crowley: The Biography* for Crowley's relationship to the Roerich expedition).

Even if we put Gurdjieff's accounts together, what we really have is a spectacular geographical setting for a series of sermons, most of which present more questions than answers.

We begin on what has been called the "roof of the world." Among the world's highest, the Pamir Mountains form a kind of junction with the Himalayas and the Tian Shan, Karakoram, Kunlun, and Hindu Kush ranges. In the Karpenko expedition, the tough ascent of the northwestern slopes of the Himalayas proves fatal for one Baron X. "Ardent occultist" Baron X and his guide are killed in an avalanche. One suspects this offers Gurdjieff's view of occultists' value in real exploring, while the lesson encourages people to guide themselves from instinct rather than external authority.

We soon meet a remarkable man, a *fakhr,* which we are told, tongue-in-cheek, is Turkoman for "beggar." Clothed in rags, he is in fact (!) an "ez-ezounavouran" which seems to be a Gurdjieffianism for a "man who was working on himself for the salvation of his soul, or as Europeans would say, a fakir." We then have the usual swipe at European mentalities. Europeans misunderstand fakir: a *fakhr* takes from people by way of their religiosity; a *lourie,* on the other hand, takes advantage of their stupidity. *Lourie* means "gypsy." For conveying the meaning Europeans wrongly ascribe to *fakir,* Turkoman uses the word *ez-ezounavouran:* "he who beats himself." One feels Gurdjieff is pulling a leg. *Fakr* is Arabic for poverty, usually denoting a Sufi.[31]

The ez-ezounavouran is a gifted healer and heals Vitvitskaia's neck goiter. He is given an interesting past: once a *top-bashi* or chief of artillery for the Emir of Afghanistan, he returned to Khorasan (ancient Parthia including parts of Iran, Afghanistan, and Turkmenistan) after being wounded in a rising against Europeans.[32] He had joined a monastery of Persian dervishes near Kabul and had also been a Baptist.

Karpenko asks what kind of life could be lived if he lived it in accordance with the Above; what kind of life was worthy of the name "man"? Gurdjieff says he will put the old man's answer in a work titled, "The astral body of man, its needs and possibilities of manifestation according to law." Gurdjieff didn't, but Papus published *his* medical findings on the same subject after touring Europe and Russia in 1894–95 (his doctoral thesis was passed in 1894). Papus concluded there were three kinds of diseases: physical, astral (connected to vitality), and diseases of the mind.

Gurdjieff's closest companions all receive cures from the old man of their maladies without recourse to Western medicine. And this raises a possibility too, for at the time Russian experimental medicine was greatly interested in cures from the Himalayas, or secreted in remote cultures on the empire's fringes. It is possible Gurdjieff was researching such things, or since he didn't just say so, he was trying to imply he'd "been there and done that" already.

Just in case anyone should try to trace Karpenko, Gurdjieff conveniently tells us he was shot by natives from the riverbank and, severely wounded, died two years later in a town in central Russia. Most of Gurdjieff's fictional companions disappear in a similar manner. Professor Skridlov, for example, disappeared, *leaving no trace* "at the time of the great agitation of minds in Russia," a reference to the Revolution.[33]

Skridlov also is given a colorful past. They met, says Gurdjieff, when Gurdjieff was a "guide" in Cairo. Chance encounter led to a journey in pursuit of the Nile's source—somewhat *vieux jeu,* since John Hanning Speke had discovered it in 1859 (Lake Victoria). Gurdjieff says they shared an interest in antique rugs, certainly true of Gurdjieff. However, all this is by the by, since the Skridlov episodes are designed to show how parts of the psyche may be integrated to advantage. For example, on one expedition, Skridlov "reached a turning-point in his general inner psyche [and he] began to be activated not only by his thoughts, but also by his feelings and instinct."[34] The unity of three faculties is illustrated as instincts began to predominate or, as is said, "to take the initiative," giving us a formula: feeling + instinct = initiative.

Gurdjieff now says he wanted to go to Mecca "in the hope of penetrating into the secret heart of this religion" and finding answers to certain questions "I considered essential." This might also be considered *vieux jeu,* since Hanning Speke's sometime friend Sir Richard Burton had brought off the very rare feat of a non-Muslim on the Hajj, entering Mecca in 1853. Anyhow, Gurdjieff did not find what he sought: "I found nothing." What he was seeking, he says, he found rather in Bukhara, nicely situated on the Central Asiatic Railway, "where from the beginning the secret knowledge of Islam has been concentrated, this place being its very center and source."[35] Gurdjieff says he settled on Bukhara after making a point of acquainting himself with a group of Sarts returning from Hajj. It transpires Skridlov shares his fascination for Bukhara, intending to go there and the Samarkand region to solve an archaeological problem—all tall stories!

However, uppermost in the imaginary archaeologist's dream destinations was the remote region of Kafiristan in northeast Afghanistan, bordering on what is now the extreme west of Pakistan. Whether elements of this account were based on the alleged 1900 trip to the Pamir range and India is unknown, but there is something to be gained from aspects of the account as to Gurdjieff's beliefs, if nothing else.

Kafiristan (named after its population of polytheist *kafirs;* that is, nonbelievers) was renamed Nuristan ("Land of the Enlightened"), a province of Afghanistan, after many of its population were force-converted to Islam in the 1890s. That is to say, soon after Englishman Sir George Scott Robertson explored the country in 1895–96, Emir Abdur Rahman Khan invaded and converted the Kafirs, subjecting them to centralized Afghan government. Until Robertson's visit, it was regarded as quite impossible for a European to penetrate Kafiristan's remoteness. Obviously, such did not deter Gurdjieff, at least in his imagination.

Following Sir Richard Burton's example, Gurdjieff and Skridlov disguise themselves: Gurdjieff as a *Seid,* a direct descendant of the Prophet, and Skridlov as a Persian dervish. Gurdjieff says they trained for about a year, which seems quite absurd, learning Persian chants and growing their hair. They then get a train from old Merv (now "Mary") to Chardzhou in Turkmenistan, a flat-bottomed boat up the Amu-darya River (once known as the Oxus), and on to an appointment with destiny.

All the distances and times in the narrative now come in threes, so they approach Kerki (now Atamurat, Turkmenistan) "nine days" (3 × 3) out of Chardzhou—a journey of about 200 kilometers—while "on the third day" the boat runs aground. Then it is "already the third day the steamer has been stationary," when thirty-six (3 × 12) hours later, it runs aground again. One almost expects to read, "On the third day he rose again from the dead . . ." A well-described array of humanity share the boat, with all the classes finding their own company separately and harmoniously, including "an Armenian going to buy Kirghiz rugs on the spot," as well as fusiliers and sappers of the Transcaspian Regiment, on leave.[36] This all chimes in with the history. Baron Alexandr Gerngross (1851–1925), imperial Russian Army general, served in Turkestan from 1891 to 1897 with responsibility for land surveys for the Trans-Caspian Railway. Appointed commander of the Transcaspian Infantry Battalion in August 1897, Gerngross then commanded the border guards units of the Russian Ministry of Finance through 1901.

At Kerki, Gurdjieff and company must leave the boat for a *kobzir*, a kind of elaborate raft kept buoyant with inflated goatskins. This takes them about 160 kilometers to Termez, where there is a drama about a sack of money given to Gurdjieff and Skridlov by a Sart intended for someone else. This is honestly reported to the next Russian border post they come to; one wonders if General Gerngross got to hear about the mysterious, and quite possibly fictitious, sack of unearned tiangi. The moral of the story is obvious.

Gurdjieff and Skridlov leave the river by an unprepossessing Afghan fort at a place associated with Alexander the Great's attempted invasion of India and Oxus crossing. The place indicated may have been what is today Al Khanoum (or "Lady of the Moon"), though that is considerably farther up the river from Termez than Gurdjieff suggests. Many Hellenistic artifacts and archaeology have been found there, a place where the river seldom looks more than a gray bifurcating stream surrounded by panoramas of gray stony flats with high cliffs and escarpments above them that change color and shade with the sun's height: a Martian landscape with an unsettling atmosphere of infinity.

They then head south and soon come to a central settlement of the Afridis (a Karlani Pashtun tribe), in a region considered the heart of Kafiristan, the lost world of legends surrounding the coming of Alexander in 327 BCE. One of the legends concerned a fair-skinned European-looking race living high up in the Hindu Kush. In fact, such a people lived and live there today—the Kalash—but DNA testing fails to support any alleged descent from Alexander's Greek soldiers.

Gurdjieff leaves the Afridi settlement toward Chitral, now across the Afghan border in Pakistan, but in 1900 an area critical to British campaigning to secure India's Northwest Frontier—the famous Relief of Chitral had taken place in 1895: recent history. Gurdjieff says an old man approached him, a Greek speaker who addressed him in Greek. So much for the one year's effort at disguise—*to be recognized as Greek in Kafiristan!*

The next day another man "of a certain monastic order well known in central Asia" places a note in Gurdjieff's hand. It is in Greek: an invitation to the monastery. The old man, it transpires, is "self-freed" so "all men were respected there," all, that is, who strove toward the One God, Creator of all nations and races without distinction. Highly Masonic, one might think: the family of Man.

The old man was once a Christian missionary whose mother was a Greek, who on a mission to Afghanistan was captured by the Afridi while traveling through a "certain Pass" (the Khyber, surely!),[37] unless this be a Gurdjieffian pun, for in *Tales,* Beelzebub's word for time is *Heropass,* so the "certain pass" could be time; that is, the man (a hero?) has slipped through time. Then, one might suppose, the Greek "mother" was Alexander the Great's army's homeland, but this is all conjecture.

The man has the reputation of being an "impartial man." The word *impartial* is that given to the nature of Beelzebub's study of the human race. Gurdjieff must now, it seems, make contact with certain adepts of a "World Brotherhood," who live in their monastery. This should seem oddly familiar to fans of John Huston's 1975 movie of Kipling's 1888 novella *The Man Who Would Be King*, where Masonic symbols have overwhelming spiritual resonance for Kafiristanis who worship the mysterious (to them) Englishman. It seems such cross-fertilization has occurred in Gurdjieff's mind too.

The party is introduced to possibly the most profound figure in *Meetings*, Father Giovanni, an Italian who had served as a Catholic priest. *Giovanni* is of course the Italian for John, and John is one of the most revered names in ancient Masonry and gnostic traditions. The key date of Masonry has always been June 24, Saint John the Baptist's Day: midsummer, the time of the annual Masonic feast, when new Masters may be appointed.

Another minor observation: when Gurdjieff learns from the old man about the World Brotherhood, among whom all men who strive to honor the One God without distinction are respected, it takes place at what is called by Gurdjieff without explanation, an *askhana,* where they *eat lunch.* One notices a resonance with the Persian for Masonic Lodge: *farāmūš-ḵāna.* As mentioned earlier, the Turkish word for lodge is *tarikat,* from *tariqa,* the Sufi "path." The collective meal is masonically significant.

Giovanni offers to help them once; that is, they reveal their true aim and identity: this might strike one as asking for a password, as well as the Gurdjieffian stress on finding what one should aim for. The visitors enjoy free access to the monastery but for one building where the sheik lived, intended for those "who had attained preliminary liberation" (a degree attainment, or the usual Buddhist concept?).

Irrespective of religion "to which he had formerly belonged," anyone could enter the World Brotherhood. "All were united by God the Truth."[38] This is surely ideal Freemasonry presented as allegory, and one simply wonders why it has gone unremarked upon as such—but then there has been and still is so much prejudice about the Craft. Imagine if Freemasonry had only ever been discovered in the mountains of Kafiristan and nowhere else at all, practiced among an obscure, mysterious ethnicity; would not the world then have marveled at this "ancient" revelation wherein men of all faiths and nations can find true universal brotherhood? Would there not be students clamoring to associate with it, films, documentaries, and so on? Of course, it's a message you might well have to hide in an obscure mountain, for if many governments heard it, for the first time at least, it would be suppressed or taken over and distorted, only ever allowed to exist in its fullness in fiction! Perhaps this was Gurdjieff's point, for there is a cynicism in wisdom that is not cynical at all.

Skridlov is openmouthed at what he hears: "the possibility of transmuting faith in oneself"! How the world could do with even one ten-thousandth of "this all-penetrating faith" that now inspired him! Giovanni warns Skridlov that he doesn't understand the human psyche as well as he does archaeology: "Faith cannot be given to man." It is not from the senses. Understanding does not come from ordinary reason; it needs experience, knowledge from being. "Understanding is the essence obtained from information intentionally learned and from all kinds of experiences personally experienced." This sounds like Gurdjieff, of course, a bit clumsy compared to the inspiration he has poured into Giovanni's best lines. I should put it this way: *you cannot teach consciousness.* Gurdjieff says to give faith verbally "is like wishing to fill someone with bread merely by looking at him." So true: the despair of all true teaching. Knowledge that affects only the memory, and is not enlightened into understanding, is worse than useless. There is in the whole sequence the suggestion of a liberating gnosis, and that is why *Meetings* comes slowly to an end soon after this point. As if to say, *Now it's your turn.*

But before the dénouement, we meet Brothers Ahl and Sez whose task is to explain "various aspects of the essence of divinity." They tell us that the brotherhood has four monasteries: one in Kafiristan, one in Pamir, one in Tibet, and one in India. When brothers are in Kafiristan, "the soul of every one of us experiences pure heavenly pleasure and tenderness."[39]

There is more Gurdjieffian philosophy that adds up to the idea that one must have lived *with one's whole being.* Again Gurdjieff promises he's going to impart it in another book on the divine body of Man, but such never appeared. But then, he has already said that you cannot get people to understand by words. The truth is spoken all over the world, every day, but is it *lived?*

After the encounter, Gurdjieff and Skridlov part, with Gurdjieff returning to Tiflis and to Alexandropol to see his family. They meet again in 1916, so we are told, at the spa town of Piatigorsk in the north Caucasus. They converse for the last time on the summit of Mount Bechow while Gurdjieff is living in Essentuki. Skridlov says he's been suffering from panic attacks and cannot control his subconscious from getting in his way with bouts of hysteria. Every time he sees something that points toward his Maker, he weeps uncontrollably. Giovanni had rooted in him "a revaluation of all values."[40] Before he met Giovanni, all "manifestations and experiencings" flowed from his vanity. Meeting Giovanni "killed all this," and from then on there gradually arose in him that "something"—something "which has brought the whole of me to the unshakeable conviction that apart from the vanities of life, there exists a 'something else,' which must be the aim and ideal of every more or less thinking man, and only this makes him happy and gives real values, instead of illusory 'goods' with which in ordinary life he is always and in everything full."

Gurdjieff is saying that we need that "something." He needed it too; that's why he went looking for it.

TWELVE

Two More Bullets

Trying to find precisely what George Gurdjieff was up to between 1900 and his coming to Moscow in 1912 is only slightly less tricky than trying to piece together something true and coherent about his first twenty-three years, presuming he was born around 1877.

The original foreword to what he perhaps intended to be his last work, *Life Is Real Only Then, When "I Am,"* begun on November 6, 1934, promised his readers nothing less than "almost all of the previously unknown mysteries of the inner world of man which I have accidentally learned."[1] That is certainly not what we have. He stopped writing on April 2, 1935. It remains unfinished. Still, there exists sufficient information for a reasonably sized booklet, though nobody could tell from its contents that it was intended to deliver nearly all the unknown mysteries of the inner world of man.

From its pages emerges a strange narrative about, among other things, three stray bullets in the leg, the same bullets referred to earlier. The first bullet was allegedly fired in Crete and was the agent by which Gurdjieff was carried unconscious to Jerusalem; but what of the other two, dated 1902 and 1904?

TROUBLE IN TIBET

He says he was in the mountains of Tibet. It was a year before the brief Anglo-Tibetan war, when the British army, led by explorer Colonel Francis Younghusband (famous for traversing the Gobi Desert), demonstrated imperial government fear of a Tibetan rapprochement with Russia by entering Tibet in force to establish dominance with the deaths by rifle and Maxim gun of nearly a thousand Tibetan defenders on the road to the holy city of Lhasa. It was not one of imperial Britain's finest moments, but there were reasons, if not excuses, for it.

What was Gurdjieff doing—or not doing—in this political hot spot? There is a perennial story that he helped the Dalai Lama collect taxes from monasteries, though why the young spiritual leader of the Tibetan people might have called on the "Russian" Gurdjieff for such services might seem inexplicable—could he not trust his own?—unless the request came from an intermediary with close Russian connections, that is.

Gurdjieff has been much confused with Agvan (or Avang) Dorjiev (1853–1938), a Mongolian who served as trusted intermediary between the 13th Dalai Lama and the imperial Russian government, but no evidence has yet emerged to join this interesting figure directly and unequivocally to Gurdjieff. The British came to regard Dorjiev as a spy.

Was Gurdjieff seeking something: knowledge of Tibetan medicines perhaps?

According to *Life Is Real,* he was looking for danger.[2] As part of what Gurdjieff calls his research on the human psyche, he deliberately courted "sharp, energetic events" such as civil wars and revolutions to observe the extraordinary mental state of people engaged in conflict. He says he had sought conversation with various revolutionaries over the previous years, first in Italy, then in Switzerland—almost certainly referring to the Monte Verità ("Mountain of Truth") anarchist community at Ascona, founded in 1900—and "more recently" in Transcaucasia (the rise of Bolshevism and Armenian nationalism). Rather than let us conclude such activity suggests intelligence gathering or simply thirst for excitement, he says that from it all has arisen in him a new aim: "I must discover at all costs some manner or means for destroying in people the predilection for suggestibility which causes them to fall easily under the influence of mass hypnosis." *Ah!* So that's it; he wants to preserve people from being hypnotized and so prevent war—Good! The point—at last. Here is a man who could concur with American poet Jim Morrison's question: "Do you know we are ruled by TV?" Finally, perhaps, we have the point of the stray bullet narratives. They have made him wonder what makes people get so excited as to cast conscience aside and march to the beat of another's drum (convinced it's their own). The realization, if that's what it is, he relates to personal revelations he says struck him on the edge of the Gobi Desert, whither he was taken after being wounded in Tibet. He then jumps from the saving-people-from-mass-hypnosis realization to his decision to establish an institute to prepare "helper-instructors" to put into the lives of people what he had learned. Having decided on Russia as suitable locus, the *Life Is Real* narrative jumps to Moscow in 1912.

Very interesting, but it's still unclear how Tibet, before the British invasion, was a conflict situation, though politically there was tension, with acute wariness on the British side of Russian spies and provocateurs.

Perhaps there's a small clue to his activities in what he tells us about some of his company in the mountains of Tibet. After being shot by a stray bullet, he says three good European physicians and two "specialists in Tibetan medicine"[3] attended to him: all five, he says were "sincerely devoted" to him. Few travelers to Tibet can have had such fortuitous company in the event of accident. It seems churlish to deny the conclusion that this might well have been something of a medical expedition.

The conditions for such contact were propitious. The 13th Dalai Lama had acquired a skillful intermediary with imperial Russia in Avang Dorjiev (Nawang Lobsang Dorjee, also *Dorzhiev*), a Buryat monk who studied in Drepung monastery, became Tsanshab (debate partner) and Emissary of the 13th Dalai Lama to Czar Nicholas II, and built contacts between Lhasa and St. Petersburg, resulting in the first Tibetan Buddhist temple in Europe—the Kuntse Choeling Datsang, erected in St. Petersburg in 1909–1915, largely paid for by the Dalai Lama.

In fact, contacts between the imperial Russian court and Tibetan medicine went back to the 1850s when the Buddhist Buryat lama Sultim Badma (died 1873), rechristened Aleksandr Aleksandrovich Badmayev, arrived in St. Petersburg in 1857. Appointed to the Nikolayevsky military hospital, he was authorized to practice the three-humor-based herbal medicine the Southern Siberian Buryat doctors shared with Tibet. On his being baptized in 1861, Czar Alexander II became Badmayev's godfather. Badmayev established a Tibetan pharmacy—the first in Europe—on Suvorovsky Street in St. Petersburg, inviting his younger brother Zhamsaran to join him.

Rechristened Pyotr Aleksandrovich Badmayev, Zhamsaran became the leading advocate of Tibetan medicine in Russia, with a clinic on the Poklonnaya Hill just outside of St. Petersburg, publishing a translation in Russian of the first of the Four Tantras of the Knowledge of Healing (the *Gyushi*) in St. Petersburg in 1898. Blavatsky's cousin, Count Witte, Minister of Finance, was one of his patients.[4] The Buddhist-Tibetan angle chimed in with rising enthusiasm for mysticism: a reaction to materialist atheism and its catastrophic, revolutionary potential.

Badmayev had political ambitions for Russia involving the annexation of Tibet, Mongolia, and Manchuria. In 1895, Badmayev's agents, disguised as pilgrims, entered the Forbidden City of Lhasa and met up with Agvan Dorjiev, teacher to the child Lama (the 13th). For helping these agents, the czar gave Dorjiev a monogrammed watch in 1896. In 1898, a significant court figure supported by Witte, Prince Esper Esperovich Ukhtomskiy (1861–1921), orientalist, poet, and patron of Badmayev's medical "school," introduced Dorjiev to the czar, to whose inner circle Ukhtomskiy belonged, at the czar's summer residence at Limardia in the Crimea.[5] Publisher of his university teacher spiritual philosopher Vladimir Solovyov's works, and with political interests in equal rights for Molokans, Jews, and Armenians, as well as being inspired by theosophy, Prince Ukhtomskiy sounds as if he could have served as model for Gurdjieff's Prince Yuri Lubovedsky.* Like Gurdjieff, Ukhtomskiy was also a serious collector of Chinese and Tibetan art. From 1899 the prince attempted to organize a joint Russian-German expedition to the Turfan Oasis in Chinese Turkestan to dig for early Buddhist Graeco-Indian art. When he failed to inform the court, however, adversaries accused him of encouraging German spies into an area of Russian special interest. The significance of this oasis we shall see shortly.

Unfortunately, a second visit by Dorjiev to Russia in 1901 attracted too much public notice, suggesting Tibet might become a Russian protectorate; Britain was alarmed. The *Saint Peterburgskiye Vyedomosti* ("St. Petersburg Gazette"), edited by Prince Ukhtomskiy, tried damage limitation with a published disclaimer. What with the Kushka Line, and now *this,* the British had cause for dismay. Younghusband correctly perceived Dorjiev had been "worked" by Badmayev. The czar did not seriously entertain the protectorate idea, but when the British tried to contact the Dalai Lama and the Viceroy of India's communications were ignored, the path was set for Younghusband's invasion in the winter of 1903–4. Prince Ukhtomskiy would write a book on the Younghusband mission: *From the Land of Lamaism: On the English Campaign in Tibet.*

This is the historical setting in which one can place Gurdjieff's account. Russian "geographical expeditions" and the like were certainly used for intelligence purposes, and it would seem likely, if his account of the five medical practitioners with Tibetan specialities is true, that Gurdjieff was linked to such a fact-finding expedition, which by its nature was secret. The connection may have come about, as we shall see, as a result of Gurdjieff's meeting around this period with a Russian aristocrat, or "power-possessing person," as he calls such dignitaries in an effort to undignify them.

---

*Michael Benham strongly disagrees with the idea that Ukhtomskiy was Gurdjieff's model for Prince Lubovedsky "because in checking I have found Gurdjieff to be quite honest in naming his friends and companions" (Michael Benham, e-mail to author, October 5, 2016).

Given the covert nature of the operations and the need to keep them "tight," probability suggests that if Gurdjieff participated in such a medicine-fronted fact-finding initiative, then he probably knew, or knew of, Dorjiev and Badmayev. Such connections and others we shall consider in the next chapter may have significantly affected his closer connections with old Russia and burgeoning Russian esotericism that led to his decision to base himself there in 1911–12. It may be significant that when observed by British intelligence officer John Godolphin Bennett in 1920–21 in Constantinople, Gurdjieff was identified, or confused, with Dorjiev, though they looked in no wise alike, although their names (if we pronounce Gurdjieff as he did himself: *Gyorjeff*) might be confused. More likely, it was their connections that provided meat for suspicion.

There is a curious little section of *Tales* where Gurdjieff somehow blames the Anglo-Tibetan war for knocking on the head the possibility that what he calls the "fifth teaching," that is, religious teaching, promoted by "Saint Lama," though much corrupted by time, could bring enlightenment to the world. Beelzebub says he knows this because he "happened by chance to be an eyewitness of all those lamentable events there."[6] He says "by chance" which only adds to the murk. Further into *Tales,* Beelzebub explains that Saint Lama's contemporary pupil, chief of the seven enlightened beings who came to advise the Tibetan government not to kill the invaders, and a saint-to-be himself with a destiny of global spiritual importance, was yet killed by a "stray bullet" when trying to warn the people of the decision not to kill: a disaster, says Beelzebub, for the "nearly perfected" remaining six, disoriented without their predestined leader. The Anglo-Tibetan war is presented as a bunch of blind people blundering into a spiritual (or arguably, diplomatic) process they did not understand, and which blindness served only to wreck. After this, nothing Gurdjieff tells us adds to any sense of historical reality concerning his presence there, though it is certainly odd to see a repeat of the ubiquitous stray bullet hitting a key, if possibly imaginary, spiritual figure. It is all most disconcerting for anyone interested in establishing what really might have taken place regarding Gurdjieff.[7]

Gurdjieff says in *Life Is Real* that *his* bullet wound was followed by three to four months of unconscious life, then a year of "physical tenseness and unusual psychic contrivance," whatever that might mean.[8] The narrative concerning the Tibet wound only picks up—and then oddly—*after* his account of the next bullet, suffered in the Caucasus at the end of 1904, whose subsequent events reunited him, he says, with the place where he recuperated from the *previous* stray bullet, which struck him in Tibet! Little is ever straightforward in Gurdjieffland!

The story picks up, bizarrely, with him now recuperating on the edge of the Gobi Desert near the city of Yanghissar (Xinjiang province) in Chinese Turkestan, where the air is unlike anything on Earth, he tells us, from a place that is neither heaven nor hell but something of unmatchable purity between them.

A problem here is that Yengisar (as it is now called) is a good 800 kilometers west from the Gobi Desert's edge. Strangely perhaps, Turfan Oasis, where Dorjiev's patron Prince Ukhtomskiy wished to excavate, is considerably closer to where Gurdjieff says he recovered, on the straight line northeast from Yangisar to the Gobi. We may recall Gurdjieff's claims to cattle droving in the region.

Gurdjieff says the five physicians left him when he returned to consciousness, being left with one Tibetan and a very young Kara-Kirghiz for company. We then find ourselves in similar territory to the Karpenko version of the Pamir and India expedition, even down to details. He thinks he will leave with the Kara-Khirgiz's camels for one of the valleys near the peak of Mount Alexander III. Gurdjieff says he had "information" that he could find military topographers of the Turkestan Topographical Administration "among whom was one of my very good friends."[9] He first intended to go with them (in what capacity?) before joining a large caravan to Andijan (where Vitvitskaia was heading when he met her in "The Material Question" before she was to join the "Seekers" at Chardzhou in January 1900), whence he intended to return by train to his relations in the Transcaucasus.

Having in the previous six weeks fully recovered, he starts to think, at night with the full moon out. The thinking becomes intense. He realizes his past errors and sees how he should have dealt with every case. It becomes too much, and he almost passes out.

He then recalls the passages of his thoughts. He has attained powers unlike any man of his epoch, perhaps greater than any man ever. He had powers of concentration such that, with a few hours' preparation, he could kill a yak at 10 miles distance, or in twenty-four hours accumulate forces to put an elephant to sleep in five minutes. And yet, for all that, he could not "remember himself" at a given moment, to actually be his real self, and not be influenced by his nature or circumstances. Driven by appetites, he could not "re-collect" his being and manifest it at will.

He decides he needs a regulating factor to keep himself "awake," centered on his real being. He can't understand why this had never occurred to him before. But he *should* have been able, for he was born in the image of God, and God is everywhere, and in him everything is connected. *Then he too must have within himself all the possibilities and impossibilities God has.* Between him and "self" may only be a difference in scale. He is God of the outer world and of his world, and like him, Gurdjieff suddenly sees *he too* is God of his inner world: "He is God and I am God!"[10] This seems like the kind of personal revelation that got Sufi saint Al-Hallaj crucified in 922 CE in Baghdad when he declared *"ana'l-Haqq"*—"I am the Truth!"

Breathless, Gurdjieff's inner monologue continues. God's relationship to the universe should be mirrored in *his,* and in his power to subordinate things below him to his will. *Why had he not seen this before?* We may well ask; it is basic Gnostic doctrine for the liberated and truly enlightened, for only such a person can deal with the implications on any realistic level of what he is saying, for the words themselves just make fools drunk and unbalanced persons mad.

Everything tells him, Gurdjieff, that God represents absolute goodness, all-loving, all-forgiving. How, why, should such a One send away from himself one of his nearest, for no more than the pride of youth, unformed: the "Devil"? Gurdjieff appears to imply here that what has been called the Devil is a living aspect of the unfolding divine cosmic economy, and, like the Peacock Angel of the Yezidis, the proud one, whose spirit is so evident in Man, serves God's archangelic purposes on Earth.

Gurdjieff realizes he needs a "reminding factor." This, he sees, was what made God put one of his beloved sons in such an invidious situation. It was part of God's self-realization. Therefore, Gurdjieff decides he too must, even in his own small inner world, create a beloved factor from out of himself: an unending source. How could he produce something out of himself that would remind him of the essential? He concludes that he must willingly *cease to use the power he owns:* the power of telepathy and hypnotism, or as he calls it "hanbledzoin" (goodness knows why). This power, he says, has for the previous two years been "spoiled and depraved" by himself—something of a confession. To deprive himself of it, to deprive himself of using its power to satisfy "most of my vices," to live with others always conscious of what he has forsaken, *this* will remind him of himself.[11]

He will, as it were, be giving his only begotten son—the Godlike power he has developed within him—to be a ransom for many; he will thereby willingly become vulnerable and serve. What Gurdjieff is here proposing is a highly idiosyncratic and spiritually peculiar form of kenotic Christian mysticism—emptying himself—but then it could also be Sufic mysticism, or something quite universal, depending on where you position yourself.

Gurdjieff says he made an oath, an oath so liberating he got up and ran around the spring like a young calf. The oath nonetheless reserved the use of his powers for "scientific purposes" such as viewing distant cosmic centers through the use of a medium or the cure of cancer "by suggestion." All this happened about two years prior to his return to the same place, on the edge of the Gobi Desert, between vegetation and divine sparseness. By the second sojourn, he was free, he felt, of the "automatic influences" of other people in his mentation. He had dedicated himself up to that time, he said, to understanding the purpose and significance of man. Now he had the new aim—to free man from being hypnotized into insane actions of loveless barbarism or simply inane, life-wasting stupidity. This set him on the road that would eventually lead to Moscow in 1912 or 1913.

But how had he come to be at that curious spot of self-revelation again?

This is the story of the third bullet.

THE CHIATURA TUNNEL

Toward the end of 1904, while Aleister Crowley wondered what to do about *his* personal revelation that came to him as the famous *Book of the Law* in a rented apartment in Cairo in the April of that year, Gurdjieff says he was near the Chiatura Tunnel in the Caucasus when another stray bullet hit him in the leg. What was he doing at the Chiatura Tunnel? The setting is reminiscent of the Ekim Bey story in *Meetings* where Gurdjieff climbs at the Suram Pass where the Sruamski Tunnel was engineered to hasten the passage of oil from Baku to the Black Sea. In fact, Chiatura is about 40 kilometers north of the Suram Pass, though the terrain is similar: sharp crags, exposed mountains and deep misty ravines. More particularly, it is about 60 kilometers northwest of Gori, birthplace of Josef Stalin. The Gourians, or rebels of Gori, were at the time up in revolutionary arms, asserting independence against encroaching imperial power that trampled on workers' claims to fair wages and conditions. This conflict was one of several that presaged the general emergency of 1905 when Czar Nicholas II approved violent countermeasures to prevent revolution.

The tumult at the tunnel was probably connected to the Chiatura mines, mines that produced more than half the world's manganese supply. Thirty-seven hundred miners worked eighteen-hour shifts in the mines, where they slept, without baths, ever black with carbon. German company Krupps was, at the time, a major investor in mining operations, so it is likely Gurdjieff's revolt was linked to destabilizing industrial unrest and repressive countermeasures to encourage foreign investment. A year later, in 1905, Chiatura would be the only Bolshevik stronghold in mostly Menshevik Georgia. Stalin whipped up the miners, establishing a print press, protection racket, and "red battle squads." Mines that refused to pay up were destroyed; miners were armed. Clearly, late 1904 marked the buildup to the excesses of 1905. And Gurdjieff placed himself there, in the thick of it.

Gurdjieff presents himself caught between the Cossacks, supporting the czar, and the Gourians. What this actually meant is impossible to say. Conjecture might mislead, but as events unfolded, and even from Gurdjieff's own testimony, it's clear something fishy was going on. Nevertheless, Gurdjieff insists the bullet that struck him was a stray. Who would want to shoot Gurdjieff, a man of good intentions? We might well ask.

Were the Gourians trying to sabotage the tunnel, or blockade it, or picket it?

Wounded, Gurdjieff says he was put on a donkey and carried to a mountain cave.[12] A barber-physician returned with two Khevsurs, those extraordinary chain mailed local mountain warriors we met previously in the Ekim Bey story. Weak, a young Khevsur cared for him. After a while Gurdjieff could get about with a stick and visited a "secret meeting" of the Khevsurs. This may have been revolutionary, or it may have been a reference to secret rites Khevsurs have held at places sacred to them in the mountains.

Gurdjieff says he fled from people under a "revolutionary psychosis." While nonvindictive, this gives an impression of what he thought of the Bolsheviks, and history surely proves the wisdom of the assessment, even though it may not of course have been his opinion at the time. Besides, he is really evenhanded, since fleeing from the area he recognizes he was at risk not only from the "revolutionary psychosis" but also from "national psychosis," presumably the Cossacks. The psychosis simply means people were prevented from independent action and thought by something alien that had them in its grip. Put more brusquely—they were all mad! He had to get out fast.

He says that taking into consideration his "prospects for the future"—the familiar strain of Gurdjieffian irony—that is to say, his chances of getting out alive, he decided on Transcaucasia, though still at risk of capture by one or another faction or persons unknown. He endured "incredible physical sufferings," finding it hard to maintain an ordinary demeanor. As nationalism increased among Armenians and Tartars, his "universal appearance" meant that either side could see him as their enemy if suspicion and paranoia were abroad.

To escape the heat he headed east with a friend who had assisted his recovery, to Transcaspian Ashkhabad. Then his friend disappeared. He went to the city center hoping to meet "someone of my acquaintance." He had, after all, according to the "Material Question," done unforgettable corset business in that place and would have been known to quite a number of the city's inhabitants.

Then he saw a tall man with a long beard in European clothing passing by a *chaikhana* (or teahouse). Speaking Armenian, the man calls him: "Ah! Black Devil!" Gurdjieff recognized the man at once: a distant relative, a former police court interpreter exiled for making love to the chief of police's paramour. The man knew something of Gurdjieff's plight. The missing man, he told Gurdjieff, was not arrested "seriously," but there were "dangerous revolutionaries everywhere." And what's more, Gurdjieff's name was on a list of disturbers of the peace. Did Gurdjieff have a reputation as an unpredictable oddball? He decided to exit as soon as possible, despite lack of funds.

Gurdjieff says he headed east again. If so, he would surely have taken the Central Asiatic Railway to Andijan and the border territory with Xinjiang province, China. From the railway, he got to Yanghissar in Chinese Turkestan, where the story turns full circle again. There he says he was cared for by "old friends of mine" and found again the place where he had recovered from the second bullet, the one suffered in

Tibet, the one he said in *Life Is Real* had led to a veritable rebirth and an oath to dedicate his powers only to the benefit of knowledge that would help the human race.

The implication of all this is that Gurdjieff wants us to believe he could somehow see what was coming—the three bullets indicate three fundamental conflicts—and believed it incumbent upon him to bring to people's attention their own power to see the unconscious *play* of mankind (in which people *thought* they were conscious) for what it was, and to wake up in, and from it, to wash away the common dream that piled into nightmares, and to save themselves through profound self-knowledge and self-awakening.

The question, as ever, was *how*.

THIRTEEN

Holy Mother Russia!

There are numerous references to Gurdjieff being in the vicinity of the Pyramids in *Meetings*. His tasks there range from working as a guide around ancient sites, on account of vaunted language skills—Arabic, Greek, and Italian—to assisting with Skridlov's search for the Nile's source and other archaeological matters, through to personally investigating the meaning of the Sphinx. In this connection, Gurdjieff's supposed copy of a map of "pre-sand Egypt," allegedly taken from an original left by a prince in the possession of an Armenian priest, plays a part. Now that it has been discovered by geological examinations of parts of the Sphinx's base at Gizeh that its stone blocks have experienced exceedingly long historical periods of wet weather, observers naturally wonder whether Gurdjieff's pre-sand Egypt might provide the clue to an ancient civilization considerably older than the established periods of Egyptian dynasties (pre-3500 BCE), of which the body, if not the existing head, of the Sphinx, might be a surviving monument. The Sphinx never fails to offer a riddle, and it clearly intrigued Gurdjieff.

None of the Egypt stories can be dated with any degree of meaningful accuracy, since they could all be fabrications for his various interweaving plots. Nothing in them shows real intimacy with the country, but one might be inclined to give Gurdjieff the benefit of the doubt that he was there at least once for some purpose or other, partly on account of the repetition, but more particularly because there is a story in *Tales* that might match him up with a historical, rather than fictional, personage.

Meetings assures us that the pyramids were the location for his first encounter with the passionate, seeking spirit he calls Prince Yuri Lubovedsky, who was "drawn to the study of the occult sciences."[1] One might from this wonder, as suggested in the previous chapter, whether the prince at the pyramids was inspired by Prince Esper Ukhtomskiy, who visited the pyramids with His Royal Highness Nikolai, heir to the Russian throne, in 1890, and who included a color map of Egypt in the second volume of his popular account of that extensive oriental tour.

However, a curiously similar account of meeting a prince to that of *Meetings* occurs in *Tales,* where in chapter 34, devoted to Russia, Beelzebub finds himself walking by the pyramids one morning when an elderly gentleman addresses him out of the blue, not as "Black Devil," but as "Doctor."[2] Beelzebub finds the old boy's "vibrations" sympathetic and his conversation agreeable. The gentleman is an "important power-possessing being," a conceit of Gurdjieff's for an aristocrat, whom he wishes to reduce to objective sociological, even experimental status—Beelzebub being effectively Gurdjieff's superego or psychic power-being, before whom all terrestrial life is reduced.

Conversation turns to the vices of Russians, and the elderly fellow acquaints Beelzebub with the sad facts of mass alcoholism in his native land, a vice that has reached such uncommon proportions that his compatriots have appointed him head of "The Trusteeship of People's Temperance." The man requests Dr. Beelzebub, whose reputation for knowledge of the psychological aspect of addiction has reached him, to assist the trust in St. Petersburg. This suits Beelzebub's plans, he says, for he wants to clear up all the details regarding the nature of the psyche of groups and individuals, and Russia seems a good place to accomplish that, while serving the common good at the same time.

A detail in *Tales* enables us to connect the narrative with historical fact and a historical personage. Arriving in St. Petersburg, Beelzebub endures such a rotten time, with every kind of harassment frustrating his plans to assemble a chemical laboratory, that he decides to leave. Patrician Russians are grieved to hear of it, and try to persuade him otherwise. On the eve of quitting, Beelzebub is requested by "the important Russian" to stay until after the czar has dedicated the great building designed as a vanguard against alcoholism: "The People's Building of the Emperor Nicholas II."[3]

On December 9, 1900, a *New York Times* article was headlined, "St. Petersburg New 'Palace of the People'; Immense Building for the Masses to be Opened Dec. 19. Dining Room to Seat 2,000. Concert Hall, Opera House, and Other Attractions—The Work of the Committee of Temperance." "His Royal Highness the Prince Oldenbourg [*sic*]" is named as the St. Petersburg Committee of Temperance's chairman. The actual opening by Prince Oldenburgsky on December 25 was reported on page 1 of the *New York Tribune* the next day as follows:

The Prince of Oldenbourg, president of the Government Temperance Committee, at noon to-day declared the People's Palace open to the public. After the inaugural ceremonies the Prince and twenty of the higher army officers, including the commanding generals, along with high officials, noblemen and ladies, dined side by side with peasants and the families of workingmen.

Gurdjieff was one of those invited to the event (hardly a social distinction in itself) and was subsequently granted an audience with the czar. Gurdjieff described the rather awkward occasion in *Tales.** According to Benham, omitted from the published version of *Tales,* but present in an early draft, was Gurdjieff's statement that the "power-possessing being" (Prince Oldenburgsky?) had heard of him and had been trying to meet him.

A *New York Times* article of October 2, 1904, noted that

---

*Royal Court events were also published in the *Saint Petersburg Gazette,* edited by Prince Ukhtomskiy. Michael Benham has asked several Russians to check for the announcement in that paper but to date has had no response (e-mail to author, October 5, 2016).

Prince Oldenburgsky, the czar's brother-in-law, was concerned with unusual new medical treatments.[4] That the prince was involved with experimental medicine as well as temperance should come as no surprise. Military hero of the 1877–78 Russo-Turkish war, Prince Alexander Petrovich Oldenburgsky (1844–1932) had with his own money founded the Imperial Institute of Experimental Medicine, approved by Czar Alexander III in November 1888 and opened on Aptekarsky Island on December 8, 1890. The institute is mentioned by Gurdjieff in "The Problem of Old Age" in his third series (*Life Is Real*). Oldenburgsky's motto was, "The right man in the right place." Was Gurdjieff the right man? The institute was attached to the Nurse Community of Saint Trinity, of which the prince was also a trustee, just one of several charitable enterprises the prince concerned himself with. In 1897 he chaired the Antiplague Committee, while his experimental medicine institute worked on the latest bacteriology in an effort to cure cholera.

Oldenburgsky seems to be the inspiration behind Gurdjieff's aristocrat in *Tales,* if not the Yuri Lubovedsky character of *Meetings.* In *Tales* he appears to be behind an auspicious, though risibly orchestrated, "interview" between the czar and Gurdjieff/Beelzebub: a cramped, awkward occasion, very different from Dorjiev's relatively grand reception. Inconclusive the brief encounter may have been, but immediately after it, Beelzebub's problems with state bureaucracy regarding his laboratory suddenly evaporate.[5] Despite this, Gurdjieff, with justified chip on shoulder perhaps, is still aggrieved by a racist adjutant described as a "Mama's darling" who considered Gurdjieff a savage, his not being Russian and somewhat Asiatic in appearance (this must truly have cut).[6] Indeed, the grievance must have gone deep because, laboratory or no, Beelzebub decides to leave St. Petersburg after his unforgettable "supreme presentation" to the czar, whose humanity Gurdjieff saw all too clearly, to head for Europe and other continents. Beelzebub says he returned to Russia many times, but "for other affairs," after which he would observe the utter destruction by Bolshevism of everything positive attained in those years.[7]

Two other details are worth mentioning with respect to Duke

Alexander Petrovich of Oldenburg. After the Russo-Turkish war, he was instrumental in constructing and developing a high-class spa resort at Gagra, on Georgia's north Black Sea coast, where he built a palace and tropical park. It is always possible that this is where Gurdjieff, whose career shows a fondness for spa towns, especially in Georgia and around Essentuki, may possibly have encountered the prince—though he never mentions the place—rather than the arguably more romantic setting of Egypt.

While the czar and his family were reduced to soldiers' rations in revolutionary captivity in autumn 1917, Oldenburgsky emigrated to France, where he lived at Biarritz until his death. Gurdjieff visited Biarritz in July 1926, an occasion marked by Orage's wife accusing Gurdjieff of having poisoned her husband with bad caviar. One wonders about the real purpose of the visit. Perhaps it was merely pleasant relief; perhaps Gurdjieff had another agenda, as he so often did.

PAPUS IN RUSSIA

It might seem that for Gurdjieff a move to St. Petersburg in late 1900 was premature, but for another esotericist, the period proved beneficial, at least in the short term, and looking briefly at the contrasting experience of Dr. Gérard Encausse (Papus) will help us to picture the developing esoteric milieu in Russia in the first decade of the twentieth century.

After organizing Paris's Spiritist & Spiritualist Congress of 1889, Papus proceeded to establish his Independent Group for Esoteric Studies, whose aims involved gathering all data of occult science, educating members to a high level, training lecturers in all branches of the occult, and studying spiritism, magnetism, and magic in theory and practice. Papus formed an umbrella environment for all esoteric interests, gathering able men to take responsibility for the various branches while reaching out with an effective marketing program. Above all, perhaps, he revived a French Martinist Order. It was perhaps this that put him to thinking seriously about relations with Russia, an environment he felt drawn to.

Between 1802 and 1816, French counterrevolutionary and counter-rationalist philosopher Joseph de Maistre (1753–1821) was in St. Petersburg, where he wrote *Soirées de St. Petersbourg* ("The St. Petersburg Dialogues"), a theodicy on the role of the mystery of innocent sacrifice in bringing men to God through the historical process. Papus was aware Joseph de Maistre reestablished St. Petersburg as a Martinist center. Its influence still resonated a century later. In 1900 the Grand Duke Nicholas, a Martinist affiliate, presented Papus to his nephew Czar Nicholas II. The last czar of Russia was also, like his forbear Alexander I, initiated into Martinism. Séances were part of Martinist life.

Papus had done much to prepare the ground before that. Between August 13 and 21, 1892, Papus and his colleagues organized a Franco-Russian festival with a grand tombola at the Tuileries Gardens for the benefit of Russian victims of poverty and cholera, as well as poverty-stricken French people. On the tombola committee sat Mademoiselle A. de Wolska; Papus; his publisher Chamuel; Mr. Karin-Karinski, Russian captain of artillery; Monsieur Leonard of the journal *La Vie Russe* of St. Petersburg; and Serbian artist, art critic, and travel writer Prince Bojidar Karageorgewitch (1862–1908) of *La Revue de Paris*.

L'Initiation's opening pages for October 1896 were dedicated to Papus's "Message from French Spiritualists" addressed to "A.S.M.I. Nicolas II, Emperor of Russia," who had just arrived in Paris for a state visit.

> Above all the political discussions, outside all religious communion (although we respect all), we pursue, silently and unknown, our researches whose aim is to illuminate Science by Faith, and it is from regenerated science that we demand positive proofs of the existence of God and the immortality of the human soul. . . .
>
> Now the great secret law of history has been revealed by one of our masters, Fabre d'Olivet, in his "Philosophical History of the

Human Species," and developed by another of our masters, Saint-Yves d'Alveydre, in his "Missions." This law, known to Egyptian initiates 1600 years before our era, teaches us that three grand Principles direct the march of all events; these being: divine Providence, Will, and Destiny. . . .

The Empire which takes as its line of conduct the maxim "Force permits the right" banishes by this act all Providential influence, dedicates itself to destiny, demanding of terror, force, and all the diplomatic ruses the respect due to God alone before it all shortly comes crashing down, devoured by its own errors. . . .

That Your Majesty deigns to receive with benevolence our Salute and that She [Benevolent Will] immortalize his Empire by total union with divine Providence; such is the dearest wish of those who beg Your Majesty to accept the homage of their most profound respect.

GÉRARD ENCAUSSE (PAPUS)[8]

The April 1900 issue of *l'Initiation* opens with an account of Papus's trip to St. Petersburg recently undertaken: "During a stay of some weeks in St. Petersburg among good friends whose cordial reception still enchants our memories, we were led to study a medium whose experiences suggested to us several reflections that could interest our readers. This medium, *Sambor* by name [meaning "lonely warrior"], is a man still young, of nervous temperament, lymphatic, blond, and who has already produced excellent séances."[9] The account goes on to describe Sambor's feats, such as escaping from heavy metal bonds without apparent effort, producing a child's disembodied voice, raising objects with a phosphorescent glow and transporting them to other rooms, and self-levitation. Papus does not tell his readers who his very cordial friends were or what he was actually doing in Russia other than witnessing spiritist séances.

Sambor is interesting because it is almost certain Gurdjieff would have known of him or had something to do with him. We should recall his statement that he made it his business to make contact with all sizable organizations involved with theosophy and spiritualism in the

1900s and was himself called upon to demonstrate manifestations from beyond this world.

Russian telegraph operator Stephan Fomitch "Sambor" (died 1902) was promoted as a powerful materialization and telekinesis medium. Russian journal *Rebus* reported a series of sittings with him between 1896 and 1902. Count Perovsky-Petrovo-Solovovo (1868–1954) of the British Psychical Research Society investigated Sambor and discovered fraudulence in his methods. We might be the wiser had he investigated Gurdjieff's claims, but nobody but Gurdjieff seems to have recorded his spiritist feats. Gurdjieff would long after claim his operations supported the cause of science, that he was as committed to exposing fraud as was the count. Curiously, Solovovo was quite impressed by Sambor until an accomplice supposed to be holding Sambor's hand intentionally released it.[10] Gurdjieff, as we have seen, pointed out tricks connected to positioning of hands in séances; he of course should have known!

Papus was clearly taken in, though it should be stated that the count could not prove all of Sambor's marvels were explicable by fraud. It is of course possible that Gurdjieff was clever enough to see the direction the tide was going in terms of credibility, and perhaps realized there might be a limited future in spiritist phenomena and he might need more strings for his bow. With so much obscurity surrounding Gurdjieff's actual activities, it is impossible to say. I do not see any reason, given the nature of his printed accounts and his own admissions, for automatically giving Gurdjieff the benefit of the doubt. He seems to have been perpetually faced with contrary drives, as we all are.

Having established Martinist lodges in Russia in 1897, and a Martinist Order there in 1899, Papus introduced to the imperial couple, Nicholas and Alexandra, his spiritual master Monsieur Philippe, a simple man and effective healer-by-prayer from Lyon. At Philippe's first interview with the couple at Compiègne, 50 kilometers northeast of Paris, in 1901, the saintly healer made an unforgettable impression. According to Jean-François Var, "Up until his death, in spite of intrigues and cabals, he was treated as a friend and *confidant* by Nicolas and Alexandra, to whom he had predicted the birth of the much-desired male heir [Alexei Nikolaevich, born August 12, 1904]."[11]

According to leading French Martinist and colleague of Papus, Victor-Émile Michelet, "Nothing was decided by Nicolas II and his wife in Russian politics without Philippe's assent."[12] Foolish opponents said Philippe obtained his all-powerful influence by necromancy or vulgar spiritism. Michelet encapsulates Philippe's power over the sovereigns, "A lady of the imperial court having said, joyfully, to the czarina 'I saw Monsieur Philippe' received the reply from the imperiatrix, 'One does not see Monsieur Philippe, he is pure spirit!'"[13]

Papus visited Russia again in October 1905. France's ambassador to Russia, Maurice Paléologue (1859–1944) has left us this anecdote in his *Mémoirs*. After he arrived in St. Petersburg, powerful figures sought Papus's advice regarding the formidable crisis facing Russia: riots and general strikes were spreading across Moscow and the country at large. He was immediately summoned to Tsarskoye Selo, and a brief conversation with the emperor and empress was followed the next day by Papus's organizing an elaborate séance, or demonstration of necromancy. Besides the sovereigns, His Majesty's aide de camp, Captain Mandhyka, afterward on the General Staff and governor of Tiflis, also attended the secret liturgy. By "intense condensation of will, or prodigious exaltation of his fluidic dynamism," the spiritual master Papus managed to evoke the ghost of the very pious Czar Alexander III; unmistakable signs, said Paléologue, attested his presence. Despite the anguish gripping his heart, Nicholas calmly asked his father whether or not he should react against the current of Liberalism that threatened Russia. The ghost replied, "You must, at all costs, crush the revolution that has begun; but it will be reborn one day, and will be even so much more violent that you'll wish the repression of today had been more rigorous. No matter! Courage my son! Do not stop fighting!" While the amazed sovereign absorbed this overwhelming prediction, Papus claimed he could use his magical powers to conjure an avoidance of the predicted disaster, but the conjuration would only be effective so long as he existed on the physical plane. Then, solemnly, he performed the required rites. Papus would die on October 25, 1916, and the protection ended. Within a year . . .

The French government's concern that Papus was a loose cannon was matched by the Orthodox Church's concern over Papus and Monsieur Philippe's growing influence on the czar and czarina. While Papus and Philippe left officially, the correspondence continued, but in their absence, Rasputin stepped in—a different kettle of fish.

It is interesting to wonder what Gurdjieff would have made of all this. After his brief encounter with the czar in 1900, Gurdjieff never again enjoyed the monarch's presence, but then again, according to *Life Is Real*, he had made an oath to forgo personal use of his powers, save for science, so may have had little to demonstrate. What he could do, it seems, was to advocate some kind of personal liberation for those he came into contact with. To the czar and his family, this might have seemed more socially revolutionary than sacred in intent. Gurdjieff had no great vested interest in the social system as it was. What had it done for him?

The fact is, we can barely locate Gurdjieff at all to any useful purpose between 1904 and 1912–13, when he says he moved to Moscow with the intention of establishing his own institute, perhaps having got the "institute" idea from Prince Oldenburgsky's Imperial Institute for Experimental Medicine. In his Institute for the Harmonious Development of Man, Gurdjieff would be his own czar. After all, no king had come to Beelzebub for advice since King Ahaziah (2 Kings 1:2), and he had paid the price.

THE UNIQUE WORK BROTHERHOOD

Were it not for Stalin's vindictive savagery, we should probably never have known that there has been but one chink in the cavern of darkness that surrounds our knowledge of Gurdjieff during this period. In 1937–38 Stalin purged senior Soviet staff. Among the victims of Stalin's personal paranoia was the talented Gleb Ivanovich Bokii (1879–1937).

A remarkable individual, Bokii was born in Tiflis of Ukrainian stock, matured in St. Petersburg, and graduated from the Petersburg Mining Institute in 1896. His revolutionary career began early. A Marxist by 1900, Bokii joined the Russian Social Democratic Labor Party with loyalty to the Bolshevik faction of the party headed by Lenin. Come the revolution, he became deputy head of the feared *Cheka* secret police in 1918, though recoiled personally from the extremity of terror measures of that and subsequent years. In 1921 his cryptographic skills brought him into the *Spets-Otdel,* or Special Agency. He began to share mystical ideas with Alexander Barchenko (1881–1938), a Martinist Freemason who believed in a Himalayan Shambhala or Agarttha. In fact, Barchenko took it that the enlightened beings were the original "communists." He believed communism was the social manifestation of an esoteric secret and hoped to influence high-ranking members of the party with the idea that communism had a spiritual potential untapped. They used the once "imperial" Institute for Experimental Medicine to conduct investigations into telekinesis and paranormal mind control.

In the 1920s both men were behind the exploitation by Soviet Joint State Political Directorate, OGPU, of theosophist, mystic, artist, and explorer Nicholas Roerich and his wife Helena. But that is a story for later.

On May 16, 1937, Bokii was arrested and charged with conspiracy in Stalin's Great Purge. Brought before the Military Collegium of the Supreme Soviet on November 15, he was sentenced to death. He was shot that day. Barchenko faced the firing squad on April 25, 1938. Based on Bokii's confession, this is what interrogators concluded in a document intended for consumption by superiors:

> At his interrogation the accused confessed that he became a mason
> in 1909. The Lodge he joined was created by the well-known mystic
> Gurdjieff who after the Revolution emigrated to the West. His suc-
> cessor was Dr. Barchenko. In addition, Bokii confessed that he was

the head of an anti-Soviet spiritualist circle whose members were occupied with foretelling of the future.

In the depositions of the SPEKO [*Spets-Otdel:* Special agency decoding foreign intel] collaborators arrested after their chief, is mentioned a commune organized by Bokii in a country house, where members, men and women, got drunk together, practiced communal bathing, sang dirty songs. In a word, behaved indecently outside working hours. As is well-known, Gurdjieff organized in emigration an "Institute for the Harmonic Development of Man" whose members tried in every way to reach the depths of "one's own I," including in "sessions," briefly in collective drinking orgies. It is possible that the use of alcohol, removing the psychic safety barriers, actually was practiced in Bokii's commune, who was to an extent a follower of Gurdjieff. [14]

Bokii named others associated with the "lodge" activities: Nicholas Roerich and his wife Helena; Dr. K. N. Riabinin (a close associate of Roerich who would travel with him to Tibet in 1927); B. Stomoniakov; I. M. Moskvin; and Sergei Merkurov, party supporter, esteemed sculptor of Alexandropol, and Gurdjieff's cousin. The lodge was called the "Unique Work Lodge," which has also been translated as the "United Labor Lodge," which puts a more political slant on it.

Of course, we could never have been sure just how much the conditions of interrogation influenced what Bokii actually confessed, or to what precise degree his interrogators embellished what was obtained from the victim's mouth. What we can now say, however, is that the idea of a Gurdjieff-created Masonic Lodge in 1909 has arisen through a misunderstanding.

The alleged 1909 Gurdjieffian lodge originated when the late Nicolas Tereshchenko provided Michael Benham with translated passages from the Russian book *Tibetan Medicine in Russia: The History in Fates and Faces* (Tatiana I. Gregova, St. Petersburg: Aton, 1998). The work contained portions of transcripts of secret police interrogations of Gleb Bokii, from which we have quoted above.

Not only has Benham researched all the supposed members and found no links to Gurdjieff, but new Russian material demonstrates that the Soviet accusation of a Gurdjieffian Masonic Lodge was false.* In the wake of new Russian biographies of Bokii and and Barchenko, we now know a lot more about both of them. Complete transcripts of Bokii's interrogations expose Bokii's alleged confession as having been subjected to an interrogator's heavy editing to make it fit the official communist party line that there existed a Masonic conspiracy. Bokii's original words show supposed members such as Gurdjieff and Roerich had nothing to do with Bokii's group.

In fact, the United Labor Brotherhood (ULB) was a Buddhist/ Communist commune established in Moscow in 1923 by Barchenko. It had no connection to Masonry. Barchenko's descendants have preserved his written instructions to members and they indicate derivation of idea from Blavatsky and Saint-Yves d'Alveydre, with no trace of any of Gurdjieff's idiosyncratic ideas.[16]

---

*The Bulgarian Boris Spiridonovich Stomoniakov (1882–1941) was Soviet Trade Representative in Berlin 1920–1935, while famed Russian actor of the Moscow Art Theatre, Ivan Mikhaiovich Moskovin (1890–1946) was a Presidium member of the Soviet Union and chief of the USSR's Supreme Council of National Economy's personnel section.

The revelation that there was in fact no 1909 Gurdjieffian Masonic Lodge comes from Michael Benham, who mistakenly originated it (e-mail to author, October 4, 2016). Among Russian works that have corrected this misapprehension, Benham cites Professor Andrei Znamenski's *Red Shambhala: Magic, Prophecy, and Geopolitics in the Heart of Asia* and Oleg Shishkin's "The Occultist Aleksadr Barchenko and the Soviet Secret Police (1923–1938)" in *The New Age of Russia: Occult and Esoteric Dimensions.*[15]

According to Benham, "Nicholas Tereschenko's father was a noted Russian (Ukranian) Freemason. Nick wrote a number of books about Gurdjieff's ideas mostly in French. I knew him well when he returned to Australia in the last years of his life. He never mentioned any connection between Freemasonry and Gurdjieff's ideas."

Nevertheless, a link between Barchenko and Gurdjieff does exist, but it is indirect and refers to a much later period than the alleged 1909 lodge. Znamenski writes in *Red Shambhala*, "The blueprint for the ULB was G. I. Gurdjieff's United Labor Commonwealth which Barchenko learned of from his close friend Peter Shandarovsky, a former member of Gurdjieff's circle who chose to remain in Russia."[17] Benham suggests this much later link with Gurdjieff explains stories of Gurdjieff's Essentuki talks late in World War I circulating in Moscow after Gurdjieff had left Russia.*

As for the rest of the period running up to the outbreak of the First World War in 1914, we can only say that while Freemasonry was permitted in Russia after 1906, and a new, progressive Masonry appeared that admitted women, we know very little about it. As for what Gurdjieff himself was actually doing during that period we have scattered comments from him that mutually jostle each other into a cloud of dust. From the testimony of "The Material Question"—designed to shear "dollar fat" from Americans—it would appear he devoted much time to "coining it." He says that the business he preferred, and which was very profitable, requiring no fixed residence, was the "trade in carpets and antiques of all kinds."[19] He says that after five or six years of feverish activity, he "liquidated" all his affairs and, "near the end of the year 1913," went to Moscow to realize "what I had taken on myself as a sacred task." He had, he declared with justifiable pride, "amassed a million rubles and two invaluable collections" of old and

---

*There is also a link between Barchenko and Gurdjieff's follower, P. D. Ouspensky. Before 1923, while living in St. Petersburg, Barchenko wrote two novels: "Doctor Black" (*Doktor Chernyi*, 1913) and "From the Darkness" (*Iz Mrak*, 1914). According to Leonid Heller, "his [Barchenko's] multi-volume novel 'Doctor Black' was only published in 1991."[18] While still requiring analysis, it appears that the novel's prototype was, as Heller suggests, "Barchenko's guide to the esoteric sciences, Petr D. Uspensky.". Benham is of the view that this work of Ouspensky's favors the idea that Ouspensky already "fancied himself as something of a teacher/guide before he met Gurdjieff" (Michael Benham, e-mail to author, October 5, 2016).

rare carpets, porcelain, and Chinese cloisonné (enameled ware). His aim was to put into practice ideas on which the institute would be based: "to create around myself conditions in which a man would be continually reminded of the sense and aim of his existence by an unavoidable friction between his conscience and the automatic manifestations of his nature."[20] This formulation of his modus operandi rather suggests self-hypnosis and a discomfiting psychic ambiguity.

Materially speaking, Gurdjieff had finally achieved what his father had not, regaining the fortune his father had lost: "that was about a year before the World War."

According to this account, the institute idea first got going in Moscow in 1913: "In Moscow and a little later in St. Petersburg I arranged a series of lectures which attracted a number of intellectuals and men of science, and the circle of people interested in my ideas soon began to grow." He was selling again, but a different kind of ware to that he had peddled across Central Asia.

Arguably, Gurdjieff truly belonged in prewar Russia, his proper context—the place where he makes most sense; the position he aspired to.

According to *Life Is Real,* his Moscow work, begun in 1912, was nearing completion when war broke out. Does this mean he'd had enough of it and was looking for something else to do, or did he have extended plans and ideas? We shall never know, for history played the role of fate and smashed practically all plans to smithereens.

In *Life Is Real* he says he was just getting inured to war, when "esteemed lady" "Madame Russian Revolution" sowed injuries and consequences that made his work in Moscow impossible.[21]

FOURTEEN

The Struggle of the Magicians

On Tuesday, September 13, 1932, at the Café de la Paix, Paris, Gurdjieff began writing the booklet *The Herald of Coming Good—First Appeal to Contemporary Humanity.* Introducing it, he maintained the day marked precisely twenty-one years since he had sworn to lead "in some ways an artificial life, modeled upon a program which had been previously planned in accordance with certain definite principles." This life he described as a "burden," an "absolutely unnatural life" at odds with, and irreconcilable with, traits established by his maturity. He says he wanted first to prevent people from automatically opposing him, and second to prevent people from feeling enslaved to him and losing initiative. To call this odd is to call it Gurdjieffian.

The word *artificial* is intriguing, for it is precisely the word Aleister Crowley used to describe Gurdjieff's scheme after visiting his institute at Avon in February 1924.[1] Perhaps Gurdjieff was sensitive to such a criticism, or knew it all along. Twenty-one years would take us back to 1911. Unfortunately, other than allegedly making the oath, we do not know what Gurdjieff was doing in September 1911. But we know what other relevant persons were doing.

According to Levan Khetaguri, Ph.D., who has studied early twentieth-century Tiflis (Tbilisi), the city attracted many esoteric teachers and schools in that period, including followers of Blavatsky, Rudolf Steiner, the Dalcroze school of dance, and Norwegian nationalist and spiritual symbolist writer Knut Hamsun (1859–1952).[2] Prominent Tiflis aristocrat and member of the Constitutional-Democratic Party Prince David Iosifovich Bebutov was a Freemason and scientist with close links to the Moscow power élite; he held a lodge at his apartment at 8 Dmitrovsky Lane, St. Petersburg.

A new kind of Masonry emerged after the events of 1905. It had little of the ceremonial, included women, insisted on strict secrecy, and was intended to cross the political divides and unite Russians in common cause according to universal principles.[3] Gurdjieff may have been involved with it. That Rudolf Steiner's analogous work had reached Tiflis is significant. In September 1911 (when Gurdjieff allegedly made his oath) spiritual teacher and scientist Rudolf Steiner gave a talk at Neuchâtel, Switzerland, saying that individuals became aware of the call of the spirit-being Christian Rosenkreutz when they reached a personal crisis, where there was a real threat of danger or even suicide; at such a point an adept could begin a new life of service, guided by the spirit of Christian Rosenkreutz. It seems oddly appropriate to Gurdjieff's position, and his evident need to alter his tack again. From 1910 to 1913 Steiner's "Mystery plays" were being produced in Munich, while Steiner worked with Marie von Sivers on his new art of movement, called "Eurythmy," launched in 1912. Expelled from Annie Besant's Theosophical Society in 1913, Steiner launched his Anthroposophical Society, which quickly gathered devotees.

There was a tremendous surge of interest in esoteric spiritual development. In 1912, Aleister Crowley became British head of Theodor Reuss's Berlin-based *Ordo Templi Orientis* and effectively launched the order proper. The following year Crowley was in Moscow, putting on a popular music and dance show (the Ragged Ragtime Girls) and writing *The Gnostic Mass* for use in the order. He may also have been operating as an intelligence asset in association with the British consulate in Moscow.

Gurdjieff had some artistic ideas of his own, though how well formulated at this stage is unclear. His arrival in Moscow in 1912 or 1913 was inaugurated by advertisements in the local press for a ballet called *The Struggle of the Magicians,* presented by a "well-known orientalist"; that is to say, Gurdjieff had the idea of the ballet, though unperformed it was still only an idea, but we may suppose the ballet was alive enough in his imagination, just waiting for actualization. The following statement appeared at the end of the original Russian newspaper notice about *The Struggle of the Magicians:*

> Initially I. G. G. planned on staging the ballet himself, not sparing any expense, but his friends have dissuaded him from doing so and suggest that he present "The Struggle of the Magicians" to the repertory office of the Bolshoi, which, as everyone knows is undergoing a lengthy "ballet" crisis.[4]

One of the artists at the center of the Bolshoi ballet crisis was Vasilii Geltzer. Interestingly, *The Struggle of the Magicians* was dedicated to Geltzer. As Benham has observed, this is the only dedication to another person by Gurdjieff, a fact completely overlooked to date. An outstanding mime who may be described as a "remarkable man," Geltzer worked on the libretto for *Swan Lake.* Since Geltzer was knowledgable about Russian folk tales, his presence at the Bolshoi at the very time Gurdjieff was researching the country's folk traditions suggests some kind of a relationship about which we otherwise know nothing.

Gurdjieff distributed a prospectus announcing a center for esoteric knowledge. This appears as a salesman's trick to stimulate interest, anticipation, and mystery, to seed the subconscious without having to appear in person and attract opprobrium. For a magician, the first step to establishing something is to imagine it. He was probably nervous as to how he would be received, his not being Russian and having arrived "loaded." Besides, had he intended to manipulate the artistic side of an already intense and highly sophisticated, globally influential artistic scene, his personal wealth might have been a handicap. The rich were supposed to be patrons, not entrepreneurs of their own art, or system, if they had one. Meanwhile, Gurdjieff conducted a lucrative carpet business, buying in Moscow and selling for profit in St. Petersburg, adept as ever at targeting the weak spots of clients.

He eventually followed up his ballet ad with an essay distributed to followers. Just what constituted being a follower of Gurdjieff at this time has never been explained. It seems to have meant you liked him, heard his stories, and would do things for him. His modus operandi was always to keep himself back and let the followers play heralds; word of mouth was a great selling tool. He wanted a machine. His essay was called "Glimpses of Truth," and in 1915 he wanted someone to publicize what he was about, based on it.

The piece is written as a clever account by an unknown person who has seen the ballet ad in *Golos Moskvi* ("Voice of Moscow") and who has been informed its author had spent years in the East and was now a dance master in St. Petersburg and Moscow. The ballet ad now appears as the first step in a mystery plot. *Something is missing. What is it?* The intrigued person called "A" braves the snows to reach a dacha far from Moscow, where he hears Gurdjieff expatiate at length on Hermes Trismegistus's *Emerald Tablet*—a concise alchemical compendium from the late antique period famous for its dictum: "As above, so below; to work the miracle of the One Thing."

Gurdjieff expounds the basic microcosm-macrocosm theory associated with Rosicrucianism and Hermetic Freemasonry, how individuals relate to mankind and mankind to the universe, which universe is mirrored within each person. Gurdjieff adds the Pythagorean element by showing that the laws sustaining the universe express a musical harmony, with the musical octave of seven notes separated by two gaps $(7 + 2 = 9)$, and the relation of these numbers holds the key to all, and above all, the Unity that underlies the creation. As with an octave, the eighth represents the new beginning. This knowledge is, he says, already within everyone. Gurdjieff's role is to help the aspirant realize all this for himself or herself and *in* himself and herself: to recover the knower and the known. Know thyself: know all.

The Gurdjieff of "Glimpses" says his ballet contains secret dances he saw in the East containing vital knowledge that will make for good, as opposed to bad, art, which is based on bad, or incomplete, knowledge. Voicing a theory already expressed by French esotericist Joséphin Péladan in terms of "Tradition," Gurdjieff asserts an objective art: not mere opinion or emotional shading of one person's feelings, but the art that commands, that of the Sphinx and Orpheus, reducing the questioner to silence while opening his or her being, if fit to receive. The implication was clear: give Gurdjieff an opening, and you would be opened up to objective art.

"Glimpses" concludes with a nice Gurdjieffian trick. The traveler asks his friend the time and finds Gurdjieff's talk has taken practically no time at all. A nice one: *there is no time in the transcendent world,* and Gurdjieff's transcending message can be absorbed quickly—ideal for the modern world. Gurdjieff put out his stall. His product: the "Great Knowledge." His schtick (arguably): *dancing,* when he'd worked that out in practice, that is. He was clever. He started not with his presence, but his absence. The rest could be left to the imagination of the one who had lost something.

You.

And people came to the conceptual maypole he had erected. Not immediately, and not very many, but sufficient to get a ball rolling. Gurdjieff's cousin, sculptor and communist Sergei Merkurov was, to all intents and purposes, already a friend.

Gurdjieff's most significant follower is generally agreed to have been Pyotr Demianovich Ouspenskii (1878–1947) who encountered the "actor" Gurdjieff in the war's darkening days of 1915 and was impressed. Mathematician, esotericist, journalist Ouspensky was not used to playing second fiddle. He'd already written *The Fourth Dimension* (1909) and *Tertium Organum* (1912), a work that interested both Gurdjieff and artist Casimir Malevich, for it expressed mystical dynamics as potential science and vice versa. Ouspensky could be impressive himself and serve as herald, telling his contacts in St. Petersburg that Gurdjieff was significant. Already, in February and March 1915, Ouspensky had lectured on his travels to the East, especially India. Attracting over a thousand visitors to each of his lectures, "In Search of the Miraculous" and "The Problems of Death" at the Alexandrovsky Hall of the Petersburg Town Duma, Ouspensky could in due course turn his many visitors and inquirers on to Gurdjieff, who seemed to have in him what Ouspensky had traveled far to find.

The rather open-hearted, sensitive intellectual Ouspensky was struck by the way Gurdjieff constantly spoke outside of the box. He spoke neither like Indian yogis nor like Western scientists; in this sense his ideas seemed to emanate from an unknown source. Gurdjieff didn't seem to care much about scientifically established theories. For example, while most people understood the idea of our solar system as having been a fairly constant feature of the created cosmos, Gurdjieff saw a vaster evolutionary scheme and would say that the moon was in the early stages of becoming something like the Earth, that the sun would disappear, and the Earth, if it advanced properly, could become a sun to the moon, which could then be a new Earth. And to be a sun meant to be an intelligent being. As the Hermetists had taught for millennia, the Earth and all planets had their own life of active intelligence. That man could not see this was a sure sign that man was not properly switched on, or in. The heavenly bodies were not simply "objects of man's knowing." Indeed, when Ouspensky suggested man could think, Gurdjieff repeatedly told him in their meetings that machines can't think or, especially, *do*. They are machines, whereas *men* were responsible. Becoming a real man was not inevitable. A machine could not be responsible. Most things that passed for art or culture were inevitable mechanical reactions, usually ending in some kind of violence. Man could not be *objective*, because he was driven by his appetites, identified with his emotions, prone to break off any direction, easily distracted and sent off elsewhere from his goal (if he ever had one), and all effected by a persistent programming from anterior sources other than his own "will-less" will. He was not a free man; he was one in a series of numbers, and indeed, he could hardly be said to be one at all, for he was unaware of his nothingness. Gurdjieff, clearly, *was* something.

Their first meeting took place just after Ouspensky's Petersburg lectures, when he traveled to give them in Moscow just after Easter 1915. He met a sculptor who told him about a "Caucasian Greek," Gurdjieff, who had a group engaging in occult investigations and experiments. Ouspensky was able to connect this man with the alleged "Hindoo" who had advertised his forthcoming ballet, *The Struggle of the Magicians* (black and white) at the end of 1914. The sculptor was probably Gurdjieff's cousin Merkurov, and with great effort he persuaded Ouspensky to meet a man who seemed to be able to make objects appear in people's minds and to captivate their wills and fascinate their need for miracles. Ouspensky was in search of miracles but claimed to be completely skeptical about reports of such. He seems to have been a rationalist in search of the irrational or, better perhaps, unrational. He had come to the right place.

Their first encounter occurred, Ouspensky says, in a Moscow café where small dealers and commission agents gathered, not an artistic or intellectual setting. Ouspensky saw *with* his eyes a man, "no longer young," in a black bowler and black overcoat with velvet collar, with piercing eyes and big moustache; but *through* his eyes he saw a figure in a gold turban and white burnoose, with the face of an Indian raja or Arab sheikh. He seemed to have been in disguise, almost too obviously so. He spoke incorrect Russian with a Caucasian accent: a voice in which one would not normally expect to find exposition of philosophy. The accent, in short, was "common," apparently socially careless. Nevertheless, Ouspensky warmed to Gurdjieff's economy of expression. He said clearly what he meant, and Ouspensky learned that Gurdjieff's work was connected with psychology and involved something of chemistry. The teaching reminded Ouspensky of a Brahmin who taught that you could improve or at least change a man's moral or psychological nature by removing certain chemicals from the organism. Gurdjieff said there might be similarities, but the meaning between different schools could be totally different. Similarity of ideas or methods "proved nothing." Gurdjieff was clearly well into his habitual practice of *unmaking* the minds of those he got into serious conversation with. His tools were the tools of disconcerting the unexpected, trumping the clever statement, leading on, but done in a matter-of-fact tone that maintained attention, even as the interlocutor's sense of reason would begin to wobble internally. It is interesting that Ouspensky moved his conversation on to the use of narcotics. Gurdjieff seemed to know a lot about them but made it clear that those who used psychoactive substances properly were people with deep knowledge of the "human machine" and could administer substances correctly and with great discipline so as to improve mental performance, not inhibit it.

They then went by carriage to a flat in the direction of Sokolniki. Contrary to expectations engendered by Gurdjieff's complaints in the carriage about the expense of his apartments, they turned up at a cheap apartment suitable for a provincial schoolteacher, where three or four young men and what Ouspensky took for two schoolmistresses gathered in a room with barely any furniture, above a municipal school. Where were the notable, not unnamed, significant artists and professors who had taken an interest in his work Gurdjieff had mentioned in the carriage?

The persons gathered had responded to the document "Glimpses of Truth" mentioned above. They used unfamiliar terminology and were indefinite about the doctrine imparted to them, speaking of "work on oneself." Ouspensky felt their answers seemed artificial, learned for the occasion, so to speak. They were of a low rank of Moscow's "intelligentsia" as Ouspensky judged them: nice and decent but not highfliers. Gurdjieff asked Ouspensky the journalist whether "Glimpses of Truth," whose very long account they had now heard read, could be published in a paper. Ouspensky judged it ill-suited for the purpose, as it had no beginning or end and was too long for a paper.

Ouspensky got on the tram back to Moscow's center with a deter-mination to see the strange man again. He saw him every day for the rest of the week before heading back to St. Petersburg. Ouspensky had felt a need during their first meeting to break out and laugh and sing, as though having been freed from school detention.

Subsequent meetings added to the mystery. When he tried to ascertain where in the East Gurdjieff had obtained his insights into the "miraculous," Ouspensky just couldn't tell exactly from what was said where Gurdjieff had really been. Gurdjieff said he had two groups working at different levels. Members paid one thousand rubles a year and combined meetings with him with their ordinary lives. When Ouspensky opined that the fees were high for those without private means, Gurdjieff said they had to be high, as he could only give atten-tion to small numbers of pupils and that it would be wrong of him to spend his own money on the organization of the work. It was not meant to be a charitable work and those who were weak in life would be weak in the work; the strictures of having to help themselves find places of meeting and places to perform experiments made them more worthy of what they strove to attain.

One might argue that such a conviction would suit someone out to fleece the uninitiated, but self-help is the alternative to charity, and only those who can help themselves are in a position to give to charities; this is a Masonic principle. One must be free to undertake the work. A person subject to charity is not free. Still, a thousand rubles was a lot of money . . .

Gurdjieff said he had far too little spare time to be able to afford to waste it on people who would in all likelihood prove to be hopeless cases. He needed people who could respond to the needs of the work. If the pupil should go to Cairo, for example, then the means must be available. "People do not value a thing if they do not pay for it," said Gurdjieff.

Ouspensky doubted whether the pupils he had seen would in fact have been able to pay the fees, and wondered whether he, Ouspensky, might be able to put Gurdjieff in a position where he might get proper funds, as one would for an archaeological expedition or scientific work. He rather liked that Gurdjieff's talk was devoid of sentimentality, or sugary humanitarianism. When Ouspensky asked if joining the work involved obligations of secrecy or personal obligations to Gurdjieff himself, Gurdjieff said that a man was not capable of such things, as he was one man one day and another man the next; the man who made the promise might be different tomorrow. There was as yet no real "I." Disciples were free to come or go. When Ouspensky asked about Gurdjieff's alleged former companions, experts in their fields who had shared their knowledge with one another (an early Rosicrucian injunction), Gurdjieff was silent, then slowly looked into the distance: "Some have died, some are working, some have gone into seclusion." Ouspensky felt Gurdjieff was "acting" in some way, as if to deflect Ouspensky's line of questioning. He got a similar response when he asked what Gurdjieff really knew and where he got it from (he was perhaps thinking of a newspaper interview). Gurdjieff said that Ouspensky's talks about India had been in the papers, and he had asked his pupils to study them and work out what on Ouspensky's search his point of End would be. Gurdjieff said that his pupils knew his "End," while Ouspensky was still on the way there. If I read this bit of somewhat sly and subversive mental trickery correctly, what Gurdjieff was saying was that places to go in search had only one point: their end. Ouspensky's "end" was his fundamental unconscious intention, which revealed itself only obscurely in the nature and incidents of his search. Therefore, there was little or nothing to be gained from places passed through in themselves, but only in what the search would bring (its "end"). Gurdjieff also implied that you could reach the End, or purpose, of the search in one place without exotic trips. Travel for health or fun, by all means, but don't kid yourself. If one may quote the moral of the *Wizard of Oz,* the end of the rainbow leads back home. He was also saying, "Don't ask me these questions; the answers won't satisfy you," and he was saying, I think, "We all reckoned you'd end up coming to *me.*" Clever as Ouspensky was, one feels that to a certain extent, he was putty in Gurdjieff's wily hands. The sense that Ouspensky had more than met his match became compelling. He wanted what he was soon convinced Gurdjieff had.

It was mathematician Andrei Zaharoff who introduced to Gurdjieff a major figure in the St. Petersburg arts scene, Thomas Alexandrovich de Hartmann (1885–1956), whose ballet *The Pink Flower* (1907), featuring Vaslav Nijinsky, so delighted the czar at the Imperial Opera that he exempted de Hartmann from military service. De Hartmann's wife, Olga (1885–1979), a famous opera singer, joined him on the theosophical adventure that led to Gurdjieff and a life of adventure and heartache around the unpredictable teacher of dance.

In 1915 Muscovite-born doctor and psychologist Leonid de Stjernvall (1872–1938) and his wife Elizabeth joined Gurdjieff, drinking with him at Phillipoff's café in St. Petersburg, where he worked. Stjernvall's calm demeanor could be turned to advantage as a negotiator when conditions worsened as Russia's defeat by Germany and the abdication of the czar on March 2, 1917, hit home. Gurdjieff left St. Petersburg with his wife, St. Petersburg–born Julia Osipovna Ostrovska (1889–1926), just before, in February 1917. *Gurdjieff married?* Yes. Some time between 1912 and the war he'd met and married his beloved Polish wife, Julia. She would dance for him as priestess. Gurdjieff wanted everyone to dance, but the world war carried on. For Gurdjieff it was all psychosis, and he didn't want his followers caught up in it.

FIFTEEN

Octave and Enneagram

Everything *is* vibrations, I believe. Everything *is* going on a sort of [electronic drone sound] *hmm . . . mm . . . mm . . .* all the time. I mean *you're* breathing, and speaking, and he's inhaling, and those people over there are whistling, and I'm humming, and so all this is [staccato syllables] *go*-ing-*on*-all-the-*time* . . . like that.

JOHN LENNON IN CONVERSATION WITH
VICTOR SPINETTI, BBC ARTS PROGRAM *RELEASE*, 1968

What Gurdjieff did wish to impart was his will for his followers' salvation. In order to escape, you had to know you were in prison. If you thought you were free, you could never tunnel out. And to tunnel out, you best needed a group. And Ouspensky served to enlarge the group and with it, presumably, Gurdjieff's income, though it should be noted that Gurdjieff made it difficult for people to join his meetings with Ouspensky in St. Petersburg. They were held almost spontaneously, and he worked on the basis that those who really wanted to be part of the work would make sure they were at the ready. Those who came easily would leave easily and try to live easily. The work was not easy. Breaking out of prison is not a walk in the country. Part of Gurdjieff's kit for mental freedom emerges in P. D. Ouspensky's account of Gurdjieff's teachings in Russia during World War I: *In Search of the Miraculous: Fragments of an Unknown Teaching.*

It must have been disconcerting for Ouspensky and his fellow disciples to be hearing of the law of the "Octave," and the "law of three" and the "four principles" and the "ray of creation" while the war was going so badly for Russia, and the economy disrupted by shortages and gathering industrial unrest. After the devastating battle of Tannenburg destroyed the Russian second army at the end of 1914, the Russians were consistently ground down by the superior condition of German forces. Ouspensky remembered seeing a cart in the public streets filled with prosthetic legs, still to be attached to soldiers who had not yet had their real ones torn off by German shells. Here we find some of the emotional attraction for what Gurdjieff was unfolding. How had the war happened? What made people do these terrible things to one another? Why was it going on? Why couldn't people just stop and wake up and realize how pointless it all was? Why was everything so driven—and so plainly driven to destruction? Could you stop or prevent what appeared to be sheer force of Fate, a vibratory wave that carried people away—from themselves. The adjective of fate is fatal. In Russia, the only ones likely to benefit from the carnage were the interior, parasitic forces of destruction and chaos: the Bolsheviks with their promised workers' utopia (and of course those who profited from prosthetic limbs).

Gurdjieff appeared to have the answers to explain why people were so controlled, so blindly driven, and why it was that an initial will to do something was so easily thwarted, with energies simply wasted in oblivion. For ill directed as they were, the Bolsheviks had will, and indifference to feelings. As Martinists might observe, they had will, but no belief in providence, or desire for God.

For Gurdjieff, there was not really anything wrong with the universe as such, but it required understanding, inner understanding, not just knowledge of it. People, however, were in no position to make good use of such knowledge as was available. Following the basic pattern of esotericism with regard to the "fallen faculties," human beings were basically disintegrated, their left hands not knowing what their right hands were doing. One second they were identified with their feelings, the next their thoughts, then their bodies, then their dreams. The control was lost in the identification. They must learn to stand aside. The real "I am"—already "aside" because uninvolved—was not the temporary being or relative self caught up in the action, so to say. So when a person was standing in a crowd and a patriotic song was sung, and the manipulative urge came to join the crowd and shout, or sign up for the army, and believe the promises and threats, Gurdjieffian man, that is, the "real man," observes, stands aside from the feeling, looks at the character in himself who is gagging to let go and join in, and puts him in his place. Such a being is objective. Wherever you put such a one, you would get a better result; this was someone who had mastered himself. If only there were such ones leading Russia in her hour of agony! Gurdjieff had the idea of starting a new generation; its seed members would have to go back to first principles.

Gurdjieff's first principles consisted of an idiosyncratic amalgam of esoteric lore from largely gnostic traditions blended into his own scheme. Ouspensky took Gurdjieff's "ray of creation," for example, with its "great chain of being" of seven extending from the Absolute, through all worlds, all suns, the sun, all planets, the Earth, and finally the moon (the nascent new world), as something refreshingly original in relation to current theory. Gurdjieff's picture suggested an organic, interior involution and evolution of consciousness within all things in constant motion, yet subject to divine will, which human beings have a portion of, if they ever but know it and employ it. If they do, they serve the "white magicians," for that is what they have become; if they are ignorant, they serve the black. The broad system, however, is very familiar to anyone who has studied any number of Neoplatonic, Gnostic, and Hermetic texts from the ancient world, the Middle Ages, and the Renaissance. It just so happened that the so-called Age of Reason and scientific progress had in the eighteenth and nineteenth centuries consigned the great

Tradition largely to the scrap heap and imprisoned man in a false and ultimately destructive mind-set. Besides, Gurdjieff was never claiming he was saying anything new. Perhaps he expressed things in a relatively new way, but he believed the truth had always been out there (or *in* there), so to speak, but that it needed activating again, in living fact. What was obscured in the East needed resurrecting in the West. Man was basically caught up in his own disfigured nightmare, and he must wake up and abstract himself, by his own efforts. He couldn't trust to any supposed ineluctable progress or automatic evolution of humanity to the Good. Furthermore, he could not simply leave the "spiritual stuff" to organized religion because organized religion had practically lost touch with the essence of the Tradition. Alternatively, the "word" was spoken, but not enfleshed.

All the prophets and spiritual guides had begun with a pristine spiritual truth, a real experience, not just a belief, but it always ended up going the wrong way. The Christian Church started with a liberation of the spirit and had become by stages an oppressive doctrinaire monolith that then progressively shattered. There were shards of truth in it. Likewise, according to Gurdjieff, Muhammad the prophet had an authentic vision of the divine source of life, but his followers had argued over details, persecuted one another, lost the spirit of the thing, and abused it in destructive wars and perennial conflicts that kept the absolute light and love of God out of "ordinary people's" minds and lives, and all in exchange for an insurance system based on imposed performances prescribed by conflicting orders of priests. Everywhere, practically, the story was the same: no religion was innocent. Good intentions thwarted by disintegrated and manipulative human nature. Ideals, of themselves, were useless. The individual, not the mindless mass, was the seed-unit of new creation. And individuals could grow by working together.

If you wish to read in more detail about what Gurdjieff showed to Ouspensky during the war, you may consult his book *In Search of the*

Miraculous. It should be borne in mind that Ouspensky had a logical mind and was always trying to get Gurdjieff's "system" into systematic scientific or scientific-like shape. He recognized that in this way, Gurdjieff's ideas would stand a better chance of impacting the next generations than if he took the purely esoteric path of spiritual knowledge for the relative few. Gurdjieff could see sense in this, though he had scant respect for the attitudes prevalent in modern science and technology, and one cannot help seeing that Gurdjieff tried in his way to give Ouspensky material for such an exposition, but somehow, one senses that it was not really Gurdjieff's intention, or only a possibly minor or component part of it, though he could see its value. Ouspensky was somewhat blind to Gurdjieff's sense of humor, and his use of creative analogy; that is to say, Ouspensky was somewhat literal in his approach. Gurdjieff taught through pictures and stories, analogies and parables, and through surprises, shocks.

One can see something of Gurdjieff's authentic method in his advertisement for his intended ballet *The Struggle of the Magicians.* He has the concept, plants it in the public mind, and sees what comes of it: perhaps a ballet, perhaps something else. All things are possible. Gurdjieff's great gift was to turn people on to the possibility of self-transformation. He then appears to have improvised, with both practices and ideas that might get the mind out of its accustomed state and into a dynamic of, admittedly, painful change. The drawback was that disciples very quickly tended to fall into a mind-struck awe of the teacher as a personality instead of focusing on what was being taught and experienced. Ideally, Gurdjieff wanted people to teach themselves. He wanted to start them off. The idea was that he'd get something going, the group would grow, and he would appear at intervals, to steady the tiller or shake things up a bit. The hope was to encourage more, even better teachers, but as so often in the history of esotericism, the charisma of certain individuals creates a stasis in the followers in the leader's absence, followed by the appearance of other teachers claiming leadership roles, and then the inevitable splits and sects and recriminations. All this occurred in Gurdjieff's lifetime, and subsequently. It has been this biographer's intention to try to stick as closely as possible to Gurdjieff himself, lest we start to get the filtered view. Ouspensky, it should be realized, filtered Gurdjieff to some extent, through his own rationalistic priorities. Of course one can always argue that the filtered view is a legitimate *development,* but with such developments this biography is not concerned.

Three primary concepts continue to shape Gurdjieffian thought and practice, and we first hear of them in Gurdjieff's discourse with Ouspensky and his fellow disciples in St. Petersburg and Moscow during the war. The first, already mentioned, is the ray of creation, which, while having historic antecedents, does contain some curious and apparently original elements. In Neoplatonism, the "great chain of being" explains how the pure spirit of the primal One can descend by degrees to become mucky blackness and mortal materiality in the world familiar to humans. What has happened is that the One's substance descends through grades of being: archangels, angels, intelligences of stars, planets, and on to Earth, organic life, and the nether regions below the earth. In this process is involved a diminution of spiritual substance, so gross matter is, as it were, what is left after the light has been progressively dimmed through distance from the source, as the flavor of tea diminishes as the tea bag is repeatedly used. In Neoplatonic theurgy, this situation is not all bad because man has *nous,* mind, a fragment of the divine, and through activating this, one can transmute the inert substance and raise it sacramentally to the highest through ritual and prayer. For though man as material being is distant from the One, through progressive initiation, his mind can be joined to the One, and what at first appears a descent into the darkness can become a circle of redemption, as mind flies or flees to the One beyond the created order. Well and good.

Gurdjieff's cosmic ecology asks us to look at the moon. He recognizes that it is involved at the most fundamental level with our survival on Earth; it turns the tides, providing rhythm, and all living things respond to it. Rather than being seen as an inert lump at the end of its cosmic life (as science at the time imagined), Gurdjieff sees the moon as something that is at the first stages of new life; like a fetus to Mother Earth, taking of her nourishment. Thus, organic life on Earth is sending its digested food up toward the moon in a refined state, and in course of time, this will conglomerate into an atmosphere, followed by living things. The nasty side of the picture is that *Man feeds the moon.* The unrealized potential of man, his most subtle body, will, if it has not attained a truly conscious will independent of the mortal "astral" body, simply be absorbed into the moon's feeding system, as we human beings absorb the various kinds of food, including oxygen and nitrogen, that come our way. In this sense, the moon, for Gurdjieff, serves a dual purpose. It is the promise of continued life, for in its birth (or rebirth) it reflects the will of the Absolute at the crown of the ray of creation, and reflects it (completing a cycle); but it is also an existential warning. Fail to secure understanding of the knowledge that is in us, and a human life, even at its most subtle and spiritual levels, simply becomes food for the moon. Here we see the ancient duality of the moon as ambiguous goddess expressed in a gnostic setting. The moon then becomes a kind of image for the relative God of the creation familiar to radical Gnostics, who saw this demiurge or "workman" deity as a subdeity, ignorant of the Absolute, and eager to suck out of man his mysterious divine "pneuma" or spirit accidentally sewn into him, the seed from the highest Being that longs for its source.

We see here Gurdjieff's fundamental cynicism for Man in his natural state. If he is to survive this natural condition, which for Man the individual is fundamentally hopeless, and which hopelessness makes him do such terrible things, he is going to have to subvert the natural tendencies inherent to life in the universe.

Thus, if anyone should think Gurdjieff an organic philosopher in the sense of the modern "Green" movement, they would be mistaken, for the currently espoused idea that all Man has to do is harmonize with Nature and respect it, at his own expense, is, according to Gurdjieff, a risible folly. Capitulation to the natural order will be

Man's absolute undoing, for he will simply add to the lunar digestion, and man's spiritual potential will evaporate in a cosmic belch. Nature is to be respected, but as far as the highest potential in man is concerned, nature is not to be trusted entirely; it is like the Venus flytrap, and mad nature keeps pumping, pumping green slime, high on methane and ordure, while Man is mashed up through the generations in the teeth and guts of it. Wake up, sleepyhead! You're going nowhere.

Why human beings end up going nowhere, even when they've made serious decisions to do something is revealed in Gurdjieff's conception of the "Octave." We all know the feeling that just when something gets going, all kinds of opposition and irritations gradually grind us down, and we find ourselves swerving from intended paths into subdivided problem areas, which become all-absorbing, until we forget what we set out to do or produce very different results, sometimes worse than where we started. One thinks of Traiano Boccalini's satire on the reformation of the whole wide world (*News from Parnassus*, Venice, 1612). Great minds are summoned to Parnassus to discuss ways of saving Man from his follies. All kinds of ideal schemes are suggested, but objections are found to every suggestion. In the end the collective wisdom of the enlightened assembly is to lower the price of vegetables—at which humanity, gathered at the foot of the mountain attending the deliberations of the enlightened, rejoices exceedingly! So much for reforming the world! Similar attempts are being pursued (as I write) in a vain attempt to reform the EU. Results will conform to Boccalini's satirical conclusion.

Gurdjieff reckons if we better understood the underlying rhythms and vibrations of life in relation to the cosmic order, we should put our foot in it less often.

Man's potential for breaking free of limitations is what he calls "consciousness," or the "fourth body." This body has potential power over the mental body (thought), which has power over the astral body (feelings, the soul), which has power over the physical body, fed from the elements. Gurdjieff uses the image of a carriage where the driver of a carriage (the mind) must be awake to the language and voice of the "master" (the fourth body), so as to control in turn, the horse, by correctly feeding it, which will pull the carriage (physical body). How these bodies are connected (reins, harnesses, and so on) also needs attention. Papus had published a series of amusing cartoons of this analogy in the French periodical *l'Initiation* during the previous decade, and this clever sequence (showing graphically the result of the driver losing grip of the reins and so on) may be what inspired Gurdjieff, which Ouspensky took to be original. Since Gurdjieff saw consciousness as the only hope for immortality within the solar system—for while the astral body could outlive the body, it would fade of itself without the "master," while reincarnation was rare—the issue was how to attain and most importantly, *maintain* consciousness against the general down-tending nature of the ray of creation and the buffeting of its internal cycles. Contrary to the comforts of much religion, survival after death was not by any means a given; the moon beckoned, so to speak. Furthermore, despite the love of the Absolute for his creatures, the Absolute had established the laws of the universe and did not intervene. The ordinary deuce will never beat the ace of trumps. God won't cheat on the rules. Two and two will always be four. Man had to use what he had or could find (this too was the practical logic of Yezidism). Those with a clear vision of the Absolute had left keys, but they had to be self-realized. Man's situation on Earth is truly perilous.

Jesus knew he had to die but according to Gurdjieff found a way to maintain a link with the disciples, through giving them his real body and blood. The Last Supper was a magical ceremony, where the disciples became, as it were, "blood brothers," for without the shedding of blood, as Jewish scripture teaches, there is no redemption. These words had a deeper meaning. The disciples had to take the food of Christ into themselves not solely as symbol (bread and wine) but actually. The facts of life could not be escaped but by spiritual consciousness maintained by right feeding and listening to the master. This Gurdjieff called "esoteric Christianity." "I am" with you always. Know thyself.

What man thinks of "consciousness" is not so. Gurdjieff says ordinary conscious awareness is changing in character and application all the time. He is relatively conscious at any given time of something or other, but he is not conscious that he is not fully conscious; he thinks he is conscious, and his consciousness is then centered on his thought, and his thought is limited as a result. The consciousness that ultimately matters, the "master," requires work, clearing away confusions of faculty. One must *remember oneself* above the function of acts or thoughts. It's not at all as easy as it sounds, but it is a vital piece of self-knowledge. It might take a bullet in the leg to wake oneself up to self-remembering. This idea of shock value is central to Gurdjieff's practice and explains many of the difficulties people had with it, and still have with it. People like the "meek and mild" but don't care for the "hard sayings." Running is fun, but the harness chafes.

Gurdjieff sees it not simply as a necessity of practice but simply an analogy of the way the universe itself operates, positively and negatively. No process is truly linear. There are no perfectly straight lines in the organic universe. We need to wake up, or "come to." The best experiences are those when we can actually remember being alive ourselves at that point, not simply remembering what happened but ourselves being alive at that moment: a "self" we didn't know about, or had forgotten. Such moments have the character of eternity or timelessness, and they promote living faith through knowledge that something has happened, not in the outside world, but in the core of being itself, where the bush burns and the divine voice is heard.

FROM SEVEN TO EIGHT

According to Ouspensky, following Gurdjieff, "The 7-tone scale is the formula of a cosmic law which was worked out by ancient schools and applied to music."[1] Gurdjieff used the diatonic scale (*diatonic* meaning "through the tones") both as an image for the septenary exhibited by the ray of creation, and also for its inner organization, which could be applied to practice. He chose the scale of C major: *do* (C), *re* (D), *mi* (E), *fa* (F), *so* (or *sol*) (G), *la* (A), *ti* (or *si*) (B), and on up to *do* (C) again. The scale has seven notes that, resolving and resuming on the eighth tone, make the octave. It will be noted that the octave has two semitone intervals, between *mi* and *fa* (there is no E-sharp or F-flat), and between *ti* and final *do* (there is no B-sharp or C-flat). Gurdjieff saw great significance in this. In the diatonic scales, a semitone is always separated by at least two full tones. Since music, like everything else in Gurdjieff's scheme, is a vibratory system, Gurdjieff saw this phenomenon as an exhibition of the principle that all human and natural developments are characterized by a kind of inner "kink" inherent to the nature of involution down from the Absolute. Each phase or cycle of development involves two discontinuities. There is no even progression in any such phase or cycle. For Ouspensky, this principle was news.

Gurdjieff took this idea of discontinuity as an analogy of the principle that a development can be knocked off course at two points, even reversed if insufficient energy is applied at the right points to the momentum. Negative energy, as it were, conglomerates at these points: resistance that man by nature is too "untuned" himself to allow for. One must apply an additional shock at such points, either applied from the outside or from within, by conscious discipline. There is involved here an intuition of a kind of fault in the creative scheme, but it in fact serves the overall harmony, could we but see it *objectively*. And harmony is key to the idea: hence the Institute for the Harmonious Development of Man.

Gurdjieff found himself in the same Platonic and Neoplatonic universe familiar to Renaissance philosophers and Hermetists who enjoyed the idea of the harmony of the spheres, with the universe a kind of musical instrument whose melody can only be captured through intense meditative understanding and inner ascent in imagination.

Taking the analogy further, the "shock" needed from *ti* to *do* must be greater than the earlier shock (*mi* to *fa*) because the octave's vibrations—think of a string—at this point are of a higher pitch. It takes more energy to get amplitude from a string when it is tight than when it is loose: the higher the pitch, the higher the resistance. Man's position on the ray of creation is therefore tougher "going up" than the divine involution "going down"; the descent from the Absolute acquires accumulated force, enabling smooth descent from *do* to *ti* and from *fa* to *mi*. The analogy here is in singing where more breath is required to go to higher pitch than for the voice to go down the scale. I suspect demonstrating this would have constituted, for Gurdjieff, an "experiment."

Esoteric music expert Joscelyn Godwin and others have observed that Gurdjieff could have chosen different scales, or scales from other cultures, with differing results. Had he taken D major he would have had two internal semitonal intervals, giving the scale a pleasing internal harmonic symmetry within seven notes. Furthermore, this D scale had a claim for

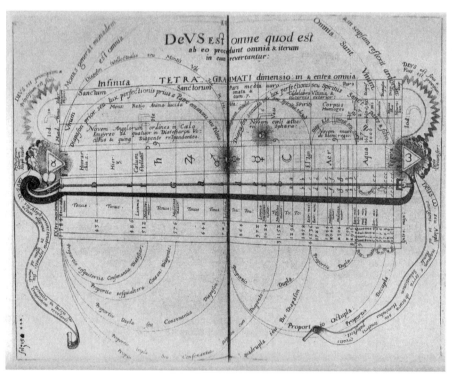

The "Great Monochord" in Robert Fludd's Anitomiae Amphitheatrum (1623, 314–15) showing correspondences between the diatonic scale and God's self-expression in the angelic hierarchies and the material universe.

ancient primacy since it was the Dorian or first mode familiar to medieval musicians, being also the diatonic Phrygian mode of ancient Greece. Even more striking is that in Plato's *Timaeus,* this mode was employed by the Demiurge for the construction of the world! One feels that Gurdjieff's choice of the modern C major was partly arbitrary, and perhaps not the best illustration of a cosmic law coming to us from ancient schools.

It may be that Gurdjieff's choice of the C major derives from its having been sourced directly or indirectly from the works of Paracelsian, Hermetic, and Neoplatonist physician Robert Fludd (1574–1637).

We know this Englishman's works were available in Russia. Indeed, Fludd's "Great Monochord" in his *Anatomiae Amphitheatrum* (1623), where we see a great string strung between Light Aleph and Dark Aleph at the base, representing the twin faces of the Absolute in extension, seems practically repeated in its basic principle in Ouspensky's simplified diagram of Gurdjieff's cosmic octave:[2]

C Absolute as ALL
   } Semitone shock/"spark" supplied by creative will of Absolute
B All created worlds
A Galaxy-Milky Way
G Solar System—Sun
F Planets
   } Semitone filled by organic life on Earth, receiving planetary
     influence
E Earth
D Moon
C Absolute or Nothing

It should also be noted that the ancient Gnostics used the seven-toned scale, attributing to each note the seven Ionian vowels A, E, H, I, O, Υ, Ω. This helps us to understand some of the curious vowel chants in ancient

Gnostic texts, for astute observers will note that the Gnostic name for God, IAΩ, is visible at the precise center and at the extremities of the septenary scale (from *scala,* meaning "ladder"), with harmonious di-tonal vowel sounds on either side of the central Pleromic or radiant "I": "He" is Alpha and Omega, beginning and end.

Fludd's monochord is not identical, for Fludd wishes his string to encompass the three worlds familiar to Hermetic occultists: the earthly, the ethereal (celestial), and the supercelestial (hierarchy of angels). Like Gurdjieff, Fludd made his scheme fit his priorities, for it should be stressed these diagrams are analogies only, expressing principles, but there is much fluidity in application. For example, in Fludd's image for the incarnation of God through the form of universal man (based on Ezekiel's famous vision), the traditional ninefold angelic hierarchy won't fit, so in Fludd's highest octave he combines the Holy Trinity of Father, Word, and Spirit, with man's higher faculties of *Mens, Intellectus, ratio,* and Will. Likewise, the traditional four elements in the lower region octave are, by adding mediant categories, stretched to seven: *earth,* salt *water,* fresh water, *air,* middle air, higher air, *fire.* The schemes are not absolute; systems can be viewed dynamically as interpenetrating multiverses.[3]

Gurdjieff's triune principles of active, passive, and reconciling/ neutralizing bear comparison with Fludd's use of kabbalistic ideas of God's twin powers of acting and nonacting.

The octave principle is applied by Fludd to make many points about the harmony of the creative universe, in relation to man's body and, notably, food processes. Gurdjieff does pretty much the same, without the benefit of Fludd's wonderfully skillful artist-engravers. It seems hard to imagine Gurdjieff had not seen and taken Fludd's detailed syntheses of the octave deeply into his ideas of relation between microcosm and macrocosm, and his conviction that music is the mirror of reality.

What Gurdjieff, like Freemasonry, calls the "rule of three" is strongly evident in Fludd, to such an extent indeed—when expressed by Fludd in the form of the pyramid—that one suspects that when Gurdjieff claims in *Meetings* to have been a guide to "the Pyramids,"

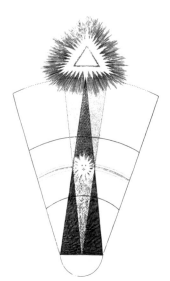

Diagram of interlocking "pyramids" from Robert Fludd's Philosophia sacra et vere Christiana Seu Meteorologia Cosmica *(Frankfurt, Officina Bryana, 1626, 212), showing how the regions between the highest empyrean worlds and the lowest material realms contain qualities from the highest and lowest creation.*

he just might have been thinking of the geometric pyramids Fludd uses to express the idea of the two points of created plenitude converging on a higher point. When Fludd wishes to express diagrammatically the cosmic duality of light and darkness, he shows a pair of interlocking triangles or "pyramids," as he calls them.

Fludd at least knew *he* wasn't being original with his monochord. The single-stringed instrument had been used for teaching students about the "great chain of being" since antiquity. Likewise, the ancient Egyptian pyramids became a teaching source for Renaissance Hermetists without knowledge of hieroglyphics. Fludd in the second volume of his *History of the Technique of the Microcosm* (circa 1620, p.190) describes the pyramids as the true key and gateway to philosophy, and to every science. Fludd uses pyramids to describe the relation of the descending soul and participation of the elements. The elements come into man through his food, and Fludd's comments on the subject of food are highly reminiscent of Gurdjieff's: "The body is formed of food, hence of the four elements. This inert matter is vivified by the soul, which is of another order of existence altogether. The wonderful harmony of these two extremes [illustrated by interlocking pyramids] is brought about by the *Spiritus Mundi,* the limpid spirit, represented here by a

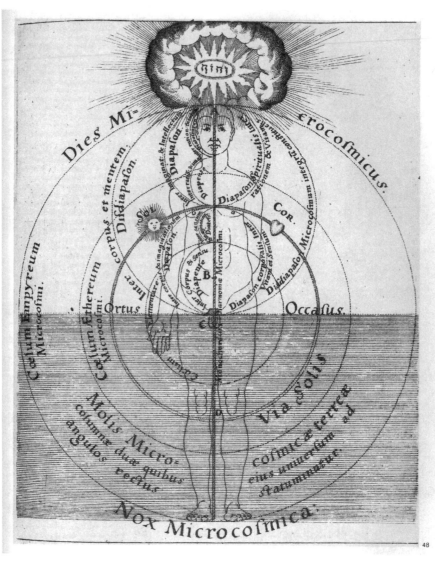

Engraving from Robert Fludd's Tomus Secundus De Supernaturali,
Naturali, Praeternaturali Et Contranaturali Microcosmi historia, in
Tractatus tres distributa *(Oppenheim, Theodore de Bry, 1619, 275),
showing how the Spiritus Mundi (Spirit of the World), depicted as a string
(monochord), harmonizes the elemental nature of food with the soul, even
though of polarized orders of existence. The string indicates the three worlds
(shown as concentric circles of the Empyrean, Ethereal, and Elemental
"heavens") man's soul must pass through in descent to earth and ascent to
heaven. The stages are again expressed in terms of the "music of the spheres"
where the Monochord expresses the Harmony of the Microcosm (Man).*

string. It extends from God to earth and participates in both extremes. On it are marked the stages of the soul's descent into the body, and its re-ascent after death."[4] From this Gurdjieff might well have deduced that the making of an "astral body" (subject to the stars) is an effort of man's ingestion of proper food in conscious relation to higher being.

NINE IN THE CIRCLE

Fludd's numerical Hermetism also give us insight into another image that Gurdjieff introduced into his Moscow and St. Petersburg meetings, according to Ouspensky. Gurdjieff's most famous transformational glyph is known as the enneagram, which is not a prognostic medical procedure but a simple work of geometry. You can of course divide the circumference of a circle into practically as many parts as you like. The more interesting results come from equal divisions from two to nine. How one connects the points on the circumference governs the nature of the image. People have long intuited deep meanings to the figures thus produced. Divide a circle into five, and you have the basis for the pentagram (with all its fascinating coincidences of internal angles); play your lines right, and you may easily produce a figure with some magical or symbolic potential, depending on the significance you choose to locate in the numbers. Magician John Dee believed a sevenfold circle of seven-sided figures to be very useful in summoning angels; Aleister Crowley likewise, and Crowley went on to develop his own sixfold magic sigil: the "unicursal hexagram" (because it can be drawn "in one" without pen leaving paper).

Gurdjieff knew that geometrical projection had close analogy to alchemical projection and would tell his students that his enneagram contained the secret of the philosopher's stone (obtained by projection), a theme long ago taken up avidly in Michael Maier's Hermetic works published contemporaneously to the works of Fludd, and similarly illustrated. The "stone" is famously the agent of transformation from a lower material state (lead) to a golden or spiritual state: a satisfying analogy for the work of reintegrating the faculties behind the "master."

In the enneagram, the key number is nine, traditionally associated with the divine spiritual sphere beyond the eighth sphere of fixed stars. The universal Man in Hermetic thought should extend his range from the lowest to the highest, with nine the limit of the symbolic numbers. The universal Man is the "I am" of Gurdjieff's system. We may note from Fludd that the three orders of being consist of threes squared: nine orders of angels in the Empyrean heaven; nine spheres of the Ethereal (celestial) heaven; and nine regions of the elemental world. The nine orders of angels Fludd relates to the four notes of the *diatessaron* (the fourth) and the five of the *diapente* (fifth), so the musical harmony analogy is carried all the way to the "top," so to speak.

Interest in finding graphic form for the nine orders of angels in the Empyrean led seventeenth-century Jesuit Hermetist Athanasius Kircher (1602–1680) to produce a ninefold geometrical figure. It served as a frontispiece to his *Arithmologia* (Rome, 1665).

We see the deity as an eye in a triangle, surrounded by three interlocking triangles, produced by dividing a circle into nine. The figure then radiates rays from the nine orders of angels produced at the points of the three triangles to the celestial spheres below of the seven planets surrounded by the fixed stars. It is fascinating that Kircher took a pictorial motif from Egyptian hieroglyphs; namely, the wings attached to a sphere he took to indicate evolution in time, to which everything below the angels is subject. The fascination comes from comparing this with Gurdjieff's insistence when showing Ouspensky *his* version of an enneagram that the figure must be viewed as being in dynamic motion; it symbolized a *moving*, multidimensional system: a living symbol. In Kircher's engraving the figure is seen above a Hebrew scholar with an open book revealing the stars of Solomon and David (formed from the circle divided into five and six respectively) who sits opposite Pythagoras with his famous theorem.

Even more interesting then is that in the section of Ouspensky's book (*In Search of the Miraculous*) dealing with the enneagram

Possible proto-"enneagram" construction from Frontispiece,
Arithmologia *(Rome, 1665) by Athanasius Kircher*

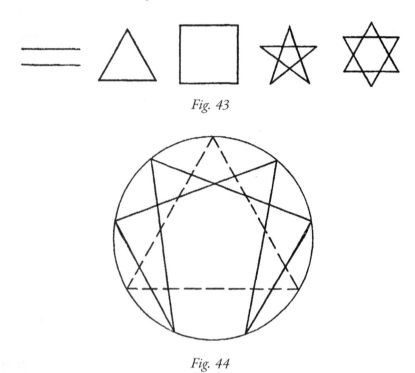

Fig. 43

Fig. 44

(fig. 44), the discussion is preceded by an explanation (fig. 43) of the generation of four figures obtained by dividing the circle into three, four, five, and six.

All of these can be seen in Kircher's engraving below the "enneagrammatic" presentation of the rays of creation. In Ouspensky's book, the figures (triangle, square, pentagram, hexagram) are given Egyptian, Hindu, Persian, and Hebraic provenance. It might seem strange then that Ouspensky takes Gurdjieff at his word when he quotes Gurdjieff as saying what he will see next is unlike theosophy or "Western occultism," "completely self-supporting and independent of other lines," and that "it has been completely unknown up to the present time." We see a diagram of the Gurdjieffian enneagram. While exponents of Sufism have claimed it as being derived from their ancient sources, I see nothing to fight about as to its origin. It does not take a great deal of effort to produce it. If, for example, one takes Kircher's glyph as template, one need only shift two triangle baselines, one to the left, one to the right, and you have Gurdjieff's enneagram. One should recall Gurdjieff's insistence that he habitually altered anything to make it his own after his grandmother told him as a boy to be different. Gurdjieff tells Ouspensky the symbol "cannot be met with anywhere in the study of 'occultism,' either in books or oral transmission. It was given such significance by those who knew, that they considered it necessary to keep the knowledge of it secret." We are told it expresses the law of seven united to the law of three. The three is visible in the horizontally based triangle, and the seven is the seven notes of the octave with the two shocks, that is, the "missing" semitones, added numerically.

Ouspensky saw a great deal in it, and like all such figures you can find what you're looking for, for the universe answers the yearning soul, and cross-fertilization of numbers rendered symbolically meaningful can be a surprisingly fulfilling exercise. It's worth noting that when the figure is harmonized into three interlocking triangles (as Kircher has it), we have three perfect equilateral triangles whose internal angles are all 60 degrees, adding to 180 degrees, where 8 and 1 is nine. We could make a lot of that, for there we have an "octave" and the number of the tonic of the scale.

As far as exercise goes, Ouspensky states that Gurdjieff began to apply his enneagram to his dance movements in 1922, drawing on the floor at the Prieuré a huge enneagram, positioning his dancers at the key points, and then choreographing their movements into relations with one another. The movements could not look anything but meaningful and fascinating, for they were dealing with fundamental relations. But one cannot help remembering Blake's dictum: "God is not a spiritual diagram."

Gurdjieff would add on to his itinerary things that emerged in his discussions with new people he met. One feels this side of the arrangement was greatly satisfying to him when the momentum of his operations started to build up at, most unfortunately, the very time the internal geometry of imperial Russia was collapsing on itself.

SIXTEEN

The International Alliance of Ideological Workers

That Gurdjieff had acquired followers had never been so obvious as when an awestruck Ouspensky saw an apparently transfigured Gurdjieff off from St. Petersburg's Nikolaevsky Station in February 1917. From that point, biographies of Gurdjieff have focused as much on the familiar (to Gurdjieffians) names of de Hartmann, Hinzenberg, Stjernvall, de Salzmann, Ouspensky, and later, Orage, Toomer, Heap, Howarth, Taylor, and the others, as on Gurdjieff himself. They needed him, and in some curious way, he needed them, to a point.

From Alexandropol in June, Gurdjieff telegrammed Ouspensky, offering him a "rest." In September, Elizaveta de Stjernvall's husband showed her a letter in which Gurdjieff practically ordered him to terminate his affairs, leave his chattels, and join him that month.[1] Liquidation again! Given the imminence of the October Revolution that delivered Russia's capital to uncompromising Bolsheviks, Gurdjieff must have resembled a moustachio'd Moses extending a staff of comfort from the Promised Land.

In these circumstances, he was an attractive proposition. Gurdjieff had tremendous charisma, willpower, and physical strength and was inured to conflict situations; in fact he could thrive in them. To him, his followers were like the flecks of startled color and form in a Kandinsky painting. His dance-gymnastics had that quality: abstractions of planetary movements; vital forces vibrating, like iron filings jerking round a magnet. He wanted to make his planets shape up into orbit; he would test them. This way he could turn the awful civil war erupting across Russia into a positive, magical event. He would wield the brush—and a revolver.

After meeting the Hartmanns, the Stjernvalls, and others on the Black Sea resorts of Sochi and Uch-Dere (50 kilometers north of Prince Oldenburgsky's resort at Gagra), Gurdjieff sensed the Bolsheviks' predatory menace. He chose familiar turf to the east—the mineral waters territory between Mineralni Vodye and Kislovodsk in Russia's Stavropol Krai 250 kilometers northwest of Tbilisi in the north Caucasus. Gurdjieff rented rooms suitable for quartering separate families in the pretty town of Essentuki and began a roster of household tasks, profitable labors, and what Ouspensky—reacting against Gurdjieff's new regimes—disparagingly called "numbers": various counting tricks and dances of Bektashi dervish origin. A sign was put up outside the collective residence: INTERNATIONAL ALLIANCE OF IDEOLOGICAL WORKERS.

Already severely strained caring for his followers, Gurdjieff was disturbed to see his own ragged, skeletal family turn up in the streets: mother; brother Dmitri with wife and daughters Anna and Luba; sister Anna and husband Feodor, their children; youngest sister Sophia plus fiancé. Fleeing a Turkish advance on Alexandropol, they had walked to Tbilisi, procuring carts to Essentuki. Gurdjieff's father had refused to leave. Ivan's eldest son was now saddled with some eighty-five persons. Sending out the professionals to find jobs, Gurdjieff opened his "Philosophical Working Community" to the public for evening talks and dance displays. Followers were put severely through their paces. Gurdjieff dissected weaknesses, insisting pupils confront them by going against familiar grain. He said he was like a coachman; if the horse veered to the left, he pulled them to the right. It hurt.

Returning to Alexandropol with Feodor in July 1918, Anna learned her father had succumbed to mortal wounds inflicted by Turkish forces on June 26; they moved to Feodor's family home near Mount Ararat. Feeling the pinch, Gurdjieff adopted a line he expressed in "The Material Question": "In every circumstance of life always strive to combine the useful with the agreeable."[2] His extraordinary plan to keep things moving in a situation where towns and villages were switching daily from White Army to Red, then to the Cossacks, was to launch a scientific expedition to assess the extraordinary prehistoric dolmens of the Caucasus. Yes . . . *the dolmens*. Science. Objectivity. This trek would take them to Tuapse (where Ouspensky would join him again) and Sochi on the Black Sea coast and then southeast to Tbilisi, spared from fighting. Gurdjieff's convincing arguments, combined with pupil Pyotr Shandarovsky's useful job in the Bolshevik administration, secured passports, equipment, and financing.[3] Gurdjieff informed all comers that his word was to be absolute law on the journey; to make his point clear, a revolver sat on the table before him.

Media vita in labore sumus. Like Lara in *Doctor Zhivago*, Ouspensky worked for the Reds in the local library; Dmitri stayed to secrete valuables, and on August 7, 1918, a train of wagons and horses left Essentuki in the cause of science. The dolmens were there, all right (3000–2000 BCE), and still are. Most resemble huge stone ovens with megalithic roofs, sometimes with a "porch" and often carved with circular patterns. Usually there is a round hole in the walls. Peasants used them for chickens. Who knows their ancient purpose?

The journey was extraordinarily tiring, full of close shaves; privation was normal. Gurdjieff's main worry was to save the young men from Red Army conscription; the Whites made gains daily. He had a Red pass and a White one: on two sides of the same sheet. Gurdjieff repeatedly charmed away threats, even from bandits who took their rifles. They encountered kindness from Cossacks, Armenians, and a Pole called Philipovich at Solohov near Sochi. An engineer, Philipovich suffered from fainting spells after a malevolent hypnosis experience. Such was his joy at Gurdjieff's curing him completely that "Pan," as he was known, joined Gurdjieff and stayed all the way to Paris. No wonder Gurdjieff would say to New York listeners that it was "as if miracles were being performed for us." They felt "under supernatural protection"; five times they crossed Bolshevik and White Army lines. Their attitude to each side was, he said, "impartial, as if we were not of this world." Even though "surrounded by infuriated beasts of people," an attitude of good will was elicited from both sides, "even though adopted unconsciously and purely instinctively." Despite the loss of reason from those "in the grip of a psychic state," Gurdjieff maintained there was an instinct in all humans for distinguishing good from evil in an objective sense, and despite circumstances, this persisted. He believed the combatants were "instinctively sensing in my activities the living germ of that sacred impulse which alone is capable of bringing genuine happiness to humanity"[4] On this basis, getting out of that "real hell" was not, he claimed, "due entirely to my well developed ability to discern and play upon the slightest changes in the weaknesses of the psyche of people in a psychosis of this kind." Everywhere was devastation, but they were preserved.

In January 1919, Essentuki fell to White Russian General Deniken, who moved down on Sochi. Gurdjieff's exhausted party caught a boat to Poti, whence a train cradled them to Tbilisi, under Georgian Menshevik control. In a short-lived independent Georgia (the Russian *Tiflis* was dropped for *Tbilisi*), Tbilisi saw the first proper, or more familiar, manifestation of the Institute for the Harmonious Development of Man.

TBILISI

Having left his two most valuable collections in Petrograd and Moscow, and suffering from *angina pectoris* with a temperature of 104 degrees, Gurdjieff begged to borrow a pupil's diamond ring for a night's food for everyone. But when Tbilisi's flourishing carpet trade opened its doors, Gurdjieff's health improved. Sufficient funds poured in to encourage seeking the new republic's Ministry of Education's support.

The ministry authorized the institute on October 6, 1919. Promises of a proper building failed to materialize, however, so Gurdjieff leased a hall. From this nucleus was cemented a new inner core of Gurdjieffians.

Teaching composition at the city's Conservatory, Thomas de Hartmann met stage designer Alexander de Salzmann (born 1874), whom he'd known in Munich, and Salzmann's wife, Jeanne, who taught "eurhythmics"—not be confused with Steiner's eurythmy—at the Military School Hall. Salzmann had married nineteen-year-old Jeanne Matignon Allemand in Hellerau, north Germany. There she had taught the dance method taught her by Emile Jaques-Dalcroze in Geneva, where she was raised. Intrigued by Gurdjieff's "sacred gymnastics," she let him dominate her lessons.

Olga Ivanova Lazovich (Olgivanna), daughter of a general from Montenegro and married to Salzmann's partner, Latvian Valdemar Hinzenberg, in a local cabaret called The Peacock's Tail was equally intrigued, having seen Jeanne's pupils at Gurdjieff's dances. When Olgivanna asked for work, Gurdjieff asked what she wanted. "Immortality," she replied. *Could he help?* He could.

Having already bonded so strongly on the Caucasus trek, the other women did not warm to Olgivanna. But they welcomed experienced dancer Elizaveta Galumnian Chaverdian (Lili), just one of those attracted to packed-out lessons.

In spring 1919 Gurdjieff learned from brother Dmitri of his father's death, a direct consequence of Turkish army aggression, and that the White Army had discovered Gurdjieff's hidden cache in Essentuki and destroyed his Petersburg porcelain collection. Filing a complaint, Dmitri was told the owner would have to claim. Less than gallant, Gurdjieff sent Olga de Hartmann on the perilous mission, giving her a suicide pill "in case of extreme necessity."[5] There was little left to collect. Returning with two carpets she was told to go to Armenia with her husband to learn Armenian music, and to perform—all part of "working on themselves." They returned to find the group summering at the Borjhomi spa resort. Back in Tbilisi, "rehearsals" proceeded for

The Struggle of the Magicians. Beekman Taylor considers this more a "work task" than a serious attempt at the ballet's somewhat vaporous conception.[6] Highly intellectual Frank Pinder of the "British Economic Mission" to the White Russian Army observed rehearsals. He had already met Ouspensky and connected him to A. R. Orage, whence came Ouspensky's "Letters to Russia" in Orage's *The New Age* magazine, and the seed of Gurdjieff's most advantageous relationship.[7]

Grief returned in January 1920 with news that the Turks had raped and killed Gurdjieff's sister Anna, slaughtering her husband Feodor and their children before razing Baytor, Feodor's village. Only their boy Valia escaped, emerging from hiding to traverse an incredible 240 kilometers to Tbilisi by foot and train.

In the summer, Gurdjieff decided it was time to pack up and head for Constantinople, a remarkable choice given what had happened to his family. At Batum on the Black Sea coast, amid Rothschild's oil refineries, the core group (minus Lili and Olgivanna) departed in early July a few days before the Soviet Army's arrival. Gurdjieff had managed to get an Armenian passport, dated June 29, 1920. The "so-called Special Georgian Detachment" only permitted him two small diamonds and two carpets of the many he brought from Tbilisi. All the carpets he'd distributed to members were confiscated. In his attempting to recover them after the Bolsheviks seized Batum, only two of twenty were recovered, sent by diplomatic bag from the Finnish consul to the Stjernvalls.[8] Nevertheless, having sold everything for a song in Tbilisi, Gurdjieff thought he still had good money, with his carpet profits, but in Constantinople Tbilisi's currency proved worthless.

SEVENTEEN

Stateless Person

Gurdjieff had packed up and left many times, but he had always come back home. Now there was no home, and he was in his early forties.

It has often bothered observers as to why Gurdjieff alienated most of his followers. Surely, the question is why he ever spent so much time with them in the first place. He might have fantasized about a group of seekers of truth, but none of his followers matched up to his "remarkable men," and indeed, there were more women than men, and no Vitvitskaia with her intriguing "Thais-like" characteristics. Judging by his behavior, he doubtless fancied most of the women at one time or another. We should not have heard of any of the followers, save arguably Ouspensky, but for the Gurdjieff connection. Thomas de Hartmann trained under Rimsky-Korsakov, yes, but the world knows Rimsky-Korsakov. They must all have doubted themselves, especially in Gurdjieff's presence. He picked on them as a matter of policy. Was it all well intentioned? I suspect he was disappointed. I think he would have loved to hear Jim Morrison sing, "I need a friend who doesn't need me." He played ball with his ego, and it was a big ball. It may not have demanded *him,* but it demanded respect, and got it: hard to find a friend for such a one, or two. Was his wife a comfort? We don't know. We know he loved her; there were no children.

CONSTANTINOPLE

Strapped for means to support his group as he was, he had obviously "done" Constantinople before; he knew where to go and what to do. He found ample premises in Pera, the European district, renting an apartment on Kumbaraci Street and later at 13 Abdullatif Yemeneci Sokak near the Galata Tower, close to the dervish house of the Mevlevi Sufi Order, followers of Rumi. There at the Khanen Gate, Ouspensky, just arrived, joined Thomas de Hartmann at the *sema* ceremony of the whirling dervishes. Gurdjieff explained to the mathematically minded Ouspensky that the whirling was based on counting patterns.

Luck, Gurdjieff says in "The Material Question," brought him immediate business success: the resale of a large consignment of caviar, and the sale of a ship. Fast work. He held "office" in the Black Rose café, a focus for White Russians. When not conducting business he directed movements classes and demonstrated publicly on Saturdays before many local Turks and Greeks, fascinated, he says, by the music he'd written with Hartmann.[1] Continuing to make money "by every possible means," Gurdjieff drafted lecture synopses on movements, music, and painting in relation to objective science, sitting on trams or boat hopping across the Bosphorus to Kadiköy, where he healed pathological ailments by hypnosis, all the time aware that the clock was ticking. Governing parties of "Young Turks" were fiercely nationalistic: their ire turned on Greeks and Armenians.

Soon after Ouspensky's arrival—he'd been sending Gurdjieff pupils—Olgivanna and daughter Svetlana turned up. Gurdjieff was looking for a way out but had visa trouble. Turkey's alliance with Germany, and the Salzmanns' and Hartmanns' prewar experience of that country, made Germany attractive; Gurdjieff determined on the West.

According to Beekman Taylor, a file on Gurdjieff from India led British intelligence agent John Godolphin Bennett (1897–1974) to observe Gurdjieff in Constantinople, but the file actually concerned Buryat "spy" Dorjiev. This account strains belief somewhat. Dorjiev looked nothing like Gurdjieff, of whom photographs had appeared in Russian journals; history had moved on from the Anglo-Tibetan war. Still, intelligence is far from infallible. According to intelligence specialist Richard B. Spence, Bennett was in Constantinople on "special duties" but "whether he served the military, SIS or some other entity is unclear."[2] Young Bennett's outstanding success in ingratiating himself with senior reformist Prince Sabahaddin of Thrace (1879–1948) and other Turkish figures would in time make MI5 and the Foreign Office suspect Bennett of running with the hare and hunting with the hounds. In July 1921 the twenty-three-year-old orientalist came face to face with Gurdjieff "by accident" when dining with Prince Mehmed Sabahaddin. That Bennett was mightily impressed by Gurdjieff's perceived link to higher being only made Gurdjieff himself look suspect.

JOHN GODOLPHIN BENNETT, PRINCE SABAHADDIN, AND GURDJIEFF

Prince Sabahaddin was nephew, through his mother, to sultans Abdul Hamid II (died 1918), Mehmed V, and Mehmed VI, and enjoyed access to the royal palace. He was, however, committed to fundamental reform in Turkey, advocating the rights of Armenians and Greeks to equality. While he was against separatism, he argued that Turkey's economic success depended on a reversal of the centuries-old dhimmi status of Christians in Turkey. This view brought him into close contact with Turkey's Freemasons. Sabahaddin's Liberal Party and his association with the Young Turk political spectrum had seen him banished from the country twice (he had visited England). Returning after the war in 1919, the prince made a powerful impression on British intelligence officer John Bennett. The following year, Satvet Lutfi Bey (Satvet Lütfi Tozan) introduced Bennett to the prince in Istanbul.

Bennett had undertaken an intensive course in Turkish at London's School of Oriental and African Studies and, having proved himself to the intelligence services a remarkably adept linguist, was posted to

Constantinople after British and Arab forces had forced Turkey out of its old Eastern empire with the end of the war. Bennett became British liaison officer to the Ottoman war ministry, a sensitive position.

In Bennett's book *Gurdjieff: The Unknown Teacher,* the intelligence officer offered a colorful account of what attracted him to the company of the prince and to the prince's admired friend, Gurdjieff. Bennett claimed he had seldom encountered a place where East and West blended more perfectly than Sabahaddin's palace of Kouron Chesme (Kurucesme) in Constantinople. There, Sabahaddin introduced Bennett to the world of Universalist spirituality, lending Bennett Édouard Schuré's highly influential book, *The Great Initiates,* which bound the pioneers of religion to a common underlying spirituality often betrayed by those who dominated religious life after their deaths. Sabahaddin was deeply committed to both Islamic and Christian spiritual traditions. The prince also introduced Bennett to Winifred "Polly" Beaumont, who was living in Turkey and who would become Bennett's wife. But above all, the prince introduced Bennett to the man who would change his life fundamentally and forever.

In 1921 Prince Sabahaddin telephoned to tell Bennett of a guest he had invited to dinner whom he thought Bennett might profit by meeting. The prince informed Bennett he had not seen the man since 1912, but time had not dimmed his impression of someone unusually interesting. Bennett said he couldn't catch the man's name over the phone but learned subsequently Gurdjieff had recently arrived from the Caspian region. Further investigation brought out the usual gossip in the bazaars that the man was a great traveler and linguist, familiar with all oriental tongues, believed by Muslims to be a convert to their faith and by Christians to be joined to some obscure Nestorian sect. Bennett learned from the prince that he had first met Gurdjieff by chance when returning from Europe to Turkey after the Young Turk revolution of 1908. The prince had, he said, only met Gurdjieff three or four times but believed he belonged to a group of occultists and explorers with whom he had traveled far and wide. The prince believed Gurdjieff had entered into the hidden brotherhoods of Central Asia, and that perhaps explained why he always profited from their talks. The prince proved cagey after that, or so it seemed to Bennett.

And then they met. Bennett was bowled over. Recollecting years later, Bennett gushed. In Gurdjieff, East and West did not simply meet; differences of that kind were annihilated. Gurdjieff did not distinguish race or creed. Bennett was astonished to find a man who, though scarcely acquainted with European languages, nevertheless combined a thorough knowledge of oriental philosophies with good working knowledge of physics, chemistry, biology, and modern astronomy. Gurdjieff was even at home making insightful comments on Einstein's new and fashionable theory of relativity and on Freudian psychology. One might have asked Bennett, "What do you think they read in Moscow and St. Petersburg?" It is obvious Bennett in his youthfulness was making assumptions about Gurdjieff based on his manner of speech, the way he looked, and his linguistic skills.

Bennett recognized that Gurdjieff's knowledge of languages did not extend beyond the Caspian, though Gurdjieff could manage a limited blend of Azerbaijan Tartar and Osmanli Turkish. His Turkish displayed, Bennett observed, an accent of unexpected purity, not out of place in the imperial Ottoman court.

Gurdjieff didn't affect the look of an Eastern sage. Though of medium height, the muscles of his rippling neck and powerful build commanded respect. And then there were the piercing eyes and the huge moustache curled into points below the bald dome. And of course, the mystery. . . . Very little could be ascertained of his life before he appeared in Russia in 1914. It was as though he had come from another world.

Though Bennett would eventually invite Gurdjieff's ire, and certainly the hostility of Ouspensky, who would accuse Bennett of stealing his material when running Gurdjieffian groups in England, Bennett's real life began after meeting the mysterious teacher. He would spend decades trying to understand where Gurdjieff had "got it all from," a quest that led him to bring Sufi spirituality into the forefront of post–

World War II spiritual discourse, and which would take him into even stranger waters, and much controversy.

Bennett's sympathy with Prince Sabahaddin got him, temporarily perhaps, into even deeper trouble with his paymasters. Sabahaddin was a controversial figure all round—a follower of French sociologist Émile Durkheim (1858–1917) who had a left-wing approach to progress—the prince is credited with introducing sociology to Turkey. By 1924 British intelligence considered Bennett "violently anti-British" with communist associates.[3]

There is another factor. Throughout 1921 and 1922, while military attaché to Constantinople's British Embassy, Bennett represented claims of twenty-two heirs of the late Sultan Abdul Hamid to inherit the sultan's Mesopotamian oil fields, worth billions. This embarrassed substantial British interests, which also had a claim, though it would be abandoned at the 1922 Lausanne Conference, while U.S. Standard Oil contested that since Iraq was now a free state, exploitation rights were open: *to them*.[4] It is likely this issue influenced Bennett's intelligence reputation and might also explain in part Gurdjieff's later claim to have gained income from oil investment and may have been a factor in his meeting Bennett chez Prince Sabahaddin.

The volatile political situation in Constantinople, the accelerating storm against Greeks and Armenians, meant that Gurdjieff could not see a way to staying in Turkey. He would have to go west, confident of fresh support through his extending web of personal connections.

In August 1921 Gurdjieff took the train to Berlin. Renting rooms in Schmargendorf in the capital's southwest, he set to work. Jeanne de Salzmann took him to Hellerau near Dresden, to the house where she had taught the Dalcroze system, described in Dalcroze's foreword to *Rhythm, Music, and Education,* as a seeking after "the connection between instincts for pitch and movement . . . time and energy, dynamics and space, music and character, music and temperament, [and] finally the art of music and the art of dancing."[5] Eurhythmics united body and mind. A photograph has survived of Gurdjieff in Hellerau: lean, lithe, very dapper in a suit, brogues, and cane, his shaved head glowing with vigor, a very fit man in his mid-forties. Hypnotic powers of suggestion would not, however, make the owner yield the property; he had another option. Despite Otto Hellwig at Uhlandstrasse 61's printing a German pamphlet about the institute's "Methode" (oddly signed: "G. J. Güdschijew-Georgiadis"), Gurdjieff accepted an invitation to London, abandoning his HQ at the Cristal Café, from which venue, incidentally, follower Tchesslav Tchechovitch—recently freed by Gurdjieff's agency from incarceration in Budapest as a suspected spy— has left us a story showing Gurdjieff would not do *anything* for cash, even when strapped. A modestly attired woman approached him for help with a mentally handicapped son. Gurdjieff offered help at a modest price, but on learning from the café proprietor she was a wealthy widow who regarded the son as a burden, Gurdjieff told her to stick her fifty thousand marks—she had upped her offer on being uncovered—as she was a "whore mother," not a loving mother. I like this story; Crowley would have done likewise. Better the devil you know.

Gurdjieff hit London on February 12, 1922, rather behind Ouspensky, who had been there since October, invited to translate his *Tertium Organum* by theosophist Lady Beatrice Rothermere. Gurdjieff was invited to address Ouspensky's group in Kensington. A faux pas of Ouspensky's at Lady Rothermere's precipitated a brief return to Berlin, where Gurdjieff bought electronic equipment to assemble to give patients the impression he was "up to date": shades of Ashkhabad!

Returning to England for two talks in March, he had a brief row with Ouspensky and decided Paris would be better for him, even though asked to establish his institute in England. He felt he would be lost in England; he sensed its lost-in-suburbia character and insular, tepid culture and desired rather to be at a global radix of ideas: Paris was the place. He'd just visited it with Olga de Hartmann to see her cousin. He said he would send over instructors to England and took care to cultivate Lady Rothermere's generosity.[6] As for Germany, its stuttering economy, social discontent, and perhaps moral atmosphere did not encourage confidence; Paris felt better all around. There were between 45,000 and 100,000 Russian exiles in Paris; he could get a grip on that.

The Salzmanns greeted Gurdjieff in Paris on Bastille Day 1922. In "The Material Question" he says he had only 100,000 francs left. Ouspensky accompanied Lady Rothermere and Yorkshire industrialist Ralph Philipson over to the rescue. An agreement was reached to finance short-term projects. The pound was strong, the franc weak, the mark rate collapsed; Gurdjieff felt Paris as sound as sterling: British cash would grow there. It arrived in the form of English students whom dour Ouspensky screened as Gurdjieff's secretary.[7]

Gurdjieff needed premises. Enter Dalcroze instructor and Paris Opéra ballet director Jessmin Howarth, discovered by Alexander and Jeanne de Salzmann. The Dalcroze studio in Rue de Vaugirard in Montparnasse was empty for the summer. They took it.

Meanwhile, *New Age* editor A. R. Orage, primed by Ouspensky to hear Gurdjieff in London in February, headed for Paris. Encouraged by Gurdjieff, who so loved liquidating affairs, Orage sold his magazine *The New Age* for one hundred pounds, investing the proceeds in a year's instruction with his new idol. He told friends he'd gone to find God. Aged forty-nine, Orage should have found him already; he was a theosophist, after all. More student dues came from English Jungian alienist James Carruthers Young, impressed by Gurdjieff's movements. And Gurdjieff could expect more work with alcohol and drug addicts, whose families, as with the "whore mother" in Berlin, offered substantial sums.

Gurdjieff believed that one who had found the way he pointed to would not be prone to accidents—being in tune with the hidden harmony of the cosmos. A blind man, after all, is more bound to slip than one with sight. It may be strange then that Gurdjieff did not shudder when Olga de Hartmann found a château at Avon in the Fontainebleau Forest that could house a hundred pupils: the Prieuré des Basses Loges. Formerly the house of a religious order, it had also belonged to the

Dreyfus family. The sale price was about 700,000 francs, worth roughly $40,000 or £8,000. How Gurdjieff must have longed for the million rubles he took with him to Moscow a decade earlier! In *Life Is Real,* he lamented the material resources he'd left in Russia, gone forever: "If within three months I didn't have at least one cool million francs, I would go up the chimney, also forever."[8] He also lamented he "spoke no Western European language," reflecting bitterly in 1924 on the "amount of nervous energy I wasted during these first two years in France, at moments when I felt what I said was not translated properly."[9] This was not the way to enter a colossal mortgage.

He decided to rent the property for a year at 65,000 francs with a six-month option to buy. The reasoning was that with the franc falling, it made sense to postpone buying as long as possible, taking advantage of the strong pound. Heavily in debt, he and the group moved in on September 30, 1922. On the one hand, he must have felt like a pasha, surveying his sultanate, surrounded by admiring women—if only his father could have seen him! On the other he must have entertained serious doubts about what he had taken on.

To serve the excessive borrowing—a loan was arranged in London— he would have to divide his time between Paris and Avon, *commuting* to pay off the debt. "This was the first time I departed from the fundamental principle I had imposed on myself fifteen years before [1907] namely, to take on myself sole responsibility for the accomplishment of my work, without accepting material help from outside." Until that time, "I did not owe a cent to anyone." He told Dr. Louis Berman in New York in 1924, in answer to "The Material Question," that he sometimes had to work twenty-four hours a day, the pressure calling on "superhuman" efforts.[10] Sensing vulnerability, his enemies increased; Gurdjieff's health was badly shaken. Nevertheless, he saw his way to balancing books and even paying off some of the loan in the first six months.

He says he went into partnership with some businessmen on financial ventures, selling a block of oil shares at a good price. He also opened two restaurants in Montmartre and sold them profitably once up and running. He had no *carte d'identité,* so all this was technically illegal business. He said it went against the grain of his spiritual nature and caused disturbing inner experiences. He particularly regretted having to spend time in the dives of Montmartre trying to cure a drunk who didn't want to be cured, while encountering the jealousy and opposition of others. While some might think he was having a hoot of a time late nights in the clubs and bars, as he put it, "I would not have wished such revels even for my bitterest enemy."

In *Tales* Gurdjieff gave a puritanical, caustic, and bitter picture of Montmartre in 1922 and its hypocrisies and sexual debasement. He noted the prostitutes were all foreign; the reputation of the French for lewdness was unearned. The corruption came from, and was doled out for, foreigners. He described "the Duke's Tour," a predictable round of brothels and lowlife for visiting aristocrats, plutocrats, and democrats. Montmartre in Gurdjieff's mind was simply dreadful. He obviously saw the club *L'Enfer,* with its open mouth of ruddy hell near the Moulin Rouge, and took it literally. It was a long way from Bukhara.[11]

He struggled on, making "superhuman efforts regardless of the disastrous consequences that might ensue for me."[12] He reached breaking point. In Fontainebleau Forest one night, he fell asleep at the wheel of his car. He had never fallen asleep against his will before, he said. He caught a chill that wouldn't pass. All business had to cease, but the bills kept coming. Everything he was trying to achieve was threatened once more. After ruminating on the terrace of the Grand Café, he decided to go to America.

While Gurdjieff struggled to finance the debt, life in the Prieuré seemed to its members calm and orderly. In mid-October 1922, Orage and modernist New Zealand short-story writer Katherine Mansfield (1888–1923) moved in. One wonders if Gurdjieff found some outlet for his inner turmoil and external pressures—the police observed him, thinking him a Mason who used hypnosis—in his practice of "stepping on corns"; that is, shocking pupils into self-observation by undermining their egos. It is the

feature of Gurdjieff instruction that recurs time and time again in followers' accounts of their experience. No one could escape his penetrating,
sphinxlike eye. If you couldn't take it, you left. The press began to take
an interest. First, the Paris *Excelsior* reported on the "mystic temple in the
depths of Fontainebleau Forest"; then on February 23, 1923, the *London
Daily News* printed Orage's first installment (of four) on Gurdjieff's ideas.
Gurdjieff was providing "aids to meditation," Orage wrote. The story
shared the front page with the discovery of Tutankhamun, a fortuitous
coincidence. The *New York World* carried a full page on the Prieuré later
that year. Rumors spread: Gurdjieff was a hypnotist. He made his followers do odd things, it was said. Others said he knew the answer to happiness in life. An American woman said she'd heard someone had seen
him in Tbilisi; he was just an Armenian rug merchant who catered to
sex-starved old maids and human derelicts.

Gurdjieff did do strange things. Some have seen his "toasts to idiots" based on Masonic toasts. Gurdjieff, in observations reminiscent
of Thackeray's *Book of Snobs,* insisted there were twenty-one levels of
idiocy (3 × 7). I recall a German philosopher friend telling me of the
"law of the conservation of stupidity" by which the more a person was
convinced of the rightness of his actions, the more stupid he was likely
to be. Certainty, then, was likely to mean hell. Dictators lead us astray:
they're always sure, aren't they? This is the kind of thing Gurdjieff was
getting at. Man is a floppy idiot by and large, barely able to walk by
himself, never mind think clearly. So it is healthy to toast the idiots.
Gurdjieff was a "unique idiot." Orage a "super idiot." Children were
"candidates for idiocy," All true, when you think about it.

With his mind set on America as the best means of "shearing the
sheep," and perhaps even finding an alternative, and cheaper, home,
Gurdjieff organized and trained pupils for public demonstrations in
1923. From his new apartment on the Rue du Commandant-Marchand
between the Place d'Étoile and the Bois de Boulogne, he journeyed
out to the Prieuré to supervise movements to music, and to teach par-
ticipants tricks using mnemonics. Numbers stood for words: number

forty-two meant "thank you," for example. The number forty-two really *is* the common answer to the meaning of life! But numbers could also stand for notes on a piano. Words could stand for numbers. Pupils learned Morse code. This enabled an off-stage person to conduct artists on stage by pure code. The interplay of code and word or music could be mesmerizing, making a startling feature of the performances enacted in the United States in 1924.

Pressure persisted. Lady Rothermere would no longer assist; she was backing Krishnamurti, T. S. Eliot, and Ouspensky in England. Gurdjieff was anxious to reach a point when he could let his pupils organize their own lectures and demonstrations. If only they'd pay their own fares to America!

Gurdjieff decided to try out the gathering show at the Théâtre des Champs-Élysées, noted for its comedy. If in debt, well, why not make it worse? The show would cost 300,000 francs; he believed "Higher Powers" would conform to the law that a definite spiritual aim pursued with unflinching will earned success. Just as he feared the precipice, his mother showed up carrying an object he'd given her for safekeeping at Essentuki: a brooch formerly belonging to a Grand Duchess. Miraculously she hadn't dared touch it, despite her privations. She was relieved to hand it to him.

The brooch saved the day, but think what it could have done for the Prieuré if he had decided instead neither to do the public show nor make the trip to the United States. Was that perhaps the will of Providence? Why should Providence be stingy? The good fortune bolstered his resolve. America would tip the balance in his favor. He was, in fact, gambling. But the odds looked good. It was a friendly Jaques Hebertot who introduced the dances at the Prieuré on the open days, and it was Hebertot who had the lease for the rental of the Théâtre des Champs-Élysées.

Between December 13 and Christmas Day, the expensive theater hosted two matinées, and evening performances, with a "scratch" orchestra of thirty-five rather than Hartmann's hoped-for hundred. In her final month of pregnancy, Jeanne de Salzmann danced the lead part. The prospectus promised three of one hundred parts of "The Art of the Ancient East." The first part included the famous "stop" exercise that so impressed both New York audiences and Russian art connoisseur, impresario, and founder of the innovative *Ballets Russes* Sergei Diaghilev (1872–1929). After the first night, Olga de Hartmann asked Gurdjieff how he thought it had gone. He said: "Never think of result; just do."[13] There was some encouraging press. The institute now looked more than a crazy gimmick: "judge the tree by the fruits." The show had music, discipline, commitment, and originality. But it was still peculiar; it might intrigue or repel. Similar reactions greet performances of the movements today. Gurdjieff maintained his authority stemmed from Eastern monastic traditions unknown and inaccessible to Westerners; many were prepared to take this at face value; many still are.

Orage took over from Ouspensky in the main work of screening pupils; he would take the work to the States and seed it, in readiness for Gurdjieff's personal appearance. Ouspensky, on the other hand, at the end of 1923, found that he could not remain connected with Gurdjieff. He said he had stopped understanding him completely. Was Gurdjieff veering "off-message?" Any such judgment presumed consistency. Gurdjieff liked surprises. Then again, Ouspensky had always wanted clear answers from Gurdjieff, and frustrated with Gurdjieff's generalities and personal impositions, he had left him before. Perhaps Ouspensky found the showmanship aspect difficult to handle; perhaps there had been too few miracles and too little sense of real personal fulfillment. But Gurdjieff had rather spoiled him for anything or anyone else; Ouspensky was now stuck with trying to make the best of what he had learned, in the hope of what he might yet learn.

The Paris performances lost money. Now Gurdjieff would really have to shear "dollar fat" from the Americans. It was that, or bust.

This is where we came in. On January 5, 1924, Gurdjieff and his troupe sailed for America from Le Havre.

After midnight drinks and snacks in Juliet Rublee's Manhattan apartment at 242 East 49th Street on April 8, Dr. Louis Berman asked how the institute was funded. Gurdjieff offered his tour-de-force extended begging letter we know as "The Material Question," pleading his case of how he'd done it all by himself with little help for years and only now found himself in terrible debt, a debt he was giving his health and life to repay.

Moved by Gurdjieff's story, what else could the good doctor do? Berman told Gurdjieff it would be an honor to "lighten the enormous burden you have voluntarily taken on yourself." A check appeared. Gurdjieff thanked his "God-given brother." Then a "Lady L" made a speech. She too gave money for his "Great Work." Gurdjieff said he'd pay it all back in eight years. He didn't; he couldn't.[14]

Gurdjieff returned to the Prieuré in June. Wartime intelligence officer Frank Pinder burgled his papers, hoping to unmask Gurdjieff; nothing came of it.* Gurdjieff couldn't pay the full price for the property, but he had a mortgage. Money from the States was outstanding. Gurdjieff went to work in Paris at full tilt, moving to a new apartment at 47 Boulevard Pereire, just north of the Parc de Monceau. Orage found few buyers for certificates of membership. Orage charged $120 for an induction course in New York, but payments for a spell at the Prieuré were proportionate to income. While appearing fair, it could be taken as exploitative. It takes guts to take the rich for a ride, and by and large, as Gurdjieff understood, the rich really aren't interested in spiritual enlightenment, certainly not in paying for it. They expect it at the doorstep with a bow. Gurdjieff would have liked to interrupt rudely their conceit but seldom got the chance. Wealth requires insulation, like ingots in a vault.

He was in a dark place. Nathan Jean Toomer, an exception to the

---

*Pinder would return to Gurdjieff's entourage in 1937; Gurdjieff forgave him. An account of why Pinder rifled through Gurdjieff's papers when Gurdjieff was in America before fleeing the Prieuré and what happened years later when Pinder returned to see Gurdjieff again can be found in *Gurdjieff: A Master in Life* by Tcheslaw Tschekhovitch (chapter entitled, "The Justice of the Master: Forgiveness," 157–61). I am grateful to Michael Benham for this information.

rich-boy story, well off and sincere, sailed to France without realizing Gurdjieff just wanted to close the gates.

Then, on or about July 5, 1924, near Chailly, Gurdjieff crashed his 10 CV Citroën (top speed 65 km/hr). It seems he might have eaten and drunk too much at an Armenian restaurant lunchtime session, but that was hardly unusual. Stories about the crash and its aftermath vary wildly. He apparently swerved into a field to avoid a car coming out of a crossroads. He told one pupil the steering wheel snapped, and he'd thrown himself clear to avoid a tree on which he would otherwise have been impaled. Another account says a gendarme lifted him gently from the front seat, unconscious with a serious head wound. One account has him comatose for days; another that he was able to walk with a stick after a few days asleep. One thing seems fairly clear. He was not his old self for quite a while and, some would say, ever again. Ouspensky opined frontal lobe brain damage might permanently affect his thinking capacities. Gurdjieff would write in *Life Is Real*: "By some miracle my shell did not crack."[15] *He* didn't think he was permanently damaged.

Nobody will ever know if Gurdjieff had not somehow conspired in his own demise: a desperate way of halting the pressure that had been building for years. His wife Julia was not well; female devotees surrounded him. He was tempted. Would he not say he had been leading a consciously "artificial life"? And could one truly say it had been working? He had American followers. He had English followers. He'd done his thing—and the pressure was still on, worse even. And he was far from home among people he couldn't feel close to; he could understand them morally; he could classify them. He could psychoanalyze them, by his lights. But he could not find the kind of fellowship you could find in Transcaspia with a suspicious policeman who doesn't care whether you live or die but at least, somehow, knows where you're coming from.

Gurdjieff was lonely. And loneliness is a drag. He would sulk; then he would gather his forces and rise above mundane feelings. Then he would turn inward again, retire to his room. But now, after the accident, he was ill, by God, perhaps unbalanced. Ouspensky told followers in London that Gurdjieff was never the same after it: "His mind had deteriorated and left him in delusion."[16] Orage's fiancée Jessie Dwight, an American Gurdjieff never took very kindly to, and advised Orage to leave, described the Prieuré as having been hit by a wave of unreality: "A form of madness went on . . . when there were fifty others all behaving so oddly. . . . In spite of slammed doors. Gurdjieff recovered and that almost makes me believe he was a superman."[17] *Almost* believe . . . Jessie never really dug Gurdjieff; he came between her and her loved one. Orage said you couldn't judge Gurdjieff like other men. *How could you judge him then?*

Gurdjieff had bonfires made on the grounds of the Prieuré. He would haul his pained body into a chair to watch the gorgeous flames, emblems of spirit, garments of the phoenix resurrected from ashes. Olga de Hartmann thought he drew some special power from fire. Of course he would; nothing occult in the power of flame to call us to the elemental truths; the ocean can do it, mountains also, and the air, the right air—the air between the Gobi and the Turfan Oasis. But that was long ago and far away.

How to recapture that long ago and far away place? Gurdjieff decided he could no longer run about like an athlete, but his mind could. He could write. He could write his way out of the compressed misery of protracted disappointment and night after night of unremitting bloody work.

He would, he thought, write a masterpiece that would say it all. The word of God-man from on high, the arch-word of Beelzebub, who had come to Earth with nothing but good ideas and seen the world's response: incredulity, hostility, hatred, or, maybe even worse, blind, mindless worship. To hell, and from the fires he would weave tales, curling up with the flames from the bonfires of the Prieuré in the autumn-winter of death and promised rebirth. Gurdjieff went underground, into the soil of his memories and fantasies. He would dig and dish the dirt on the whole human race: the vilest clan of scumbags ever known.

EIGHTEEN

Doctrine

An Objectively Impartial Criticism
of the Life of Man

In August 1924, two months after the accident, Gurdjieff assembled the summer students on the lawn before the Prieuré and informed them he was closing the institute. They would have to be out in two days. He then put up a list as to who could stick around. When Lili Galumnian found she was not on it, she pleaded. Gurdjieff wouldn't budge; Lili got a job as a lavatory attendant until she had enough to leave France. Olgivanna Hinzenberg went to America where she would fall for another outsize ego, architect Frank Lloyd Wright, who, in due course, would himself be intrigued, occasionally cowed, but not seduced, by Gurdjieff.

Gurdjieff was going to be a writer; it was his way of recovering and of shielding himself. Now all responsibility would be to *the book*. Those remaining would help transcribe and translate it, from Russian or Armenian, or both, spoken and written—accounts differ. Not all the stylistic faults of what would become *Beelzebub's Tales to His Grandson* can be ascribed to loose translation. Orage declared the first version inaccessible to ordinary readership; perhaps he didn't have the heart to say that the revision was also unpublishable, except by, and for, aficionados. Perhaps he recognized its value as therapy for Gurdjieff. Gurdjieff's frontal defense remained that its value far exceeded any quibbles about mere *style*. Its importance is that it reveals, for those willing and equipped to dig into its tonnage, Gurdjieff's mind and idiosyncratic take on the world and its inhabitants, and that is the aspect we shall concentrate on, for it is valuable.

You may recall Maud Hoffman's comment in her 1924 article on Gurdjieff that there was an absence of *philosophical* lectures during her sojourn at the Prieuré. In some respects, the book aimed to satisfy on this score, accomplished in an oft-witty but grotesquely overblown satirical prose, strangely reminiscent in essential spirit of the genius of *Gulliver's Travels*.

What are the Gurdjieffian doctrines within this "objectively impartial criticism of the life of Man"? Can we refine the excavated ore into a series of confined points and postulates?

I think we can.

Behind everything is an eternal creator. At sunrise, one should greet the sun as the symbol of him and pray—or as Gurdjieff expresses his conception of prayer, consciously try to contact the subconscious as if it were conscious—pray that unconscious factors not inhibit the whole duty of being, which is to rise and awaken to our "COMMON ENDLESS CREATOR."[1]

Many of Gurdjieff's most peculiar ideas are really an ironic joke of Gurdjieff's in response to common theories of biological evolution, as taught by "education" today. If man understood what scientific "evolution" *really* intended, he would lose faith in existence. Beelzebub tells the story that the soul of the ordinary man, at death, simply goes to feed the moon, so that eventually the moon will reproduce organic life like Earth—and *that,* for all intents and purposes, is man's biological purpose in the organic scheme of things. But as we say, this is a shocking, "sick" idea, and men must be protected from it, lest they become depressed and cease serving nature. (Egyptian philosophy, note, identified the moon with Isis: goddess of *reproduction*.)

To limit man's awareness of his earthly predicament, lest he stop reproducing the required matter, higher powers long ago put in man the organ "Kundabuffer." This imaginary organ buffers, or prevents awareness while distorting reality. A side effect is that mankind, unlike other "three-brained" beings elsewhere in the universe, no longer develops naturally the objective reason proper to a three-brained being. Earthman is *un-man:* disharmonious and brainwashed by sensory data, a being dependent on exterior impressions for registration of pleasure and enjoyment, a creature as stimulable and suggestible as Pavlov's dogs or Sando the half-witted Armenian woman Gurdjieff hypnotized in Kars. This is Gurdjieff's assessment of empiricism, and it is very close to that of Fabre d'Olivet.

The fundamental myth of Gurdjieff's story is held in common by the cosmoclastic or extreme Gnostics who told of a Creator of the material cosmos who "knows no higher than himself"—like the moon ignorant its light is the sun's—and feeds off man's subtle energies, keeping man ignorant of what he really is. Man is devoured by nature and is never intended to wake up. This creator-God or demiurge is a false absolute. He is, if you will, the detached Ego of the universe. His mentality is reflected in the egoist on Earth who has imagined God like that, and who imagines everything revolves around him or her for his or her delectation, and who feeds off and destroys others: the parasite.

The holy spirit of man is not at home in this spiritless world, or *world perceived as spiritless,* as it appears to the spirit to be. Kundabuffer prevents men from ever knowing what true Men, "remarkable men," are fully made of. They therefore fear and hate anything that comes from on high, spending their fated days in irrational behavior, such as periodically killing their fellows, or building empires of sand—often in the name of God, *their God.*[2]

Such is *psychosis:* sickness of psyche or mind.

The reason that it is the moon that feeds on soul in the story is that the moon turns the tides of Earth and represents the feminine-passive in esoteric symbolism: the seductress who drugs the foolish suitor, with the association of madness and the fatality of ever-pumping, greenish mucoid, mindless, reproducing nature. *Yuck!*

The fatal quality of Man is vanity. His ego cannot bear being insulted. Correct valuing of men is always taken as offensive undervaluing, and as an insult. Ordinary men are only respected by ordinary men—and that rarely! Truth is foreign to humankind, for man is alien to "objective reason," which is truth.[3] The laws of men are not sought for their original root in objective morality but to protect the vain and the pretentious who, insisting on power over others, cannot govern themselves.

The cure for this is the constant reminder of personal death, death of ego, and the utter waste of the life truly unlived. Better to die to the ego voluntarily and begin the rebirth of new eternal life, and work to make real the spirit that rises.

Contemporary literature and art, says Gurdjieff, lacks any call to the highest, but plays to human folly and weakness. It is a futile dream on the way to futile death. Its idea of art is not of the Sphinx or the ancient prophets but serves the small minds and the quest of personal vanity. Any knowledge that can waken people up is regarded as heresy, either hushed up, ignored, or severely repressed, its authors regarded as pariahs. Most people serve the "power-possessing beings" whether they know it or not. They do not act; another acts through them. They do not think; another thinks through them. They do not live; another lives through them. They think they have power. In fact, they are overpowered by another, whom they serve. Capitalist culture, if it is permitted to become totalitarian, is a culture of mercenary automatons. Bolshevism denies the truth of Man absolutely and is tyrannical.

Human beings are pacified and made to accept the spurious "fame" of mediocrities whose vanities keep men and women unconscious, obsessed with colossally irrelevant details. Sport is a drug to deflect mass consciousness. Mankind is entertained to death. From above, the seriousness with which human beings obsess on the trivial is risible, tragic. Tell the people X is "famous" or has been given an award; X is listened to, even if, or especially if, he or she is an idiot of high degree. The media is a killer.

Gurdjieff's collective, objective idea of the "power-possessing beings" bears great kinship with the Gnostic conception of the "archons" or invisible rulers of the universe who conspire against man's consciousness—they who whisper "Crucify him!" that soon becomes the public shout, and public, democratic will—to silence the truth. But as the Gnostics say, they nail *their* man to *their* tree. And do not see the one above, laughing at them. The governed will is not a free will. If one man is true, and a hundred false, democracy is tyranny. To end a tyranny, you need topple only one; *what happens when the whole society is corrupt?*

Man has a fantasy of reason that he perceives as reality. He dwells in a false world of false values.[4]

The first victim of Kundabuffer is common sense. Things are done not because they are good but because people are afraid. Kundabuffer prevents voluntary action; work is only done by fear. People work for money for fear of poverty. Fair and just government is not respected unless people are afraid. You don't have to see the bomb, just be made to fear an idea of it. Negative ideas are more potent than prison sentences, more insidious than whips.

Common sense is right relation and adaption to circumstances—this is the gift Melek Tawus brings to man in Yezidism: intelligent initiative. Gurdjieff's system is, if you like, to remove the residuum of Kundabuffer, for Gurdjieff tells a story that the actual organ *Kundabuffer* has been long removed but has nonetheless distorted the functioning of what remained.

In chapter 15 of *Tales,* Beelzebub comes to Earth to witness a young firebrand intellectual who has wormed his way to power: lacking common sense, he is out of kilter with reality. Thinking, feeling, and body instinct are all disharmonious, but *Boy! Is he smart!* He can destroy in months a civilization that took centuries to build! This is Gurdjieff's warning from the story of Atlantis. And what is the clever intellectual's message to get power? The government is not *fair! I,* he promises, will give you your "human rights." How often have we heard this tripe from the smooth politician?[5]

In short, Kundabuffer as resistance-to-truth generates psychosis, sickness in the mind: derangement in the world. In a kundabuffered world, the one who has worked his way out of the residuum of Kundabuffer becomes suspect to those who have not.[6] He is the "enemy of the people." In the words of Saint Paul, "They crucified the lord of glory" (truth).

Time is subjective; our sense of it is not absolute. It is an image of eternity, a characteristic of creation in extension, experienced as movement, and as such, measurable, but the measure is in relation only to other phenomena at any particular point. Time can be transcended when one is in harmony with the creative source of time.[7] This is basically Platonist, but Plato believed the ideas went back considerably before Greek thought arose, as did Gurdjieff. Eternal ideas, ideas about eternity, are eternal, and have always been in Man. Our sense of vast ages is, as it were, but seconds to one in eternity. There is, ultimately, no time.

All things created will be destroyed forever, except those in which "objective reason" is fixed.[8] The only hope in man is the only hope in man.

A phrase repeated dozens of times, tiresomely in *Tales,* refers to the "abnormal conditions of ordinary being-existence." This is life conditioned by the disharmony of misperception, to which man is accustomed by habit, and therefore taken as "reality." In chapter 17, on the "arch-absurd," we can see how much of Gurdjieff's fundamental myth is informed by the esoteric staple of the fall of the faculties. He says the "instinctive sensing of reality" is absent in mankind, especially those born in recent periods. There has been a fall from reality, an inability to see aright; the lens is distorted, if not shattered, and can no longer reflect the *One* behind all existence. The ordinary ego is not the divine being that is proper to Man. Man hardly knows he's alive. For this reason he cannot see the simple laws of number that structure the inner life of the cosmos: the heptaparaparshinokh, or sevenfoldness, for example.

The number three is also critical. Gurdjieff has been deeply touched by the Orthodox Trinitarianism that has become critical to Christianity, but which is widely misunderstood. Faith, Hope, and Love are three living principles discernible in life at every level of being, as "Father, Son, and Holy Spirit." Faith is father to hope; the spirit engendered by familial harmony is Love. Gurdjieff identifies conscience with faith. The awakening of conscience opens the door to faith. The Gnostics identified Faith with Wisdom.

Gurdjieff believed the true essence contained in Christianity was very, very ancient, preceding even the historical Egyptians, a view shared to some extent incidentally by church father Clement of Alexandria (circa 200 CE). Gurdjieff insists throughout *Tales* that the first teachers and practitioners of these sacred principles are to be accorded genuine, wholehearted respect, by living the principles out in real life, not just uttering them parrot fashion. They point to a primal harmony of being: indeed, to myriads of interweaving harmonies. Human being is divided into competing races when humanity fails to see that which once united our being. Here is perhaps the greatest challenge of our times.

The law of three also stands for the dynamic forces of affirmation, denial, and reconciliation, symbolized in the triangle. These relate also to faith (affirmation), hope (denial of despair), love (reconciliation), and the whole gamut of phenomena where positives and negatives are transcended on higher planes, in physics (namely: attraction, resistance, fusion; quantum physics) and philosophy (Hegelian thesis, antithesis, synthesis).

We have already in chapter 15 looked at the extension of the law of three in the enneagram. It became employed as a hypnotic glyph related to dynamic energy flow or movement. Gurdjieff's movements aim to harness perpetual energy forces within and without, above and below, at the eternal "moment" expressed as the circle. In classical astrology, the *ninth* represents the divine, spiritual world beyond the seven planetary spheres and the eighth sphere of the fixed stars. Nine is the "aim" or "End" Finding, and maintaining an aim is a vital component of Gurdjieff's teaching. You can't even go wrong if you haven't got so much as an aim. Without an aim, man is a machine. Beyond nine: *One,* the source of being. Creation extends into manifestation by "involution" from the One and can return by "evolution" *via* Gurdjieff's ray of creation. Yes, Gurdjieff "stole" his ideas—from some excellent banks!

These and other harmonies were, Gurdjieff asserted, visible to our remotest ancestors, and fragments have been passed on through time. Kundabuffer has not mastered every single one! In a sense, Gurdjieff echoed the assessment of post-Enlightenment esotericists that the so-called enlightenment of the eighteenth century, insofar as it was rationalistic, materialistic, and externally sense based, was a "black-out," generating cold, isolate thought incapable of seeing beyond sensory limits and relative measurements. Nevertheless, history shows the fundamental loss of Tradition goes back to the beginnings of recorded history, though Gurdjieff is unimpressed by the idea that the history we know marks anything like the beginning of civilization. That is what the "map" of pre-sand Egypt is all about. It's a pointer to look further, explore deeper. Man has lost powers as much as he has gained certain others, but the ones he has lost are those he needs to employ wisely the ones he has gained. We stand at a crossroads.

There is some hope of recovering essential knowledge. Gurdjieff coins the word *Legominism,* one of the least ridiculous of Gurdjieff's many neologisms in *Tales,* to denote the transfer of long-past insight or information of events. A classic of such memories is that of the "Flood," where degeneration and psychic disintegration necessitated erasing primordial civilization. This is why the Gilgamesh story was so important to *Meetings,* and to Gurdjieff. Blake, of course, had been there before,

for he too had found "objective reason." Blake speaks of "three powers in man for conversing with paradise that the Flood did not sweep
away." By the *Flood,* Blake meant the flood of time and space. And the
three powers for conversing with paradise—the kingdom of heaven
within—are poetry, painting, and music, which can all express the
unity of the original faculties of man: *dance* can unite all three. This
is why Gurdjieff set such great store on dance as a sacred activity. One
could argue that the place for the sacred dances is in a church, or something like it; it may yet happen. The point was that people can learn
profound truths through gesture and art, using the body to untap the
spirit and *vice versa.*

There are many more perceptions of good sense in *Tales,* though it
needs editing to about one-fifth of its current length and to be recast
in clearer sentences, with spiritual understanding of its wise, humorous
contents; then *Tales* would enjoy considerably greater currency. As an
editor, in this case, Orage failed dismally to serve the purpose he so
wished to serve. But he made a start, and he had the aim.

Gurdjieff knew the essence of his message was in the book and
took to having it read as the content of meetings. This could stimulate
complaint; one lady was outraged at having paid money merely to hear
someone reading from a book. "Is that it?" she cried. She had a point.
But Gurdjieff himself enjoyed listening to it and found it very funny,
though few could see why he was laughing. Intrinsically, it is funny, for
Tales is a potential banana skin under the foot of contemporary humanity. One day, perhaps, the gag will explode on the world, and we may all
see the Joke.

As Beelzebub tells his grandson, "I must tell you that when I used
to exist among your favourites [human beings], it was always difficult
for me to refrain, as your favourites say, from 'laughter,' when one or
another of the learned beings there delivered a 'lecture' or related to
me personally about some past events, of which I had myself been an
eyewitness. These lectures or 'stories' there are crammed with fictions

so absurd that even if our Arch-cunning Lucifer or his assistants tried to invent them, they could not succeed."[9]

Mankind must work at salvation from derangement. The spirit has to be, as it were, worked into being; it is not an automatic process. We must engage willingly. The first step is also the last: *Know Thyself,* or would you rather be eaten by the moon?

NINETEEN

The Beast 666 and the Black Devil

The first half of the twentieth century provided set and setting for two outstanding and near contemporary magi, each with their own devotees. Having known several Gurdjieff aficionados over the years, I have sometimes observed the supposition that Gurdjieff dismissed Aleister Crowley from the Prieuré as something unclean, whereas Crowley's devotees tend to treat Gurdjieff either with a casual interest or indifference. It is odd because both men, with respect to their teaching, had far more in common than emphases that differentiated them. Many of Gurdjieff's cherished attitudes were expressed succinctly by Crowley: love as the uniting of opposites, for example; the importance of will, and the idea that the cosmos falls into line with the correctly orbiting will; this wisdom they shared. Gurdjieff's real "I am" is analogous psychologically to Crowley's "True Will" and "Holy Guardian Angel"; the emphasis on ego conquest; the desire to pick holes in vanities and tread on corns was endemic to both men's relations with the outside world. Both believed in candid sex education, though their views on sex otherwise were probably incompatible. The cosmic, Olympian perspective and humor were enjoyed and employed by both, despite great disparities in cultural background. Even their oriental adventures chime in at certain points. When Gurdjieff claimed to be in Tibet at the end of 1903, Crowley, only a year previously, had explored the neighboring Karakorams. When Gurdjieff was penetrating spiritualistic circles, Crowley's good friend Everard Feilding was secretary of the Psychic Research Society in London. Both Crowley and Gurdjieff had a special regard for the Yezidis. Like Gurdjieff, Crowley, with kindred Masonic interests, focused on Moscow in 1913, both using the same expression—*lynx-eyed*—for watchful policemen in Russia. Crowley had even investigated Fontainebleau as a potential HQ in the new year of 1920, nearly three years before Gurdjieff, and from 1924 to 1929 their residencies in Paris often overlapped.

Perhaps they were too close to get on personally. Like Groucho Marx perhaps, neither wanted to join a club that would have him as a member. They were, anyhow, competitors in the game of esoteric leadership, whether they liked it or not. It rather reminds one of the old contest between the Beatles and the Stones: the bands had time for one another; the fans were often partisan.

Were Crowley and Gurdjieff at odds? Let us examine the evidence.

Crowley gained access to the Prieuré on February 10, 1924. He was met by Major Frank Pinder (1882–1962), a "hell of a fine fellow," according to Crowley. Former intelligence officer Pinder had first encountered Gurdjieff in Tbilisi and, like former intelligence officer John Bennett, had become attached to Gurdjieff. Gurdjieff himself was in the United States when Crowley arrived. Crowley's record:

> Gurdjieff, their prophet, seems a tip-top man. Heard more sense and insight than I've done for years. Pinder dines at 7:30. Oracle for my visit was "There are few men: there are enough." Later, a really wonderful evening with Pinder. Gurdjieff clearly a very advanced adept. My chief quarrels are over sex (I doubt whether Pinder understands G's true position and their punishments, e.g. depriving the offender of a meal or making him stand half an hour with his arms out. Childish and morally valueless.[1]

Admittedly, the two men did not meet on this occasion, but Crowley's sense and generosity of spirit are evident. Even the "oracle" encouraged the view that Crowley's law of Thelema ("Do what thou wilt shall be the whole of the Law; Love is the law, love under will; Every man and every woman is a star") could be advanced by others, as he believed it had been through history. Crowley's view of sex was more libertarian than Gurdjieff's; indeed, for Crowley, sex was properly a form of spiritual worship and could be used by adepts as the prime form of holy magic. Gurdjieff's views were never stated systematically, but in general sex was related to the health of the body and to reproduction primarily, though his own practice and self-criticism suggests he linked sex to selfish appetite and to the fundamental idea of family in a fairly conservative sense, but Gurdjieff did not respect individual women outside of family ties in the way that Crowley tried to. Gurdjieff's view of women was fundamentally traditional, though he obviously fantasized about a Vitvitskaia-Blavatsky-type free ideal.

Beekman Taylor concluded that Gurdjieff's personal view of women would be a letdown for contemporaries today who might otherwise find his ideas "cool."[2] I don't know of any support for Pinder's account to Crowley of specific punishments at the Prieuré, nor is it clear what these punitive measures might have been for; they are not incredible. Crowley himself had some of his students adopt a questionable penalty for using the word *I* during set periods; failure earned a razor cut on the arm. This rather had the effect of making students timid and nervous of themselves rather than ego conquerers. Interestingly, this was a similar response to some of Gurdjieff's students' experience of being shouted at, or psychologically and physically tested, as Gurdjieff was wont to do in his "shock-therapy" mode. Some people suffered temporary trauma in the face of Gurdjieff's powers to humiliate; stories persist of a few cases where Gurdjieff probably misjudged the right point to apply shock. People were always free to leave; some wished they had never come in the first place. Then again some people doubtless feel that way after an experience in a poorly staffed hospital. However, Crowley's methods were softening. In 1924 Crowley was trying to recover from a severe physical and psychological breakdown, and his views were changing, particularly with regard to nonspiritual interpretations of his doctrines. He was becoming a gentler, more tolerant person.

Gurdjieff's impact on Crowley's subconscious is interesting too. Throughout February and March 1924, Crowley was having supervivid dreams, occasioned by heroin shortages (the drug being the only effective cure for extremely chronic asthma attacks), holed up in his hotel bed most of the day in the Rue Vavin, Paris. Later in February, Crowley experienced, "Another dream Gurdjieff driving a dagger (my skean dhu) through open hand of a fat woman disciple. Question concerned the acquisition of power of holy man to reduce fat of their disciple in large chunks . . . the rest gone, or so nearly so that effort to recall would snap thread of main sentence."[3]

The skean dhu (Gaelic *Sgian dubh*) is a small, one-sided household knife secreted in the kilt hose with the hilt only showing. The dream is of course open to interpretation. Is the fat woman somehow a projection of Crowley himself, who had a strong feminine aspect to his nature? Most likely the idea mixes two things. First, the competition between Gurdjieff and Crowley to rehabilitate drug-addicted persons, as we shall see shortly—Crowley claimed to be the world's greatest living psychologist—expressed as the power of "reducing fat." Second, Gurdjieff's stated desire to "shear the dollar-fat Americans." The dagger would represent Gurdjieff's will to achieve this, then being worked full tilt in New York and Chicago, as well, I suspect, as representing a kind of menace, or potential treachery that Crowley may have intuited or secretly feared. The skean dhu is, after all, a secreted weapon, and it is plunged into an open hand; that is to say, a freely offered hand (or handout?).

On Sunday, March 22, 1924, at 9:50 p.m., Crowley confided the following to his diary:

Went out to dine instead; talked 93 [law of Thelema] to Hope Johnstone [Charles Hope Johnstone (1883–1970), photographer]. We agree remarkably on most points, even to astonishingly small details, e.g. making almost identical joke on Women's Suffrage and Democracy. We discussed Gurdjieff at some length—also with agreement. He began: "What do you think of etc." I retorted: "How do you know I know anything about it?" He seems to have taken it for granted that I should know. No doubt at all that the Gods sent me there [the Prieuré]—in the one three-day period when my health allowed such excursion. It is therefore important. *Question:* can I work with them at all, to complete them, as I proposed to myself, by taking on all those who will not fit into his very artificial scheme.[4]

Crowley clearly had the idea of cooperation with the Prieuré in mind. He believed he could "complete" them, an interesting idea suggesting he thought Gurdjieff was missing something, perhaps the full sanction of the "Gods," or the explicit Thelemic principle and literature. Since it is well known certain students left or were kicked out (one for being too flirtatious, for example), Crowley was willing for Gurdjieff to pass them on to him to see if he could do for them what Gurdjieff could not or would not, or even complete their esoteric development. There is also the suggestion that people Gurdjieff had failed to "get off" drugs or alcohol might fare better under Crowley's less hypnotic regimen, though given Crowley's condition at the time, this was something for the future! He had had some limited success on this account before, but Crowley found, like Gurdjieff, if the person did not really want to end the addiction, help was of little avail. And that went for himself too.

The reference to the "Gods" sending him to Gurdjieff's establishment is interesting. There might just have been a covert suggestion of Secret Service interest in Bennett's activities, or even Gurdjieff's, on account of suspected links with Nicholas Roerich and Dorjiev. Bennett had been three months at the Prieuré in the summer of 1923, during which time Bennett became convinced Gurdjieff had the knowledge

Silver

Blue

Custom Sun Shield provides a perfect fit for YOUR vehicle – Say goodbye to flimsy cardboard solar shades that don't fit properly and let in heat and UV light. Composed of a triple laminate construction, the Custom Sun Shield's exterior surface reflects destructive UV rays, thereby reducing the fading and aging of your car interior while the foam core center acts as an insu~~ ~~ ~~and~~ keeps your vehicle cooler. Accordion-folds allow for simple placement and storag~~ ~~ ~~ ~~ visors hold it in place. Optional Storage Bag protects and holds your Sun Shiel~~'~~ specify year, make, model, and whether it's a two-door or four-door. Availab~~'~~ allow up to two weeks for delivery. Made in the USA.

22105T Custom Sun Shield **$79.95**   Optional Storage Bag **$11.95**

Designed for commercial use

This 20' Heavy-Duty Tow Rope is better than a chain because ~~ ~~ stretches ~~ ~~

TO ORDER

(₅-7897) • **Fax: 1.800.543.8633** • **Online: SportysToolShop.com**

Holds up to
100 F

Extends to over
Crevice Cleaning T
you remove all
deck with
is 23/

to transform the human being to a higher level of evolvement. While Gurdjieff tried to persuade Bennett to stay, Bennett felt financially constrained and returned to England to earn money. Though he expected to return, he would not meet Gurdjieff again until 1948. Ouspensky seems to have had a hand in turning Gurdjieff against Bennett.

It is possible that Crowley was killing two birds with one stone in visiting Gurdjieff's competing self-development institute: sniffing out Bennett, if he was there, for intelligence purposes, while offering to take on those unsuitable for Gurdjieff's "artificial scheme." However, Crowley makes no reference to Bennett, though he may have obtained information from Pinder on a "need to know" basis. The intended offer certainly exemplifies Crowley's cheek; he was not in the least awed by Gurdjieff, unlike many disciples then and now, for whom any mild criticism is condemned as wiseacreing, a clumsy word extracted from translations of Gurdjieff. One wonders what word *he* used for vapid intellectualism.

Perhaps even more curious in terms of synchronicity is the fact that after Crowley's visit in February 1924, Pinder, while in charge of the Prieuré, rifled through Gurdjieff's personal papers looking for evidence of . . . *what?*—then left, not reappearing in Gurdjieffian circles until 1937. Gurdjieff destroyed all his personal papers in 1930. *If* Gurdjieff avoided Crowley, it may just have been possible that he and Bennett were sensitive to intelligence interest.

Gurdjieffian myth suggests Crowley was ejected from Fontainebleau. The story comes from the late James Webb's book *The Harmonious Circle:*

> Crowley arrived for a whole weekend and spent the time like any other visitor to the Prieuré; being shown the grounds and the activities in progress, listening to Gurdjieff's music and his oracular conversation. Apart from some circumspection, Gurdjieff treated him like any other guest until the evening of his departure. After dinner on Sunday night, Gurdjieff led the way out of the dining room with

Crowley, followed by the body of the pupils who had also been at the meal. Crowley made his way toward the door and turned to take his leave of Gurdjieff, who by this time was some way up the stairs to the second floor. "Mister, you go?" Gurdjieff inquired. Crowley assented. "You have been guest?"—a fact which the visitor could hardly deny. "Now you go, you are no longer guest?" Crowley—no doubt wondering whether his host had lost his grip on reality and was wandering in a semantic wilderness—humored his mood by indicating that he was on his way back to Paris. But Gurdjieff, having made the point that he was not violating the canons of hospitality, changed on the instant into the embodiment of righteous anger. "You filthy," he stormed, "you dirty inside! Never again you set foot in my house!" From his vantage point on the stairs, he worked himself into a rage which quite transfixed his watching pupils. Crowley was stigmatized as the sewer of creation, was taken apart and trodden into the mire. Finally, he was banished in the style of East Lynne by a Gurdjieff in fine histrionic form. White-faced and shaking, the Great Beast crept back to Paris with his tail between his legs.[5]

Webb places this alleged encounter in July 1926, over two years after the above accounts. But Crowley's diary reveals he only sailed to France from Tunis on July 19, and "failed to arrive in Paris" on August 2, but was there five days later, being thrown out of the Vuillemont hotel on the Champs Elysées, presumably for lack of money.[6] Furthermore, Webb's account gives no source whatever for the story,* nor is there

---

*Michael Benham has kindly informed me that an unpublished manuscript by Gurdjieff pupil Ethel Merston—"A Cloth of Bits and Pieces," held at City of Westminster Archives Centre, London—apparently refers to some hostility enacted on Crowley by Gurdjieff at the Prieuré, which Merston attended from 1922–27. A summary of Merston's memoir in Patterson's *The Gurdjieff Journal* vol. 8, issue 2, states, "'Crowds' of Americans now came as well as many others, including Aleister Crowley, the only person she [Merston] ever knew Gurdjieff to turn out after only a few days." In the context of all else contained in this chapter, the snippet may be fairly regarded as inconclusive (Michael Benham, e-mail to author, October 14, 2016).

any contemporary evidence from any member of the institute to support the account. If Webb did have privileged information, it is only fair to make the point that Gurdjieff may have been unbalanced by the death in June of his wife, Julia, after a protracted fight with cancer that Gurdjieff felt he could, had he been at peak health and power, have done more to prevent. Also his mother had died at the Prieuré the previous year.

Also supporting the idea of bad odor from Gurdjieff regarding Crowley is author and publisher Charles Stanley Nott's account of Crowley's being within the Prieuré precincts in 1926 and chatting to a boy there, saying "something about his son who he was teaching to be a devil." Nott then says Gurdjieff spoke to the boy, who had no more to do with Crowley while Gurdjieff kept an eye on him.[7] By this time, Nott already had a fixed idea about Crowley and must have been miffed to find him close to the idol he'd chosen.

Nott (1887–1978) does not give us the full rejection story. He would have done, had he known it. Deeply devoted to Gurdjieff, Nott had already decided to eschew Crowley—whom he had met in Paris to discuss publishing—for Gurdjieff. Crowley did not have a son in 1926, but he might have been having a joke about Leah Hirsig's son Hansi, who was fond of Crowley and wrote to him as "Beast" and behaved willfully, like a "little devil." Gurdjieff wasn't running a Sunday school either! One can well imagine Gurdjieff watching Crowley closely for other reasons than he had a terrible reputation, largely undeserved. If Gurdjieff had any inkling of Crowley's powers of perception, or intelligence connections, or any doubts about Bennett or Pinder, that would also have added to a certain guardedness.

However, apart from Webb, writing in 2000, no other such account has surfaced. Crowley never voiced publicly any animosity or displayed any vindictiveness regarding Gurdjieff, nor *vice versa* that we know of, though biographer Paul Beekman Taylor for some reason calls Crowley a "witch," a member of a "coven," which statements have no truth in them whatsoever. He furthermore reports a very un-noxious, quite benign visit of Crowley to the Prieuré sometime in the summer of 1926 in his book *Shadows of Heaven: Gurdjieff and Toomer*. Following an account left by Edith Taylor, the author's mother, Beekman Taylor describes a formal lunch at the "Paradou" (a residence in the Prieuré grounds), with Gurdjieff entertaining his niece Lucia, his brother Dmitri, his sister Sophia, "Campananci," Nikolai de Stjernvall, Jeanne de Salzmann, Jean Toomer, Thornton Wilder, "Blackmur," and Aleister Crowley. Beekman Taylor recorded that someone invited the Beast "in anticipation of a combat of magical powers, but apparently both he and Gurdjieff behaved well."[8] This is a very different slant again on Crowley's summer 1926 visit.

On December 29, 1927, the long association of Gerald Vincent Yorke and Aleister Crowley began when they met for the first time at the Hotel Foyot opposite the Luxembourg Palace. Yorke was sole witness to a half-hour encounter Yorke said he organized between Crowley and Gurdjieff at a Paris café. The magi eyed one another warily. As Yorke recalled to Gerald Suster, "They sniffed around one another like dogs, y'know. Sniffed around one another like dogs."[9] This is obviously interesting because it cannot have occurred before early 1928 and no later than spring 1929, when Crowley's legal residence in Paris was withdrawn. Anyhow, if the Webb story were factual, a subsequent meeting would have been unlikely.

A last word from the wonderfully intelligent poet, political activist, artistic patron, publisher, and style icon Nancy Cunard (1896–1965), who had moved to Paris in 1920 and remained in France until the war. She was also, after 1933, a friend and admirer of Aleister Crowley, whom she regarded as an artist and significant "mind." When John Symonds was writing his biography of Crowley (published in 1951), Nancy wrote to Symonds regarding her old friend: "He [Crowley in 1943] then told me a beautiful little anecdote about that ghastly Gurdjieff. I'll bet it's true. He was indignant at Gurdjieff."[10]

It is clear from this remark that Nancy already had views about

Gurdjieff ("ghastly"). Webb's story could hardly be described as "a beautiful little anecdote," however recounted. However, Crowley's indignance at someone was usually earned. One suspects, and suspicion is all, that Crowley had reason to feel his dignity had been offended by Gurdjieff at some point. In that sense, Crowley's dream may have been prophetic: a hand extended and refused, perhaps. As for Nancy's feelings about the "ghastly" Gurdjieff, it is important to recognize she was close friend and confidante for many years to American poet and writer Solita Solano (1888–1975), whose fellow lesbian friends formed a group around Gurdjieff chiefly in 1935–38, which they called "The Rope," following advice from Gurdjieff (Nancy was not a lesbian and did not succumb to Gurdjieff's charisma). Gurdjieff believed lesbian sex indicated an imbalance somewhere, and when he tried to get Solita to consider this, she told him it was not something she wished to discuss with him. Even though The Rope disintegrated in 1938, Solano continued to associate with Gurdjieff as his secretary, but if anyone knew anything an independent woman would consider ghastly about Gurdjieff, it was Solita Solano. On the other hand, Nancy was exceptionally well connected, and there were always stories going around of Gurdjieff's extreme psychological methods and exposure of weaknesses. Perhaps he tried it on Crowley. Perhaps Crowley saw through it.

TWENTY

The Long Ascent

Then there were the women. Some women are drawn to "psychic" men, or men who disturb their peace of mind, stirring emotion. Some women feel they gain something from giving themselves to chosen gurus. Gurdjieff gave, and he took. He ate the moon.

Jeanne de Salzmann and Elizaveta de Stjernvall gave birth to sons— Gurdjieff's—even while their husbands worked with him (Leonid de Stjernvall, unable to father a child, was overjoyed at "son" Nikolai's birth in Tbilisi in 1919). Jessmin Howarth bore his daughter in 1924 (Cynthia, known as Dushka); Gurdjieff's wife was alive at the time. In 1927, Lili Galumnian had a son from Gurdjieff. Edith Taylor bore him a daughter, Eve, in 1928. According to Beekman Taylor, there is "some evidence" Olga de Hartmann and Jessie Orage both parried Gurdjieff's sexual advances in 1930. Jessie complained to her husband about Gurdjieff's sexual predations, only to be told Gurdjieff was not "a man."[1] By which we may suppose Orage meant not a man to be judged by ordinary codes of behavior, a great man. *Droit de seigneur* still operated. Gurdjieff does not appear to have experienced "remorse of conscience" over interfering with other people's marriages, either by making himself available to the attraction of wives, or by his perennial advice that often seriously disturbed couples. Gurdjieff exercised power; he believed it was a beneficial power, and many believed it. He had, he claimed, pushed himself to extremes and come out the better for it; he

302

was sure he knew when enough was enough when it came to others: first shock, then pain, then reward. Such a relationship required faith, a lot of it. Why were people prepared to put up with so much from him? Is faith its own reward? We have not seen battalions of holy enlightened genii emanating from Gurdjieff's fold. We have not seen the miraculous, whose explanation Gurdjieff sought so avidly in his youth. Where are all the harmonized people; we can only say, they're working on it, constantly: hard work, better than being moon-eaten.

I suspect the problem may have something to do with the nature of the "psychic." Gurdjieff's fortunes went into a long decline after the car crash of 1924; still, he attracted sympathy as well as opprobrium, and he had his fun and shared himself with those closest to him. His inner circle wanted to protect him even as they sought his protection. But the fact is he was on a course that essentially combined religion (the sacred) with his idiosyncratic form of shock psychotherapy (waking people up), and he seems to have been blind to the contradictions involved. The evidence suggests his ideas of the sacred were formed in too close a relation to hypnosis and spiritualism, and how these fields could enhance his own powers. Was he obsessed by his own powers? What was the Prieuré, if not folie de grandeur?

The fundamental limitation, as I understand it, is that Gurdjieff confused the triune nature of man, perennial in Gnostic thinking, with the *faculties* of the psyche. It is a staple of Gnostic thought that there are three types of human being: hylic (or material, that is flesh-aware), psychic (aware of "soul," possessing faculties but in need of spiritual salvation), and pneumatic, that is "spiritual." Spiritual people are awake and aware and know it and are "saved" already. There has been a tendency to internalize these three types of being from the beginning; this has consequences. We divide a person into three. Gurdjieff never budged from his three-brained hypothesis. Solita Solano, Kathryn Hulme, and their friends' reports of conversations with Gurdjieff, recently published, show that he clung to the idea like an orthodoxy; it was axiomatic for him.[2] Thus the hylic (material) becomes Gurdjieff's body instinct; the psychic becomes Gurdjieff's *feelings*, and the pneumatic, the thinking faculty—what he called mentation. By doing this, you place the spiritual within the dimension of the *psyche*, hence Gurdjieff practically identifies the spiritual with the psyche that has received the spirit: what he calls "objective reason" (recall the *nous* of Plotinus). You effectively seek "God" or even the essential "I am"—Gurdjieff's "inner God"—*within the realm of psychic experience.* Thus prayer, for Gurdjieff, means the consciousness addressing the unconscious. Such must place an impossible strain on the psyche.

In traditional Gnostic psychology, the spiritual cannot be "sourced" *within* the psychic realm. To a limited extent this is understood in Gurdjieffian practice; one has to open to the "higher," but the dimensions of the Work are psychic dimensions. The Gnostic and Neoplatonic "daimon" or "Holy Guardian Angel," on the other hand, is not of the psychic world ("My kingdom is not of this world"; John 18:36). Crowley, for example, considered it wise to think of the Holy Guardian Angel as an independent being of another dimension, lest it be confused with "self."

Also, regarding psychic functions, Blake and Jung both envision a quaternity of *functions,* not a trinity of brains. The four functions of the psyche, according to them, are reason, feeling, sensation, and *intuition.* One can see Gurdjieff's three brains in the first three, but where is intuition? In Gurdjieff's conception, intuition stands as a quasi-spiritual experience or benefit seen as the outcome of the first three functions being harmonized. Intuitive experiences then are easily identified with spiritual experiences. All this has repercussions in Gurdjieff's view of man having practically to "make" a body that cannot be eaten by "the moon." One almost thinks of ectoplasm, and it seems that Gurdjieff's idea of spirit is a highly refined *substance.* Gurdjieff was essentially a rationalist, and that has its appeal.

Now, this may all seem quite abstract, but the unwinding of these conceptions practically shapes what occurred to Gurdjieff in the years after the crash. Although a now highly remarkable, self-made, and extremely winning, soulful personality, Gurdjieff seems to have stopped seeking, content to let others believe he had *found*.

BREAKING WITH OLD FRIENDS

When the ascent is steep, it may feel as if we are in decline. We are in decline when the going is easy and fast, for we are heading downhill and think we're doing well.

There would be another seven trips to the United States (1929, twice in 1930, 1931, 1934, 1939, 1949).* It seems transatlantic crossings took the place of his past regular forays east on the Trans-Caspian railway—how many realize how much of Gurdjieff's oriental explorations were spent sitting on the train that trundled from Krasnovodsk to Ashkhabad, to Merv, to Chardzhou, to Bukhara, to Samarkand, to Tashkent, to Andijan? He went west, but there was no seeking, no discovery, no fresh insight, just diminishing returns from Orage and Jean Toomer's initially tireless exercises to raise money on the institute's behalf, always an uphill and unenlightening struggle, always, arguably, in vain.

In January 1926 the wealthy owner of the Taos Ranch in New Mexico, patron of arts Mabel Dodge Luhan (1879–1962), succumbed to Toomer's persuasion and offered Taos to Gurdjieff as a center for the institute. Toomer took her $14,000 on Gurdjieff's behalf, but Gurdjieff

---

*Gurdjieff was, however, in New York in 1935, owing to an accident. After he arrived in New York on April 25, 1934, he lost his passport. For three days starting June 12, 1934, he advertised the loss of his wallet containing his passport in the *New York Times*. Stuck in America, he risked deportation after his visa ran out on April 23, 1935. Having pursued the possibility of special American citizenship through Senator Cutting, and Soviet citizenship through Washington's Soviet Embassy, he obtained a German *Fremdenpass* (Aliens' Passport) on April 14, 1935. A passport stamp shows he arrived at Bremerhaven on June 4, 1935. Michael Benham used this information on the Fremdenpass to disprove Bennett's claim that Gurdjieff made a secret trip to Central Asia at this time (Michael Benham, e-mail to author, October 7, 2016).

did not want to disappear in New Mexico. Odd then that he claimed to value the inaccessible monasteries of the East. Odd that no one made it clear to Mabel that they wanted the cash but not the ranch, and took it. It wasn't enough, but it was enough for Mabel Luhan, whose generosity dried up when she realized she'd been had. In June of that year, Mrs. Gurdjieff, Julia Osipovna Ostrovska, died of cancer. Gurdjieff believed he might have saved her by willpower had he not been laid so low by the accident.

In 1927 Orage, to his master's displeasure, married Jessie Dwight. Orage then informed Gurdjieff that *Tales* was not in a state fit for the public. Gurdjieff's depression is evident throughout his often confused, personal remarks in the unfinished *Life Is Real,* begun in November, tired by "black thoughts," exhausted, insomniac in Montmartre's night cafés in the wee small hours.[3] His recently finished *Meetings,* he wrote, indicated "other ways of perceiving reality" while the "third series" would show his "discoveries touching reality, and if desired ever merging with it."[4] The fragments of *Life Is Real* let the cat out of the bag as far as showing that he was spending most of his active hours in Paris, and sometimes New York, grafting in the antiques business. The writing is often crazy and neurotic; he never refers to a single cultural or political event in Paris.

On May 6, 1928, self-locked in his room, he made a vow of austerity and "to remove from my eyesight all those who by this or that make my life too comfortable"[5] While he might shock through outrageous acts those who had become too dependent on him, to wake them, or alienate them for mutual good, making oaths as a way of structuring his life, including his past life, had become habitual as a means of control when major plans failed. On another occasion he decided emphatically to divide his day into three: the first part for egoistic bodily pursuits, the second part for making money, the third for "science" or humanitarian service. He was often frustrated, disappointed, and run down, but then, he could always surprise with fresh energies and personal magic.

Orage's last visit to the Prieuré in 1928 completed the revision of *Tales,* while Gurdjieff polished the considerably more readable *Meetings with Remarkable Men.* Then—the 1929 stock market crash. As global depression bit, the numbers of Americans at the Prieuré dropped off to a trickle. Gurdjieff only wanted Americans; would only tolerate opening a letter from an unknown person if there was a cheque in it. The institute was intended to be self-financing; something he could set up, appoint instructor-managers for, and leave a free man. It didn't happen; failure rankled.

Gurdjieff never intended to bear his followers for life, so it's not altogether surprising he couldn't stop alienating old friends, but they weren't that old in the scheme of things. And what is a "friend" from the higher perspective? Olga de Hartmann got the cold shoulder in 1930. In 1931 Gurdjieff castigated those who'd clung to Orage's groups in New York. According to Gurdjieff they'd misunderstood his intentions, thinking the Work was all about self-observation. He'd only wanted to start clubs. Now new members would have to pledge to have nothing to do with Orage and would be divided into three: exoteric, mesoteric, and esoteric. Orage apparently made the pledge and returned to England, where he died in 1934, Gurdjieff, he said, having nothing more to teach him.

In 1933 the Prieuré was repossessed. Fed up, Toomer retired from the Chicago group. Gurdjieff was back in the States in 1934, guest of Frank Lloyd Wright and the Work-devoted Olgivanna, whose daughter Svetlana got sick of Gurdjieff lording it over the house at Taliesin, Wisconsin, observing reactions and treating everyone "like guinea-pigs in his laboratory"—an old habit.[6]

Back in Paris, Gurdjieff attracted interest from a fascinating group of expats, all enjoying Paris's relative freedom for lesbians, a freedom born out of the late nineteenth-century Parisian occult sympathy with androgyny: a subject Gurdjieff never entertained. Solita Solano, Elizabeth Gordon, Louise Davidson, Alice Rohrer, Kathryn Hulme, Georgette Leblanc, and Margaret Anderson were sometimes joined by

Jane Heap, back from her English Work groups, for drinking sessions, toasts to idiots, and instructional exercises for becoming aware of the three brains. Gurdjieff advised them that on the slopes of consciousness they should ascend roped together; he would guide them, so they called the group "The Rope." They found him a loving, great, insistent character, a sage whose talk was therapeutic and spontaneity stimulating. He found them a relief and was probably more fascinated by them than he would admit. He said their collective "emanations" *killed him*, not literally. He once took Kathryn Hulme to a private club in Montparnasse full of men and naked girls dancing together with just a bit of silk round the middle. He asked her to choose one, or if not, she could strip too and let him choose her; she didn't know how to take it but was moved in a deep way she couldn't grasp.[7]

Before his death in 1934, Alexander de Salzmann introduced Gurdjieff to his friend, spiritual poet and parasurrealist René Daumal (1906–1944). Daumal and Gurdjieff enjoyed a fruitful conversation resumed occasionally over the years till Daumal's premature death, when he left unfinished his *Mount Analogue: A Novel of Symbolically Authentic Non-Euclidean Adventures in Mountain Climbing* to delight successive generations. Columba Powell and I wrote a movie script inspired by Daumal's "mountain that cannot not exist" in 1994, called *The Gatecrashers.* There are echoes of Gurdjieff's "seekers after truth" in Daumal's group of curious explorers in search of a mountain no one believes is possible. The last song of the proposed film: Lou Reed's "There Is No Time."

Gurdjieff taught that automatons are made when they allow an exterior force to live through them, act through them, speak through them. Adolf Hitler demanded the surrender of the will, and millions, not knowing their own, gave it to him. Hitler would have made an intriguing character in *Beelzebub's Tales to His Grandson* and another object lesson on the price of sleep.

THE WAR

June 14, 1940, saw Hitler's army goose-stepping into Paris. Valia Anastasieff, Gurdjieff's nephew, joined the resistance; what would Gurdjieff do with his German-issued Fremdenpass and his "stateless" status? The latter unavailing in the United States, he considered Cuba, but the expense and his ineligibility for an exit visa proved prohibitive.

On Christmas Eve 1942, he was luckily granted a French-German *Certificat d'identité de l'Office des Emigrés Caucasiens en France,* a jolly present. With the tide turning slowly against Germany, German ID papers might have served him ill. Thanks to a connection, his Caucasian immigrant status was secure. Jeanne de Salzmann, meanwhile, trekked from Geneva to Paris for visits to Gurdjieff's apartment in the Rue des Colonels Renard and movement classes in the Salle Pleyel, Tchesslav Tchechovitch being the sole member from the Constantinople days, among artists, the aged, and infirm folk unwanted for forced labor in Germany or concentration camps.

Considering Gurdjieff hoarded all kinds of savory foods, meats, tobacco, and liquor, it seems he had developed a way of working black market contacts and mollifying Germans, who were running an administration forbidding the sale of meat four days of the working week in a city where rats proliferated because cats were eaten. Never charged with collaboration, he was known as a generous old resident who fed the local poor, and gave treats to children and money to starving artists, buying paintings that filled his apartment. Gurdjieff's creditworthiness for wartime luxuries was a mystery covered by tales of credit-inducing oil shares until Paul Beekman Taylor uncovered the true source of Gurdjieff's good fortune in his book, *Gurdjieff's Invention of America* (2008).[8]

Racehorse breeder François Dupré owned the luxury Plaza Athenée and George V hotels. In early 1939, his wife Anna Stefanna (Anci) was suffering from a terminal illness. Diagnosed as inoperable, a painful tumor by her liver brought Gurdjieff in as a last resort. Gurdjieff followed a manual reconnaissance of chest and abdomen by placing his right palm over the tumor. Within a day, the pain was gone. Anci became devoted to the miracle man and, prompted by Jeanne de Salzmann, persuaded her husband to support Gurdjieff. Dupré wanted nothing to do with Gurdjieff personally but complied until December 31, 1942, when Anci announced she was pregnant. Dupré told the stunned Anci he was impotent. The father was René Daumal's friend Luc Dietrich, who did not take responsibility.

Thanks to Dupré's good relations with the Wehrmacht, Anci obtained an *Aussweiss* to pass through to Switzerland with Jeanne de Salzmann for an abortion performed by a gynecologist friend of Jeanne's. Returning to Paris, Anci and Dupré reached an amicable agreement. Dupré's German connections and subvention would keep Gurdjieff in sauce till the end of the war. The miracle served Gurdjieff well.

Liberated on August 25, 1944, Paris's new administration arrested Dupré for collaboration but released him on his paying an enormous fine. Gurdjieff was detained for a day or so for possessing dollars under his mattress but released as an old man who did not understand the crime. Gurdjieff could receive guests from outside France again, who were relieved the old boy still stalked the land of the living.

TWENTY-ONE

The Grave with No Name

In 1944 Foreign Office man Robert Cecil was working as secretary to Sir Stewart Menzies, known to insiders as "C," head of SIS and Britain's code-breaking organization. A pupil of Aleister Crowley, who had hoped Cecil might succeed him, Cecil read Ouspensky's *A New Model of the Universe.* It took him down another route on his search for inner happiness. Cecil and Crowley's mutual friend Frieda, Lady Harris, informed Cecil that Ouspensky was in America. Ouspensky's representative, Harley Street doctor Kenneth Walker, told Cecil new members were forbidden until Ouspensky's return. Meanwhile, Cecil should avoid John Bennett, whom Ouspensky accused of stealing his teachings.

A fortuitous diplomatic posting to Washington, D.C., in 1945 brought Cecil to Ouspensky's home at Franklin Farms, Virginia. There he was coldly, rigorously interviewed. Teachings were secret; contact with Jane Heap's London group was forbidden. Ouspensky, wrote Cecil, "was by nature a shy, constrained person, in whom some of the springs of human sympathy seemed to have dried up as a result, perhaps, of his too rigorous efforts to 'remember himself.'"[1] Weekend Work tasks at Franklin Farms were grim.

Ouspensky died on October 2, 1947. Deciding to send his pupils to Gurdjieff, Ouspensky's widow gave Cecil the diplomatic task of sweetening the "return" by personally taking gifts to Paris: $500 for Gurdjieff and a bale of fine silk for Madame Salzmann. In 1948

Cecil arrived at Gurdjieff's small apartment on the first floor, 6 Rue des Colonels Renard. Through the front door, a dark corridor; two rooms on the right overlooked the street. The first was for readings and meetings, the second for dining. There behind a long table sat Gurdjieff. The gifts were deemed inadequate to compensate for "the long years of self-exile." Cecil asked what he should telegram to Madame Ouspensky. Gurdjieff's eyes twinkled: "You out of mouse make elephant!"

Cecil returned for dinner, struck by Gurdjieff's "gruff, but insinuating voice; the very bulk of the man with his controlled economy of movement. . . . All these aspects contributed to the general impression; but underlying them was the sense of being in the presence of immense power, irradiated, even in moments of simulated wrath, by benevolence."[2] Cecil, touched by Gurdjieff's *baraka,* or blessing, wanted to bask in the "vivifying presence" and was soon doing movements with Madame Salzmann playing piano in the Salle Pleyel's large, bare room. "All three 'centers,' intellectual, physical, and emotional, were involved and the latter was emphasized in certain movements by intoning a phrase such as 'Lord, have mercy!'"[3]

Gurdjieff would give exercises and insist his French Work groups define their aim. The exercises were varied and tough: "If it wants sugar, give it salt," urged Gurdjieff. Asceticism was not for its own sake; "intentional labour and voluntary suffering" could "produce substances that go to the making of the second body, the one capable of surviving death."[4] Gurdjieff told one questioner, "You must never believe. Everthing must be looked at critically."

Cecil went on one of the many car trips Gurdjieff enjoyed, this one to Vichy. Meant to last two days, the trip was curtailed when it appeared a female pupil called "blonde numéro cinq" had been called to Gurdjieff during the night and told "to strip." Cecil was shocked; fellow pupil Count Bobby de Pomereu shrugged his shoulders, saying, "If you seek God in me, you will lose both God and me."[5] Cecil later heard of the Sufi teacher's practice of *Malamati,* meaning "to incur blame"—the idea being to disintoxicate followers from idolizing the teacher. One might look at this critically.

It is interesting that Cecil, having problems reconciling work with family commitments, took Gurdjieff's advice that "no way can begin from a level lower than the Obyvatel [good bourgeois]." That followers must before all observe ordinary duties to self, family, and society is a basic Masonic injunction for members. Spiritual development cannot be built on a foundation unable to support fundamental duties.

Gurdjieff's approach to communication was changing rapidly. In spring 1943 meetings occurred on Thursdays; by early 1944 a second group met on Tuesdays (about fifty were now involved altogether). In 1948 it seemed to Cecil the doors were swinging wide open.

One day Jeanne de Salzmann invited Cecil to her apartment on the Rue de Bac. Knowing he'd been in touch with Bennett's English group, she wanted to know if they had any money. By August Bennett was reconciled with Madame Ouspensky, whereafter Mr. and Mrs. Bennett visited Gurdjieff, promising financial support; Gurdjieff would take Bennett's pupils "in batches through the purifying fires that consumed guests at the Master's table."[6] Bennett came to Paris and enjoyed as many fruitful meetings with Gurdjieff as he could, trying to make up for lost time and opportunities.

Cecil was sensitive to what he perceived as the "squeezing out of the French." People came without having been screened, bemused by Gurdjieff. Others could not take robust humor mixed with religion. When some just gaped, he would say, "You look at me like cow in front of newly painted gate." Esoteric tradition seemed cast to the wind. Cecil wondered why. Was it to establish an outward-looking structure before his death? Unlikely. Gurdjieff was, observed Cecil, more an agent for disintegration of groups, perpetually setting frustrating obstacles. He appointed no successor and established no hierarchy. Individuals did receive tasks with regard to publishing, especially *Tales* (or *All and Everything*). If the new policy wasn't a desperate throw in the encroaching shadow of nuclear annihilation, Cecil considered it a "spasm" like that which had made him produce *Herald of Coming Good* then prevented its distribution in 1933.

Pamela Travers (1899–1996), world-famous author of the *Mary Poppins* books that draw so much wise magic absorbed from Gurdjieff, had a different view. Having first encountered Gurdjieff in the 1930s, possibly through A. R. Orage (he published one of Travers's poems in *The New Age*), Travers saw Gurdjieff's late explosion of communicative energy in a different light. It was, she wrote in her essay on Gurdjieff, "a period that for those who had known him earlier was richer than any that had gone before. For a little over three years new adherents and old pupils bringing their own pupils and children, flocked to his small crowded room to listen to a reading of one of his manuscripts—*All and Everything; Meetings with Remarkable Men; Life Is Real Only When I Am*—to hear him play on his small hand accordion the music he had composed for the different chapters, or to sit at his table and receive the bounty of his teaching in whatever form it might be given. 'If take, then take!' was one of his favorite aphorisms—no sipping, no trifling—and for many the special nourishment that was offered in addition to the delicious edibles was indigestible, hard to stomach."[7] In this, at least she agrees with Cecil that unworthy guests approached the master's table. But then, to Gurdjieff, idiots only differed in degrees where enlightenment was concerned.

Travers, who would spend the rest of her life serving the Gurdjieff Society with exacting study series, profound research, and much personal attention, writes of Gurdjieff's merciless stripping off of masks. Those who took it might see Gurdjieff's own mask fall, revealing a human being full of sorrow and compassion. "I am" was crucial, but so were "Thou art" and "He is." "Gurdjieff," Travers concluded, "now belonged to the world for the brief time that was left him."[8]

Perhaps Gurdjieff knew the end was near. In late 1948, supported by Lord Pentland, a member of the Virginia Ouspensky group, he went on a high-energy trip to the States. It would be his last, and he gave it everything he had, attending movement classes with sixty pupils at Carnegie Hall, holding court at Childs Restaurant, giving talks, and encouraging groups. Returning in early 1949 to France, there was talk of expansion. A young London architect came to assess the château de Voisins near Rambouillet for a new Prieuré. But as the "Zeros"—as Gurdjieff called dollars—started rolling in again, Gurdjieff was visibly swollen with dropsy, his movements laborious. Nevertheless, he emulated his teaching: one must live, really live, until one dies. Retirement was for knackered horses and insurance companies.

Cecil had a last interview in the summer of 1949 in Gurdjieff's inner sanctum, surrounded by boxes of Greek halva, Turkish loucoum, cheeses, figs, pistachio nuts (but not books). Gurdjieff smoked Russian cigarettes through a wooden holder and drank Turkish coffee. "Well," he said, "what question?" Cecil asked Gurdjieff how he, Cecil, could convince himself that the world he was sitting in was the real world, or was the real world rather the one he inhabited as a bureaucrat in London? Gurdjieff smiled: "God help—also Devil."

On October 27 the American Hospital in Paris admitted Monsieur Gurdjieff. Suffering great pain, he died from cancer of the pancreas on the morning of October 29. On November 2, at the Cooper Union Convocation, New York, architect Frank Lloyd Wright received the Peter Cooper Medal for the Advancement of Art. Having completed his part in the ceremony, Wright asked permission of the chairman to make an announcement: "The greatest man in the world has recently died. His name was Gurdjieff." Few present had ever heard of him.

Gurdjieff's grave at Avon is remarkable for two rough standing stones, one taller than the other, at opposite ends of the lawned plot. In the far right corner is a perfectly squared stone seat.*

There is no name, and no time.

---

*Masons may note the symbolism: two rough ashlars and the perfected squared stone in a sequence of three.

Notes

PREFACE.
CAVEAT LECTOR

1. Gurdjieff, *Meetings with Remarkable Men,* 29–30 (hereafter referred to as *Meetings*).

CHAPTER I.
THE ENIGMA ARRIVES

1. Passenger Records, Ship Manifests, State Immigration Officers' Lists, held by the Statue of Liberty–Ellis Island Foundation Inc. www .libertyellisfoundation.org (accessed December 12, 2016).

2. Gurdjieff originally traveled on a pre-Soviet imperial Russian passport. When this expired, ever resourceful, Gurdjieff twice used the local Soviet passport issued by lawyer Peter Shandarovsky in Essentuki in 1918. That the United States did not recognize the Soviet Union until 1933 may have helped Gurdjieff pull it off. Shandarovsky was probably only able to issue passports to local inhabitants. This would explain why Essentuki is given as Gurdjieff's birthplace on immigration records for February 1930. Gurdjieff got his Armenian passport in Batumi. I am grateful to Michael Benham for this information (e-mail to author, October 4, 2016).

3. See Taylor, *G.I. Gurdjieff, A New Life,* 15–18 (hereafter referred to as *New Life*).

   In eight United States Immigration entries, Gurdjieff's age is given as follows: 13 Jan 1924, age 47; 23 Jan 1929, age 52; 18 Feb 1930, age 53;

11 Nov 1930, age 53; 6 Nov 1931, age 54; 25 Apr 1934, age 56; 8 Mar 1939, age 62; 17 Dec 1948, age 71. Only in the February 1930 entry is Gurdjieff's birthplace listed as Essentuki. Here, Benham believes Gurdjieff probably used the Soviet passport Shandarovsky issued him in Essentuki in 1918.

Regarding a possibly earlier birth date in the 1870s, Michael Benham cites information given to Paul Beekman Taylor by George Kioutzidis, great-grandson of Gurdjieff's paternal uncle Vasilii (through Vasilii's son Alexander. Vasilii had market gardens near Kars. George Kioutzidis recalled that his grandfather Alexander, born in 1875, said that Gurdjieff was about three years older than he.

Gurdjieff's U.S. Census return for 1 Apr 1930 records his occupying an apartment at 204 West 59th Street, New York City. No documentary evidence was required; Gurdjieff gave his age as 57, which would make his birth date 28 Dec 1872.

In *Meetings,* Gurdjieff specifically fixes the ages of his fellow young seekers, Sarkis Pogossian and Ekim Bey, and implies the same for Piotr Karpenko—as the same as his own. It is impossible to construct a plausible chronology starting from 28 Dec 1877 that matches their likely ages while having Pogossian graduate from the seminary and Gurdjieff at Ani before Nicholas Marr began excavations there in summer 1892.

In final support of an earlier birth date than 1878, Benham observes Gurdjieff's remark that he retired to a monastery in 1892 to reflect on his situation. As Benham puts it, "It is difficult to imagine him doing this at age fourteen. (He would have been fifteen only at the end of 1892.) It is, however, possible to construct a fairly plausible chronology (compressing slightly in some places the lengths of time between events claimed by Gurdjieff) starting with a birth date of December 28, 1872, primarily from his account in *Meetings* and other sources supplemented by additional historical information" (Michael Benham, e-mail to author, October 4, 2016).

4. Taylor, *New Life,* 32.

5. Michael Benham (e-mail to author, October 4, 2016) draws attention to Bernard Metz's "extensive notes of Gurdjieff's philosophical talks at the Prieuré right through 1923 and beyond. These notes are cited by J. Walter Driscoll in 'Notes of Talks by G. I. Gurdjieff 1918–1946' as [Bernard Metz Notes on Meetings with G. I. Gurdjieff and A. R. Orage in London, Fontainbleau and New York between November 1921 and February 1924.]

23 pages. [missing pages 19–23.]" (brackets in original). According to Metz, "These notes are in the order in which I got them, meeting by meeting. They are almost all verbatim expressions from Mr. O[rage]. or Mr. G[urdjieff]. taken down at meetings, or immediately afterwards, so take them for what they are worth. All notes are from Mr. O[rage]'s meetings unless otherwise stated." These can be found at "Notes of Talks by G.I. Gurdjieff: Three Compilations; With Bibliographic Notes by J. Walter Driscoll," 6. http://www.gurdjieff-bibliography.com/Current/1504_a_insert_notes-8-talks-by-G_pg18_2004-07-06-go-to-press.pdf (accessed November 10, 2016).

According to Benham, Bernard Metz was "Gurdjieff's real secretary (not Olga de Hartmann as she thought) and traveled at the same time as Gurdjieff to America in Jan 1924, Jan 1929, Feb 1930, Nov 1930, and Nov 1931, sometimes on different vessels" (Michael Benham, e-mail to author, October 4, 2016).

CHAPTER 2.
REVIEWING THE SITUATION: A BIRTH

1. Taylor, *New Life,* 13.
2. Ibid., 14.
3. File 47, Description 2, n. 25, cited in Taylor, *New Life,* 13.
4. Ihsan, *Atrocités Grecques en Turquie,* 2:144.
5. File 489, Description 6, n. 2036 1807, cited in Taylor, *New Life,* 12. Beekman Taylor's account is also informed by the collective monograph in Gordeziani, *The Greeks in Georgia,* 5–8, which employs records from Ekepad indicating the Turkish origin of Pontus Greek settlers there.
6. Gurdjieff, *Meetings,* 40.
7. Ibid.
8. Ibid., 41.
9. Spinage, *Cattle Plague,* 210.

CHAPTER 3.
WAR BABY: AN EDUCATION IN KARS

1. Jung, *The Spirit in Art, Man, and Literature,* 4–5.
2. Gurdjieff, *Beelzebub's Tales to His Grandson,* 21 (hereafter referred to as *Tales*).

3. Ibid., 61.

4. Ibid., 26.

5. Gurdjieff, *Meetings*, 250.

6. Ibid., 42.

7. Michael Benham's information (e-mail to author, October 4, 2016) is that Avetik Melik-Sargsyan, who runs a "Gurdjieff Center" in Gyumri, Armenia, has found these wax cylinders in Moscow, though, if intact, they have yet to reach the public ear.

8. Gurdjieff, *Meetings*, 34–36.

9. Smith, "The Chaldaean Account of the Deluge," 219 (translation of tablet 11).

10. Heidel, *The Gilgamesh Epic and Old Testament Parallels*, 2–4.

11. Kreyenbroek, *Yezidism: Its Background, Observances and Textual Tradition*, 185.

12. Paraphrase of John 5:39.

CHAPTER 4.
DEAN BORSHCH
AND OTHER ENTHUSIASMS

1. Petsche, *Gurdjieff and Music*, 43–45.

2. Gurdjieff, *Meetings*, 52.

3. Ibid., 53.

4. Gurdjieff, *Tales*, 12–13.

5. Gurdjieff, *Meetings*, 53.

6. Ibid., 62.

7. Ibid., 61.

8. Ibid., 65.

9. Ibid., 67.

10. Ibid., 66.

11. Henry Korman obtained his information from Pir Khidir for a two-part essay, "Gurdjieff and Yezidism" in *The Gurdjieff Journal*, vols. 17–18.

12. Gurdjieff, *Meetings*, 58.

13. Ibid., 59.

14. Ibid.

15. Gurdjieff, "The Material Question," 252, appended to *Meetings* (henceforth abbreviated to "MQ").

CHAPTER 5. THE SPIRITUAL QUESTION

1. Gurdjieff, *Meetings,* 71.
2. Ibid., 64.
3. Ibid., 82.
4. Ibid., 83.
5. Ibid., 69–70.
6. Ibid., 69.
7. Consult: Bernheim, *De la suggestion dans l'état hypnotique et dans l'état de veille;* Bernheim, *Souvenirs latents et suggestions à longue échéance,* 17, 97–111.
8. Gurdjieff, *Meetings,* 43–44.
9. Gurdjieff, "Hypnotism," chapter 32 in *Tales,* 341 ("I chose for myself the profession of what is called there 'physician-hypnotist'"); "Beelzebub as Professional Hypnotist," chapter 33 in *Tales,* 354.
10. Michael Benham to author (e-mail, October 5, 2016), "Correct. It took me years to track this down from a clue in the first draft of *Beelzebub's Tales.*"
11. Gurdjieff, *Tales,* 26.
12. Ibid., 27.
13. Gurdjieff, *Meetings,* 70.

CHAPTER 6.
MAD ABOUT THE GIRL:
OR HOW TO GET TO TIFLIS IN A HURRY

1. Gurdjieff, *Meetings,* 201–2.
2. Ibid., 203.
3. Ibid., 205.
4. Ibid.
5. According to Benham (e-mail to author, October 5, 2016), "All references say 1895."
6. Gurdjieff, *Meetings,* 200.
7. Wcislo, *Tales of Imperial Russia,* 26.
8. Rogers, *The Esoteric Codex,* 145.
9. Johnson, *The Masters Revealed,* 19–22.
10. Ibid., 23.
11. Ibid., 32.

12. Gurdjieff, *Meetings,* 109.

13. Ibid., 84.

14. Ibid., 110.

15. Ibid., 86.

16. De Windt, *A Ride to India across Persia and Baluchistan,* 11–12.

17. Ibid., 5–7; 12.

18. Ibid., 13.

19. De Windt, "Tiflis," in *A Ride to India.*

20. Gurdjieff, *Meetings,* 111.

CHAPTER 7. BOOKS: FURNITURE OF THE MIND

1. Ross, *The Politics of Sub-National Authoritarianism in Russia,* 46–47.

2. Carlson, *No Religion Higher Than Truth,* 21.

3. Ibid., 21–23. See also Maria Carlson's paper: "Fashionable occultism: spiritualism, theosophy, freemasonry, and hermeticism in fin-de-siècle Russia" for a general overview in Rosenthal, ed., *The Occult in Russian and Soviet Culture.*

4. Leighton, *Esoteric Tradition in Russian Romantic Literature,* 27.

5. I am grateful to Frank van Lamoen, Curator, Stedelijk Museum, Amsterdam, for his assistance in locating esoteric works in the Russian State Library archives, and for general advice on Russian esoteric publishing.

6. Russian State Library catalogue of 1918 Masonic manuscripts (V. S. Arsenyev collection) compiled by K. A. Maykova, 1974. See Carlos Gilly, "Iter Gnostico-Russicum," in *500 Years of Gnosis in Europe.* Exhibition catalog, Bibliotheca Philosophica Hermetica Publications (Amsterdam: In de Pelikaan, 2002), 54. Other collections of the Russian State Library are rich in esoteric classics, such as the D. Popov collection and the S. S. Lanskoy collection.

7. Kasinec and Kerdimun, "Occult Literature in Russia," 361.

8. Aksakov, *Animizm i spiritizm,* 3.

9. Janet Flanner and Solita Solano papers, Library of Congress. See http://hdl .loc.gov/loc.mss/eadmss.ms003029 (accessed November 12, 2016).

CHAPTER 8. IN SEARCH OF BROTHERHOOD

1. Gurdjieff, *Meetings,* 112.

2. Ibid., 86.

3. Mirzoyan and Badem, *The Construction of the Tiflis-Aleksandropol-Kars Railway.*

4. Ibid., 20.

5. Gurdjieff, *Meetings,* 86.

6. Ibid., 86–87.

7. Ibid., 87.

8. Ibid., 90.

9. Ibid.

10. Ibid., 92.

11. Report on the state of the Kars province for the years of 1890–1905, *Osmanlı Belgelerinde Ermeni-Rus İlişkileri.* Ankara: Başbakanlık Devlet Arşivleri Genel Müdürlüğü, 2006, as well as National Archive of Armenia, f. 1262, op. 3, d. 38. Cited in Mirzoyan and Badem, *The Construction of the Tiflis-Aleksandropol-Kars Railway,* 13.

12. Gurdjieff, *Meetings,* 208.

13. Ibid.

14. Ibid., 209.

15. See "Ani Ruins Reveal Hidden Secrets from Below," Turkis Hurriyet Daily News KARS—Cihan News Agency, August 26, 2014, http://www .hurriyetdailynews.com/ani-ruins-reveal-hidden-secrets-from-below.aspx? PageID=238&NID=70875&NewsCatID= (accessed November 12, 2016):

> New underground structures have come to light in Ani, one of Turkey's most breathtaking ancient sites. History researcher Sezai Yazıcı says the ancient city's structures should be promoted.
>
> The underground secrets of the historic Ani Ruins, an ancient, 5,000-year-old Armenian city located on the Turkish-Armenian border in the eastern province of Kars, have been revealed.
>
> While speaking at the recent "International Ani-Kars Symposium," history researcher Sezai Yazıcı said secret water channels, undiscovered monk cells, meditation rooms, huge corridors, intricate tunnels, unbelievable traps and corners that make one lose their sense of direction were just some of the unknown underground structures located at the ancient site.
>
> Yazıcı said a number of experts, academics and researchers attended the Kars Symposium, which was held at Kars' Kafkas University from Aug. 14 to 16. At the symposium, Yazıcı's presentation titled, "Underground Secrets of Ani," drew a lot of attention since no previous publications on the underground structures had been mentioned before.

"In 2011 while working on a United Nations project in order to promote Kars and to reveal its historical and cultural heritage, I came across some pretty interesting information. One of the most important names of the first half of the 20th century, George Ivanovic Gurdjieff, who spent most of his childhood and youth in Kars, had chosen [to stay in] an isolated place in Ani along with his friend Pogosyan where they worked for some time together in the 1880s. One day, while digging at one of the underground tunnels in Ani, Gurdjieff and his friend saw that the soil became different. They continued digging and discovered a narrow tunnel. But the end of the tunnel was closed off with stones. They cleaned the stones and found a room. They saw decayed furniture, broken pots and pans in the room. They also found a scrap of parchment in a niche. Although Gurdjieff spoke Armenian very well, he failed to read Armenian writing in the parchment. Apparently, it was very old Armenian. After a while, they learned that the parchments were letters written by a monk to another monk," Yazıcı said, speaking about how he became interested in the underground structures.

"Finally, [Gurdjieff and his friend] succeeded in understanding the letters. Gurdjieff discovered that there was a famous Mesopotamian esoteric school in the place where they found the letters. The famous school was active between the sixth and seventh centuries A.D. and there was a monastery there," he added.

Yazıcı said Gurdjieff was the first person to mention the monastery that was located under the Ani Ruins.

"Gurdjieff's discovery, nearly 135 years ago, could not have been confirmed until the excavation works of 1915. Years later, an Italian excavation team confirmed that it was a monastery. Before Gurdjieff, many travelers also observed that a significant population had lived in caves or rock houses in Ani," he said.

"The tunnels are above [sic] 500 meters in Ani. Most of underground structures and caves were used as houses. The metrical sizes of most of the underground structures have been measured and maps have been made for most of them," the researcher said, confirming that there were currently 823 underground structures and caves in Ani today.

Yazıcı said among the most important underground structures were the Giden Gelmez Tunnel, Yeraltı Anisi (Underground Ani) and Gizli Kapılar (Secret Doors). "On the other hand, Ani also has four complicated structures. It is very difficult to reach some of them. It is time to mention these underground structures in the promotion of Ani. The Culture and Tourism Ministry should put signs showing the places of underground structures and build walking paths. Underground structures draw great interest in the world," Yazıcı said.

The drawback of the article from the historical perspective, rather than its obvious tourist publicity value, is that Yazici seems to accept Gurdjieff's story at face value, referring to "Gurdjieff's discovery," while the impressive photographs that accompany the article are captioned in conformity with Gurdjieff's ideas. An image captioned "Prayer room of a monastery," for example, is revealed as an empty underground room, with no outstanding feature to suggest its purpose.

16. *Meetings*, 90.
17. Ibid., 113.
18. Ibid., 91.
19. Ibid., 93.
20. Ibid., 99.

CHAPTER 9. THE YEZIDIS

1. For Joseph's (Yusef) essay, "The Yezidis" in *Devil Worshippers; The Sacred Books and Traditions of the Yezidis,* see Guest, *The Yezidis—A Study in Survival,* 151–52.
2. Drower, *Peacock Angel, Being Some Account of Votaries of a Secret Cult and Their Sanctuaries.*
3. Kreyenbroek, *Yezidism,* 92.
4. Drower, *Peacock Angel,* 171.
5. Kreyenbroek, *Yezidism,* 99.
6. Guest, *The Yezidis—A Study in Survival,* 202.
7. Irenaeus, *Adversus. Haereses,* 1.13.
8. Yusef (Joseph), *Devil Worship: The Sacred Books and Traditions of the Yezidis,* 38.
9. Drower, *Peacock Angel,* 7.
10. Layard, *Nineveh and Its Remains,* chapter 8, 188, n. 1.
11. Layard, *Discoveries Among the Ruins of Nineveh and Babylon,* chapter 8, 188-89.
12. Kreyenbroek, *Yezidism,* 244–47.

13. In 1895, for example, Oswald Parry's *Six Months in a Syrian Monastery* (London: Horace Cox) included Cambridge orientalist E. G. Browne's translation of both the *Jelwe* and *Meshef Resh*. In September 1891 the Bibliothèque Nationale, Paris, acquired a manuscript (BN Syr. MS. 306) of the same works, copied by one Abdul Aziz, a member of the Syrian Orthodox Church who lived in the predominantly Yezidi village of Bashiqe.

14. Drower, *Peacock Angel,* 126.

15. Kreyenbroek, *Yezidism,* 92.

16. Ibid., 127.

17. Martin, "In Iraq, Ancient Sect Quietly Lives on Faith," *St. Petersburg Times* (April 26, 2004). Reporter Susan Martin's interview with Yezidi teacher Hamed: "We respect other religions—everyone who respects God, we respect him. Why can't they respect us?" www.religionnewsblog.com/7017 /in-iraq-ancient-sect-quietly-lives-on-faith (accessed December 13, 2016).

18. Gurdjieff, *Beelzebub's Tales to His Grandson,* 53.

19. Yusef (Joseph), *Devil Worship,* 39-40.

20. Hooke, *Middle Eastern Mythology,* 127.

21. "Gurdjieff & Yezidism, Part One," from *The Gurdjieff Journal—Fourth Way Perspectives*; website of The Gurdjieff Legacy Foundation: http:// www.gurdjiefflegacy.org/40articles/yezidism.htm; Note 4 source-reference to: Sami Said Ahmed, *The Yazidis: Their Life and Beliefs;* ed. Henry Field (Miami: Field Research Projects, 1975, Study No 97).

22. Kreyenbroek, *Yezidism,* 29–31, 50–52.

23. John Guest photographed the inscription on the mausoleum of Zein ed-Din Yusuf, in Cairo—a relic of the 'Adawiyya tariqa in Cairo. Guest, *The Yezidis,* plate 24.

24. Frayha, "New Yezidi Texts from beled Sinjar, 'Iraq,'" 38–39.

25. Kreyenbroek, *Yezidism,* 57–61.

CHAPTER 10.
DO-IT-YOURSELF GURDJIEFF AND
UNACCOUNTABLE JOURNEYS

1. Nicholson, *The Legacy of Islam,* 221.

2. Gurdjieff, *Meetings,* 270.

3. Ibid., 264.

4. Gurdjieff, *Tales,* 686.

5. Ibid., 687.

6. Gurdjieff, *Meetings*, 72.

7. Ibid., 72–73.

8. Cansdale, *Qumran and the Essenes*, 27; cites from De Saulcy, *Narrative of a Journey Round the Dead Sea and in the Bible Lands*, 146–47.

9. Gurdjieff, *Meetings*, 178–79.

10. Nicholson, *The Legacy of Islam*, 215.

11. Rumi, quoted in Iqbal, *The Life and Work of Jalaluddin Rumi*, 4.2034.

12. Ibid., 4.3000–29.

13. Gurdjieff, *Meetings*, 182.

14. Gurdjieff, *Life Is Real*, 12.

15. Gurdjieff, *Meetings*, 183.

CHAPTER II.
TRAVELING TALES AND
BULLETS IN THE LEG

1. Gurdjieff, *Meetings*, 192.

2. Ibid., 193.

3. Ibid., 195.

4. Ibid., 196.

5. Ibid., 197.

6. Ibid., 198.

7. Ibid., 147.

8. Ibid., 135.

9. Ibid., 136–37.

10. Ibid., 141.

11. Ibid., 142.

12. Ibid., 148.

13. Ibid., 149.

14. Ibid., 152.

15. Ibid., 154.

16. Ibid., 160.

17. Ibid., 161.

18. Ibid., 163.

19. Ibid., 165.

20. Šūštarī, cited in "Freemasonry ii. In the Qajar Period" Encyclopaedia

Iranica. www.iranicaonline.org/articles/freemasonry-ii-in-the-qajar-period (accessed December 13, 2016).

21. Gurdjieff, *Meetings,* 255–56.

22. Ibid., 257.

23. Ibid., 259.

24. Ibid., 259–60.

25. Ibid., 261.

26. Ibid., 209.

27. Ibid., 230–31.

28. Ibid., 210.

29. Ibid., 212.

30. Ibid., 211.

31. Ibid., 214–15.

32. Ibid., 222.

33. Ibid., 225.

34. Ibid., 226.

35. Ibid., 227.

36. Ibid., 233.

37. Ibid., 238.

38. Ibid., 239–40.

39. Ibid., 242.

40. Ibid., 245.

CHAPTER 12. TWO MORE BULLETS

1. Gurdjieff, *Life Is Real,* 5.

2. Ibid., 20.

3. Ibid., 11.

4. Saxer, "Journeys with Tibetan Medicine," 25–29.

5. Ibid., 35–38.

6. Gurdjieff, *Tales,* 431.

7. Ibid., 439–40.

8. Gurdjieff, *Life Is Real,* 11.

9. Ibid., 15.

10. Ibid., 18.

11. Ibid., 19.

12. Ibid., 12.

CHAPTER 13. HOLY MOTHER RUSSIA!

1. Gurdjieff, *Meetings*, 119.
2. Gurdjieff, *Tales*, 362–63.
3. Ibid., 374.
4. Taylor, *New Life*, 35.
5. Gurdjieff, *Tales*, 378.
6. Ibid., 376.
7. Ibid., 379.
8. Papus (Dr. Gérard Encausse), *l'Initiation* 33, no. 1 (October 1896): 1–3.
9. Papus, *l'Initiation* 47, no. 7 (April 1900): 1.
10. Perovsky-Petrovo-Solovovo, Count, "My Experiments with S. F. Sambor"; "On the Production of Spurious 'Spirit Raps.'"
11. Var, "Philippe, Anthelme-Nizier," in *Dictionary of Gnosis & Western Esotericism*, 948.
12. Michelet, "Marc Haven & 'Mr. Philippe,'" in *Les Compagnons de la Hiérophanie*, 102 (author's translation).
13. Ibid.
14. Taylor, *New Life*, 39.
15. Znamenski's *Red Shambhala*; Shishkin "The Occultist Aleksadr Barchenko and the Soviet Secret Police (1923–1938)" in *The New Age of Russia: Occult and Esoteric Dimensions*.
16. Shishkin, "The Occultist Aleksadr Barchenko and the Soviet Secret Police (1923–1938)," 84.
17. Znamenski, *Red Shambhala*, 60.
18. Heller, *The New Age of Russia*, 203, note 15.
19. Gurdjieff, *Meetings*, 270.
20. Ibid.
21. Gurdjieff, *Life Is Real*, 20–21.

CHAPTER 14.
THE STRUGGLE OF THE MAGICIANS

1. Crowley, *Diary*, Sunday, March 22, 1924, 9:50 p.m.
2. Khetaguri, "Gurdjieff and Twentieth Century Culture" (speech given at Tbilisi State University "Javakhshvili," supported by the Embassy of Italy, March 7, 2007).

3. Hosking, *The Russian Constitutional Experiment,* 196–97.
4. This Russian newspaper notice, its translation, and the information about Vasilii Geltzer that follows it was brought to my attention by Michael Benham (e-mail to author, October 7, 2016).

CHAPTER 15. OCTAVE AND ENNEAGRAM

1. Ouspensky, *In Search of the Miraculous,* 180.
2. Ibid., 132.
3. Godwin, *Robert Fludd,* 42–43.
4. Fludd, *Tomus Secundus De Supernaturali,* 274–75.

CHAPTER 16.
THE INTERNATIONAL ALLIANCE
OF IDEOLOGICAL WORKERS

1. Stjernvall, *Daddy Gurdjieff,* 98.
2. Gurdjieff, "MQ," in *Meetings,* 272.
3. Taylor, *New Life,* 58.
4. Gurdjieff, "MQ," in *Meetings,* 274–75.
5. De Hartmann and de Hartmann, *Our Life with Mr. Gurdjieff,* 81.
6. Taylor, *New Life,* 69.
7. Ibid., 70.
8. Gurdjieff, "MQ," in *Meetings,* 282.

CHAPTER 17. STATELESS PERSON

1. Gurdjieff, "MQ," in *Meetings,* 283.
2. Spence, *Secret Agent 666,* 192.
3. UK National Archive, WO 339/21087, Capt. JG Bennett, and Foreign Office 371/15232, cited in Spence, *Secret Agent 666,* 192, 202.
4. See *New York Times* archive, December 2, 1922, "To Fight for Billion and Rich Oil Lands for Sultan's Heirs: Alvin Untermyer Sails Today to Press Claims of 22 Princess & Princesses. AT LAUSANNE CONFERENCE: Immense Oil Holdings in Mesopotamia Now the Object of World Diplomacy."
5. FragmentsOfragments website. https://fragmentsofragments.wordpress .com/2012/04/19/a-man-named-gurdjieff (accessed November 16, 2016)

6. Gurdjieff, "MQ," in *Meetings*, 284.

7. Ibid., 285.

8. Gurdjieff, *Life Is Real*, 22.

9. Gurdjieff, "MQ," in *Meetings*, 285–87.

10. Ibid., 287–88.

11. Gurdjieff, *Tales*, 408.

12. Gurdjieff, "MQ," in *Meetings*, 289.

13. De Hartmann and de Hartmann, *Our Life with Mr. Gurdjieff*, 111.

14. Gurdjieff, "MQ," in *Meetings*, 296.

15. Gurdjieff, *Life Is Real*, 22.

16. Taylor, *New Life*, 122.

17. Ibid.

CHAPTER 18.
DOCTRINE: AN OBJECTIVELY IMPARTIAL CRITICISM OF THE LIFE OF MAN

1. Gurdjieff, *Tales*, 53.

2. Ibid., 59–61.

3. Ibid., 63–64.

4. Ibid., 66–68.

5. Ibid., 76.

6. Ibid., 78.

7. Ibid., 80–81.

8. Ibid., 82.

9. Ibid., 217.

CHAPTER 19.
THE BEAST 666 AND THE BLACK DEVIL

1. Breeze, "AC Diaries," February 10, 1924.

2. Taylor, "Gurdjieff and Women," in *New Life*, 231.

3. Breeze, "AC Diaries," February 1924, 7.

4. Ibid., 55.

5. Webb, *The Harmonious Circle*, 315.

6. Breeze, "AC Diaries," July–August 1926.

7. Nott, *Teachings of Gurdjieff*, 121–22.

8. Taylor, *Shadows of Heaven*.

9. Suster, *The Legacy of the Beast*, 92–93.

10. Symonds, Scrapbook of letters to John Symonds when writing "The Great Beast," folder no. 96.

CHAPTER 20. THE LONG ASCENT

1. Taylor, *New Life*, 233.

2. Solano and Hulme, *Gurdjieff and the Women of the Rope*, 10.

3. Gurdjieff, *Life Is Real*, 7.

4. Ibid., 8.

5. Ibid., 30.

6. Taylor, *New Life*, 240–41.

7. Baker, "No Harem: Gurdjieff and the Women of the Rope," para 3.

8. Taylor, *Gurdjieff's Invention of America*, 264–68.

CHAPTER 21. THE GRAVE WITH NO NAME

1. Cecil, "The Will and the Way," 20.

2. Ibid., 26.

3. Ibid., 27.

4. Ibid., 28.

5. Ibid., 30.

6. Ibid., 33.

7. Travers, *George Ivanovitch Gurdjieff (1877–1949)*.

8. Ibid.

Bibliography

Ahmed, Sami Said. *The Yazidis: Their Life and Beliefs.* Edited by Henry Field. Miami: Field Research Projects, 1975.

Aksakov, Aleksandr N. *Animizm i spiritizm.* 2nd ed. 1893. St. Petersburg: V Demakova, 1901.

Algar, Hamid. "Freemasonry ii. In the Qajar Period." In *Encyclopaedia Iranica,* 2012. www.iranicaonline.org/articles/freemasonry-ii-in-the-qajar-period (accessed November12, 2016)

Baker, Rob. Review: "No Harem: Gurdjieff and the Women of the Rope." 1997. www.gurdjieff.org/rope.htm (accessed November 12, 2016)

Bernheim, Hippolyte. *De la suggestion dans l'état hypnotique et dans l'état de veille.* Paris: Revue Médicale de l'Est, 1883; published 1884: Octave Doin, Paris; éditions Harmattan (2004).

———. *Souvenirs latents et suggestions à longue échéance.* Paris: Revue Médicale de l'Est, 17, 1886.

Breeze, William, ed. "AC Diaries." Unpublished manuscript. Yorke Collection. Warburg Institute, University of London.

Cansdale, Lena. *Qumran and the Essenes: A Re-evaluation of the Evidence.* Tübingen, Germany: JCB Mohr, 1997.

Carlson, Maria. *No Religion Higher Than Truth: A History of the Theosophical Movement in Russia 1875–1922.* Princeton, N.J.: Princeton Legacy Library, 1993.

———. "Fashionable occultism: spiritualism, theosophy, freemasonry and hermeticism in fin-de-siècle Russia. *The Occult in Russian and Soviet Culture.* Ithaca, N.Y.: Cornell University Press, 1997.

Cecil, Robert. "The Will and the Way" (unpublished manuscript).

Crowley, Aleister. "Diary." Unpublished manuscript. Yorke Collection. Warburg Institute, University of London.

De Hartmann, Thomas, and Olga de Hartmann. *Our Life with Mr. Gurdjieff.* rev. ed. San Francisco: Arkana, 1992.

De Saulcy, Félicien. *Narrative of a Journey Round the Dead Sea and in the Bible Lands; 1850 and 1851, including an Account of the Discovery of the Sites of Sodom and Gomorrah.* 2 vols. Edited by Count Edward de Warren. London: R. Bentley, 1854.

De Windt, Harry. *A Ride to India across Persia and Baluchistan.* London: Chapman and Hall, 1891.

Drower, E. S. (Ethel Stefana). *Peacock Angel: Being Some Account of Votaries of a Secret Cult and Their Sanctuaries.* London: John Murray, 1941.

Fludd, Robert. *Tomus Secundus De Supernaturali, Naturali, Praeternaturali Et Contranaturali Microcosmi historia, in Tractatus tres distributa.* Oppenheim: Theodore de Bry, 1619.

Frayha, Anis. "New Yezidi Texts from beled Sinjar, 'Iraq.'" *Journal of the American Oriental Society* 66 (1946): 18–43.

Godwin, Joscelyn. *Robert Fludd.* London: Thames & Hudson, 1979.

Gordeziani, Rismag, ed. *The Greeks in Georgia.* Tbilisi, Georgia: Tbilisi State University, 1990.

Guest, John S. *The Yezidis—A Study in Survival.* New York: Routledge, Kegan and Paul, 1987.

Gurdjieff, Georges I. *Meetings with Remarkable Men.* New York: EP Dutton, 1963.

——. *Beelzebub's Tales to His Grandson.* Milton Keynes, UK: Aziloth Books, 2011.

——. *The Herald of Coming Good.* Lynnwood, Wash.: Holmes Publishing Group, 1987.

——. *Life Is Real Only Then, When "I Am."* London: Penguin Books, 1999. Reprinted with prefatory note by Valentin Anastasieff, Aziloth Books, 2011.

Heidel, Alexander. *The Gilgamesh Epic and Old Testament Parallels.* Chicago: University of Chicago Press, 1949.

Heller, Leonid. *The New Age of Russia: Occult and Esoteric Dimensions.* Edited by Birgit Menzel, Michael Hagemeister, and Bernice Glatzer Rosenthal. Munich: Kubon & Sagner, 2011.

Hooke, Samuel Henry. *Middle Eastern Mythology.* Harmondsworth, UK: Pelican, 1978.

Hosking, Geoffrey A. *The Russian Constitutional Experiment: Government and Duma 1907–1914.* London: Cambridge, 1993.

Howarth, Jessmin, and Dushka Howarth. *It's Up to Ourselves: A Mother, a Daughter, and Gurdjieff—a Shared Memoir and Family Photo Album.* New York: Gurdjieff Heritage Society, 2009.

Ihsan, Ahmed. *Atrocités Grecques en Turquie.* Vol. 2. Constantinople: Imprimerie Ahmed Ihsan & Cie, 1921.

Iqbal, Afzal. *The Life and Work of Jalaluddin Rumi.* Oxford: Oxford University Press, 1999.

Irenaeus. *Adversus. Haereses.* 1.13. In *The Ante-Nicene Fathers.* Edited and translated by Alexander Roberts and James Donaldson. Grand Rapids, Mich.: William B. Eerdmans, 1981.

Johnson, K. Paul. *The Masters Revealed: Madame Blavatsky and the Myth of the Great White Lodge.* New York: SUNY, 1994.

Jung, Carl. *The Spirit in Art, Man, and Literature.* London: Ark, Routledge, 1989.

Kasinec, Edward, and Boris Kerdimun. "Occult Literature in Russia." In *The Spiritual in Art: Abstract Painting 1890-1985.* New York: Abbeville Press, 1986.

Korman, Henry. "Gurdjieff and Yezidism." *The Gurdjieff Journal,* vols. 17–18.

Kreyenbroek, Philip G. *Yezidism: Its Background, Observances and Textual Tradition.* Texts and Studies in Religion 62. Lewiston, N.Y.: Edwin Mellen Press, 1995.

Layard, Austen Henry. *Discoveries Among the Ruins of Nineveh and Babylon.* New York: Harper and Bros., 1853.

———. *Nineveh and Its Remains, A Narrative of an Expedition to Assyria.* London: John Murray, 1867.

Leighton, Lauren. *Esoteric Tradition in Russian Romantic Literature.* University Park: Pennsylvania State University Press, 1994.

Merston, Ethel. "Miss Merston at the Prieuré." *The Gurdjieff Journal.* Vol. 8, no. 2.

Michelet, Victor-Émile. *Les Compagnons de la Hiérophanie, Souvenirs du movement hermétiste à la fin du XIX siècle.* Paris: Dorbon-Ainé, n.d.

Mirzoyan, Sonya, and Candan Badem. *The Construction of the Tiflis-Aleksandropol-Kars Railway (1895–1899).* Leiden, Netherlands: Historical Justice and Reconciliation, 2013.

Moore, James. *Gurdjieff: The Anatomy of a Myth.* Boston: Element, 1991.

Nicholson, R. A. *The Legacy of Islam*. Oxford: Oxford University Press, 1931.

Nott, Charles Stanley. *Teachings of Gurdjieff: A Pupil's Journal*. London: Penguin Arkana, 1990.

Ouspensky, Pyotr Demianovich. *In Search of the Miraculous*. New York: Harcourt Brace & World, 1949.

Papus (Gérald Encausse). *L'Initiation* 33 (October 1896).

———. *L'Initiation* 47, no. 7 (April 1900).

Petsche, Johanna. *Gurdjieff and Music: The Gurdjieff/de Hartmann Piano Music and its Esoteric Significance*. Leiden, Netherlands: E. J. Brill, 2014.

Perovsky-Petrovo-Solovovo, Count. "My Experiments with S. F. Sambor." *Journal of the Society for Psychical Research* 30 (1937).

———. "On the Production of Spurious 'Spirit Raps.'" *Journal of the Society for Psychical Research* 6 (1893).

Rogers, Mark. *The Esoteric Codex: Theosophy; Alchemy I*. Raleigh, N.C.: lulu .com, 2013.

Rosenthal, Bernice Glatzer, ed. *The Occult in Russian and Soviet Culture*. Ithaca, N.Y.: Cornell University Press, 1997.

Ross, Cameron. *The Politics of Sub-National Authoritarianism in Russia*. Edited by Vladimir Gel'man. Surrey, UK: Ashgate Publishing, 2010.

Saxer, Martin. "Journeys with Tibetan Medicine: How Tibetan Medicine Came to the West. The Story of the Badmayev Family." Master's thesis, Institute of Social and Cultural Anthropology, University of Zurich, 2004.

Shauman, T. *Tibet: The Great Game and Tsarist Russia*. Oxford: Oxford University Press, 2000.

Shishkin, Oleg. "The Occultist Aleksadr Barchenko and the Soviet Secret Police (1923–1938)." In *The New Age of Russia: Occult and Esoteric Dimensions*. Edited by Birgit Menzel, Michael Hagemeister, Bernice Glatzer Rosenthal. Translated by Josephine von Zitzewitz. München: Kubon &Sagner, 2012

Smith, George. "The Chaldaean Account of the Deluge." In *Transactions of the Society of Biblical Archaeology* 2: 213–34. London: Longmans, Green, Reader & Dyer, 1873.

Solano, Solita, and Kathryn C. Hulme. *Gurdjieff and the Women of the Rope: Notes of Meetings in Paris and New York, 1935–1939, and 1948–1949*. London: Book Studio, 2012.

Spence, Richard B. *Secret Agent 666, Aleister Crowley: British Intelligence and the Occult*. Port Townsend, Wash.: Feral House, 2008.

Spinage, Clive A. *Cattle Plague: A History.* New York: Kluwer Academia, 2003.

Stjernvall, Nikolai de "Val." *Daddy Gurdjieff.* Geneva: Georg, 1997.

Suster, Gerald. *The Legacy of the Beast: The Life, Work, and Influence of Aleister Crowley.* York Beach, Maine: Samuel Weiser, 1990.

Symonds, John. Scrapbook of letters to John Symonds when writing "The Great Beast." Folder No. 96. Yorke Collection. Warburg Institute, University of London.

Taylor, Paul Beekman. *G.I. Gurdjieff, A New Life.* Utrecht, Netherlands: Eureka Editions, 2008.

———. *Gurdjieff's Invention of America.* Utrecht, Netherlands: Eureka Editions, 2007.

———. *Shadows of Heaven: Gurdjieff and Toomer.* Newburyport, Mass.: Red Wheel, Weiser, 1998.

Travers, Pamela L. *George Ivanovitch Gurdjieff (1877–1949).* Toronto: Traditional Studies Press, 1973. Previously issued as "Gurdjieff" in *Man, Myth and Magic: Encyclopedia of the Supernatural.* London: Purnell, 1970–1971, serialized in 111 issues, bound as 12 volumes.

Tschekhovitch, Tcheslaw. *Gurdjieff: A Master in Life.* Toronto: Dolmen Meadow Editions, 1990.

Var, Jean-François. "Philippe, Anthelme-Nizier." In *Dictionary of Gnosis & Western Esotericism.* Edited by Wouter J. Hanegraaff. Leiden, Netherlands: Brill, 2006.

Wcislo, Francis W. *Tales of Imperial Russia: The Life and Times of Sergei Witte (1849–1915).* Oxford: Oxford University Press, 2011.

Webb, James. *The Harmonious Circle: The Lives and Work of G. I. Gurdjieff, P. D. Ouspensky and Their Followers.* New York: G. P. Putnam's Sons, 1980.

Yusef (Joseph), Isya Muksy. *Devil Worship: The Sacred Books and Traditions of the Yezidis.* White Fish, Mont.: Kessinger Publishing, 2005.

Znamenski, Andrei. *Red Shambhala: Magic, Prophecy, and Geopolitics in the Heart of Asia.* Wheaton, Ill.: Quest Books, 2011.

Index